DEVELOPMENT CENTRE STUDIES

FINANCIAL SYSTEMS AND DEVELOPMENT:

WHAT ROLE FOR THE FORMAL AND INFORMAL FINANCIAL SECTORS?

BY
DIMITRI GERMIDIS
DENIS KESSLER
AND
RACHEL MEGHIR

D1416987

DEVELOPMENT CENTRE
OF THE ORGANISATION FOR ECONOMIC CO-OPERATION AND DEVELOPMENT

Pursuant to Article 1 of the Convention signed in Paris on 14th December 1960, and which came into force on 30th September 1961, the Organisation for Economic Co-operation and Development (OECD) shall promote policies designed:

— to achieve the highest sustainable economic growth and employment and a rising standard of living in Member countries, while maintaining financial stability, and thus to contribute to the development of the world economy;
— to contribute to sound economic expansion in Member as well as non-member countries in the process of economic development; and
— to contribute to the expansion of world trade on a multilateral, non-discriminatory basis in accordance with international obligations.

The original Member countries of the OECD are Austria, Belgium, Canada, Denmark, France, Germany, Greece, Iceland, Ireland, Italy, Luxembourg, the Netherlands, Norway, Portugal, Spain, Sweden, Switzerland, Turkey, the United Kingdom and the United States. The following countries became Members subsequently through accession at the dates indicated hereafter: Japan (28th April 1964), Finland (28th January 1969), Australia (7th June 1971) and New Zealand (29th May 1973). The Commission of the European Communities takes part in the work of the OECD (Article 13 of the OECD Convention). Yugoslavia takes part in some of the work of the OECD (agreement of 28th October 1961).

The Development Centre of the Organisation for Economic Co-operation and Development was established by decision of the OECD Council on 23rd October 1962.

The purpose of the Centre is to bring together the knowledge and experience available in Member countries of both economic development and the formulation and execution of general economic policies; to adapt such knowledge and experience to the actual needs of countries or regions in the process of development and to put the results at the disposal of the countries by appropriate means.

The Centre has a special and autonomous position within the OECD which enables it to enjoy scientific independence in the execution of its task. Nevertheless, the Centre can draw upon the experience and knowledge available in the OECD in the development field.

Publié en français sous le titre :

SYSTÈMES FINANCIERS ET DÉVELOPPEMENT :
Quel rôle
pour les secteurs financiers formel et informel ?

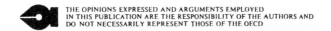 THE OPINIONS EXPRESSED AND ARGUMENTS EMPLOYED IN THIS PUBLICATION ARE THE RESPONSIBILITY OF THE AUTHORS AND DO NOT NECESSARILY REPRESENT THOSE OF THE OECD

*
* *

This study was undertaken as part of the Development Centre's programme on the theme of the Financing of Development. The study was carried out under the direction of Dimitri Germidis, Head of this research programme.

Also available

"Development Center Studies"

NEW FORMS OF INVESTMENT IN DEVELOPING COUNTRIES: Mining, Petrochemicals, Automobiles, Textiles, Food, by Charles Oman (1989)
(41 89 02 1)ISBN 92-64-13188-4, 368 pp.   £28.00   US$48.50   FF230   DM95

THE WORLD ECONOMY IN THE 20TH CENTURY by Angus Maddison (1989)
(41 89 05 1)ISBN 92-64-13274-0, 160 pp.   £17.00   US$30.00   FF140   DM58

FINANCIAL POLICIES AND DEVELOPMENT by Jacques J. Polak (1989)
(41 89 01 1)ISBN 92-64-13187-6, 234 pp.   £17.00   US$29.50   FF140   DM58

DEVELOPING COUNTRY DEBT: THE BUDGETARY AND TRANSFER PROBLEM by Helmut Reisen and Axel van Trotsenburg (1988)
(41 88 01 1)ISBN 92-64-13053-5, 196 pp.   £14.00   US$26.40   FF120   DM52

RECYCLING JAPAN'S SURPLUSES FOR DEVELOPING COUNTRIES by T. Ozawa (1989)
(41 88 05 1)ISBN 92-64-13177-9, 114 pp.   £11.00   US$19.00   FF90   DM37

"Development Centre Seminars"

THE IMPACT OF DEVELOPMENT PROJECTS ON POVERTY. Seminar organised jointly by the OECD Development Center and the Inter American Bank (1989)
(41 88 07 1)ISBN 92-64-13162-0, 100 pp.   £9.00   US$16.50   FF75   DM33

ONE WORLD OR SEVERAL? Edited by Louis Emmerij (1989)
(41 89 04 1)ISBN 92-64-13249-X, 320 pp.   £19.50   US$34.00   FF160   DM66

Prices charged at the OECD Bookshop.

The OECD CATALOGUE OF PUBLICATIONS and supplements will be sent free of charge on request addressed either to OECD Publications Service, 2, rue André-Pascal, 75775 PARIS CEDEX 16, or to the OECD Distributor in your country.

TABLE OF CONTENTS

Acknowledgements 9
Preface 11
Executive Summary 13

Chapter 1
FINANCIAL DUALISM IN DEVELOPING COUNTRIES: MAIN FEATURES AND ISSUES

I. Financial Dualism: Formal versus Informal Financial Sectors 23

   A. The Alternative Financial Systems in Developing Countries 24
   B. The Extent of the Informal Financial Sector 39
   C. Salient Features of the Formal and Informal Financial Sectors 46

II. Causes and Effects of Financial Dualism 50

   A. The Informal Financial Sector is a Response to the Shortcomings and Excessive Regulation of the Formal Financial Sector 50
   B. The Formal Sector is Hampered by the Structural Dualism of Developing Economies More Than It Contributes to It 53
   C. The Effects of Financial Dualism 55

   Concluding Remarks 57
   Notes and References 59

Chapter 2
STRUCTURE OF THE FINANCIAL SYSTEMS IN DEVELOPING COUNTRIES

I. The General Lay-Out of the Financial Circuits 61

   A. The Configuration of the Financial Systems 63
      1. Formal Sector Financial Institutions and Markets 63
      2. 'Semi-Formal' Bodies: Savings and Credit Co-operatives and Credit Unions 81
      3. The Various Informal Sector Mechanisms and Operators 85
   B. The Completeness of the Financial Systems 108

II. The Respective Shares in Financial Circuits 113

   A. Credit in the Developing Countries 113
   B. The Importance of Capital Markets 119
   C. The Shares in Deposits and Lending 121

D. Lending and Deposit Rates 126
E. The Role of Social Security and Insurance 134

Concluding Remarks 138
Notes and References 140

Chapter 3

OPERATIONS AND PRACTICES OF THE FORMAL
AND INFORMAL FINANCIAL SECTORS

I. Localisation of Activity.. 145

A. The Urban Bias of the Formal Financial Sector 148
B. The Localism of the Informal Financial Sector 151

II. Access to Financial Services 154

A. Characteristics of Clientele..................................... 154
B. Size of the Sums Involved 156
C. Use of Funds.. 158
D. Collateral Requirements....................................... 164
E. Lending and Deposit Procedures............................... 165

III. Cost of Financial Intermediation and Interest Rates 170

A. Operating Costs.. 170
B. Debt Discipline 175
C. Differential Formation of Interest Rates 179

IV. Market Interlinkages in the Informal Sector...................... 188

A. Land-Lease and Land-Mortgage Loans 189
B. Labour-Related Loans 189
C. Product-Related Loans.. 189
D. Final Remarks... 191

Conclusion 192
Notes and References 193

Chapter 4

REDUCING THE GAP BETWEEN THE FORMAL
AND INFORMAL FINANCIAL SECTORS

I. Costs and Benefits of Financial Dualism 200

A. Assessing the Potential Effects of Financial Dualism 201

1. On the Mobilisation of Savings............................. 201
2. On the Allocation of Resources 202
3. On the Efficient Use of External Resources 203
4. On the Effectiveness of Macroeconomic and Macrofinancial Policies 204
5. On Equity.. 205

B. Determining the Costs and Benefits Involved 206

II. Country Policy Attitudes... 207

6

III. Strategies and Recommendations 214

    A. Integration or Linkage? 214
    B. Measures to Progressively Reduce the Gap 215
    C. Policy Recommendations 217
          1. Pursuing Appropriate Monetary and Financial Policies 217
          2. Improving the Formal Financial Sector 222
          3. 'Organising' the Informal Sector 232
          4. Promoting Linkages Between the Two Sectors 234

    Concluding Remarks 238
    Conclusion 239
    Notes and References 240

BIBLIOGRAPHY 243

ACKNOWLEDGEMENTS

We express our gratitude to the following institutions, which provided support in various forms for the implementation of the research related to this project:

- The Swedish Savings Banks Association;
- The Swedish International Development Agency (SIDA);
- La Caisse des Dépôts et Consignations (France);
- Finafrica (Italy);
- The Office for Development Research and Policy Analysis of the UN;
- The Asian Development Bank;
- IFC;
- UNIDO;
- The East-West Center (Hawaii);
- The International Savings Banks Institute.

For the country case studies, the Development Centre called upon the co-operation of the following researchers, from both OECD and developing countries:

- Prime Nyamoya and Marcellin Dayer (University of Burundi): *Burundi*;
- Arnaldo Mauri (Finafrica, Italy): *Ethiopia*;
- Jean Masini (IEDES, France): *Togo*;
- Mojmir Mrak (RCCDC, Yugoslavia): *Zambia*;
- Birger Möller (University of Göteborg, Sweden): *Zimbabwe*;
- Jean-Louis Lespès (University of Orléans, France): *Senegal* and Mauritania**;
- Srinivasa Madhur and C.P.S. Nayar (National Institute of Public Finance and Policy, India): *India*;
- Dibyo Prabowo (Gadjah Mada University, Indonesia): *Indonesia*;
- Hans Dieter Seibel (University of Cologne, FRG): *Indonesia**;
- Pan A. Yotopoulos and Sagrario L. Floro (Stanford University, USA): *the Philippines*;
- Denis Kessler and Carlos Pardo (CEREPI, France): *Mexico*.

Their valuable assistance enabled the Development Centre to extend this project and cover a larger variety of experiences.

I would also like to express my heartfelt gratitude to the late Uno Tenfält of the Swedish Savings Banks Association, whose unfailing support and enthusiasm for this work was a major source of inspiration.

Dimitri Germidis
Head, Research Programme

* The case studies on these countries have essentially covered the subject from the point of view of "social protection".

PREFACE

The Development Centre has undertaken over the past three years a series of research projects in the field of domestic savings mobilisation in developing countries within its "financing of development" programme. The present volume constitutes the synthesis of case studies covering Bangladesh, Burundi, Ethiopia, India, Indonesia, Mauritania, Mexico, Philippines, Senegal, Thailand, Togo, Zambia, Zimbabwe.

The international financial crisis is having far-reaching effects on developing countries. In a number of cases it has created major difficulties which have altered the conditions necessary for financing economic growth so that development financing has shifted from external to domestic sources of funding. The deficiencies and inefficiencies in the domestic financial mechanisms of developing countries have therefore become more obvious.

The heterogenous nature of financial systems – more commonly called financial dualism – is characteristic of a number of developing countries and it has become accepted practice to contrast the formal financial sector with the informal one. Yet it is equally important to recognise the great diversity which exists within each of these two sectors. The difficulty lies in accurately defining the precise dividing line between these two subsets.

The informal financial sector is characterised by: i) the fact that operators are above all individuals; ii) the importance of personal relationships and iii) the flexibility, rapidity and ease of transactions in the absence of regulations.

The formal financial sector is frequently a legacy of colonial times or the result of imported systems. In developing countries, the vast majority of formal financial systems are characterised by a high degree of control by public authorities. Formed of a mosaic of banking and non-banking agents, the formal financial system calls upon specialised agents, both within a geographical context and at the sectoral level. This proliferation of institutions contrasts with the atrophy of markets.

A fundamental question to be raised is whether monetary and financial dualism is an expression of the inefficiencies within the financial system. Either the importance of the informal sector, and in some cases its dualism, results from the shortcomings of the formal sector and the "financial repression" seen in a number of developing countries or, according to a second view, the informal sector is more a function of duality in both social and economic structures existing in developing countries.

Beyond its impact upon institutions, monetary and financial dualism also affects the efficiency of economic, monetary and financial policies.

Reducing financial dualism can be justified both on economic and social grounds. The establishment of a balanced economic, monetary and financial environment is one of the prerequisites – though not the only one – for more regular and balanced high growth rates. A reduction in dualism should favour a rise in the household savings rate and a rise in the national savings rate. Moreover, with an increase in the volume of savings, the reduction in

11

dualism should be accompanied by an improvement in the quality of the savings. However, it is important to question the degree to which financial dualism should be reduced.

Some experts – and, indeed, the monetary authorities of a number of developing countries – think that these two sectors should be integrated. The strategy of integration requires designing the means for total absorption of the informal sector: to integrate by institutionalising it. Others, including the authors of the present volume, believe, on the contrary, that the two sectors should be linked and should complement each other. Integration would be a long-term process. The informal sector, they say, has beneficial effects which would disappear if its role was taken over by the formal sector. The concepts of *solidarity* and *mutuality*, often the very bases on which informal savings and credit groups are set up and operated, would not survive the institutionalisation of these bodies. It would always be more advisable to look for better linkage between the two sectors. For this to succeed, both would need to evolve and change simultaneously.

Following an in-depth analysis of the features of financial dualism and a presentation of the forms and modalities of functioning of the informal financial sector (based essentially on the case studies mentioned above, supplemented by work done by the Asian Development Bank, the IFC, the Caisse des Dépôts et Consignations, the East-West Center, etc.), the authors have analysed various attempts undertaken to reduce financial dualism and establish a bridge between the two sectors. They have formulated additional measures to be implemented both at the microeconomic and macroeconomic levels. The ultimate objective of course is to contribute to an increased and better allocation of domestic household savings for development.

In implementing this ambitious research programme the Centre enjoyed the co-operation, both financial and intellectual, of many national and international institutions and research centres, as well as the expertise of numerous specialists to all of whom I address our very warm gratitude.

Louis Emmerij
President
OECD Development Centre
March 1991

EXECUTIVE SUMMARY

Context and Aims of the Study

The international financial crisis which broke out in 1981-82 marked the end of a period of abundant and cheap external capital flows towards the developing countries which were thus increasingly forced to rely on the mobilisation of domestic resources to finance their development. This sudden and forced conversion served to underline the deficiencies and inefficiencies of existing financial circuits in the developing countries. At the same time, the link – though not the direction of causality – between financial development and economic development has come to be recognised.

The financial systems of most developing countries are characterised by the co-existence and operation side by side of a formal financial sector and an informal financial sector – a situation commonly denoted as "financial dualism". Theoretically, the formal sector would refer to an organised urban-oriented, institutional system catering to the financial needs of the monetised modern sector, while the informal sector, itself unorganised and non-institutional, would deal with the traditional, rural, subsistence (non-monetised) spheres of the economy. The reality is more complex, however; the dividing line is not so clear-cut. Indeed, the interpenetration between the two sectors in terms of the operations and participants (lenders, borrowers, savers) involved, geographic location, the nature of activities, also results in a sometimes substantial flow of funds – in both directions – between them.

This study is based on the results of case studies undertaken in Burundi, Ethiopia, Togo, Zambia, Zimbabwe, India, Indonesia, the Philippines and Mexico. Additional studies on Mauritania, Senegal and Indonesia covered the subject from the point of view of social insurance practices. For certain aspects of the finance issue – notably financial markets – other countries for which the relevant data was available were included in the sample (among others, Thailand, Nigeria and Brazil).

As regards the formal financial sector, two main cases may be distinguished: the first is that of a closely "regulated" financial sector where government control over and intervention in the activities of financial institutions is extensive, often at the expense of the development of financial markets; the second is that of a more "liberalised" financial sector where financial institutions have greater leeway in carrying out their intermediation activities, and where market mechanisms are promoted. In between these two theoretical archetypes, there is a whole range of ways and degrees to which control is exercised. For example, controlled financial systems such as that of Ethiopia can be contrasted with the more liberalised systems of Zimbabwe, the Philippines and India; in between, the financial systems of Mexico, Indonesia, Burundi and Zambia could be described as "mixed and evolving" towards more liberalised policies. Regulation by the public authorities may be carried out through the markets (Zimbabwe, the Philippines), or through direct control of financial institutions (India, Indonesia).

Analysis of the informal financial sector must be placed in this context. It is undoubtedly true that the structure and functioning of the formal financial sector largely determine the nature and extent of the informal sector, but it must also be recognised that the informal financial sector has a dynamism of its own. In fact, gauging the extent of the informal sector – whatever the proxy used (monetisation of the economy, size of participating population, volume of transactions) – is difficult because, by definition, informal transactions are not subject to official controls and regulations. Figures for the share of informal credit may range from 30 to more than 80 per cent of total rural credit, for example.

Two main arguments are usually put forward regarding the causes of financial dualism. One sees the informal financial sector as a response to the shortcomings of the formal financial sector which result from "financial repression", that is, the close regulation of the financial system and the various restrictions that the government imposes on the activity of financial institutions – interest rate controls, exchange rate controls, reserve requirements, regulation of competition, etc. Strict credit controls lead to credit rationing by institutions which translates into reduced access to funds for a large share of the population that cannot fulfil the stringent eligibility criteria. The proponents of this thesis contend that financial liberalisation, i.e. removing the fetters on the formal sector, would reduce the activities of the informal financial sector.

According to the other line of argument, monetary and financial dualism can be explained more by the intrinsic dualism of economic and social structures in the developing countries and the rural population's attachment to traditional values and customs than by the inefficiency of the formal sector. Thus the formal financial sector would itself be subjected to dualism more than it engenders it. Those who subscribe to this thesis favour a more regulated financial system and hasten to point out that even in a liberalised financial system, the informal financial sector is still present.

The results of the case studies rather suggest a combination of the two above analyses regarding the causes of financial dualism. The informal sector – whose strength lies in the fact that it is firmly rooted in traditional values and practices and that transactions are flexible and speedy – responds to the needs of those segments of the population who, for whatever reasons, have found themselves excluded from the formal sector. Alongside those who have no access at all to formal funds, this includes people who do have access to formal sources but who seek to supplement bank loans with informal funds or to take advantage of the speed of delivery of informal credit or to better integrate themselves into their community by participating in neighbourhood associations. In other words, dualism can be ascribed as much to financial repression as to the population's attachment to traditional modes of behaviour.

Whatever the causes, financial dualism can have an adverse impact on development by affecting the accumulation and distribution processes of the developing countries and hence their rate of economic growth. Sectoral and regional disparities are created as regards the mobilisation and allocation of funds (rural savings are siphoned off to urban centres), and a growth rate differential is introduced between economic sectors as their development becomes a function of their access to the different credit sources available. Negative effects on equity result from the fact that the informal financial sector's clients are usually the small and poorer borrowers who must choose between higher-cost informal credit and no credit at all.

Dualism also undermines efforts by the public authorities to implement a consistent economic, monetary and financial policy, since objectives are difficult to define in the absence of aggregate economic indicators (informal sector activities do not appear in national accounts). By nature, the informal sector escapes taxation, while a dualistic financial structure makes the sources of money supply and monetary targets difficult to define; nor is regulation through volumes or interest rates efficacious when there is a considerable amount of liquidity outside the banking sector. Moreover, the capital flight which takes place through informal channels weighs heavily in the definition of monetary objectives.

Against this backdrop, therefore, the objective is to analyse the overall framework for financial intermediation in the developing countries – that is, formal and informal financial circuits in parallel – from the point of view of their structure, organisation, operations and practices, as well as the economic policy environment to which they are subjected. By underlining the similarities and differences of functioning, and identifying those areas where the two sectors are complementary and those where they are substitutable, one may uncover points for potential "bridge-building" between them. Indeed, there is a growing consensus that financial development and financial deepening cannot be achieved by focusing attention on formal sector institutions and markets alone – the tenacity of the informal sector, if anything, testifies to that. By the same token, the informal sector cannot be left to its own devices if financial dualism and its impact on development are to be reduced.

Structure and Operations of the Formal and Informal Sectors

The ensemble of financial circuits in the developing countries is composed of the formal and informal sectors together. Each of the two sectors is quite diverse with regard to the institutions, markets, mechanisms and operators involved.

From the institutional point of view, the developing countries would seem to be well-endowed. Their *formal financial sector* can be represented on three levels. The first level is that of the central bank which, in the developing countries, often oversteps the prudential functions it is assigned and assumes an increasingly interventionist role in local financial activity. Another characteristic of financial activity is the predominant role of the Treasury, as gauged by the share of claims on central government in domestic credit. The second level is composed of a myriad of banking and non-bank financial intermediaries, including commercial banks, merchant banks, development banks, savings banks, building societies, postal savings networks, specialised financial institutions, social security schemes, provident funds, and insurance companies. As for the third level, i.e. capital markets, developing country experiences are multifarious, ranging from the relative atrophy of money, bond, or stock markets in Africa to what the IFC has labelled "emerging capital markets" in certain Asian and Latin American countries.

In a number of countries (India, Zimbabwe and Zambia, for example), savings and credit co-operatives and credit unions are of growing importance. They may generally be labelled *"semi-formal" entities* insofar as there is often no registration or regular supervision, although rules of functioning may be laid down by law. The main significance of the co-operative movement is that it provides an alternative form of financial intermediation for small-scale savers and borrowers and that it is based on the concept of self-help through mutual solidarity. Its generally satisfactory overall performance has prompted governments to take a more active interest in it as a potentially viable means of mobilising funds and distributing loans.

Turning to the *informal sector*, one of the most striking features is the wide variety of links between lenders, borrowers and savers, ranging from simple credit arrangements to complex financial intermediation mechanisms. Three basic types of informal financial operators can generally be distinguished: individual moneylenders, groups of individuals organised mutually, and partnership firms.

Individual moneylenders include friends, neighbours, relatives, landlords, professional moneylenders, input dealers, output processors, produce and itinerant traders, market vendors, storeowners, etc. Individual moneylenders most often lend out their own funds; sometimes they accept deposits. Their credit arrangements may be non-commercial – in the sense of being interest-free – or commercial. In the latter case the credit transactions may be money-based (professional lenders), land-based (farmer-lenders) or commodity-based (trader-lenders).

Informal financial activity may also take the form of groups of individuals sharing a common bond (ethnic, residential, occupational, etc.), organised mutually and subject to rules and regulations of functioning which they themselves have laid down and agreed upon. The two main types of informal associations, which also assume a function of social protection, are: savings arrangements only (fixed-fund associations, savings clubs); and combined savings and credit arrangements where regular participation in the savings accumulation process entitles a member to loan facilities – with or without interest – from the group (mutual aid associations, rotating savings and credit associations).

Finally, the informal sector in some countries may be rather more complex and evolved, not only from the point of view of structural and operational characteristics but also in terms of the weight it carries in overall financial activity. Examples of partnership firms, such as indigenous bankers and pawnbrokers are found primarily in India, as are other non-bank financial intermediaries such as finance, investment, leasing and hire-purchase, and chit fund companies (the latter are actually an evolved form of rotating savings and credit associations, common to India). Despite the corporate structure of the latter four and the existence of legal regulations on their activity, they are included in the informal sector due to their exemption, to a greater or lesser degree, from central bank controls.

Clearly, various combinations – and not necessarily the entire gamut – of both formal and informal entities may be found in each country.

With regard to formal financial institutions, one would expect to find a central bank, commercial banks, and state-owned development banks in all cases, as was confirmed by the case studies. Interestingly, the cooperative/credit union movement was a feature common to all of the countries studied. As for the informal sector, it is by nature a reflection of the economic, social, and cultural specificity of each country.

Alongside the inventory of existing financial circuits, it is equally important to know, where possible, the *share* of each type of institution, scheme, operator, as well as the importance of financial markets, in overall transactions. Commercial banks play a prominent role within the financial sector, as evidenced by their market shares in the volume of deposits (from 40 to 75 per cent of the total) and lending (from 25 to 60 per cent). Central banks come next in the share of total gross liabilities of the formal financial system, an indication of the degree of intervention in financial activity by the public authorities. The remainder of the market share in deposits and lending is divided between specialised financial institutions (mostly development banks), social security and private insurance institutions, savings banks, postal networks and other small-savings oriented bodies, cooperatives and credit unions. Hence, their shares are relatively limited.

As regards financial markets, the ratio of market capitalisation to domestic credit varies markedly amongst the developing countries and reflects the relative weight of market mechanisms versus intermediation mechanisms as well as that of the private sector in the economy. Brazil and Zimbabwe are among the most market-oriented sample countries, with ratios of 61.4 per cent (1985) and 41.3 per cent (1987) respectively, followed by the emerging capital markets in Southeast Asia (14 to 25 per cent).

In the informal sector as well, the relative "shares" – admittedly difficult to quantify – of different schemes vary as the economic environment in which they operate changes. One of the most noticeable changes is within the moneylending profession itself: with the advent of urbanisation, new technologies and marketing procedures, it is becoming more of an urban than a rural phenomenon, while in rural areas, landlord-lenders are slowly being eclipsed by more complex arrangements with trader-lenders and storeowners.

It is also important to analyse and contrast the *operational aspects* of the formal and informal financial sectors.

Formal financial institutions are overwhelmingly urban-oriented, from the point of view of both the distribution of bank branches over national territory and the concentration of their deposit and lending activities. Poor communications and infrastructure often make it costly for financial institutions to set up shop in outlying rural areas.

Access to formal banking services is made difficult for both rural- and urban-based lower-income groups by the rigid, bureaucratic procedures that loan disbursements and deposit-taking entail. Cumbersome paperwork and processing requires literacy skills of potential clients (which is not always the case) and slows down considerably the loan disbursement process. Moreover, because of high transaction costs (loan appraisal, documentation, and legal fees), formal financial institutions prefer to deal in large sums (deposits and loans) which are beyond the means of the majority of potential clients, as are the stringent collateral requirements for loans.

Formal financial institutions tend to neglect the mobilisation of household savings, and devote their efforts instead to allocating credit and creating money. They display a triple bias with regard to both the mobilisation and allocation of resources: a preference for the public over the private sector, for large-scale enterprises and upper-income households over small-scale enterprises and lower-income households, and for non-agricultural (i.e. industry, commerce, manufacturing, construction) over agricultural loans. (Loans to the agricultural sector are primarily to large-scale commercial farming activities.) Moreover, they seek to exert control over the use of funds, notably to ensure that they are used for productive, long-term investment projects. This limits considerably their scope of action because it excludes from the outset a large proportion of would-be clients for whom consumption credit may sometimes be a requisite before productive investments can follow.

Informal financial activity is present in both rural and urban areas; though, in terms of financial activity, the informal sector is generally more important in rural areas.

Access to informal finance is relatively easy, in comparison to the formal sector, thanks notably to the flexibility of operations and loan terms (short-, medium- and long-term) to meet specific needs, the minimal red tape involved in transactions, easily understood rules and regulations, the rapid processing of requests and delivery of credit and, most importantly, the willingness to handle the small amounts which correspond to the requirements and the capacity of clients. The lower-income rural and urban households, small-scale farmers, craftsmen, and small businesses that constitute informal sector clientele require mostly short-term, often seasonal financing for consumption (housing, education, durables, ceremonial expenditures) or productive purposes (working capital for small businesses, funds for the purchase of seeds, fertilizer, equipment, the hiring of labour, or the financing of a community development project).

Transactions are based on the confidence engendered by face-to-face relationships between creditor and debtor; there is usually no collateral involved, except in some cases where tangible guarantees (such as jewellery, household appliances, etc.) or a promissory note, mortgage deed, or post-dated cheque are required by informal lenders. Security on loans is contingent upon the borrower's past savings and credit record and on social pressure to abide by certain rules of behaviour. Indeed, the link between prior savings and credit is stressed much more in the informal sector than in the formal one.

One of the central issues on the subject of formal and informal finance is that of interest rates and intermediation costs. In the formal sector, transaction costs when dealing with small clients are high, while interest rates across the board are usually fixed at low levels by the monetary authorities. Transaction costs in the informal sector are low (administrative expenses such as premises and overhead costs are low or non-existent) and interest rates are higher than in the formal sector; yet informal credit is more popular and repayment rates are higher – which is not to say, of course, that bad debts do not exist – in the informal sector.

Default risk is minimized by informal lenders in a number of ways. Information on the creditworthiness of potential borrowers can be obtained easily and relatively cheaply, since lenders usually live and work in the circumscribed area of their financial operations, which also allows for effective follow-up on outstanding loans. Lenders employ an additional means of minimizing default risk: through interlinked credit contracts, i.e. with *ex ante* or *ex post* tie-in arrangements established between the credit market on the one hand and the land, labour, or product markets on the other, through the overlapping personae of money-lenders, landlords, employers, or produce dealers. Such loans link credit transactions with the transfer of land occupancy or usufruct rights or labour services or the sale of output or the purchase of inputs, in favour, of course, of the lender. These practices seem to be on the rise in the developing countries.

As for the interest rate differential, two main arguments have emerged. The first one asserts that informal credit markets are non-competitive and that lenders who have monopolistic control are able to extract substantial rents by taking advantage of the relative inelasticity of demand for credit by informal sector clients (for the borrower, often pressured by time constraints, what counts more is the availability of credit rather than its cost). The second, opposing view is that the informal sector is competitive and that interest rates reflect the real cost of loanable funds. It is difficult to estimate the share of the various determinants of interest rates – i.e. a premium to cover transaction costs, opportunity cost of funds, a premium for risk, monopoly profits – in the global rate charged. Various empirical studies on the subject have led to differing results, particularly as regards the presence or absence of monopoly profits. What is certain, however, is that no *single* market rate of interest can be observed in the informal sector; instead, there is a multitude of credit arrangements covering a wide range of interest rates which are often a function of the relationship between lender and borrower (for example, friends and relatives may get preferential rates).

Policy Attitudes and Recommendations

There is a consensus on the existence of financial dualism, on its adverse effects, and on the need to reduce or even eradicate it. Where the views diverge, however, is on how to go about this. Should the formal and informal sectors be integrated (i.e. the formal sector expands and absorbs the informal sector) or should efforts to promote interlinkages between formal and informal operators be undertaken on a greater and more systematic scale? Clearly, the means proposed are a function of the thesis subscribed to regarding the causes of financial dualism.

Proponents of the view that the informal sector is a response to the deficiencies and inefficiencies of the formal sector focus on in-depth institutional and operational reforms in the formal sector as a remedy for financial dualism. This involves removing some of the constraints imposed on the formal financial sector – or, put differently, shifting from a policy of "financial repression" to one of "financial liberalisation" (and in particular, the liberalisation of interest rates) – as well as "deformalising" or "informalising" the formal sector, that is, adopting some of the informal sector's own practices and competing it down ("mimicry option"). By thus gradually obviating the need for the informal sector itself, the formal sector can be substituted for the informal sector and financial integration can be achieved.

By contrast, for those who perceive financial dualism as but one aspect of the overall structural dualism of the economy, the starting point for any strategy to reduce dualism is the informal sector itself, and efforts must focus on transforming it, or gradually "organising" or "institutionalising" it to some extent through linkage with the formal sector. By giving informal lenders and group leaders access to credit lines or other services, formal financial institutions can transmit, through them, to the rest of the population, the mechanics and mentality of formal financial practices.

In fact, neither of the two "solutions" is sufficient on its own, since financial dualism can be explained by both financial repression in the formal sector and the structural dualism of the economy. Hence, the policy recommendations of the *"middle of the road" approach* are a judicious mix of the two aforementioned strategies – integration and interlinkage undertaken concurrently – and they involve both microeconomic and macroeconomic measures. Moreover, in a dynamic context, integration and linkage are sequential: linkage in the short term will bring on integration in the long term. In other words, until the formal sector can cover the country's financial needs on its own, the informal sector could be used to do a part of the job (and "retail" formal credit to its clients). The challenge here resides in promoting links between the formal and informal sectors in such a way as to maximise the positive and minimise the negative aspects of each.

Alongside these measures, alternative financial instruments should be promoted, the development of insurance and social security structures should be encouraged (even when such institutions are present in the developing countries, in most cases they do not play the role they should), and the appropriate monetary and financial policies should be pursued, notably as regards interest rates, money supply, and exchange rates. Interest rate policy should involve positive real creditor rates, liberalised debtor rates (to allow more equal access to credit), and a reduced gap between borrowing and lending interest rates. This should be accompanied by deflationary measures and a policy of restrictive money supply to help protect savings against monetary depreciation. Exchange rate policy could be situated somewhere between the two extremes of liberalised capital movements and fixed exchange rates: a policy of pegging to one currency or to a basket of currencies, for example. Sectoral credit allocation policies should be redefined, and it would appear desirable for the Treasury to progressively disengage itself from excessive intervention in financial activity.

At the level of formal financial institutions, the savings and credit functions should be integrated, and multipurpose rather than specialised financial institutions should be set up. This would enhance inter-institutional competition, since banks would have a common range of activity, and avoid the duplication in financial services which may occur when there is excessive institutional specialisation. Alongside the institutional transformations, financial markets should also be developed as a means for matching financing capacities and borrowing requirements if the efficiency of monetary policy is to be really improved. Indeed, financial markets have proved to be very efficient in some developing countries, particularly in southeast Asia. Their in-depth development would require specific measures to promote organised financial markets such as futures markets for agricultural produce, stock exchanges, mortgage markets, etc.

Finally, accompanying macroeconomic policies would entail redefining sectoral credit allocation policies by replacing macroeconomic project selectivity criteria with a microeconomic and decentralised selection of investment projects through interest rates. Price control policies could also be modified to alleviate existing distortions in resource allocation.

It is highly likely that the economic, monetary and financial policies outlined above would increase the domestic rate of savings in those developing countries which decide to implement them.

There are many possible *tactics for achieving integration* (transforming the formal sector and substituting it for the informal sector) *and interlinkage* (preserving and using to advantage those characteristics of the informal sector which constitute its strength). To a large extent, these are made easier by the fact that financial flows already do occur – albeit on a spontaneous and ad hoc basis – from the informal to the formal sector and vice versa (for example, the funds amassed by mutual savings and loan associations may be deposited in accounts with a formal financial intermediary; in the opposite direction, private individuals with access to formal funds may use their position to lend informally). Efforts should therefore focus on consolidating and systematising these ad hoc initiatives. The main avenues towards attaining such a goal include: improving the formal financial sector, developing the social insurance sector, and "organising" the informal sector.

Making the formal sector more accessible may be done in a number of ways. One of the most obvious is to adopt outright those informal practices which are reproducible within formal financial circuits. (For example, the Indonesian government runs its own pawnshops, and banks in India organise chit funds, or ROSCAs.) Beyond that, simplifying structures and procedures would help keep intermediation costs low and reduce delays in loan disbursement. Decentralisation of management would allow formal institutions to be more locally adapted; they could eventually even provide guidance and assistance services on prices, markets, production and marketing techniques. Formal financial institutions should seek to provide appropriate financial services, notably for small amounts, allow for more flexible repayment schedules, and offer more consumer credit and personal loans. New formulas with regard to guarantees could also be envisaged, such as accepting either tangible assets or prior savings deposits as a guarantee for a loan. Finally, formal institutions could use informal operators as local representatives or "financial retailers" – benefitting from the latters' lower transaction costs and closer contact with target groups – by providing them with access to credit lines so that they could on-lend to their own clients, or by asking them to recommend creditworthy borrowers from amongst their clientele.

Developing the social insurance sector is another dimension of the policy for reducing dualism. The solidarity principle in the informal sector means that groups constitute in fact a collective organisation against individual and social risks; to this extent it can be said that there is a large informal insurance sector in developing countries. Thus, if the savings and credit functions of the informal sector are eventually institutionalised, alternative measures must be implemented to ensure that the social functions of such groupings also continue to be fulfilled. This may be done by developing either a social security system or the insurance sector. Financing and management obstacles, as well as the anonymity, of national social security schemes make their extension, in the short-term at least, unlikely, unless they were to adopt a more decentralised structure, with a large degree of independence granted to local bodies and methods based partly on those of informal groups.

Insurance, being more flexible, could be a more likely substitute for the spontaneous solidarity of the informal sector. The long-term, stable and financial savings generated by insurance activities (especially organisations dealing with old age insurance) would make it possible to ensure optimal financing of investments and capital. It therefore seems desirable to develop funded pension schemes or provident funds, which would be managed on the principles of mutuality. A developed insurance sector would also contribute significantly to the development of financial markets.

The challenge of *"organising" the informal sector* through closer linkage with formal sector operators resides in providing better and increased financial services to the community (by way of additional funds and guidance received) without jeopardising those characteristics of the informal sector which constitute its strength: flexibility, rapidity, transparency of procedures, personal relationships, and low transaction costs. This is admittedly a very fine line to tread.

Nonetheless, there are several possible measures which would contribute to improving the role of the informal sector in mobilising savings. Training programmes for members and group leaders of savings and credit groups, and specialised supportive services providing information on supply of production factors or marketing techniques would allow informal operators to manage more efficiently the collection and, above all, the allocation of savings. Calling on the help of informal groups to facilitate savings and credit activities is another possibility: group lending (or block lending) brings together a formal financial institution and a group of borrowers around a single transaction. The decision on how the loan received (by the group as a whole) is to be allocated among members is left to the group itself. The advantage of such arrangements for the group and its members is that they have access to additional funds over and above the limited levels of members' contributions. For the lending institution, the advantage is reduced transaction costs.

Finally, in many developing countries, the co-operative and credit union movement is seen as one of the main avenues for linkage and eventual integration of the formal and informal sectors, due to its role in providing small-scale financial facilities and its close resemblance to informal mechanisms of mutual solidarity. The institutional links may range from a simple function of assistance, including rediscounting facilities with the central bank, to national centralisation of funds collected locally.

In conclusion, while there is a consensus on the need to reduce financial dualism, only a limited number of developing country governments have as yet formulated an explicit policy to that effect. The attitudes range from "benign neglect", if not total indifference, to awareness of the problem, to an active effort for financial innovation and financial deepening.

At any rate, reducing financial dualism in developing countries calls for a multidimensional approach. It requires a dynamic programme developed both by private agents and by the government, and a far-reaching modification of economic and social behaviour patterns, as well as the appropriate adaptation of structures and procedures, all as a function of the specificities of each country.

It is not possible to transpose development models directly from one country to another. Care should be taken to avoid assuming that a policy which has proved successful in one country will necessarily produce the same effects in another country at another time. Nevertheless, the exchange of views and of experiences can only be useful in the search for the appropriate economic, monetary and financial policies to be implemented in individual countries.

Chapter 1

FINANCIAL DUALISM IN DEVELOPING COUNTRIES: MAIN FEATURES AND ISSUES

The renewed interest in financial intermediation processes in the developing countries stems largely from the international financial crisis which broke out in 1981-82 and during which external credit for the developing countries became increasingly expensive – giving rise to heavier debt burdens – and scarce. The consequent transition from strong reliance on external sources of finance to domestic financing served to underline the deficiencies and inefficiencies of developing countries' financial systems, the active development of which had hitherto been overlooked. The long-prevailing assumption that monetary and financial development was a consequence of – and not a prerequisite for – economic development, coupled with the fact that external finance had hitherto been easy, cheap and forthcoming, had placed the developing countries in a situation where they could "afford" to defer efforts for an active policy of development of the domestic monetary and financial sector. Paradoxically though, their underdeveloped domestic financial systems meant that the foreign resources channelled through them were, overall, inefficiently allocated; this had repercussions on the productivity of foreign resources, resulting in problems with repayments.

The excessive reliance on external sources of finance and the resulting atrophy of domestic financial circuits and markets also meant that the public authorities were foregoing the possibility of tapping the potential sources of savings which are present in the developing countries. These are often underestimated because the postulate that developing countries have a low or non-existent savings capacity is, unfortunately, accepted without question. The available figures on domestic savings rates in the newly industrialised countries (see Table 4.2 in Chapter 4) – which have achieved high rates of economic growth – indicate the presence of internal resources which can contribute to rapid accumulation. It is true that most of these countries simultaneously pursued an active policy of financial reform. Yet even in the least developed countries, there is a savings capacity that is often undetected and frequently neglected.

Over the last 15 years, however, a growing number of economists – Adams, Chandavarkar, Fry, Shaw and McKinnon, among others – have agreed that a well-developed financial system *does* matter in economic development, ranking *pari passu* with other necessary "inputs" such as natural resources, labour markets, management, technology, entrepreneurial ability, and this at a time when the need to relay foreign financing with domestic resources is becoming increasingly urgent and hence must be met through the reform and development of domestic monetary and financial systems.

In this introductory chapter, we shall try to set the context and define the terms of our analysis of financial dualism by succinctly presenting and discussing some of the main issues involved. The first part of the chapter focuses on the alternative financial systems in developing countries, on the difficulties involved in gauging the extent of the informal sector, and on the salient features of the formal and informal sectors. The second part discusses the causes and effects of financial dualism.

I. FINANCIAL DUALISM: FORMAL VERSUS INFORMAL FINANCIAL SECTORS

A. THE ALTERNATIVE FINANCIAL SYSTEMS IN DEVELOPING COUNTRIES

1. The Theoretical Archetypes

The informal financial sector must be analysed against the backdrop of the overall financial system in its entirety. Obviously the configuration of financial systems is not everywhere the same: some are more complete than others; some are more regulated than others. In the context of the developing countries, two main types of financial systems can generally be distinguished: those that are closely controlled and in which government intervention is extensive; and those which are more "liberalised", where financial institutions have greater leeway in carrying out their intermediation activities, and where market mechanisms are promoted.

Taking the former case first, the principal characteristic of a closely "regulated" financial sector (Type A in Table 1.1) is *i)* a quasi-fixed interest rate structure whereby real interest rates are low or even negative and little or no interest is paid on deposits. Some of the corollary effects on behaviour, allocation, organisation of the financial sector, and monetary policy include: *ii)* the delinkage of the savings and credit functions; *iii)* the implementation of sectoral credit allocation policies, either by setting target quotas or through subsidised interest rates; *iv)* the centralisation of the resources mobilised and a high degree of specialisation of both institutions and the financial products offered; *v)* inflationary pressures resulting from the transformation of short-term resources into long-term loans; and *vi)* restricted capital movements through exchange rate controls. Overall, such heavy credit control is likely to lead to credit rationing. The policy is nonetheless presented as being favourable to investment because it reduces the cost of financing; however, it undoubtedly places a brake on the development of financial markets.

The more "liberalised" financial systems (Type B in Table 1.1), by contrast, give emphasis to resource mobilisation over investment. The main characteristics in this case are: *i)* positive and variable real interest rates and remuneration of deposits; *ii)* emphasis on the link between savings and credit; *iii)* development of financial markets and the role of market forces in capital allocation, while sectoral credit allocation policies and interest rate subsidies are avoided; *iv)* multi-vocational financial institutions; *v)* a monetary policy using market instruments and designed to fight inflation, so that real interest rates remain positive; *vi)* a liberal exchange rate policy.

The features and effects of these two alternative monetary and financial policies are presented in greater detail in Table 1.1.

Table 1.1 THE EFFECTS OF ALTERNATIVE MONETARY AND FINANCIAL POLICIES

Economic and Financial Policy Type A	Economic and Financial Policy Type B
1. Principal Characteristics	
– fixed interest rate structure, with low or negative real interest rates in the formal sector	– positive and variable real interest rates
– little or no interest paid on deposits in the formal sector	– remuneration of deposits
– wide gap between interest rates in the formal and informal sectors	– reduced gap between interest rates in the formal and informal sectors
2. Effects On Behaviour	
– must favour those borrowers (mainly enterprises) who have access to formal sector institutions	– role of market forces in matching lending capacity with borrowing requirements
	– must transform idle cash holdings into financial savings
– conception of macroeconomic causality: $I \rightarrow Y \rightarrow S \rightarrow I$	– conception of macroeconomic causality: $S \rightarrow Y \rightarrow I \rightarrow S$
– scheme of finance dynamics according to which loans make deposits	– scheme of finance dynamics according to which deposits make loans
– delinkage of the savings and credit functions	– emphasis on the link between savings and credit
3. Distributional Effects	
– inflationary transfers in favour of borrowers and at the expense of savers	– rising financial returns for depositors and savers
	– creditor households and entrepreneurs gain while borrowers lose
– wide gap between lending and deposit rates which enriches the formal financial sector	– narrower gap between lending and deposit rates
– inequality between households and entrepreneurs with access to cheap credit from the formal sector and those whose sole recourse is the informal sector	– inequality between households whose resources give them access to institutional credit (they can afford the cost) and households without such access
4. Effects On Resource Allocation	
– policy presented as being favourable to investment	– policy presented as being favourable to savings
– sectoral credit allocation policies (via global credit quotas, subsidised interest rates, ...)	– allocation of resources according to the repayment capacity of sectors. No sectoral credit allocation policies
– government intervention	– priority given to market mechanisms
	– selection of investment projects through the interest rates applied

25

Table 1.1   THE EFFECTS OF ALTERNATIVE MONETARY AND FINANCIAL POLICIES *(cont.)*

Economic and Financial Policy Type A	Economic and Financial Policy Type B
5. Effects On Financial Organisations	
– a large number of specialised financial networks in the formal sector	– most banks are authorised to provide the full range of financial services
– delinkage of savings-collecting networks and institutions specialised in loan distribution	– linkage of loans and deposits
– specialised financial products	– standardised financial products
– single-purpose financial institutions	– multi-purpose (universal) inancial institutions
– centralisation of resources mobilised in the formal sector	– decentralisation of resources
– encourages the development of an overdraft economy and hampers the development of formal financial markets	– favours the development of financial markets
6. Effects On Monetary Policy	
– transformation of short-term resources into long-term loans which fuels inflationary pressures	– restrictive monetary policy designed to maintain positive real interest rates
– fixed interest rate structure by term	– variable interest rates determined by the evolution of global lending capacity and borrowing requirements (market-determined interest rates)
– administered lending and deposit rates	
– central role of the Treasury in the mobilisation, remuneration and allocation of resources	– non-interventionist policy of the Treasury in the mobilisation, remuneration and allocation of resources
– restricted capital movements	– liberalised external capital movements
– tendency for devaluation of exchange rates	– tendency to maintain strong exchange rates

Source: adapted from Kessler, D., "Foreign Indebtedness, Savings and Growth in Developing Countries", in Kessler, D. and P.A. Ullmo, eds, *Savings and Development,* Paris, Economica, 1985, pp. 351-363.

2. The Empirical Alternatives

The two types of financial systems depicted above are contrasted more in theory than in practice. In between these two theoretical "extremes", there is a whole range of possible configurations which a country's financial system can assume by combining different aspects of both alternatives to different degrees. Indeed, most financial systems appear to be hybrid. The large number of parameters involved makes it difficult to rank a given group of countries in an ordinal manner, according to their degree of "regulation" or "liberalisation".

In order to better visualise and compare the financial systems of our country case studies against the backdrop of the two theoretical archetypes, we employed a slightly more qualitative approach, focusing on eight criteria, which cover both the market and institutional aspects of the financial sector.

a) The Criteria

The criteria covering the *market aspect* included *i)* the level of real interest rates; *ii)* the extent of financial markets; *iii)* recourse to and mode of implementation of sectoral credit allocation policies, through subsidised interest rates or target credit quotas, etc.; *iv)* the extent of foreign exchange controls.

From the *institutional* point of view, we looked at *v)* the control of competition by the public authorities (the predominance of specialised as opposed to universal banks, the distribution of branches over national territory, etc.); *vi)* the public or private, local or foreign status of financial institutions; *vii)* the predominance of the Treasury in financial activity, through the share of claims on central government in domestic credit; *viii)* the role and clout of the Central Bank in determining and implementing monetary and credit policy through refinancing policies, reserve requirements, etc.

Using the information provided by the case study reports as well as supplementary statistical work on *International Financial Statistics* (IMF) data[1], each country was "graded" on a scale of 1 to 3 for each criterion, the grade "1" corresponding to a more "liberalised" market-oriented tendency, "3" marking a case of close control over the activity or institution in question, and "2" being the stage in between.

b) The Results

The graphic representation of the results takes the form of polygons around 8 axes (one for each criterion); the smaller the area of the polygon, the more "liberalised" the financial system, and vice versa, as seen from the graphic representation of the two theoretical cases "Type A" and "Type B".

With all due reserve regarding the arbitrary character of the choice of criteria and the subjective nature of the grades thus attributed, the results of this exercise are presented in Table 1.2 and Figures 1.1 through 1.10.

The graphics help to visualise the qualitative differences, i.e. the manner in which control is exercised and the emphasis given to one or another means of going about it. Many combinations are possible, as the variety of the graphics shows.

Among eight countries studied, three main tendencies can be discerned: a controlled financial system like that of Ethiopia can be opposed to the more liberalised systems of Zimbabwe, the Philippines, Indonesia and, to a certain extent, India; in between, the financial systems of Mexico, Burundi, and Zambia could be described as "mixed and

Table 1.2   REGULATED OR LIBERALISED FINANCIAL SYSTEMS: SOME EMPIRICAL RESULTS

	Asia			Africa				Latin America
	India	Indonesia	Philippines	Burundi	Ethiopia	Zambia	Zimbabwe	Mexico
Foreign exchange controls	2	2	1	2	3	2	2	2
Deposit and lending interest rates of banks ..	1*	1	2	2	1	3	2	3
Absence of financial markets	1	2	2	3	3	2	2	2
Sectoral credit allocation policies	2	2	3	1	3	1	1	1
Control of competition	2	2	2	1	3	1	2	2
Nationalisation of financial system	2	2	1	2	3	1	1	3
Predominance of the Treasury in financial activity	3	1	1	3	3	3	1	3
Central Bank intervention	3	2	2	2	3	1	2	2
Totals	16	14	14	16	22	14	13	18

N.B..   The grade 3 corresponds to a "Type A" financial system (see Table 1.1); the grade 1 corresponds to a "Type B" financial system (see Table 1.1).
* Data available only for lending rates.

evolving" towards more liberalised policies. Within these groups themselves, there are also special characteristics which can be distinguished. Among the "liberalised" countries, regulation in Zimbabwe and the Philippines, for example, is carried out through the markets rather than through direct control of financial institutions by the public authorities. This can be contrasted with India, where a close grip on the institutions of the financial sector does not seem to interfere too much with the play of market forces. Similarly, among the "mixed but evolving" countries, Mexico and Burundi can be contrasted with Zambia. In the former two countries, a predominant Treasury and Central Bank exercise considerable control over both markets and institutions – with the exception of the credit market in Burundi and the credit and financial markets in Mexico – while the Zambian public authorities seem to have a weaker hold on institutions than on markets. Indonesia differs from the rest of the group in that both markets and institutions are subject to government intervention, although this has not seemed to hinder the emergence of a financial market nor has it contributed to distortions in real interest rates or to a strong absorption of resources by the Treasury.

Figure 1.1. **TYPE A : CLOSELY REGULATED FINANCIAL SYSTEMS**

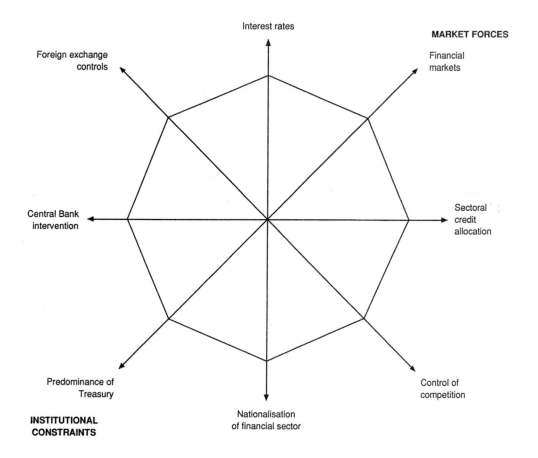

Interest rates

MARKET FORCES

Foreign exchange
controls

Financial
markets

Central Bank
intervention

Sectoral
credit
allocation

Predominance of
Treasury

Control of
competition

**INSTITUTIONAL
CONSTRAINTS**

Nationalisation
of financial sector

Figure 1.2. **TYPE B : MORE "LIBERALISED" FINANCIAL SYSTEMS**

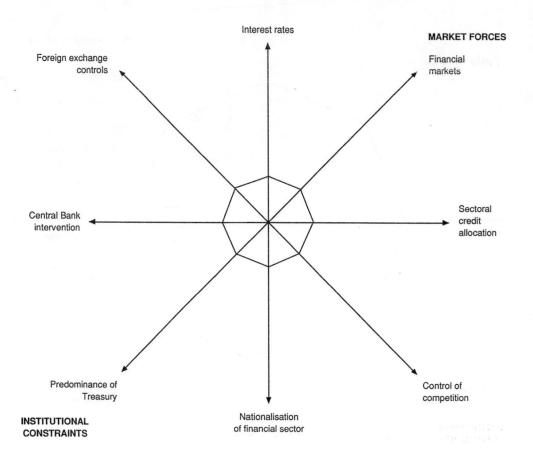

Figure 1.3. **ZIMBABWE**

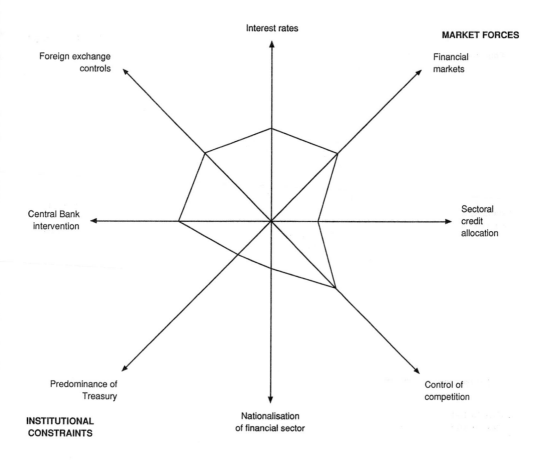

Figure 1.4. **INDONESIA**

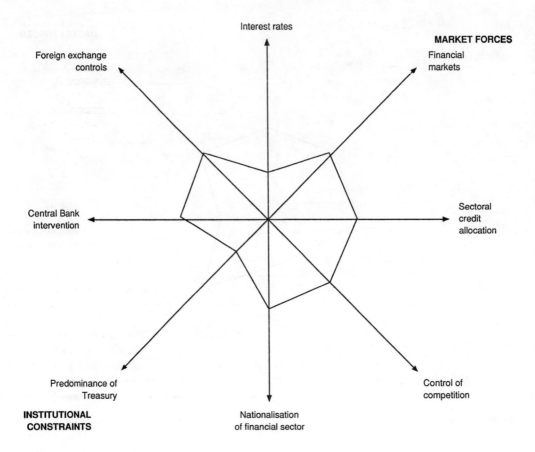

Interest rates

MARKET FORCES

Financial markets

Foreign exchange controls

Sectoral credit allocation

Central Bank intervention

Predominance of Treasury

INSTITUTIONAL CONSTRAINTS

Nationalisation of financial sector

Control of competition

Figure 1.5. **PHILIPPINES**

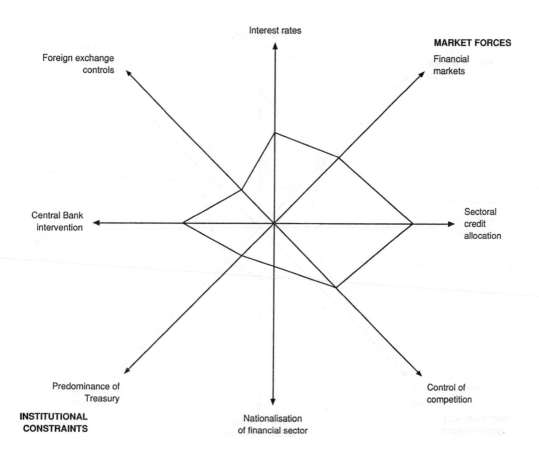

Interest rates

MARKET FORCES

Foreign exchange
controls

Financial
markets

Central Bank
intervention

Sectoral
credit
allocation

Predominance of
Treasury

Control of
competition

**INSTITUTIONAL
CONSTRAINTS**

Nationalisation
of financial sector

Figure 1.6. **ZAMBIA**

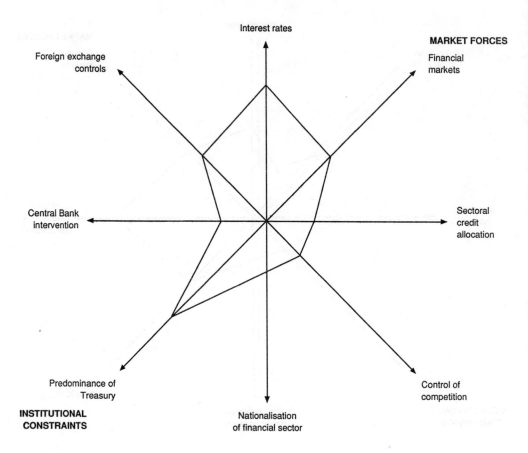

Interest rates

MARKET FORCES

Foreign exchange
controls

Financial
markets

Central Bank
intervention

Sectoral
credit
allocation

Predominance of
Treasury

Control of
competition

**INSTITUTIONAL
CONSTRAINTS**

Nationalisation
of financial sector

Figure 1.7. **INDIA**

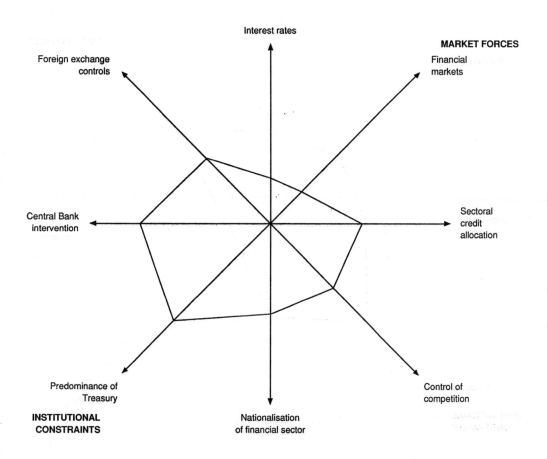

Figure 1.8. **BURUNDI**

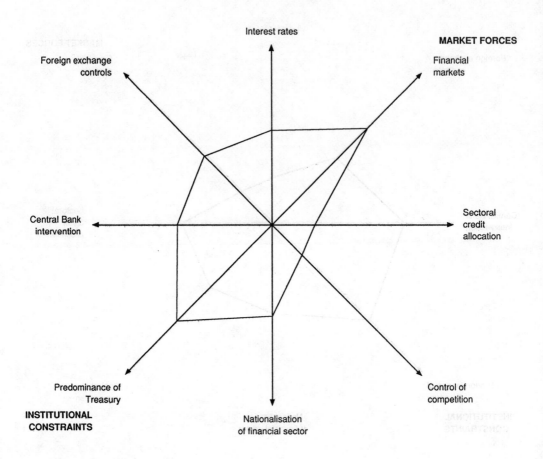

Figure 1.9. **MEXICO**

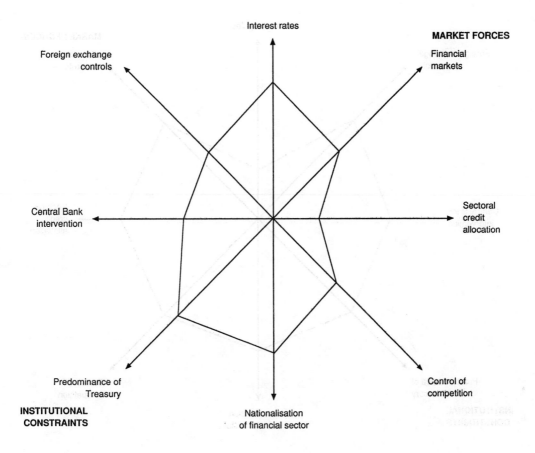

Figure 1.10. **ETHIOPIA**

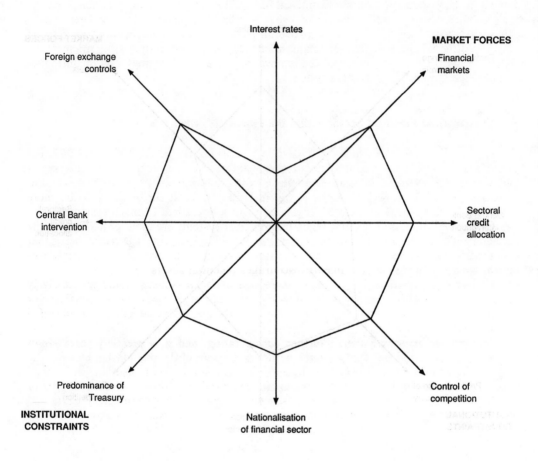

c) The Dynamic Nature of Financial Systems

It should be pointed out, however, that such a "classification" is valid only at a given moment in time. The financial systems of the developing countries are evolving: a change in the public or private status of banks, expansion of financial markets, changes in interest rate policy, etc. may indicate that some countries are moving closer to financial liberalisation while others seem to lean more towards greater regulation. Mexico, for example, is now moving in the direction of a more liberalised financial policy, after having nationalised the quasi-totality of the banking system in 1982. In the Philippines, a floating interest rate policy was adopted in 1981 as part of an overall package of economic liberalisation reform. Starting in the last quarter of 1985, Zambia introduced a liberalisation programme which included the lifting of price controls, the removal of interest rate ceilings, and the introduction of a foreign exchange auction system.

3. The Informal Financial Sector within the Financial System

It is in this context of a financial system in transition that the analysis of the informal financial sector must be placed. The question which arises is whether the structure and functioning of the formal financial sector play a role in determining the nature and extent of the informal sector. In other words, is the informal financial sector likely to be more important in the context of a closely regulated or of a liberalised financial system?

One could argue *a priori* that regulated financial systems are more propitious for the development of the informal financial sector than are liberalised ones, the reason being that credit rationing induces informal lending activity while, at the same time, the unattractiveness of deposit and saving instruments discourages potential savers.

Conversely, the transition to more liberalised financial systems would progressively curtail informal financial activity by siphoning off resources from the informal sector through positive real interest rates and consequently also short-circuiting the informal lending process.

This line of reasoning merits further consideration, and it is precisely these issues which are addressed in this study, i.e. the nature and extent of the relationship between the formal and informal financial sectors. Indeed, the case studies confirmed the presence of informal financial activity in all the economies surveyed, irrespective of their degree of regulation or liberalisation. It remains to be seen whether and to what extent the size and operations of the informal financial sector are determined by the overall configuration of the financial system.

B. THE EXTENT OF THE INFORMAL FINANCIAL SECTOR

A common characteristic of many developing countries is their dualistic economic structure, i.e. the co-existence of a formal sector and a sometimes substantial informal sector as regards the various spheres of socio-economic activity. Indeed, it must be noted from the outset that the term "informal economic sector" does not refer to one single type of activity or market, but rather includes the multitude of transactions which can be contracted informally on the commodities market, labour market, financial market, etc. At the same time, the extent of each one of these "informal markets" cannot be dissociated from that of the informal economic sector as a whole. In reference to what was said earlier, the existence of untapped sources of savings signals the presence of informal financial markets which were observed in all the case studies and on which this study will focus.

1. The Indistinct Boundaries Between the Formal and Informal Financial Sectors

It is common practice to explain financial dualism by contrasting the formal and informal financial sectors which operate side by side in the developing countries. Pushing the comparison even further, the formal sector would refer to an organised, urban-oriented, institutional system catering to the financial needs of the monetised modern sector; while the informal sector, itself unorganised and non-institutional, would deal with the traditional, rural, subsistence (non-monetised) spheres of the economy.

The reality is much more complex, however. First of all, the dividing line between the formal and informal sectors is not always so clear-cut. Informal savings and credit systems are not exclusively rural area phenomena and may in fact be quite "organised". Conversely, barter trade or even informal transactions may sometimes occur between modern sector operators.

Moreover, the two sectors are not totally independent of each other. Agents from the one often operate in or turn for services to the other, as when formal sector bank employees participate in rotating savings and credit associations (ROSCAs), lend to friends, help a relative pay his dowry, or send remittances to the extended family in communal lands. In some cases, informal sector lenders have access to formal sector funds which they then on-lend, or "retail", to informal sector borrowers. This marks a phenomenon of "money flight" away from institutionalised banking networks. In other cases, informal lenders deposit funds with formal financial institutions or engage in formal financial transactions.

Finally, it must be emphasized that each subset itself is not completely homogeneous; in fact, both are extremely diversified, whether from the point of view of the organisational set-up, the dimension or nature of activities, the operators involved, geographic (urban-rural) location, etc.

2. The Diversity of Formal and Informal Sector Operators

The formal financial sector includes commercial banks (public or private, national or foreign), development banks, specialised financial institutions, savings banks, etc., as well as the various capital markets (bond, equity, money, real estate, etc.).

Within the informal financial sector one finds, for example, moneylenders, landlords, traders, rotating savings and credit associations (ROSCAs), self-help organisations, family or tribal funds, indigenous bankers, etc. These different informal bodies do not function in the same way. In effect, the savings and credit functions are dissociated in the case of individual lenders but are linked in the case of ROSCAs and indigenous bankers. Furthermore, the nature of each one of these bodies can vary considerably, even though they may be designated by the same word. This is especially true of informal savings and credit associations whose organisation, size, and mode of functioning often differ from one region to another within the same country.

3. The Extent of the Informal Sector

This diversity of informal financial activity makes it quite difficult to estimate the actual extent of the informal financial sector within the economy. Various studies have nonetheless attempted to do so, using different means: assessing the degree of monetisation of the economy, looking at the tax base, estimating the size of the participating population or the volume of transactions. While each of these proxies is a positive step towards better defining the informal financial sector, their drawback is that they actually cover only a limited segment of the latter, and as such probably underestimate its overall extent.

a) The Monetised and Non-Monetised Sectors

One method is to try and assess the degree of monetisation of the economy. This implies contrasting the monetised sector – where money serves as a unit of measure, a means of exchange, and a reserve of value – and the non-monetised sector, which is predominantly rural and where a subsistence and/or barter economy prevail. The extent of the non-monetised sector depends on how widespread the auto-subsistence phenomenon is. In the cases of both a subsistence economy and a barter economy, no money is used and no surplus is generated. Even when there is a surplus involved, it is not necessarily in cash form. In effect, both savings and investment may be in kind: food stocks, cattle, and the hoarding of gold are examples of non-monetary savings; accumulation of materials for the construction of wells in rural areas and housing in urban areas are forms of investment in kind. Moreover, even credit transactions may be in kind, a loan of seeds being repaid with a share of the harvest.

The available figures are very approximate but nonetheless of some interest. Estimates of the size of the non-monetised sphere for Africa, Asia, and Latin America range from a low 2 per cent to a high 50 per cent of GDP. The variety and contrast is particularly marked in the African case. Indeed, Chandavarkar[2] found that, in the early 1970s, the share of non-monetised production in GDP was 49 per cent in Rwanda and 45 per cent in Ethiopia, compared to 13 per cent in Senegal, 11 per cent in Côte d'Ivoire, and 7 per cent in Zambia[3]. In Asia, the range is narrower – from $1/10$ to $1/5$ of GDP. For example, 10 per cent of production is non-monetised in the Philippines and Thailand, while this figure approaches 20 per cent for India, Malaysia, and South Korea. Of the three regions, Latin America is the most monetised; for instance, estimates set the level of non-monetised production for both Argentina and Mexico at 2 per cent of GDP.

The problem with this approach is that it limits the concept of informal savings and credit mechanisms to those which take place in kind. Yet informal financial activity can also involve cash. In other words, whereas the non-monetised sphere of the economy is indeed part of the informal sector, the informal sector itself extends beyond the limits of the non-monetised sphere.

b) The Size of the Population Concerned

Another way of assessing the extent of informal financial activity would be to consider the number of persons who are members of informal savings and credit associations. According to Bouman[4], "amongst the Bamileke in eastern Cameroon, every adult is a member of at least one savings association ..." In western Cameroon, at least three-fourths of the villagers are members of one or several *djanggi*. In the villages of Iliako Igboroko and

Toffo in southeastern Benin – two neighbouring villages of different tribal lineage – almost all the men and women over 18 years of age participate in a tontine. In Addis Ababa in Ethiopia, it is estimated that 60 per cent of the urban population participates in an *ekub* and that, among craftsmen, and especially weavers, this figure may be as high as 90 per cent. Also in Ethiopia, it has been observed that everyone is a member of at least one *idir*. In Zambia, the informal sector is no longer limited to rural areas; 80 to 90 per cent of the urban population (everyone except in the higher-income groups) participates in the informal financial sector.

The available studies thus show that membership of informal groups covers the majority of the population in developing countries, independently of age, income-level, region (urban or rural), or profession. Moreover, as many households may participate in both the formal and informal sectors, there is also a considerable overlap which is not distinguishable in the figures.

c) The Volume of Transactions Effected

The extent of the informal sector can also be gauged by comparing the volume of transactions effected by the formal and informal sectors as regards agricultural loans in rural areas or loans to small-scale entrepreneurs in urban areas, for example. The sums involved can be quite substantial in some cases. In Ethiopia, according to the 1968-1973 Development Plan, the volume of savings mobilised through *ekubs* was estimated at 8 to 10 per cent of GDP. In the case study by Mauri, the net savings of the 95 *ekubs* surveyed accounted for 44.5 per cent of total household savings deposited with the Commercial Bank of Ethiopia in July 1986. In Bangladesh, the size of the informal credit market, defined as the percentage of credit from informal sources, could be anywhere from 30 per cent to 90 per cent. However, if one takes account of all the major studies on the issue since 1974, the mean size could be estimated at approximately 60 per cent[5].

In some countries, the extent of the informal sector can be assumed from the small proportion of beneficiaries of formal credit programmes. In Zimbabwe, in 1986, only 13 per cent of small farmers received credit from formal financial sources. The remaining 87 per cent were thus obliged to turn to other (informal) sources for their financial requirements. In Nigeria, based on a representative sample from the two states of Kwara and West Nigeria, the share of the informal sector in loans to farmers was 95 per cent[6]. The informal sector represents an important share of rural credit in Zambia as well, where 57 per cent of farmers' financial needs were met by formal credit services, the remaining 43 per cent coming from informal sources. A survey by Nagle[7] of Zambian farmers found that farmers' 'self-finance' (i.e. own funds and informal sources) provided, on average, 84 per cent of the latter's required finance.

Similarly, the 1983 Agricultural Census in Indonesia noted that during the early 1980s, only 17 per cent of the total number of agricultural households received credit from the government's special programmes, which means that 83 per cent of households received no formal credit at all. By contrast, in Thailand, the share of the formal sector in meeting the rural population's credit needs is said to have increased in the last 12 years as a result of the government's policy directing commercial banks. During the 1950s and 1960s, the formal sector provided 10 per cent of the credit needs in rural areas, while in the 1980s the figure rose to 40 to 50 per cent[8]. This still leaves a substantial proportion of rural credit needs uncovered, however, and indeed it has been estimated that 52 per cent of the new loans extended to the agricultural sector in Thailand are still provided by the informal market[9].

In Malaysia, a survey in 1986 on rural informal credit[10] found that 62 per cent of all loans granted to farmers were informal. In the Republic of Korea, the Ministry of Agriculture and Fisheries estimated that 50 per cent of the average outstanding loans of agricultural households were obtained from informal sources[11].

Finally, in Mexico, formal credit covered about 45 to 50 per cent of agricultural credit needs, thus leaving considerable scope for informal sources (50 to 55 per cent of rural credit).

d) *Evolution of the Share of the Formal and Informal Sectors in Financial Activity*

Figures on the formal-informal sector shares over a longer time period are available for the Philippines and India. During the 1950s and 1960s in the Philippines, the informal sector provided more than 60 per cent of the total value of loans to the rural population. This share dropped to one-third in the 1970s, largely as a result of the various credit subsidy programmes and the massive injection of government funds into the rural sector. However, it rose again to more than three-fourths (78 per cent) in the late 1970s when the credit programmes were abruptly discontinued, leaving a vacuum which the informal sector came to fill. In India, the percentage of debt owed by rural households to informal sources (landlords, moneylenders, traders, relatives and friends) has continuously declined from 83 per cent in 1961 to 71 per cent in 1971 to 39 per cent in 1981, in large part due to the vigorous expansion of commercial bank branches (their number quadrupled between 1971 and 1981) since their nationalisation in 1969.

Estimates of the share of informal credit in urban areas are available only for a few countries. According to Ghate[12], "in India the share is estimated to be at least 30 per cent. In the Republic of Korea the size of the curb market was about 15 per cent of the deposit money bank loans in 1978 but is estimated to have declined since then. In Thailand it is estimated that outstanding deposits with the informal credit market, and loans made by it, constituted about 16.7 per cent and 20.5 per cent, respectively, of total deposits and loans." A 1983 National Socio-Economic Survey in Indonesia of households with business activities found that 89 per cent of their capital came from their own funds, 6 per cent from bank sources and 4 per cent from "other" sources, including the informal sector, which thus appears to be almost as important as formal sources for this category of the population. Finally, in the Philippines, small- and medium-scale business enterprises constituted 97 per cent of the total number of manufacturing establishments in 1980 (and accounted for 24 per cent of value added in manufacturing), yet less than 10 per cent of them benefited from formal finance, leaving considerable scope for informal sources.

Some figures are available even by type of lender. In Bangladesh, informal moneylenders covered 77 per cent of farmers' credit needs. This figure was 50 per cent in Korea, 52 per cent in Thailand, 70 per cent in India and the Philippines[13]. Within the individual moneylenders category, the share of friends and relatives is often quite substantial. According to the World Bank[14], in those African and Asian countries for which data is available, friends and relatives supply around 50 per cent of loans to farmers. In Latin America, this figure drops to 10 per cent. In Bangladesh, for example, friends and relatives are indeed the single most important source of rural credit (both in cash and in kind), accounting for 61 per cent of informal credit markets in the 1970s and with a share at present of about one-half. Alongside the latter, the rural "well-to-do" also supply around 13 per cent of total informal credit, while the surveys on the share of professional moneylenders show conflicting results, ranging from four-fifths of the total to an insignificant share. Rahman[15] estimates their share also at 13 per cent.

Table 1.3 THE EXTENT OF THE INFORMAL FINANCIAL SECTOR: SOME PRELIMINARY FIGURES

	Savings	Credit	Urban informal	Type of lender	Non-monetised production (% of GDP) (figures from late 1970s)	Population concerned
Ethiopia	Volume of savings mobilised by *ekubs* = 8-10% of GDP				45	Addis Ababa: 60% of urban population in an *ekub*. Everyone is member of at least one *idir*.
Bangladesh		63% of credit came from informal sources		Informal moneylenders covered 77% of farmers' credit needs: • 50% by friends and relatives • 13% by rural "well to do" • 13% by professional lenders	16	
Zimbabwe		87% of farmers used informal sources of credit				
Nigeria		95% of loans to farmers came from informal sources				
Zambia		43% of farmers' credit needs were met by informal sources		Commercial moneylending on the rise	7	80-90% of the urban population participates
Indonesia	93% of capital of households with business activities came from own funds and "other source"	83% of agricultural households received no formal credit				

Country				
Thailand	32% of loans to the agricultural sector are from informal markets	16.7% of outstanding total deposits and 20.5% of total loans were with the informal sector	Informal moneylenders covered 52% of farmers' credit needs	10
Malaysia	62% of all loans granted to farmers were informal			20
Korea	50% of average outstanding loans of agricultural households were from informal sources	Size of curb market (urban informal credit) was 15% of deposit money bank loans in 1978	Informal moneylenders covered 50% of farmers' credit needs	21
Philippines	Informal sector provided: • (50s and 60s) 60% • (70s) 30% • (late 70s) 78% of total value of loans to rural population	Less than 10% of small and medium scale businesses received formal finance	Informal moneylenders covered 70% of farmers' credit needs: • 29% of total no. of loans came from friends and relatives • (1982) 6% of total loan value provided by landlords • 75% of total credit to agricultural sector from traders, millers, dealers, big farmers	10
India	1961: 83% 1971: 71% 1981: 39% of debt of rural households came from informal sources	Share of informal credit in urban areas is 30%	Informal moneylenders covered 70% of farmers' credit needs	20
Mexico	50-55% of agricultural credit needs are met by informal sources			2

In other countries, however, it appears that professional moneylending and trader-lenders' activity is on the rise. In Zambia, for example, commercial moneylending has increased since the country's economic crisis of the mid-1970s. A similar evolution is taking place in the Philippines: friends and relatives provided 29 per cent of the total number of informal loans received by households in a 1983-1984 survey by Floro[16]; at the same time, the share of landlord-lenders fell from 61 per cent of total loan value in the 1950s to 16 per cent in 1978-1979 to 6 per cent in 1981-1982. They have relinquished their predominant role to traders, rice millers, input dealers, and big farmers, as a number of surveys have shown. The Floro study calculated the share of the latter in the total credit supplied to the agricultural sector to be around 75 per cent.

It is evident from the preceding pages that data on the extent of the informal financial sector is not only difficult to come by but, even when it is available, it is also quite approximate and heterogeneous. In Table 1.3, we have attempted to summarise, in table form, the figures quoted above in the text.

By its very nature, therefore, the informal sector cannot be precisely defined either qualitatively or quantitatively. Depending on the means of measurement chosen, approximations of the size of the informal sector in a given country can vary considerably. The overriding conclusion then is that, whatever the method used, there is a high chance that the result is actually an underestimate of the reality. This is largely due to the interpenetration of the formal and informal sectors in terms of the operations and participants involved, geographic location, nature of activities, etc.

The closest one can come to gauging the importance of the informal sector is by studying the diversity of relations both within the informal sector itself and between the latter and the formal sector. In the next section we present the main characteristics of both, reserving a more detailed description for Chapter 3.

C. SALIENT FEATURES OF THE FORMAL AND INFORMAL FINANCIAL SECTORS

In this section, we shall contrast the salient features of the formal and informal financial sectors by briefly describing the diversity of the operators involved as well as the principal characteristics and the relative ease of access to financial services in each case. We shall conclude by evoking some of the main criticisms directed at the informal sector.

1. The Formal Sector

a) The Diversity of Formal Sector Operators

The formal financial sector – which includes both banking and non-bank financial intermediaries – covers a vast range of institutions and intermediaries: a Central bank, a Treasury administration, commercial (public or private, national or foreign) banks, merchant banks, development banks, specialised financial institutions (both within a geographical context or at the sectoral level), savings banks, insurance companies, social security schemes, provident or pension funds, investment funds, mutual building and loan associations, and, to a lesser degree, financial markets (mainly stock exchanges). In addition, developing countries often have a post office savings system and, in some cases, a relatively successful and growing co-operative movement. From the point of view of the variety, and often the number, of institutions in place, the developing countries would seem to be well endowed.

b) Characteristics of the Formal Financial Sector

In a "regulated" financial system, there is a high degree of specialisation, or rather "compartmentalisation", of the formal financial sector, both on the regional and sectoral levels. In this context, the main activity of rural development banks, for example, is to allocate investment credits and subsidies in rural areas; both national and foreign commercial banks are mostly urban-based and cater to large-scale clients; savings banks and postal savings networks are more spread out but the collected funds are often managed by the Treasury rather than by the above bodies themselves; co-operatives, for their part, seek to replace investment banks in rural areas and to meet the specific seasonal needs of their members. It should be added here that financial markets are rare and the only securities available are usually government bonds.

In a more "liberalised" financial system, by contrast, financial intermediaries tend to be multipurpose, and markets play a more active role in the mobilisation and allocation of resources.

c) Access to Formal Financial Services

Despite the apparent proliferation of institutions, however, access to the formal financial sector is usually denied to a large part of the population. Formal financial institutions are overwhelmingly urban-based, thus excluding from the outset the rural section of the population, even though it is usually the majority. Poor communications and infrastructure often make it costly for financial institutions to set up shop in the outlying rural areas. Even rural bank branches, however, are detached from the milieu in which they operate and remain largely unaware of the local conditions and needs.

Access to formal banking services is also made difficult for both rural and urban-based lower-income groups by the rigid, bureaucratic procedures that loan disbursements and deposit-taking entail. Because of high transaction costs (loan appraisal, documentation, and legal fees), formal financial institutions prefer to deal in large sums (deposits and loans) which are beyond the means of the majority of potential clients, as are the stringent collateral requirements for loans. Often, limits are imposed on the amounts that can be withdrawn without advance notice, which is incompatible with the liquidity preference of small savers. Cumbersome paper work and processing requires literacy skills of potential clients (which is not always the case) and slows down considerably the loan disbursement process. Even opening an account can sometimes take several months until authorisation from the head office is obtained, as is the case with post office savings banks in Zimbabwe, for example.

Formal financial institutions tend to neglect the mobilisation of household savings, and devote their efforts instead to allocating credit and creating money. They display a triple bias with regard to both the mobilisation and allocation of resources: a preference for the urban over the rural sector, for large-scale over small-scale transactions, for non-agricultural over agricultural loans. This limits their scope for effective financial intermediation. Moreover, the formal financial sector is the direct link with external capital flows. Development banks are vital instruments for receiving and channelling external aid to public sector projects, while the granting of private loans often brings on the presence of foreign banks which finance major investment projects.

47

2. The Informal Sector

We shall now examine these same aspects – diversity of operators, principal characteristics, ease of access – in the context of the informal financial sector.

a) The Diversity of Informal Sector Operators

Within the informal sector, three types of lenders are generally distinguished. Individual moneylenders usually rely on their own funds (though there are sometimes cases where they accept deposits) and include: friends, relatives, landlords, rural moneylenders, agricultural input dealers, produce traders, urban curb-market brokers, etc. Informal lenders may also operate as groups of individuals organised mutually, as in rotating savings and credit associations (ROSCAs), "chit funds", informal credit unions, self-help organisations, or family and tribal associations. Sometimes, though, informal lending takes on the form of partnership firms (such as pawnbrokers and "indigenous bankers", mostly found in Asian developing countries) or companies (i.e. non-bank financial intermediaries such as informal finance, investment, leasing and hire-purchase companies) which are usually included among informal lenders due to their exemption, to a greater or lesser degree, from central bank controls.

If such is the case and informal lenders may be institutions, then to talk of the informal sector as "non-institutional" can be misleading. Nor does the term "unorganised" seem warranted since, as we shall see in greater detail in the chapters that follow, informal sector activity *is* highly "organised", with "regulatory controls" emanating not from official financial authorities but from social pressure and the borrower's desire to uphold a good repayment record which will ensure access to future loans. This is but one of the many characteristics that differentiate the informal from the formal sector.

b) Characteristics of Informal Financial Transactions

The informal sector refers to all financial transactions functioning outside the purview of the regulations imposed on the activity of the formal financial sector in terms of interest rate and credit allocation policies, reserve requirements and the like. Informal financial transactions also escape taxation. The informal sector may be characterised by the flexibility of its loan terms and operations, giving it a number of differential economic advantages over the formal financial sector.

Informal lending takes on many different forms and is present in both urban and rural areas. The operators are mostly individuals, and transactions are based on the confidence engendered by face-to-face relationships between creditor and debtor. There is thus usually no collateral involved; security on loans is contingent upon the borrower's past credit record, personal good faith and social pressure to sustain payments, while interest rate flexibility allows the lender to cover the opportunity cost of his funds and the risk of default[17]. Burdensome documentation and book-keeping requirements are also absent.

c) Access to Informal Financial Services

As a result of the flexibility described above, transaction costs in the informal sector are generally low, and thus access to informal finance is relatively easy, in comparison with the formal sector. The flexibility of loan terms and operations to meet specific needs, the speed with which requests for loans are met and, most importantly, the willingness to handle the small absolute amounts which correspond to the requirements and the capacity of the majority of the population are all signs that, to a large extent, informal financial mechanisms are more adapted to the conditions and needs of the milieu – both rural and urban – in which they operate than are formal financial mechanisms. This may also partly explain why, despite the fact that informal sector credit is usually more expensive than formal sector credit, it is nevertheless more popular.

3.　Final Remarks and Criticism of the Informal Sector

There are three operational aspects of the formal and informal sectors which deserve emphasis. First, the informal sector only extends credit, whereas the formal sector can both extend and create credit through money creation, since it can rediscount the liabilities of its borrowers with the central bank[18].

Second, as a result of the "traditional" separation of banking from commerce, the formal sector operates only in one market – the credit market – while the informal sector may operate in several. One of the features of the informal sector is market interlinkage, whereby credit transactions may be linked with transactions in input, output, land-lease or labour markets through the overlapping personae of moneylender, product dealer, landlord or employer. This is one of the most important mechanisms for reducing transaction costs and risk premia in the informal sector[19].

Third, whereas the formal sector may refuse to grant credit (for reasons of lack of collateral, credit control, sectoral allocation policies, etc.), almost all loan requests are satisfied in the informal sector, although the assessment of the associated risk is reflected in the interest rate charged[20].

Criticism of the informal sector usually focuses on three main points: the interest rates charged, the use of funds and social and macroeconomic effects of informal activity.

An oft-repeated charge against informal credit is that the spread between lending and borrowing rates is too high to be socially acceptable. Moneylenders (merchants, middle-men, landlords) in particular, are much criticised for charging quasi-usurious interest rates and taking advantage, especially in rural areas, of borrowers who often may not realise the true rate of interest they are paying and either do not know of or do not have access to alternative sources of finance, to inflate the element of monopoly profit, which is one of the determinants of informal interest rates. (The others are: the risk-free rate of interest, that is, the opportunity cost of funds; a premium for risk; and a premium to cover transaction costs.)[21] Some analyses interpret the wide spread between lending and borrowing rates as an indication that the cost of financial intermediation is very high in the informal sector and that, consequently, informal financial intermediation is less efficient than formal sector intermediation[22].

Second, since a considerable share of informal loans are for consumption purposes, it is often argued that the informal sector channels resources from savers to consumers rather than into productive investment for development, and hence depresses the overall productive capacity of the economy. Moreover, it is often argued that the informal sector has an adverse effect on equity in the economy, because it is usually the poorer sections of the population who resort to informal sector lending (since access to the formal sector is denied them) and who are thus subjected to the usurious rates on consumption loans.

Finally, since the informal sector functions outside the purview of control by the public authorities, and notably by the central bank, its existence and expansion in developing countries is thought to render official monetary and credit policies ineffective.

II. CAUSES AND EFFECTS OF FINANCIAL DUALISM

Two main arguments are usually put forward regarding the causes of financial dualism[23]. The first one presents the informal financial sector as a response to the shortcomings and excessive regulation of the formal financial sector. This line of reasoning is held by the proponents of financial liberalisation, who contend that the informal financial sector is the result of "financial repression" and can thus be reduced by removing the constraints imposed upon the formal sector.

According to the second argument, monetary and financial dualism can be explained by the overall dualism which characterises many developing countries. Monetary and financial dualism is rooted in the heterogeneous economic, social, cultural, and even ethnic structures of the developing countries. Thus, far from giving rise to monetary and financial dualism, the formal financial sector is itself hampered by the general dualistic nature of developing economies. The apparent paradox lies in the fact that economic development is expected to reduce monetary and financial dualism while, at the same time, reducing monetary and financial dualism is one of the prerequisites for a more balanced economic development. Those who subscribe to this thesis favour a more regulated financial system and hasten to point out that even in a liberalised financial system, the informal financial sector is still present.

In this section, we shall first present the point of view of the proponents of financial liberalisation, to be followed by the line of argument of those who favour a more regulated financial system.

A. THE INFORMAL FINANCIAL SECTOR IS A RESPONSE TO THE SHORTCOMINGS AND EXCESSIVE REGULATION OF THE FORMAL FINANCIAL SECTOR

According to this first thesis, defended by the proponents of financial liberalisation, the dynamism of the informal sector can above all be explained by the deficiencies and inefficiencies of the formal financial sector. The latter has proved to be too urban, too bureaucratic, too regulated, too rigid to provide the savings and credit facilities which a large part of the population needs and seeks.

The barriers set up between the institutions and financial circuits within the formal sector remove the latter from the influence of market forces. Close and constant control by the public authorities over formal financial institutions – notably the fixing of deposit and lending rates and the implementation of sectoral credit allocation policies – prevents them from adjusting to the specific conditions of the economies of developing countries. This "mismatch" is partly due to the fact that financial institutions in developing countries are modelled on those of the industrialised countries. Within the formal sector, comprehensive social insurance schemes (social security, provident funds, insurance, etc.) are often either lacking or, when they do exist, operate inefficiently. This merely reinforces the social insurance role of the informal sector.

On a wider scale, what transpires from the growing literature on the subject is that the monetary and financial policies pursued by many developing countries are unsuitable and, moreover, may even fuel dualism. These policies can be designated by the term "financial repression".

"Financial repression" usually refers to the effects of close regulation of the financial system and to the various forms of restriction that the government imposes on the activity of financial institutions – interest rate controls, exchange rate controls, reserve requirements, regulation of competition, etc. – and which, by discouraging the development of financial institutions and instruments, lead to fragmented financial markets (shallow finance)[24]. In this section we shall focus primarily on interest rate controls, sectoral credit allocation policies and minimum reserve requirements.

1. Interest Rate Controls

The most salient feature of financial repression is the control and manipulation of interest rates and the distortion this creates on the supply and demand of financial resources, as well as its effect on saver behaviour, on the choice of investment projects, and on monetary control.

The alleged aim of imposing interest rate controls is to encourage investment by keeping interest rates to borrowers low. This may be achieved either directly, by setting ceilings on loan rates, or indirectly, through ceilings on deposit rates, because banks which obtain their funds cheaply will be able to lend them cheaply[25].

In practice though, actual interest rates are distorted from the equilibrium interest rates that would prevail in a competitive market. They are officially – and arbitrarily – set and, due to inflation, usually end up being negative in real terms. Nor do they reflect the supply and demand situation in the developing countries where, characteristically, demand for credit highly exceeds supply. On the contrary, the imbalance is reinforced.

The proponents of financial liberalisation argue that negative real deposit rates discourage saving and can foster money and deposit aversion if inflation is high and rising. As negative real interest rates increase, individuals are less willing to hold financial assets and tend to invest instead in inflation hedges such as gold, jewellery, real estate, commodities and the like, which are generally non-productive. In real terms, this leads to a decline in money savings and in funds available for investment, which in turn restricts the rate of economic growth.

Interest rate controls also affect investment behaviour, since lending rates are also negative in real terms. This stimulates demand for credit and increases the supply/demand gap; at the same time, there is no leeway for adjustment via a variation in interest rates, since the latter are fixed. The resulting laxist monetary policies whereby money supply is increased to compensate for the shortfall in savings merely fuel inflationary pressures.

Controlled lending rates lead to increased credit rationing by financial intermediaries. Since the latter cannot charge a risk premium commensurate with the risk of the project they are financing, they will tend to squeeze out more profitable but riskier ventures in favour of lower-risk projects (with relatively low rates of return) and borrowers who can offer substantial security or who have a good track record. The venture capital element of financing is lost and thus not only the quantity but also the quality of investment is affected by financial repression. Moreover, banks may be tempted to inflate the effective interest rate by adding service charges such as inspection fees, notarial and documentation fees, which are deducted at loan release.

The thrust of the criticism of interest rate controls by proponents of financial liberalisation is hence that the fixing of interest rates in the formal sector at non-market equilibrium levels leads to the creation and development of an informal market in which interest rates are usually higher since they better reflect market forces (thus giving rise to positive real interest rates).

2. Active Credit Allocation Policies

Another form of government intervention in financial activity consists of setting sectoral targets for financial institutions whereby a certain proportion of their loans must be directed to a specific, priority sector or category of borrowers. Banks may be compensated for credits to priority sectors or target groups in a number of ways: interest rate subsidies, rediscount lines, lower minimum reserve requirements, lighter taxing of interest income of banks according to the borrower.

Another alternative is to set up specialised agencies, financed by taxation or cheap government borrowing, with the purpose of channelling "low-cost loans" to favoured debtors or sectors, usually agriculture.

Sectoral allocation of credit may restrict the volume of funds available to the other, non-favoured sectors of the economy, thereby raising the cost of those funds which are available to them and favouring the development of an informal sector to fill the gap. For instance, large-scale borrowers and favoured sectors crowd out other sectors and activities (farmers, small-and medium-scale enterprises, traders, etc.) on the credit market, thus making informal financial circuits their sole remaining recourse for credit.

One last point which should be stressed is that interest rates may no longer play a role in the choice of investment projects[26]. A perceived guarantee of being "bailed out" by government should things go wrong may result in unprofitable projects nonetheless being undertaken, while resource allocation through global, sectoral credit policies encourages politico-economic bargaining over which sectors should be favoured and what volumes made available.

In essence then, the liberalisation argument contends that favouring one particular sector or activity over others with regard to financial intermediation is an incentive for the non-favoured ones to turn to and develop informal financial circuits which function along their own lines regarding interest rates, collateral requirements, etc.

3. Minimum Reserve Requirements

Minimum reserve requirements are intended to ensure a certain degree of stability to the banking system and to limit money creation. In industrialised countries, levels are typically around 10 to 15 per cent of total bank deposits, but in developing countries they may be as high as 50 per cent[27].

By imposing high levels of reserve requirements which are placed with the central bank at low or even zero interest rates or invested in low-interest government bonds, the government is in essence forcing the domestic banking system to finance public debt. Banks compensate for this by paying negative real interest on savings deposits. Moreover, it makes the Treasury a "privileged borrower", thus crowding out other potential borrowers.

4. Limited Competition

Another factor which can hamper the development of the financial sector in developing countries and which deserves mention is the absence or restriction of competition, due to the fact that highly specialised institutions do not have a common ground of activity in which to compete.

Indeed, the limiting of competition may also reflect a voluntary policy of geographic distribution of bank branches over national territory: as an incentive for one bank to open a branch in certain neglected (primarily rural) areas, other banks are prohibited from establishing their branches close by, so as to avoid competition in deposit mobilisation and credit allocation.

Proponents of financial liberalisation stress that in an over-regulated financial system, where competition is also controlled, both the need and the incentive for banks to actively seek out new clients and attract deposits are considerably diminished – while the potential borrowers and savers who are not solicited in this way turn to parallel financial circuits.

To sum up then, according to this first theory which we briefly presented above, the presence and dynamism of the informal financial sector reflect the formal sector's incapacity – due to inappropriate monetary and financial policies – to adjust to the conditions of a large part of the economy. Financial liberalisation is presented by those who subscribe to this line of argument as the means of achieving a single and more uniform financial sector.

B. THE FORMAL SECTOR IS HAMPERED BY THE STRUCTURAL DUALISM OF DEVELOPING ECONOMIES MORE THAN IT CONTRIBUTES TO IT

According to the second thesis, the existence and dynamism of the informal sector are explained more by the intrinsic dualism of economic and social structures in the developing countries and the rural population's attachment to traditional values and customs of family, village or tribal solidarity than by the inefficiency of the formal sector. In this context, monetary and financial dualism can be ascribed to economic dualism. The difficulties and failures of formal sector operations are thus largely due to the general structure of the economy. The formal financial sector is itself subjected to dualism more than it engenders it.

Three examples help to illustrate this argument. The weak links between formal sector institutions and the rural masses are often attributed to the problem of the illiteracy of the latter, for which the former cannot be held responsible; yet the need to record their activities in writing is obvious. In a similar vein, communication and transportation difficulties in the developing countries are a handicap to formal sector expansion and explain in part its urban concentration. Finally, the difficulties encountered by insurance and provident fund-type institutions in expanding the scope of their activities can be imputed just as much to the prevailing social structures as to the inadequate management of these institutions. It is difficult to penetrate and compete with the close-knit village, family or ethnic ties of solidarity.

This approach to the causes of financial dualism stresses the importance of cultural and socio-political factors, alongside economic and financial ones, in explaining the resilience and vitality of the informal financial sector.

1. The Cultural and Socio-Political Factors

Cultural factors and the persistence of traditional investment habits are important in explaining the resilience of the informal sector in that they largely determine the underlying motives for saving or borrowing, as well as the means available and the forms preferred. In Burundi, Zambia, and the Philippines, for example, part of the harvest is saved to meet any unforeseen needs and to serve as seed for the next planting season. Savings in the form of gold, precious stones, jewellery and other valuables are important for prestige and ceremonial purposes. In India, great importance is attached to the possession of gold. Other material goods which serve as savings include land, housing, and cattle. In addition to being a productive resource (providing draught power, milk, meat, manure for fertilizer), possessing cattle is the traditional means of storing wealth and providing for life and risk insurance. In Burundi, Zambia, and Zimbabwe, for instance, the size of one's herd is a measure of one's status and a sign of prestige.

Savings in kind are thus widespread in the informal sector. In fact, the major share of rural household savings is in non-financial form. It goes without saying that the stronger the attachment is to such forms of wealth, the more resistant the informal sector, since there is little the formal sector can do to satisfy this type of demand.

The hoarding of money is another common form of saving in the developing countries and can be explained by a number of factors. An obvious one is the lack of accessible facilities; but even when formal financial institutions are present, potential clients can easily be deterred from resorting to them for reasons of illiteracy or because of the intimidation they often feel vis à vis the personnel and the complicated procedures involved. The absence of profitable investment opportunities and a basic lack of confidence in formal financial institutions and in the government itself are also factors which underlie the distance between formal financial institutions and a part of the population. People are often averse to having written records of their savings and lending activities which might be scrutinised by government revenue officials or could fall into the hands of members of the extended family with whom one is expected to share any conspicuous wealth. This may also be at the root of a deep-seated mistrust, particularly amongst the rural masses, of official "intrusions" into their productive and financial activities.

The population's attachment to and preference for tangible savings over other forms of saving or, more generally, for informal financial practices over formal ones, can also be explained in part by the socio-political context. Social and political instability and an ever-changing public policy do little to inspire confidence; on the contrary, they increase the attraction of tangible wealth (non-productive assets) as hedges or fuel a surge in capital flight[28].

2. Economic and Financial Factors

From the economic viewpoint, the structural dualism is reflected in the obstacles to capital formation which prevail in many developing countries: a limited capacity to absorb abundant labour, inequalities in income distribution, insufficiency of the productive apparatus in meeting the stringent conditions emerging in world trade, a marked urban bias, scarcity of capital resources, etc. The resulting tensions on the labour and capital markets are partly alleviated by the informal sector, but this merely accentuates the dualism on the labour market which is also felt in the savings and credit market.

From the financial viewpoint, the basic premise underlying the argument in favour of regulation is that capital markets in developing countries can be neither efficient nor in equilibrium and that, consequently, economic and financial activity should and can be closely regulated and controlled. It may be pointed out that this is a difficult enough task on its own, and it can only be exacerbated by the conditions in developing countries where communication is difficult and information often inaccurate or incomplete.

According to the proponents of regulation, the conditions whereby resources may be mobilised and allocated efficiently through market forces are not present in the developing economies. To begin with, if left free, the institutions themselves would not behave in accordance with the basic tenets of management, which is why they must be closely controlled and their operations verified. Secondly, the relative absence of people who are willing to assume the role of shareholders underpins the necessity for public sector resources and explains the narrowness of financial markets. The developing economies are in a state of basic disequilibrium, which means that financial markets are also affected; hence regulation is necessary and financial liberalisation is potentially dangerous.

Moreover, the proponents of regulation stress the fact that, even in those countries where financial liberalisation policies are being pursued, these have done little to counter the activities of the informal financial sector. This would seem to imply that the factors behind the existence and development of the informal financial sector are not solely financial.

To sum up then, the main thrust of this second view of the causes of financial dualism is that dualism is more the result of the overall configuration of society rather than of excessive regulation of the formal sector. Moreover, the informal sector continues to exist because the government does not really want to interfere. For obvious economic, social and political reasons which need not be developed here, the general stance of the public authorities can in fact be described as one of benign neglect towards the informal financial sector, and sometimes even disregard for the consequences, in the long term, of a persistent state of financial dualism.

C. THE EFFECTS OF FINANCIAL DUALISM

Financial dualism can have adverse effects on development by affecting the accumulation and distribution processes and hence the rate of economic growth.

The presence of non-monetised sectors in the economy are a brake on economic development for a number of reasons. The absence of money deprives individuals from a unit of measure which makes it almost impossible to make any sort of economic calculations. Second, non-monetised production and barter trade are unlikely to facilitate progress away from a subsistence economy; indeed, monetisation can be propitious for economic development because it can help boost trade with its corollary beneficial effects. Finally, non-monetisation of surpluses can be a brake on development in the sense that savings take on non-productive forms such as the hoarding of gold, silver, precious stones, jewellery. Such non-financial savings are still relatively widespread in some developing countries and will continue to be so as long as no alternative and sufficiently attractive forms of saving are offered to the public.

Financial dualism can also affect the rate of economic growth by accentuating both sectoral and regional disparities as regards the mobilisation and allocation of funds. Financial dualism introduces a growth rate differential between economic sectors, whose development becomes a function of their access to the different credit sources available. On the regional level, the formal financial sector is known to siphon off a large part of the funds collected in the rural sector, whereas the informal financial sector recycles the quasi-totality of the funds mobilised in the region where they were collected[29]. Besides the volume effect of inter-sectoral and inter-regional disparities, there is also a price effect. Usurious interest rates in the informal sector prevent small producers from accumulating their surpluses, since the latter are used to pay the interest on loans rather than to purchase better equipment, to mechanise production, or to increase their output or the size of their farm.

Table 1.4 TAX REVENUE BY TYPE OF TAX
Percentage of GNP

Country	Year	Mandatory contributions (total)	Income and corporate tax (total)	Excise duties (total)[1]	Taxation of duties (total)[2]	Social security contributions	Wealth and property tax	Other mandatory contributions
Ethiopia	1976-1978	12.20	2.88	2.71	6.24	–	0.26	0.10
Burundi	1975-1977	11.31	2.16	2.50	5.33	0.24	0.61	0.46
Zaire	1978-1980	16.54	5.90	2.47	6.63	0.76	0.04	0.75
Kenya	1978-1980	20.45	7.08	8.01	5.00	–	0.19	0.17
Togo	1978-1980	26.70	10.56	4.36	9.41	1.96	0.32	0.08
Zambia	1978-1981	22.25	8.78	10.82	1.79	0.74	0.01	0.11
Nigeria	1975-1977	20.61	16.80	0.42	3.37	–	–	0.02

– Statistical data unavailable.
1. Includes tax on turnover, sales, VAT and other levies.
2. Includes import and export duties and other fees.
Source: Extracted from Kessler, Lavigne and Ullmo, *op. cit.*, p. 30.

Moreover, the diversity of interest rates and the inequality of access to cheap credit fuel speculative behaviour and extortionary practices.

Dualism also undermines efforts by the public authorities to implement a consistent economic, monetary and financial policy. From the point of view of general economic policy, the monetary and financial dualism in the developing countries makes them particularly sensitive to both external and internal shocks. On the international level, these include fluctuations in world commodity prices, interest rates, and exchange rates; the changing absorptive capacity of trading partners; migratory flows, etc. Internal imbalances are mostly linked to fluctuations in production levels in the agricultural sector or to political or social instability[30].

Macroeconomic policy objectives are difficult to define in the absence of aggregate economic indicators. Informal sector activities do not appear in national accounts, and the extent of the non-monetised sector makes them that much more difficult to perceive.

The traditional instruments of monetary and financial policy lose much of their efficacy in a context of structural economic dualism. With regard to budgetary policy, low fiscal revenues can be explained by the fact that, by nature, the informal sector escapes taxation, while even the formal sector is only slightly subjected to taxation, on account of its narrow base. The government must therefore seek other sources of revenue, such as import or excise duties, or increase the money supply.

Table 1.4 shows some of the principal characteristics of the tax base in seven African countries. One remarks that the tax and social security contributions ratio is relatively low, between 10 and 30 per cent of GDP. As it is well known, the tax burden in developing countries is much lower than that in the industrialised countries. Moreover, parafiscal payments are low or non-existent, reflecting the absence or malfunctioning of compulsory social insurance schemes. This gap in social protection is filled not by private insurance but by the extended family or other informal sector associations which provide mutual assistance and thus substitute to a large extent for compulsory social insurance mechanisms.

As with budgetary policy, a coherent monetary policy is difficult to pursue when the sources of money supply are ill-defined. To begin with, central banks are often forced to finance the Treasury, advances to the State constituting one of the main sources of increased money supply in the developing countries. This fuels inflationary pressures and explains in part the high inflation rates which prevail in the developing countries. Moreover, setting intermediate monetary targets (in terms of the level of interest rates or the growth rate of monetary and credit aggregates) should concern the economy in its entirety, but in practice it is directed only at the formal monetary and financial sector. Finally, the uncertainty with regard to the external sources of money supply, notably in relation to the illicit export and import of capital which is channelled through the informal sector, weighs heavily in the definition of monetary objectives.

Monetary and financial dualism also places constraints on the choice of instruments of monetary policy. Neither regulation through volumes nor through interest rates is efficacious when there is a considerable amount of liquidity outside the banking sector, signalling a phenomenon of "money flight" away from institutionalised banking networks towards the informal sector.

Concluding Remarks

The preceding pages dealt with some of the main aspects of the formal and informal financial sectors and, where relevant, presented the different approaches on each particular issue.

Our attempts to "visualise" the regulated or liberalised nature of the financial systems in the sample countries brought to light some of the inconsistencies which may appear in a country's economic and financial policies. For example, it is difficult to strike a balance between the will to liberalise interest rates on the one hand, while maintaining active sectoral credit allocation policies on the other (even if the latter policies are implemented through credit quotas rather than interest rate incentives, distortions are still introduced on the credit market). To what extent Indonesia has been successful in this respect remains to be seen.

The presence of seemingly incompatible elements and the resultant hybrid nature of a country's financial system may also stem from the fact that financial systems evolve; in the transitional phase, some elements of the out-going policy may coexist with those of the in-coming one. In the case of Mexico, for instance, this explains the concurrence of the heavily nationalised banking system with efforts to develop financial markets.

It is also difficult to judge whether and how the degree of control exerted over the formal financial sector is linked to the extent of the informal sector. The disparate nature of the available statistics (which may be in terms of the number of farmers or households concerned, the share of credit needs covered, the percentage value of total loans ...) does not provide enough common ground for a relevant comparison. The case studies themselves gave ambiguous results. Zambia, for example, has one of the highest monetisation coefficients, yet 80 to 90 per cent of the urban population is said to participate in the informal financial sector in one way or another. In other cases, the informal sector is allegedly more extensive in some of the countries classified as "liberalised" (Zimbabwe, the Philippines, Indonesia) than in those labelled "mixing and evolving" (India, Mexico) which are supposedly more controlled.

However, it seems that, at least indirectly, the informal sector is affected by the spillover effect of policies in the formal sector: in the Philippines, for instance, its share in overall lending declined in the wake of an increased supply of formal sector funds to the rural sector, and subsequently rose when these were abruptly discontinued.

Two points must be kept in mind on the question of the size of the informal sector. First, it should be remembered that quantitative estimates for the informal sector involve large margins of error. Second, as the relationship between the formal and informal sectors becomes increasingly complex and diversified and the boundary between the two in terms of operators and the flow of funds becomes more and more blurred, estimating the importance of the informal sector by the residual method becomes inappropriate.

The aim of this study is to clarify the respective roles of the formal and informal sectors in the financial intermediation processes of the developing countries and to seek ways of reducing financial dualism so that efficiency may be enhanced. The structure of each sector as well as its operations and practices must be dealt with in parallel, since the two sectors together make up the ensemble of financial circuits in a given country. This will be the object of the following two chapters.

As for the causes of financial dualism, the authors contend that each of the two aforementioned theses taken on its own is an insufficient explanation; in fact, the presence and dynamism of the informal sector may be imputed to both sets of factors evoked by the proponents of each point of view. These issues, along with the effects of financial dualism, shall be taken up in Chapter 4 in the context of the discussion on the ways and means of reducing this dualism.

NOTES AND REFERENCES

1. See Chapter 2 for tables on interest rates, domestic credit, government finance, market capitalisation and volume of transactions, etc.

2. Chandavarkar, A.G., "Monetization of Developing Economies", *IMF Staff Papers*, November 1977, vol. 24, No. 3, pp. 665-721.

3. This figure is very similar to the findings of a study by Blades, Derek W., *Non-monetary (subsistence) Activities in the National Accounts of Developing Countries*, Paris, OECD, 1975. According to Blades, the monetisation coefficient in Zambia was already 93 per cent at the end of the 1960s, at that time the highest in Africa. Mrak suggests that the high proportion of the urban population (48 per cent in 1984) and the low share of agriculture in GDP (15 per cent) in 1984, according to the World Bank's *World Development Report: 1986*, may explain to a large extent the relatively high coefficient of monetisation.

4. Bouman, F.J.A., "Indigenous Savings and Credit Societies in the Third World – Any Message?", mimeo, July 1977.

5. Source for the figure of 30 per cent: Rural Finance Experimental Project (1981-82), *Baseline Survey II*, GOB and USAID.
   Source for figure of 90 per cent: Alamgir, M. and Atiq Rahman, *Savings in Bangladesh: 1959/60 to 1969/70*, Bangladesh Institute of Development Studies, BIDS Research Monograph No. 2, 1974.
   Source for figure of 60 per cent: Hussein, Md. Ghulam, "An Analytical Review of Non-Formal Credit Studies in Bangladesh", A/D/C, Dhaka, 1983. All above sources cited by Rahman, Atiq, *Domestic Savings Mobilization Through Formal and Informal Sectors in Bangladesh*, paper prepared by the Asian Development Bank for an International Experts' Meeting on Domestic Savings Mobilisation Through Formal and Informal Sectors: Comparative Experiences in Asian and African Developing Countries, East-West Center, Honolulu, 2-4 June 1987.

6. Kessler, Denis and Anne Lavigne and Pierre-Antoine Ullmo, *Ways and Means to Reduce the Financial Dualism in Developing Countries: The State of the Art*, working paper prepared for the OECD Development Centre, November 1985, p. 6.

7. Nagle, Sean, "Zambie", in Masini, Mario, ed., pour le Groupe de Travail FAO-FINAFRICA, *Profils de Finance Rurale des Pays d'Afrique*, Milano, Finafrica-CARIPLO, 1987.

8. Siamwalla, Ammar, *Thai Rural Credit System: Some Empirical Findings and a Theoretical Framework*, paper prepared by the Asian Development Bank for an International Experts' Meeting on Domestic Savings Mobilisation ..., East-West Centre, June 1987 (see note 4).

9. Ghate, P.B., "Informal Credit Markets in Asian Developing Countries", *Asian Development Review*, 1988, vol. 6, No. 1, p. 66.

10. Van Nieuwkoop, Martien, *Rural Informal Credit in Peninsular Malaysia*, Kuala Lumpur, Bank Pertanian Malaysia, 1986. Cited by Ghate, *op. cit.*, p. 66.

11. Ghate, *op. cit.*, p. 66.

12. *Ibid.*

13. Kessler, Lavigne, Ullmo, *op. cit.*, p. 27.

14. IBRD, "Agricultural Credit", *Rural Development Series*, Washington, D.C., August 1975, p. 128.

15. Rahman, *op. cit.*, p. 37.

16. Floro, Sagrario, *Credit Relations and Market Interlinkage in Philippine Agriculture*, unpublished PhD dissertation, Stanford University, 1987.

17. Ghate, *op. cit.*, p. 65.

18. See Yotopoulos, Pan A. and Sagrario L. Floro, case study on the Philippines for the OECD Development Centre, p. 5.

19. Ghate, *op. cit.*, p. 85.

20. Kessler, Lavigne, Ullmo, *op. cit.*, p. 16.

21. Kitchen, Richard L., *Finance for the Developing Countries*, Chichester, John Wiley and Sons, 1986, p. 135.

22. See Madhur, S. and C.P.S. Nayar, case study on India for the OECD Development Centre, p. 2.

23. Kessler, Lavigne, Ullmo, *op. cit.*, p. 26.

24. R.I. McKinnon and E.S. Shaw independently pioneered work on financial repression, following the earlier work of J.G. Gurley and E.S. Shaw, and R.W. Goldsmith. A summarial presentation of subsequent formalized models of financially repressed economies can be found in Fry, Maxwell J., "Models of Financially Repressed Developing Countries", *World Development*, September 1982, vol. 10, No. 9, pp. 731-750.

    See also: McKinnon, R.I., *Money and Capital in Economic Development*, Washington, D.C., Brookings Institution, 1973; Shaw, E.S., *Financial Deepening in Economic Development*, New York/London, Oxford University Press, 1973; Gurley, J.G. and E.S. Shaw, *Money in a Theory of Finance*, Washington, D.C., Brookings Institution, 1960; Goldsmith, R.W., *Financial Structure and Development*, New Haven, Yale University Press, 1969.

25. Such a line of argument is based on the assumption that funds from savers will be forthcoming despite the ceilings on the deposit rate. It also implicitly suggests that savers should subsidise borrowers.

26. Benoit, J. Pierre V., "Artificially Low Interest Rates Versus Realistic or Market Interest Rates", in Kessler, Denis and Pierre-Antoine Ullmo, eds., *Savings and Development*, Paris, Economica, 1985, pp. 35-78.

27. Kitchen, *op. cit.*, p. 83.

28. Wachtel, Paul, "Observations on Saving by Individuals in Developing Countries", in Kessler and Ullmo, eds., *op. cit.*, pp. 17-26 (see note 25).

29. Causse, Jean, "Necessity of and Constraints on the Use of Savings in the Community in which They are Collected", in Kessler and Ullmo, eds., *op. cit.*, pp. 153-181 (see note 25).

30. Gobbo, F., R. Ascari, G. Cigarini and R. Zavatta, *Economic Policy in Some African Countries: Recent Developments*, mimeo, paper presented at an International Conference on "Adjusting to Shocks – A North-South Perspective", November 1984.

Chapter 2

STRUCTURE OF THE FINANCIAL SYSTEMS
IN DEVELOPING COUNTRIES

The purpose of this chapter is to describe the functions and objectives that the formal, semi-formal, and informal operators involved in financial intermediation activity are supposed to fulfil in developing countries. This should shed light on the possible configurations that the latter's financial systems can take as well as on their "completeness", i.e. which entities are present and which are not, depending on the country. The second part of the chapter will deal with some of the quantitative aspects of financial intermediation, and notably the respective shares in financial circuits of the various entities present.

Following this, in Chapter 3, we shall assess how well they perform these functions, by focusing more closely on their actual practices and behaviour.

I. THE GENERAL LAY-OUT OF THE FINANCIAL CIRCUITS

The formal and informal sectors together encompass the ensemble of financial circuits in the developing countries. Contrary to what is widely assumed, the formal sector on its own harbours a wide variety of institutions while the numerous mechanisms and operators of the informal sector are equally diverse.

Formal financial systems in developing countries are often either a legacy of colonial times or copies of the financial set-up in developed countries. From the institutional point of view, the developing countries would seem to be well endowed, with a vast range of both banking and non-bank institutions and intermediaries making up a sometimes complex financial system. The formal sector may thus include: a central bank, a Treasury administration, commercial (nationalised or private, local or foreign) banks, merchant banks, development banks, savings banks, specialised financial institutions, building societies, social security schemes, provident or pension funds insurance companies, a post office savings network, and credit co-operatives. In some developing countries, capital markets may complete formal sector financial intermediation (see Table 2.1).

The informal financial sector, for its part, is more widespread in the developing countries, and the mechanisms and operators involved (moneylenders, savings and loan associations, indigenous bankers, finance companies, etc.) are more complex and numerous than heretofore assumed. Not only do they play a role in mobilising the savings of and channelling credit to the lower-income groups in both rural and urban areas, but they are

Table 2.1 FINANCIAL CIRCUITS IN DEVELOPING COUNTRIES

FORMAL FINANCIAL SECTOR	INFORMAL FINANCIAL SECTOR	
CENTRAL BANK AND TREASURY		
BANKS AND OTHER FINANCIAL INTERMEDIARIES		
Commercial Banks	Professional moneylenders Indigenous bankers Pawnbrokers, etc.	Loan companies Finance companies Investment companies
Merchant Banks	Trader-lenders Landlord-lenders Farmer-lenders Storeowners	
Development Banks		
Savings Banks Building Societies Postal Savings Networks Co-operative Banks/Mutual Banks	Fixed-fund associations Savings clubs Self-help organisations ROSCAs Chit funds	Housing finance companies
Social Security Institutions Provident/Pension Funds Insurance companies	Mutual Aid Associations	
CAPITAL MARKETS		
Stock Bond Money Foreign exchange	Friends Neighbours Relatives Private individuals from upper-income groups Rural financial markets Informal foreign exchange markets	Investment companies

often a major source of working capital for enterprises of all sizes, thus serving a broad spectrum of the population and not just the poor segments. They are said to provide as much as half of rural credit and a significant part of urban credit.

There are obviously structural differences between the formal and informal financial sectors, both on a global and on an institutional (formal sector) or mechanism (informal sector) level. However, in Table 2.1, we have tried to show that there are also areas of similarity with regard to the financial services provided – as well as the savings and credit needs covered. In this context, the objectives and behaviour, if not the purpose served, of commercial banks on the one hand and indigenous banks on the other, or of merchant banks and trader-lenders or of co-operative banks and ROSCAs, for example, are not always that much different from each other.

In spite of the apparent institutional cleavage between the formal financial sector and the informal financial sector, it should be pointed out that there is a growing tendency towards greater linkage – and even complementarity – of the two, as we shall see in greater depth in Chapter 4. Nonetheless, for reasons of convenience and clarity, we shall proceed in the following sections, first, with a description of the structure of the formal sector, and of the co-operative movements in those countries where they exist and, second, a discussion of the workings of the informal financial sector.

A. THE CONFIGURATION OF THE FINANCIAL SYSTEMS

1. Formal Sector Financial Institutions and Markets

In reference to the preceding table, the formal financial sector can be further schematised as shown in Figure 2.1.

The formal financial sector can be represented on three levels. The first level is that of the central bank which, in the developing countries, often oversteps the prudential functions it is assigned and assumes an increasingly interventionist role in local financial activity. At the same time, its relationship with the Treasury is affected. Regarding the second level, one may find a myriad of financial intermediaries in the developing countries; and though their nomenclature may differ from country to country, their basic purpose and orientation is somewhat similar. Developing country experiences with regard to the third level, i.e. capital markets, are multifarious, ranging from the relative atrophy of money, bond or stock markets in Africa to what the International Finance Corporation (IFC) has labelled "emerging capital markets" in certain Asian and Latin American countries.

a) Central Bank and Treasury Administration

In most countries, the central bank is the keystone of the financial sector. Usually government-owned, it is the institution through which government monetary and financial policies are implemented. Besides acting as banker to the government (keeping accounts, advancing loans, issuing bills and bonds), the central bank issues national currency, holds the country's official foreign exchange reserves and implements exchange control regulations, and performs open market operations. Its other main function is to manage, supervise, control and regulate the activities of formal financial institutions, and be a lender of last resort to the banking system in the interest of maintaining external and internal stability.

The central bank is often the instrument of financial repression (or liberalisation) since it imposes (or lifts) interest rate controls, receives the required reserves from banks, regulates credit policy through the rediscount rate, and controls the availability of foreign exchange. In fact, it is in this capacity that the central bank can overrun its role as a safeguard of the stability of the financial system and increase its degree of direct control over financial activity.

The central bank in developing countries is also well placed to go beyond its traditional functions and play an active developmental role in the economy. More specifically, it can contribute to financial development in a number of ways. An obviously direct way is to provide equity capital for financial institutions. For example, the central bank of Indonesia – Bank Indonesia – actively participates in three private development finance companies, a housing finance company, a credit insurance company for small business loans, and a commercial bank in the Netherlands. Equity capital, as well as "moral suasion", can also be used to encourage the geographical spread of branches.

Figure 2.1 **FORMAL FINANCIAL SECTOR**
Banking and non-bank financial intermediaries

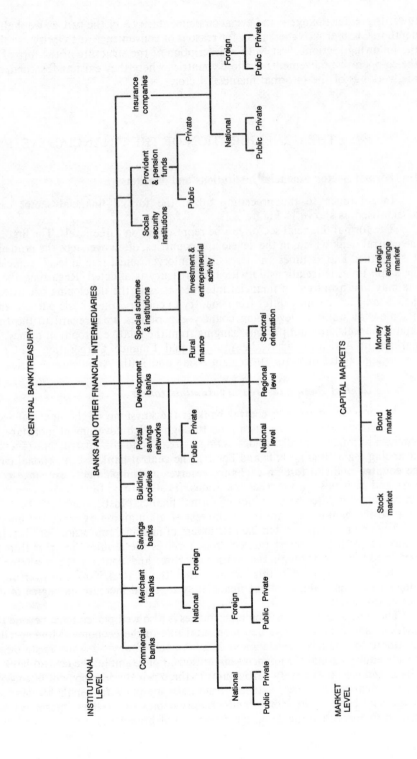

Special provisions may be made regarding sectoral lending, namely through favourable refinancing policies or by setting up or co-sponsoring (with development or commercial banks) special funds or schemes to that effect (see section (vii)). The Philippines have long been practicing preferential credit policies towards agriculture by means of favourable rediscounting facilities with the central bank. The central bank of Zambia – Bank of Zambia – has a special department which operates, in collaboration with commercial banks, a Credit Guarantee Scheme aimed at accelerating the flow of credit from formal financial institutions to small businesses.

Finally, a central bank's open market operations can encourage the growth of the money market[1], while the central bank itself can also provide the appropriate supervisory and regulatory framework for the development of a securities market. This may be reinforced by parallel "institutional efforts", as is the case in Indonesia where, in 1976, the government established a regulatory agency – the Capital Market Operations Board (BAPEPAM) – and a national investment company – PT DANARESKA – in order to promote the development of a securities market in the country. The former has elaborated operating procedures for the Jakarta Stock Exchange and supervises their execution, while the latter is responsible for encouraging the spread of share ownership. Tax incentives were introduced since 1979 in order to encourage companies to seek listing.

The Treasury

Alongside an often omnipresent central bank, another characteristic of financial activity in the developing countries is the predominant role of the Treasury, as reflected by the share of claims on central government in domestic credit.

The Treasury may be considered as the financial agent of the State. In this capacity, it manages the revenue and expenditure flows of the government. To assume this function, the Treasury has an account with the central bank which must always have a positive credit balance. In return, the Treasury benefits from a permanent credit line with the latter. Alongside seasonal cash requirements, the budget deficit generates a longer-term need for financing of the Treasury, while the resultant public debt must be regularly amortized with the central bank. The predominance of the Treasury and consequently its relationship with the central bank are hence a function of the extent of government involvement in monetary circulation. In fact, there may be potential conflicts between the Treasury and the central bank, with either one of the two institutions assuming a leadership role.

There were five countries in our sample with a high share of claims on central government in domestic credit (see Table 2.7 in section II). Over the period 1981 to 1987, the figures for India varied within the range of 40 to 45 per cent; those for Ethiopia, Burundi, and Mexico between 50 and 60 per cent; while in the case of Zambia, they were between 65 and 70 per cent, with two peak years in 1985 and 1986 when the figures reached the 80 per cent level.

b) Banks and Other Financial Intermediaries

i) Commercial Banks

Commercial banks collect resources from the public which they then use for lending, discounting, or other financial operations. Their resources are derived primarily from deposits – demand deposits, short-term deposits, savings deposits – from both households and business enterprises. More recently, commercial banks in some countries are also able to issue certificates of deposit.

Commercial banks play a large role in the provision of credit and investment funds. Lending operations are mostly short-term business credits (especially trade credit and working capital) and personal credit. Sometimes commercial banks also grant mortgage loans. Other uses of the collected funds include discounting services and investment in securities.

Commercial banks in developing countries tend to favour large-scale borrowers in the commercial and industrial sectors and concentrate their activities in urban areas. Although efforts are being made to make commercial banking services available to small-scale borrowers in rural areas – such as the use of mobile banking units in rural areas in Zimbabwe, the nationalisation of major commercial banks in India in 1969, or the specialisation of state-owned commercial banks along sectoral lines in Indonesia – agricultural lending is still usually limited to agricultural parastatals, export crop plantations, large-scale commercial farmers, mill-owners, etc.

Despite their urban concentration and bias away from agricultural lending, however, commercial banks are usually the most popular of the formal financial intermediaries in the developing countries (from the point of view of their percentage share of financial savings) if only because other financial institutions and instruments are often underdeveloped. In the Philippines, for example, they dominate the financial scene, holding around 43 per cent of the total financial resources in the country. Nationalised commercial banks in Bangladesh held 70 per cent of total bank deposits in 1984. In Zambia, three of the nine commercial banks in the country accounted for three-fourths of total deposits at the end of 1985.

ii) Merchant Banks

Merchant, or investment, banks specialise in trade finance, especially by accepting bills. They may also serve as issuing houses and underwriters, accept deposits, provide short- and long-term loans, organise financial packages and act as portfolio managers for corporations and individuals. The volume of funds they mobilise directly is usually limited, however[2].

Only three countries of our sample include merchant banks in their formal sector – Zambia, Zimbabwe and Mexico – and in all three cases they operate as accepting houses, provide financing for foreign trade, and carry out introductions on the stock exchange.

iii) Savings Banks

Savings banks may be government-owned, or run by regional or local authorities, or they may be operated as co-operatives or trustee organisations. Their principal aim is to accept household savings, especially from the lower-income groups (hence small, private savings), as well as to grant credit, to both savers and other borrowers, such as small businesses and private individuals within the same region or even community from which savings were mobilised[3].

The credit policy of savings banks is usually oriented in three main directions. Savings banks usually provide a lot of housing finance, either by granting real estate loans directly to borrowers or by serving as a channel for government concessional credit to low-cost housing, as is the case of the state-owned savings bank – Bank Tabungan Negara – in Indonesia.

Savings banks also often lend to the public sector. The government-owned National Savings and Credit Bank in Zambia, for example, has lent about 85 per cent of its total funds to the government to finance development projects in accordance with national investment priorities.

As for the third direction, greater efforts are being made in many countries to reorient or reinforce, depending on each case, credit policy in favour of small local enterprises.

iv) Building Societies

Housing finance companies (or building societies) accept deposits from savers and may lend to individuals – for the construction, purchase, maintenance or repair of dwellings – to construction firms, or to the state for the financing of low-cost accommodation. Sometimes they may also provide mortgage loans for commercial property. Potential borrowers must first save in order to qualify for a loan, and it is this incentive to qualify which often makes building societies popular with small savers.

Building societies in Zimbabwe come closest to this general description (see Box 2.1). Their widespread branch network, the variety of deposits offered, and the low minimum deposit rules (relative to other financial institutions) make them particularly accessible. By contrast, the Zambian National Building Society would seem to cater more to the urban, higher-income groups. In Ethiopia, the Housing and Savings Bank offers savings and time-deposits but its number of branches and territorial expansion has been limited so as to avoid competition in deposit-taking with the Commercial Bank of Ethiopia. Interest rates on loans were recently reduced in order to stimulate the construction sector. Public enterprises and co-operatives are the favoured borrowers, however, not individuals.

v) Postal Savings Networks

Postal savings networks use post office branches to collect small savings of households, but they do not grant loans and as such they do not create money.

One of the main assets of post office savings networks is their accessibility to a wide section of the population. From the simple geographical point of view, the widespread network of post offices can bring savings facilities closer to outlying areas. Secondly, the lower minimum deposit and minimum value per transaction requirements, compared to those of commercial banks for example, mean that small savers can actually use these services. Moreover, the lower-income and rural segments of the population find the post office setting less intimidating than a bank – they feel accepted as a customer, and not looked down upon by the clerks.

Postal savings networks also have relatively low administration costs, since mobilising savings, i.e. accepting deposits, is only one of a variety of functions performed by a post office.

The main drawback, however, is that post office savings banks do not grant loans, and thus cannot be considered as financial intermediaries proper. Most of the resources mobilised are invested in government bills and bonds, when they are not directly channelled to the Treasury. In Zimbabwe, for example, the proportion is 90 per cent. The process also tends to draw funds away from the rural areas to the urban centres.

* * *

Savings banks, postal savings networks, and building societies thus share a common function: that of collecting small, private savings which may otherwise have been hoarded or spent for consumption purposes. It should be pointed out, however, that savings banks and postal savings networks offer low interest rates, in real terms, on deposits. Where these

Box 2.1

BUILDING SOCIETIES IN ZIMBABWE

The three building societies operating in Zimbabwe play a prominent role in the mobilisation of personal savings. Together they accounted for 23.3 per cent of total savings and fixed deposits in 1984 (second to commercial banks, which collected 37.2 per cent of savings and fixed deposits).

The building societies regard themselves as "small people's banks" which provide savings facilities – including savings accounts and fixed deposits as well as various kinds of shares – that are adequately geared to the needs of savers. A minimum deposit of Z$ 20 is required to open an account[1], but group deposits are also accepted, thus still giving small savers the possibility of depositing funds. The minimum and maximum withdrawal requirements are Z$ 20 and Z$ 200 respectively, and transactions may be conducted from any branch of a building society. Banking procedures are uncomplicated and are among the fastest in the country, not least because of a comparatively high level of computerisation.

The fact that transactions are free of charge and that interest, although limited to an annual ceiling, is paid on deposits, serves to attract the lower-income groups and small savers. However, managing a large number of small accounts, at an estimated average cost of Z$ 1.30 per transaction, may be a considerable burden for a building society if clients begin using their savings account as a current account.

From the point of view of geographic accessibility, the building societies have branches, sub-branches, or agencies in all the main urban centres and in some rural areas as well. Access to building societies for rural dwellers remains relatively limited though, despite efforts by one building society to run some mobile units in outlying rural areas. Still, deposits with building societies are made throughout the country.

By contrast, lending policy is highly concentrated in urban areas (branches in Harare alone accounted for some 70 per cent of the total value of private mortgages granted) and among the middle- and upper-income groups (the average mortgage between 1980 and 1985 amounted to Z$ 14 200, well beyond the reach of lower-income groups).

The government's current policy is to urge building societies to embark upon low-cost housing schemes (so far, only one has complied). The additional resources that will be needed to do so, however, will not be forthcoming so long as restrictions on interest rates, combined with high inflation rates, result in negative returns on savings.

1.   Average exchange rate value 1985-1987: Z$ 1 = US$ 0.60.

three types of intermediaries differ is in the provision of credit. In this regard, one of the advantages of savings banks over postal networks, for example, is the fact that the former can offer a wider range of services than the latter, especially by providing credit to the private sector as well as government. Postal savings banks are more limited than savings banks in their degree of freedom to adapt financial services to local or regional needs. Building societies, for their part, may be distinguished from the other two because the resources they mobilise are, in principle, destined for a specific purpose. These factors may have contributed to the trend in a number of African countries in the 1960s and 1970s for postal savings networks to be reorganised and converted into savings banks[4].

A final question which may arise is whether or not it is cost-efficient for such institutions with so similar a function to operate side by side and compete for small savings in the relatively limited context of the formal financial sector of a developing country.

vi) Development Banks

Objectives

Usually with at least partial, if not total, government ownership (although private development banks do exist), development banks are viewed as an instrument of government policy with the mission of providing long-term finance (debt or equity which the capital market cannot or will not provide) for bankable development projects in industry, agriculture, services, infrastructure. This means that they are assigned – in theory, at least – the unenviable task of reconciling national development concerns with banking profitability criteria. The former may include such functions as:

- Contributing to the creation of employment;
- Saving or earning foreign exchange;
- Improving the distribution of income (between social classes, regions, racial or ethnic groups, men and women ...);
- Contributing to the diversification of industry;
- Modernising the agricultural sector;
- Encouraging the development of small businesses and entrepreneurial activity;
- Developing capital markets.

Clearly, these are ambitious objectives, and development banks do not always succeed in putting them into practice. Development banks are often forced to finance high risk projects (a new technology or industry, for example) which do not fulfil eligibility criteria on commercial banking terms: weak financial structure, little or no available security, the borrower has little track record, etc. Sometimes they must extend grace periods or take equity in addition to extending loans, thus increasing their exposure even more. Under such circumstances, maintaining financial viability becomes increasingly difficult. Moreover, there is the potential danger that by filling the gaps left by the private sector banks regarding investment needs, development banks may become the financiers of last resort, and be called upon to finance those projects which are unacceptable to the private sector.

Specialisation

Development banks may be specialised either on a regional or sectoral basis. While one could argue that this allows economies of scale, the limits and pitfalls of concentrating lending in one sector or region and the virtues of diversification should also be pointed out.

At any rate, in most developing countries, and in those of our sample, specialised development banks are common. Two specialised government banks in the Philippines, for example, are the Land Bank of the Philippines – set up to extend financial support for the agrarian reform programme of the government – and the Philippine Amanah Bank – established to support the government's objective of providing financial services to the Muslim segment of the population. The Agricultural Development Bank in Zambia was established to become the country's primary agricultural credit institution (agricultural lending is a common form of specialisation in development banking). Regional development banks in Indonesia were set up in each province (and are owned – wholly or partially – by the provincial governments) to mobilise savings for development investment within their region of activity.

National-level development banks are, of course, expected to play a more comprehensive developmental role in the economy, and in some cases, the objectives set may be quite ambitious. The Development Bank of the Philippines is the institution through which funds are rechannelled to development projects. The Development Bank of Zambia's "mission" is to contribute to the development of economically viable enterprises in various sectors, although not to finance individuals or small enterprises. The national development bank of Indonesia, BAPINDO, is supposed to finance long-term investment by indigenous, non-Chinese enterprises. Ethiopia's Agricultural and Industrial Development Bank specialises in medium- and long-term loans to agriculture and industry (and also short-term loans to agriculture), and also provides consultancy and technical assistance services.

Sources of funds

To the extent that development banks are primarily lending institutions, the mobilisation of household savings, especially small savings, may be of minor importance in their overall activities. Most often, development banks do not accept deposits or, if they do, they are from institutions, not individuals. Two exceptions within our sample are the regional development banks in Indonesia, for which demand deposits are one of the two primary sources of funds (the other being the refinancing of loans with the central bank), and private development banks in the Philippines, which draw their funds from household and individual savers. In most other cases, development bank financial resources may be derived from one or more of the following sources:

- Government funding and loans from other financial intermediaries;
- Shareholders, including government, national banking and non-bank financial institutions, foreign banks, bilateral development agencies, etc.;
- Refinancing of loans with the central bank;
- External credit lines, usually with multilateral and bilateral financial and/or development institutions.

Lending policy

As the recipients of government funds and of funds for on-lending from overseas agencies at concessional rates, and as the beneficiaries of favourable rediscounting policies, development banks can provide long-term loans at below market interest rates[5]. While the underlying intention of such practices is to promote long-term investment for economic development, it is important to recognise and try to avoid the risk that this can bring on of transforming the beneficiary development banks into conduits of cheap funds from government and external sources rather than reinforcing their role as intermediaries between national savers and borrowers. This has particularly been the case in the Philippines and Ethiopia, for example.

Generally speaking, lending by development banks involves medium- and long-term loans (ten to fifteen year maturity), sometimes also short-term loans, and equity, which are directed primarily towards public or private commercial, manufacturing and industrial enterprises. As far as agricultural lending is concerned, much of the incentive for both public and private development banks stems from the favourable conditions offered under government-supervised credit programmes. Although the intended target groups usually include the gamut of agricultural producers – small-, medium- and large-scale farmers, co-operatives, fishermen, marketing unions, public organisations engaged in agricultural/fisheries activities, and agro-industries – in actual practice, the principal beneficiaries are mostly medium- and large-scale commercial farmers or state farms and co-operatives.

vii) Special Schemes and Institutions

Alongside development banks, many, if not most, developing countries have a network of specialised institutions or run special schemes (under the auspices of a development or commercial bank, the central bank, or of another public authority) geared to a particular target-group or purpose. The two main concerns are rural finance and small businesses.

Rural Finance

The relative absence of financial services (both deposits and loans) for the rural sector underpins the keen interest in rural finance, and in particular the efforts made to reach the smaller-scale farmers. From the point of view of the mobilisation of resources, it appears that savings propensities in rural areas may be higher than usually assumed. A 1983 study by the World Bank on rural credit in Indonesia, for example, found that the savings propensity in the rural sector was 20 per cent[6]. Looking at it from a different angle, the case study on the Philippines showed that, in 1985, 55 per cent of rural households were net savers; moreover, the saving rate in rural households was higher than in urban households at the same income bracket except for the highest income brackets above 250 000 pesos.

However, much of rural savings goes unheeded – and unexploited – because it is largely channelled into non-financial assets such as gold, land, crops (food stocks), etc. Hence, on the mobilisation side, a way must be found to attract potential rural savings towards more financial forms.

From the point of view of the allocation of resources, it is also clear that small farmers and other low-income rural dwellers must have access to loan facilities if they are to pursue their economic activities successfully.

Although it is increasingly being recognised that there are two dimensions to the issue of rural finance, the tendency up till now has been to focus on the lending aspect. For example, rural banks were set up in the Philippines in 1952 to specialise in the extension of small loans for agricultural purposes as well as for retail trade, but they do little savings mobilisation; rather, their activity is mostly agricultural lending under supervised credit programmes. Likewise, the Agricultural Finance Company in Zambia provides seasonal loans to small-scale farmers as well as medium- and long-term agricultural financing. It is solely a lending institution, however, and its resources are external. In Indonesia, village-level organisations obtain their capital from the state commercial bank and provide short-term loans to merchants, while pawnshops receive government funds and/or loans from the central bank and provide credit (at relatively high interest rates of 2 per cent per month) for the cash needs of low-income groups, with loans of a maximum maturity of six months.

Besides central bank guidelines on interest rate policies, credit ceilings, rediscounting policies, and branch banking directives, preferential policies for rural finance may also include loan guarantee policies or crop insurance for subsidised loans. One such example is the Crop Insurance Scheme which was set up in the Philippines in 1981 with the basic purpose of encouraging banks to grant high-risk, short-term, non-collateral loans for specific commodities (corn, rice, cotton, cattle) and to provide them with some sort of guarantee of recovery of these loans. From the farmer's point of view, crop insurance not only serves to protect his capital but also enables him to obtain credit after a crop failure that would otherwise have left him in deeper debt.

Crop insurance has been made compulsory for all rice and corn farmers covered by government-supervised credit subsidy programmes. The crop insurance scheme is subsidised by government, though the farmer also contributes a small percentage share of the premium. While the scheme has undoubtedly encouraged lending institutions to extend credit to farmers, its overall impact is not significant given its limited coverage (only 5 per cent of total surface area planted with rice was covered by the scheme in 1981-82). Moreover, the accumulation of rural bank arrears seems to suggest that there is a substantial problem in terms of paying off bank claims on insurance.

Box 2.2

FINANCE FOR INVESTMENT AND ENTREPRENEURIAL ACTIVITY IN ZIMBABWE

Zimbabwe has a number of corporations and funds designed to ease the access to financial services for small entrepreneurs. FEBCO (Finance for Emergent Businessmen) is a co-operative venture between the Reserve Bank (central bank) and commercial banks whereby the former, through FEBCO, guarantees 50 per cent of the loan that a commercial bank may grant to a small businessman in commerce, industry or the services who, for lack of adequate security, would otherwise not qualify for a loan. Beneficiaries of this scheme may be sole proprietors, co-operatives, partnerships or limited liability companies. The loan investigation and appraisal procedures assumed by FEBCO reduce considerably the commercial bank's credit appraisal costs, while also serving as an advisory service for businessmen seeking to expand. Statistics from the first four years of the scheme's operation (1978-1982) showed that 62 per cent of the total loan value went to finance retail trade, while the urban-rural distribution of loans was about even.

SEDCO (Small Enterprises Development Corporation) is a government corporation which seeks to promote and accelerate the development of commerce and industry. Loans are advanced to small, viable enterprises which give an acceptable purpose for a loan application. In addition, SEDCO provides training and advice on bookkeeping and management with a view to improving both the efficiency of the enterprise and the repayment record.

Investment and Entrepreneurial Activity

Another area of prime concern for developing countries is the development of entrepreneurial activity – especially by small- and medium-sized enterprises – and productive investment. Many governments have established special schemes or institutions to this effect (see Box 2.2).

Investment houses, financing companies and securities dealers are among the public and private long-term financing institutions set up in the Philippines with the aim of expanding and modernising productive ventures, or facilitating short-term investments in other financial institutions. In Zambia, the Central Bank and commercial banks are jointly operating a Credit Guarantee Scheme in order to accelerate the flow of credit from formal financial institutions to small businesses.

In Indonesia, a more decentralised approach has been adopted. The Badan Kredit Kecematons (BKK) is one of a set of programmes that come under the control of provincial government and community organisations. These entities are generally given greater independence to determine interest rates and loan amounts. Operating at the provincial level, the BKK is simple in design, has high turnover rates and is considered highly efficient. Loans are made primarily as trade credits and for the funding of small handicraft operations. This programme has a compulsory retention component, whereby a certain percentage of the loan value is held as a savings deposit. Capital requirements are not high and, given the retention component, it does not depend heavily on external funding.

viii) Social Security and Contractual Savings Institutions

Alongside the various types of deposit-taking and credit-disbursing institutions described above, non-bank financial intermediaries – among which are social security and other contractual savings institutions such as provident funds, private pension funds, and life and non-life insurance – also play a role, which may sometimes be negative, in the mobilisation and allocation of savings[7].

Social Security

Social security institutions are compulsory, public contributory programmes which guarantee a minimum, moderate level of benefits covering one or several of the following "risks": long-term risks such as invalidity, old age, death; and short-term risks such as sickness, maternity, employment injury, and unemployment. They also provide for medical care and family allowances.

Financing of benefits may be on a pay-as-you-go or on a funded (or capitalisation) basis. In the former case, contributions paid each year by active participants are immediately used to finance benefits, while in the latter case, the fund manages contributions by individuals on their behalf, and they recover their capital and accrued earnings at a later date (i.e. upon retirement or when the contingency occurs)[8]. It is clear that only the second method of financing generates substantial financial reserves.

Hence, social security schemes may have two main functions: a social function, i.e. the long-term maintenance of the individual's income level; and an economic/financial function, i.e. the role of a supplementary instrument in mobilising internal savings and funding investment.

Regarding the savings mobilisation potential of social security[9], the level of surpluses mobilised (gross savings) depends on:

- The financing technique adopted (only a capitalised, or funded, financing technique generates reserves, and hence savings);
- The maturity of the system, insofar as a "young" system will have few maturing claims relative to its receipts;
- The demographic structure of the affiliated population, since this determines the coming of age of the system's beneficiaries and thus the length of the contribution period before benefits are claimed;
- The short-term or long-term nature of the risks covered (risk pooling through funded financing is possible and appropriate only for long-term risks);
- The impact of the economic environment, since inflation can erode the real value of reserve funds, and external factors such as recession or unemployment can affect the rates of contributions.

On the allocation side, there are three types of investment possibilities:

- Seek a maximum rate of return;
- Invest in accordance with the goals set out by a national development strategy;
- "Return" surpluses to the scheme's affiliates.

The first case entails giving a relatively free rein to management regarding the composition of the investment portfolio (though this may not always coincide with government priorities). By ensuring a constant demand for assets, social security schemes can thus contribute to a widening of national capital markets, provided, of course, that the latter can offer enough viable, long-term investment opportunities[10].

The second type of investment possibility involves the channelling of surpluses into favoured industrial sectors or social investments (schools, hospitals, roads) or into government securities, thus providing the public sector with an important source of borrowed funds. In order to achieve this, the government may impose restrictive legislation on investment portfolio composition (e.g. with some percentage compulsorily invested in government securities).

In the third case, "returning" part of the surpluses to the scheme's affiliates may be done by lowering contribution levels, increasing benefits, granting personal loans, mortgages, housing or other social facilities.

Contrary to what may be widely believed, most developing countries do have some experience with national social security schemes and provide some form of protection. Some schemes are older than others; extent of coverage, benefit levels, and the relative success or failure in mobilising and allocating savings vary widely from one country to another.

Contractual Savings Institutions

Contractual savings institutions include provident funds, private pension funds (see Box 2.3), life and non-life insurance companies. Provident and pension funds[11] ensure income payments upon retirement in the form of annuities. Life insurance companies provide protection against the risk of loss of income due to death and also sell annuities. Non-life insurance companies insure against financial losses from theft, fire, accidents, etc.

Contractual savings institutions are financial intermediaries that acquire funds from the public at periodic intervals on a contractual basis, transform these contributions or premiums into assets, and use the earnings to pay out the benefits and claims on the policies. Based on a funded financing technique, these institutions are thus centred on savings, with a view to ensuring their financial viability. In non-life insurance, funds tend to

Box 2.3

PENSION FUNDS IN ZIMBABWE

At the end of 1983, 1 389 pension funds were registered in Zimbabwe, with a membership of 569 933. Estimates by the German Development Institute[1] showed that, in 1984, roughly two-thirds of all the formally employed had some kind of pension coverage.

Pension funds in Zimbabwe may be run by insurance companies or they may be self-administered schemes. The majority of pension funds are administered by insurance companies (1 278 out of 1 389 in 1983). These schemes also cover approximately 75 per cent of all contributors and, in 1984, held 55 per cent of total pension fund assets (which were Z$ 1 668 million)[2]. The remaining 25 per cent of contributors were covered by the 111 self-administered arrangements.

The amount of personal savings mobilised by pension funds, defined as members' contributions alone, represented 45 per cent of total resources (liabilities minus reserves, provisions and sundry creditors). It is estimated that the amount of personal savings mobilised by pension funds will increase in the next few years, as the share of employees covered increases (and especially if a national pension scheme is introduced) and nominal wages rise. Nevertheless, high inflation rates throughout the 1980s, except in 1985, have caused serious erosion and mean that in real terms, the value of funds, and hence individual benefits, will decline.

From the employees' point of view, self-administered schemes are more attractive than insurance company-run schemes because the ratios of employer's to employee's contributions are, respectively, 64 to 36 per cent and 49 to 51 per cent. However, it appears that those who are the primary beneficiaries of self-administered schemes are the higher-paid, steadily employed clerks or workers who make up the middle- and high-income groups. Pension funds administered by insurance companies cater to the lower-income groups, i.e. low-paid workers who, because they change jobs frequently, do not stay on the payroll long enough to meet the minimum employment requirements which confer eligibility for benefits. For these groups, contributions to pension funds are simply a wage deduction, while pension payments calculated as a percentage of wages provide insufficient coverage after retirement. Hence there is little alternative but to fall back on traditional solidarity schemes.

1. Radke, Detlef *et al.*, *Mobilisation of Personal Savings in Zimbabwe Through Financial Development*, Berlin, 1986, German Development Institute, mimeo report.
2. Average exchange rate value 1985-87: Z$ 1 = USD 0.6.

be in the range of 120-140 per cent of annual premiums. In life insurance, the amounts are relatively higher, as an implicit savings component is included in the premiums (see Box 2.4).

The savings mobilised, particularly in the case of life insurance, are long-term, non-liquid, stable, regular, non-inflationary, and to some extent accurately determinable, depending on the degree of precision of the actuarial base.

Box 2.4

INSURANCE IN ZIMBABWE

At the end of 1983, 47 national and international direct insurers, including both life and non-life companies offering the full range of commercial and personal insurance services, were registered in Zimbabwe[1].

The insurance sector can be regarded as one of the fastest growing sectors in the country. Net revenue from premiums rose by between 20 and 30 per cent per annum during the 1980s, reflecting a growing demand for both life and non-life insurance. Between 1980 and 1984, assets of insurance companies doubled to about Z$ 1 278 million, while savings – defined as net premiums minus net claims and surrenders – were 2.6 times higher in 1984 than in 1980, and amounted to Z$ 186 million[2]. According to the German Development Institute[3], a growth rate of 25 per cent can be assumed for the insurance industry in 1985 and 1986. The insurance companies hold over 15 per cent of the country's financial reserves.

The most important branch by far is life insurance, accounting for roughly 90 per cent of assets, 82 per cent of revenue, and 78 per cent of savings in the insurance sector. This market is highly concentrated, with the five largest companies accounting for four-fifths of all assets and for almost nine-tenths of all revenue in the insurance sector.

All the companies have their head offices in Harare, with branches in the main cities and agencies in the major urban centres. Insurance companies are mainly geared to the requirements of industrial, commercial, and large-scale farming enterprises on the one hand, and of the urban, middle- and higher-income groups (for personal insurance) on the other. For instance, life insurance companies require either a regular minimum income of Z$ 400 to 500 a month – which is quite high considering that the average minimum wage in Zimbabwe is Z$ 150 a month – or a minimum premium of Z$ 12 to 20 a month. These criteria are strictly applied. It is thus not surprising that about 90 to 95 per cent of all life insurance business is contracted in urban areas with the upper strata. Life and non-life insurance business with inhabitants of rural areas and lower income earners in urban areas is therefore limited, due to their insufficient and/or irregular cash incomes and the high administrative costs of operating in rural areas.

Life insurance policies are long-term investments, and are consequently hard hit by the high rates of inflation in Zimbabwe. With interest rates at about 7 or 8 per cent and inflation rates at 10 to 15 per cent, future benefits will be badly eroded. Nevertheless, there is a growing demand for life and non-life insurance, particularly in urban areas, since the traditional forms of security – namely the extended family – seem to be slowly eroding for those who have lived and worked in towns for a long time.

Insurance companies in Zimbabwe play an important role in the economy from the point of view of investment. Total revenue is twice as high as total expenditure, leaving insurers with substantial sums of investible funds. The statutory requirements – in force since 1984 – that 60 per cent of life insurance surpluses and 30 per cent of non-life insurance surpluses be invested in approved securities have not been respected in practice. Indeed, the respective percentages were 45.6 per cent and 19.1 per cent, partly because high inflation rates have resulted in negative returns on public sector stocks. It should be pointed out, however, that other, more profitable forms of investment are also hard to come by.

In sum, despite the limited range of clients of the insurance sector in Zimbabwe, it appears that insurance companies make a major contribution to savings mobilisation and inject substantial funds into the economy. In particular, life insurers channel long-term resources from the middle- and higher-income groups (that may otherwise have been used for consumption purposes) towards investment.

1. In 1984 and 1985, some companies effectively ceased to operate.
2. Average exchange rate value 1985-87: Z$ 1 = USD 0.6.
3. Radke, *op. cit.*, p. 30.

Ideally, with all of the above attributes, contractual savings institutions could make appropriate sources for the financing of long-term investment. In fact, legislation permitting, their investment portfolio should reflect efforts to maximise yield, or at least to invest in secure and profitable assets.

As institutional investors, contractual savings institutions could contribute substantially to the development of national capital markets – through their regular demand for securities – and more generally to the financial and monetary development of the developing countries. In addition, they can be called upon by the public authorities to provide sectoral support by orienting their surpluses towards investment in priority sectors as designated by the government.

Contractual savings institutions are generally of a more limited importance than social security schemes in developing countries, although they are growing rapidly in some, notably in Asia and Latin America, and less so in Africa. Pension funds are substantial institutional investors, for example, in Malaysia, Singapore, Indonesia, the Philippines. Rapid growth in the insurance business was experienced especially in Brazil, South Korea, Chile, Venezuela, Taiwan, Columbia, Guatemala.

Constraints

One of the main constraints on both social security and contractual savings institutions is the need for contributors with a steady and regular source of income; modern sector workers often represent a minority share of the total population. On the allocation side, it appears that, so far, social security and contractual savings institutions have primarily served to channel savings into the hands of government, at the cost of limiting equity investment, the growth of the stock market, and credit to the private sector. This is largely the result of restrictive legislation requiring that a substantial proportion of these surplus funds be invested in government securities or deposited with other financial institutions (usually the central bank) at low or even negative real interest rates. Inflation and repressed financial markets too, are hardly conducive to the growth of the insurance industry.

c) Capital Markets

There are many different types of capital markets where economic units with varying financing capacities and borrowing requirements may operate.

Four main types of capital markets may be distinguished: money market, Treasury bill and government bond market, stock market, and foreign exchange market.

i) Money Market

The central bank, the Treasury, ordinary banks, and sometimes other financial institutions exchange their resources on the money market. Although the money market is usually for short-term maturities (up to two years), the bulk of activity involves day-to-day transactions.

The share of money markets in overall financial activity, as well as the volume of the financing and transactions involved, depend to a large extent on two factors: first, the role of banks in the financing of the economy; and second, the variance of the debtor or creditor position of banks within the financial system.

Generally speaking, there are few well-functioning interbank money markets in the developing countries, even though interbank borrowing and lending is requisite for efficient monetary policy implementation and domestic resource allocation[12]. One of the reasons for this is the practice in many developing countries of taxing all financial transactions, which makes very short-term overnight borrowing and lending uneconomical. This may be compounded by the fact that the ceilings set on interest rates may prevent banks from negotiating the terms of interbank loans. Perhaps more significant is the fact that, in many cases, banks have access to inexpensive and unlimited loans through central bank discount facilities, thus making interbank borrowing and lending dispensable.

Effective money markets exist in half the countries of our sample: Togo, Zimbabwe, India, Indonesia, Thailand, and Mexico. In those countries where they do not exist or where they are deficient, banks have access only to Central bank rediscounting facilities.

ii) Treasury Bill and Government Bond Market

Closely linked with the money market, the Treasury bill and government bond market is where the State issues short- and medium-term bills in order to finance its infra-annual and other term financing needs; sometimes the maturities of Treasury bills can extend up to two to three years.

On the demand side, the economic units involved are banks, households, firms, and other financial intermediaries. Treasury bills are, of course, exchanged on the money market, of which they are one of the pillars.

The size and importance of the transactions on this market depend on the financing needs of the Treasury, i.e. on that share of the government deficit which is financed through bonds and not through monetary creation. In most cases, large government deficits lead directly to an important Treasury bill market, as is the case in Mexico. Among the case study countries, Treasury bill markets are also present in Ethiopia, Zambia, Zimbabwe, India, the Philippines, and Thailand.

The rates on Treasury bills carry a certain weight in the overall structure of interest rates in the sense that they play the role of the risk-free asset rate.

Some countries also have government bonds with maturities exceeding two or three years. The existence of short-term and long-term bonds and bills, as well as their respective share in domestic financing if both are present, vary from country to country. Among those countries of our sample which have both Treasury bills and long-term government bonds – Ethiopia, Zambia, Zimbabwe, India, the Philippines, Thailand, and Mexico – long-term bonds are more important than short-term bills in domestic financing in all but India – where there seems to be more of a balance between the two – and Zambia, where a short-term horizon prevails.

iii) Stock Market

The stock market is the market where private enterprises can obtain financial resources by issuing shares and bonds, and where bond and shareholders can carry out portfolio arbitrage.

As far as equity is concerned, both the existence and the size of the equity market depend on a number of factors. First, they are inversely correlated to the size of the public sector. Clearly, in countries where the public sector is extensive, the equity market will be used only marginally as a means of channelling resources to the productive sector. A second factor is the willingness or degree of reluctance, depending on the case, of the owners of family firms to accept the idea of "going public" and opening their capital to outsiders. In this regard, taxation policies may have counterproductive effects on the development of financial markets, as they are often biased in favour of deposit interest income over dividends. For example, in Morocco, interest on deposits is tax exempt while there is a 25 per cent witholding tax imposed on dividends[13]. In other cases, equity income may be taxed twice: once as business profit and once as personal income. Stiff taxation may also discourage corporations from opening their books. However, it should be pointed out that the debate is still open as to whether fiscal incentives have any impact or not on the development of equity markets in the developing countries[14].

A final factor is the propensity of households to hold shares in their portfolios; this also reflects their degree of risk aversion. Furthermore, the attraction of the stock market is determined to a large extent by the relative returns on an investment in shares compared to monetary or real estate investments, for example. In this regard, low dividends and high inflation may be at least partially blamed for the inadequate provision of term finance.

As far as bonds are concerned, it must be noted that the growth of private bond markets depends on the willingness of subscribers to hold such assets which is, in the developing countries, seldom forthcoming. In fact in the rare cases when bonds are issued, they are mainly issued by public entreprises.

However, low or subsidised interest rates may remove the incentive to issue bonds. A striking example is the case of Indonesia where an inverted pattern of deposit and lending rates (loan rates were set below the corresponding deposit rates) which prevailed in the 1970s was aimed at keeping down the cost of government borrowing but also had the effect of encouraging firms to borrow from banks too, at rates lower than those at which they could sell any bonds[15].

Security markets exist in 35 developing countries – including India, Indonesia, the Philippines, Thailand, Zimbabwe and Mexico among the case study countries – but have generally played a minor role in domestic resource mobilisation. To the best of our knowledge, in all the other developing countries, neither shares nor bonds are issued and traded.

iv) Foreign Exchange Market

Two cases may be distinguished: those where the exchange rate is closely regulated by the monetary authorities; and those where exchange rate policy is more flexible.

Table 2.2 EXCHANGE RATE ARRANGEMENTS
as of 31 March 1988

Currency pegged to				More flexible	
US Dollar	French franc	SDR	Other composite[a]	Managed floating	Independently floating
Ethiopia	Togo	Burundi	Bangladesh	India	Philippines
Zambia			Thailand	Indonesia	
			Zimbabwe	Mexico	

a) Comprises currencies which are pegged to various "baskets" of currencies of the country's own choice, as distinct from the SDR basket.
Source: Extracted from *International Financial Statistics,* IMF, July 1988.

Administered exchange rates have long been common in developing countries. In this case, the government and the Central bank fix the external value of the currency – by pegging it to one of the hard currencies, to the SDR, or to any other composite of their choice – and enforce strict regulations notably in order to prevent nationals from exporting their capital. Within our sample, the Ethiopian and Zambian currencies are pegged to the US dollar; Togo's currency is pegged to the French franc; Burundi's currency is pegged to the SDR; and the currencies of Bangladesh, Thailand, and Zimbabwe are pegged to various "baskets" of currencies (as distinguished from the SDR basket) (see Table 2.2).

It should be remarked, however, that where there is an official foreign exchange market, it is not unusual for there to be an unofficial one alongside it, in which prices more or less reflect the true value of money and where both firms and households can acquire or sell foreign-denominated currency holdings. This has notably been the case in Mexico and Ethiopia.

In the second case of more flexible arrangements – which include both managed floating and independently floating exchange rates – economic units can trade freely on the foreign exchange market. The exchange rate itself is set at a level which more closely reflects market forces. India, Indonesia, and Mexico have managed floating exchange rate arrangements and the Philippines an independently floating one.

*   *   *

In conclusion to this section on financial markets, mention must also be made of informal financial markets although, by definition, the relevant statistical data is lacking. Indeed, there are, in some countries, informal operators and mechanisms for equity financing of informal business enterprises. The most notable examples of this are the informal sector partnership firms which are predominant in India, and especially investment companies, loan companies and sometimes finance companies which provide finance not only by making loans or advances but also by dealing in securities. The case of partnership firms is discussed in Section 3c.

2. "Semi-Formal" Bodies: Savings and Credit Co-operatives and Credit Unions

Savings and credit co-operatives and credit unions[16] are voluntary, co-operative financial organisations owned and operated on a non-profit basis by members, with the purpose of encouraging savings by providing local deposit facilities, using the pooled funds to make loans for productive or social purposes, and providing other (financial) services to members[17].

Members receive interest on deposits made regularly into a common fund from which loans are disbursed to those who qualify. The loan amount cannot exceed a fixed percentage of the member's accumulated savings or salary, while a minimum duration (usually three to six months) of membership and regular contributions are also required. Other conditions imposed may be that the loan purpose be judged sound by other members or that another member must offer a personal guarantee[18].

Loans are mostly short- to medium-term tide-over loans (usually one year) and may be for either productive or social purposes: weddings, funerals, other ceremonies; illness; social insurance; schooling; consumer durables; purchase of land or housing; and agricultural or commercial activities. Generally, though, co-operatives and credit unions lend mostly for consumption rather than investment.

Loans are usually to members, although non-members may sometimes borrow as well. Credit unions in Zambia also lend to organisations and other agencies. In the Philippines, co-operatives have innovated systems of mutual interlending schemes for the transfer of funds from surplus credit co-operatives to deficit ones; some have even grouped together and set up their own co-operative rural banks through which they link up with the formal financial sector.

Savings and credit co-operatives and credit unions have a different legal status from one country to another. In some cases, they may be full-fledged legal entities regulated by government and can thus be considered as part of the formal financial sector, as are co-operative banks in India, for instance. In other cases, they have what could be characterised as a more "semi-formal" status: in Zimbabwe, for example, there is no full, obligatory registration or regular supervision of co-operatives, but their rules of functioning are laid down by law. Finally, there are cases where the co-operative and credit union movements – even those which are government-sponsored – are considered part of the informal sector, as in the Philippines[19].

Whatever the classification, though, the systems in question can be of a highly complex and organised nature.

At the local level, co-operatives and credit unions have three basic characteristics: a common link between the members of a specific group, which may be residential (same village or area), occupational (same employer) or professional; voluntary participation; and the accumulation of savings which qualifies a member to receive credit. Groups tend to be small (20-25 members) although there are cases of co-operatives or credit unions within a firm with a membership of more than 200 (see Box 2.5).

Co-operatives and credit unions may be rural-based or urban-based, depending on the underlying motive for their creation. Rural co-operatives operate as farmers' grassroots organisations aimed at meeting the seasonal needs of their members which formal sector banks do not satisfy. Urban-based co-operatives are usually those centered around the firm or profession and serve primarily to cover short-term credit needs.

Beyond the local level, co-operatives and credit unions may be grouped into federations or attached in some way to a regional-level or national-level structure. In Togo, for example, co-operatives are grouped into a federation and contribute to a central fund on which

Box 2.5

URBAN SAVINGS AND CREDIT CO-OPERATIVES AND CREDIT UNIONS IN THE PHILIPPINES AND ZIMBABWE

Urban-based savings and credit co-operatives and credit unions are usually centered around a firm or a profession.

In the Philippines, urban co-operatives and credit unions are patronised by an increasing number of small business enterprises. The majority of credit union members are women, 90 per cent of whom are engaged in what could be called "entrepreneurship of survival", that is, street and market vending, junk recycling, umbrella repairing, manicure and pedicure services, clothes washing, and other micro enterprise endeavours.

In their lending operations, the credit unions extend loans to qualified members in amounts ranging from 300 to 500 pesos[1] with no interest. Borrowers, however, are encouraged to contribute to the capital build-up fund. Repayment of loans starts one week after disbursement.

Both the loans granted and the training in entrepreneurship provided by the credit unions are said to underpin the high success rates in these enterprises (80 per cent) and the timely loan repayments. The default rate due to business collapse or diversion of funds for emergency purposes is around 10 per cent.

Co-operatives and credit unions do not cater only to those involved in informal economic activity, however. They can also be linked with activities in the "modern" sector, as illustrated by the two Zimbabwean cases described below.

The Faith Mission Savings-Credit Society emerged from a need at the grass-roots level for savings facilities and access to credit for policemen, several prison guards and their wives. The 34 members contribute thirty dollars' savings[2] every other week (it is deducted from their wages) and the money is jointly deposited in an account with the Post Office Savings Bank. Each member is issued a book with the latest balance.

At the opposite end of the spectrum, the Savings Club and Credit Union for Air Zimbabwe Employees was an initiative which came from the company's managing director, in an effort to reduce the number of requests for advances before pay day (workers are either referred to the credit union or advised to join). At present, 256 out of 1 596 employees are members. A minimum of ten dollars per month is automatically deducted from their salary, as are repayments in the case of a loan.

Both the policemen's society and the Air Zimbabwe credit union deposit the accumulated funds with the Post Office Savings Bank at 10 per cent tax free interest and charge 12 per cent and 6 per cent annual interest on loans respectively. In both cases, the schemes are run by volunteer members who are not paid for these services.

1. Average exchange rate value 1985-1986: Pesos 19.497 = US$1.
2. Average exchange rate value 1985-1987: Z$1 = US$ 0.60.

Figure 2.2 **STRUCTURE OF THE ZAMBIAN COOPERATIVE MOVEMENT**

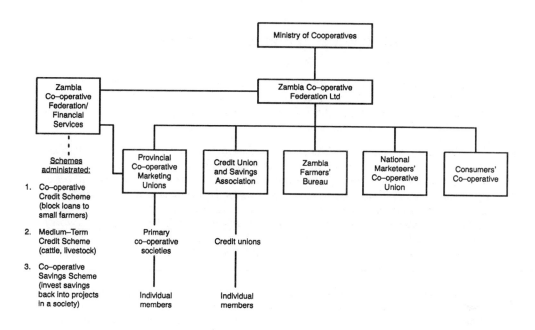

they earn interest; while in Zambia one finds a very structured and hierarchical system with local-level societies, regional-level unions and national-level federations and associations for both co-operatives and credit unions (see Box 2.6). These apex bodies seek to promote, co-ordinate and supervise co-operative and credit union activity, and to provide permanent and dependable savings and credit facilities, as well as advisory services, to the co-operative movement.

Co-operatives rely heavily for their funds on membership fees and savings deposits. In the Philippines, for example, 70 per cent of the total financial resources of co-operatives come from these sources. To the extent that co-operatives may sometimes serve as lending conduits of formal financial institutions, they may also receive credit assistance from government, local banks or external agencies, either in the form of funds to be distributed as loans as part of a national credit scheme, or by providing financial and logistical support for their operations.

It is important to realise, however, that even in those countries where the co-operative movement has proved economically viable (high repayment rates have been achieved) and membership as well as the total savings mobilised have risen, the volume of funds involved is actually rather limited. In Ethiopia, for example, the total funds of co-operatives represent 0.5 per cent of the deposits with the Commercial Bank of Ethiopia. Total credit union deposits in Togo represent less than 1 per cent of quasi-money (i.e. interest-bearing liabilities of the banking system)[20]. Similarly, when considering the number of borrowers and the total loan amounts granted to small farmers by co-operative schemes in Zambia,

Box 2.6

THE ZAMBIAN CO-OPERATIVE MOVEMENT

The overall objective of the Zambian co-operative movement is to make banking facilities available to the rural areas. In this regard, the highly organised and structured system covers an entire range of operators, from grassroots, local associations to apex bodies on a national level (see figure 2.2).

The Zambian Co-operative Federation (ZCF) Ltd. was set up in 1973 as an apex body of the co-operative movement in Zambia, while multipurpose Provincial Co-operative Marketing Unions were established, one in each province, all of them affiliated to ZCF Ltd. In addition, the Credit Union and Savings Association (CUSA), the Zambia Farmers' Bureau, and the Consumers' Co-operative and National Marketeers' Co-operative Union are affiliated with ZCF Ltd. At the local level, the Zambian co-operative movement is organised into multipurpose primary co-operative societies. ZCF Ltd. itself is responsible to the Ministry of Co-operatives on all co-operative affairs.

ZCF Ltd. and the nine Provincial Co-operative Marketing Unions own a subsidiary company, Zambia Co-operative Federation/Financial Services (ZCF/FS), which was created in 1983, to provide permanent and dependable savings and credit facilities to the co-operative movement, and to make available banking facilities to rural areas. Funds come from internal sources (membership, deposits) and government ministries, but they are mostly from donors. (ZCF/FS pays 6 per cent dividends to its members.) ZCF/FS administers three schemes: the Co-operative Credit Scheme (CCS), the Medium-Term Credit Scheme (MTCS), and the Co-operative Savings Scheme (CSS).

The CCS is aimed at small farmers with 0.5 to 8 hectares, and grants loans in kind for seasonal, agricultural purposes. The lending procedure used is a system of block loans which are disbursed down the hierarchical line, from national to provincial to primary (local) level co-operative societies or credit unions. Loans are disbursed in block form to provincial unions; the latter then disburses loans to individual primary societies in that province, which in turn lend to the individual member of the society. At each stage of the process, a good repayment record is required of the participating bodies or individuals in order to qualify for the next loan. For example, a primary society must achieve a minimum repayment rate of 93 per cent in order to qualify for the next loan. The scheme as a whole does, in fact, run a high repayment rate: 87-90 per cent. Interest charged in 1986 was 16 per cent (3 per cent to the primary society, 3 per cent to the Provincial Co-operative Marketing Union and 10 per cent to ZCF/FS).

The MTCS covers loans for wholesale and retail operations related to the purchase of hammermills, oxen, plowing equipment, cattle marketing vehicles, etc. Loans may be for a maximum of three years and are at 20 per cent annual interest.

The objective of the CSS is to invest savings back into projects in a society. Operating at a society level actually attracts non-members to join the society in order to gain access to banking facilities and take advantage of other services, i.e. the possibility to save money under safe conditions; 6 per cent interest on savings deposits; being able to save part of one's income for future investment and/or sudden expenditure.

CUSA, for its part, was set up in 1970 as the apex organisation of all credit unions in Zambia. Its objectives are to promote, co-ordinate and supervise credit union activity as well as provide advisory services. It is financed on the basis of members' shares (each member buys shares when joining a credit union) and savings deposits. West Germany provides financial support for CUSA's operational budget.

the figures are rather low compared with total agricultural credits on a national scale; co-operatives and credit unions provide services for a small proportion of the rural population. It should be pointed out, however, that this "small proportion" is usually ineligible for other loans from the formal sector.

The main significance of the co-operative or credit union movement lies in its provision of an alternative form of financial intermediation for those segments of the population that are denied easy access to the formal financial sector. In rural areas, co-operatives and credit unions may in effect be an important source of finance for small farmers, while in urban areas, they may also cater to the needs of small savers and borrowers. In this regard, they can be said to provide an alternative to non-financial savings for the households concerned.

The operating principles and social goals of savings and credit co-operatives and credit unions make them particularly suited and attractive to a small-scale urban and rural clientele (households and business enterprises) where the concept of self-help through mutual solidarity is prevalent. Moreover, the relatively high repayment rates, the use of joint liability mechanisms, the precondition that accumulated savings confer eligibility for a loan, and the generally satisfactory overall performance of co-operatives and credit unions have prompted governments in the developing countries as well as external donors to take a more active interest in them as potentially viable schemes for the mobilisation of savings – and of small savings, in particular – and conduits for government loan distribution programmes.

3. The Various Informal Sector Mechanisms and Operators

One of the most striking features of the informal sector is the wide variety of links between lenders, borrowers and depositors, ranging from simple credit arrangements to complex financial intermediation mechanisms. Upon closer examination, however, one soon discovers that the basic structures and concepts are similar everywhere; while the variants (or "variations on a theme") can be attributed to national, ethnic or village differences.

Our approach here will be to try to draw up a taxonomy of the three basic types of lenders, while drawing on the results of the case studies to illustrate certain points. The next

Table 2.3 INFORMAL SAVINGS AND CREDIT ARRANGEMENTS

	Types of links	Lenders	Borrowers
	Non-commercial arrangements	Friends Neighbours Households	Small farmers Small businesses and relatives
Individual moneylending	Commercial credit arrangements *i)* Money-based	Professional moneylenders Mobile bankers Private individuals from upper-income groups	Small farmers Small businesses and households
	ii) Land-based	Landlords Farmer-moneylenders	Tenants Small farmers
	iii) Commodity-based	Trader-moneylenders Agricultural input dealers Equipment suppliers Processors (rice millers) Produce traders Itinerant traders Market vendors Storeowners	Small farmers Small businesses and households
Associations	Savings arrangements	Fixed-fund associations Mutual aid associations Savings clubs	Small farmers Small farmers and households
	Combined savings and credit arrangements	Informal credit unions Informal savings and loan co-operatives ROSCAs (and variants)	Small farmers Small businessmen and households
Partnership firms	Financial intermediation	Indigenous bankers pawnbrokers Finance companies Investment companies Leasing companies Hire-purchase companies	Small businessmen and households

Source: Adapted from Holst, Juergen U., "The Role of Informal Financial Institutions in the Mobilization of Savings", in Kessler and Ullmo, eds., *op. cit.*, p. 123.

chapter will be devoted to a more in-depth analysis of their characteristics and mode of functioning.

The three types of informal lenders generally distinguished are: individual moneylenders, groups of individuals organised mutually, and partnership firms. Individual moneylenders most often lend out their own funds; sometimes they accept deposits. They include friends, neighbours, relatives, landlords, agricultural input dealers, processors (such as rice millers), professional moneylenders, produce traders, itinerant traders, market vendors, storeowners, equipment suppliers, etc. Among the mutual associations, one finds fixed fund or rotating savings and credit associations (ROSCAs), informal credit unions, savings clubs, mutual aid associations, self-help organisations and other types of family and tribal associations. Examples of partnership firms such as indigenous bankers and pawnbrokers are to be found primarily in India, as are other non-bank financial intermediaries such as finance, investment, leasing and hire-purchase companies. Despite the corporate structure of the latter three and the existence of legal regulations on their activity, they are included in the informal sector due to their exemption, to a greater or lesser degree, from central bank controls.

Table 2.3 summarises the principal types of informal savings and credit arrangements.

a) Individual Moneylending

Two types of credit arrangements are generally distinguished as far as individual moneylending is concerned: non-commercial – in the sense of being interest-free – and commercial.

i) Non-Commercial Moneylending

Non-commercial loans come from friends, relatives or neighbours and are quite common, as they are deeply rooted in local traditions. They may be in cash or in kind and are usually interest-free. In Zimbabwe, they are especially prevalent in urban areas, and are usually intended to help out a borrower in difficulty or to help him pay for regular expenses (such as school fees, school uniforms, etc.) or even consumer durables such as a radio, television or car. In India, what is known as "community credit" in the marine fishing villages of Kerala is actually a situation where fishermen alternate between temporary surplus and deficit positions, lending when they can so that they may borrow from others later, when and if necessary[21]. In Ethiopia, the loans are not only interest-free, but there is no fixed repayment date and in the case of default, the lender may even renounce repayment.

Ghate points out, however, that loans from friends, relatives or neighbours are not always non-commercial and that the interest charged is often no different from that of professional moneylenders, while the personal relationship serves as the collateral[22]. This seems to be the case in the Philippines, for example, where a loan of two to four kilos of rice for the next day's meal is indeed interest-free; but a loan of one cavan (44 kilos) of rice at no interest is hard to come by.

It is important to realise, however, that there are a number of factors which may place limits on the availability of credit assistance – be it with or without interest – from friends, relatives, or neighbours. This is especially the case in rural areas. Increased commercialisation and monetisation within the village economy, for example, tend to weaken personal bonds within the community. Furthermore, in case of natural disasters such as floods or drought, or an overall slump in production, all the households of the village may be affected; they will have simultaneous financial needs and will therefore be unable to provide assistance to others. Finally, the upper limit is rapidly reached on such loans, which are small in size and which must often be supplemented with funds from other informal or semi-formal sources.

ii) Commercial Moneylending

The second form of moneylending activity refers to "professional" credit arrangements, i.e. the lenders are engaged in some kind of business undertaking or in farming, but they have available capital (in cash or in kind) which they can lend to others. Commercial credit transactions in the informal sector may be money-based, land-based, or commodity-based (see Boxes 2.7 and 2.8).

Box 2.7

RURAL MONEYLENDING IN INDONESIA

In rural areas, moneylenders may be "professional" lenders, large land-owners, or persons involved in rural-based business enterprises such as processing (rice millers) or the transportation of goods. In all three cases, credit operations are largely based on an intimate knowledge of borrowers.

"Professional" moneylenders operating in villages work mostly on a small scale (e.g. a limited number of clients and volume of credit) in order to minimise the probability of encounters with the legal authorities, since their activities are illegal. Moreover, the presence of a moneylender in the village is not often welcomed by villagers and village officials. In one case, it was reported that a teacher who had lent money to neighbours at an interest rate of 20 per cent per month was forced to leave the village. Loans from moneylenders involve neither paperwork nor collateral. They may be either in cash or in kind or a combination of both. The interest rates charged vary widely – they may be up to 20-30 per cent a month – depending upon the opportunity cost of funds for lenders and the urgency of the demand from borrowers.

Two other main types of rural moneylending arrangements that involve land use or harvesting rights are "ijon" and "sewa". In both cases, the credit transaction is characterised by the farmer's borrowing in cash and repaying in kind. "Ijon" is derived from the Javanese word for green, meaning that the crop is still young. In this type of credit arrangement, the borrower transfers the rights to harvest the crop to the lender, who then assumes responsibility for, and meets the cost of, harvesting and selling the crop, his "profit" consisting of the net proceeds from the sale.

The other type of loan arrangement is "sewa", or land leasing for cash. In this case, rights to the use of the land itself rather than rights to the specific crop actually growing on the land, are transferred by the borrower to the lender. The agreements may run for a number of years or seasons and the lessee not only has considerable independence in his use of the land, but he also assumes a greater set of risks than under the "ijon" system.

Box 2.8

URBAN MONEYLENDING IN THE PHILIPPINES

Urban moneylending in the Philippines presents a wide variety of arrangements which may involve – alongside friends, neighbours and relatives – "professional" moneylenders, storeowners or market vendors, and other dealers and traders.

Professional moneylenders in urban areas are often resorted to as the only remaining source of credit when maximum credit capacity has been reached with relatives and storeowners. Lenders move about daily on motorcycles distributing and collecting a large number of small loans. One of their most notorious loan arrangements is the "five-six" scheme, that is, for every five pesos borrowed, six must be returned. Usually daily payment is demanded from the first day of the loan, although sometimes payment falls due at the end of the month. This amounts, as the case may be, to a 20 per cent daily or monthly rate of interest. Yet despite the high rate of interest charged by the local moneylenders, the level of repayment is found to be quite high. "Borrowing, however expensive, is one of the most prevalent coping mechanisms of the poor" [1].

Lending arrangements involving deferred payment on the purchase of commodity goods are the work of owners of "sari-sari", or variety stores (which are a food market, bazaar, hardware store and drugstore all combined in one). These storeowners often extend credit easily and indiscriminately in their retail operations, initially to win customer patronage and thus assure regular sales; but they gradually weed out the bad debtors and limit their credit clientele to those whose ability to pay has been well tested and proven. Those clients who may benefit from deferred payment facilities on their purchases (thus entering into a "suki relationship" with the storeowner or market vendor) are chosen on the basis of their reputation, income-level, occupation, and previous dealings. Thus it is mostly persons with stable incomes – e.g. teachers, doctors, nurses, white collar workers – and not the high risk poor (who are the majority in the town's population) who benefit from storeowner credit. Both the pricing of goods and the credit terms are flexible: lower prices and easier credit terms are allowed to customers who are close relatives or friends; other, more distant customers are charged prices which more closely reflect real transportation, storage and service costs.

From the storeowner's and market vendor's point of view, suki relationships present several advantages: the regularity of sales transactions diminishes the frequency of sales at distress prices due to inaccurately estimated turnover. Moreover, by "tying" customers to certain sellers, suki relationships allow the latter to maintain relatively high prices in defiance of direct price competition.

Another type of credit arrangement is offered by the so-called "Bombay merchants" who are in fact both traders and moneylenders since they make consigned purchases of any item on order – usually consumption items such as appliances – and sell it to the client on an instalment basis. The borrower usually pays a 100 per cent mark-up on the prevailing market price for the convenience of paying for the purchase in small daily instalments. Bombay merchants are adept at meeting borrowers' individual needs, are masters at personal relations, and have an impressive capacity for memorising accounts.

Finally, credit for the working capital of small business enterprises in urban areas of the Philippines is assured mainly by dealers and traders involved in the selling of scrap or recycled materials. Warehouse owners, or "bodegeros", finance the working capital needs of scavengers and, after a certain period, deduct the amount of the loan from the sales proceeds of the scrap or recycled material. In most cases, there is no nominal interest rate charged, although underpricing of scrap material is quite common. The next stage involves the sale of scrap material by the bodegeros to the dealer, with at least a 100 per cent mark-up. Sometimes dealers themselves give cash to bodegeros to pay cash directly to the scavengers. This credit assistance helps the bodegeros to build up their network of suppliers.

1. Keyes, William, "Approaches to Financing of Unconventional Housing, Informal Systems of Financing", paper presented at the Regional Seminar on Financing of Low-Income Housing, Asian Development Bank, Manila, Feb. 7-12, 1983. Cited by Yotopoulos, case study on the Philippines for the OECD Development Centre.

Money-based commercial credit arrangements in the informal sector usually involve professional moneylenders and sometimes private individuals. Professional moneylenders derive their spare cash from other business activities or family wealth and may or may not lend at usurious interest rates. Sometimes, in urban areas, moneylending activity attracts members of the upper-income groups with access to formal financial institutions who then lend, through middlemen, to low- and middle-income urban dwellers (see Box 2.9).

Land-based moneylending is the work of landlords and farmer-moneylenders. Landlord-moneylenders may provide food rations, cash advances, or emergency loans to tenant farmers and sharecroppers as well as seeds and working capital in between harvests. Interest is usually paid in kind and is collected with the rent. In some cases, any portion of a debt left unpaid is transferred over to the next production cycle, so that tenant farmers become, in a sense, "tied" to the land and the landlord who might then demand unpaid labour services of them.

Farmer-moneylenders are usually rich farmers – with assets for collateral and resources for leverage, and a close knowledge of the farmer-borrowers in their area – who act as local marketing agents (screening borrowers, disbursing loans, and collecting repayments) within the small-farmer community for trader-moneylenders seeking to secure themselves a portion of the output market. The latter lend to these agent farmers who become in turn lenders for the smaller farmers of the area.

Commodity-based credit arrangements are manifold and involve a wide variety of operators. Trader-moneylenders such as agricultural input dealers, produce traders, or processors (rice millers, for example), usually play a major role in rural areas by extending credits in cash or in kind to small farmers at a time when the latter are low on money. This is often attributed to the fact that traders and farmers have a countercyclical need for capital – the farmers in between harvests, and the input or produce traders at harvest time in order to channel their goods to the market. When loans obtained from traders are in

Box 2.9

MOBILE BANKERS IN WEST AFRICAN MARKETPLACES

In the larger marketplaces of West African countries, "mobile bankers" frequently carry out deposit and credit operations amongst vendors. In fact, mobile bankers are often agents for large businessmen, moneylenders, or other economically powerful individuals who, according to Miracle, Miracle, and Cohen, are "frequently members of cartels and help protect market entry by their moneylending activities"[1].

A mobile banker's activity consists of making regular – often daily – visits to market vendors and collecting their deposits from them. His fee usually amounts to one deposit per time period (one month, for example) at the end of which the lump sum less the fee is returned to the depositor. Mobile bankers also extend credit; some of the larger traders in Abidjan, for instance, may get advances of up to six times their deposits[2].

For the market vendor, mobile bankers offer the convenience of bringing banking services directly to their place of activity, during working hours – which is also the time when banks operate – and the possibility of opening a line of credit under better conditions than with a formal bank. Moreover, a survey of 44 market women in Abidjan[3] showed that the interviewees preferred mobile bankers over savings and loan associations because with the latter there are "too many disputes" whereas with the former they negotiate only with one individual and not several. Finally, market vendors see little risk in depositing their money with someone who comes around daily.

This regularity of transactions is also appreciated by the mobile bankers themselves, as it is one of the ways they may assess the creditworthiness of their clients. Indeed, their daily visits put pressure on vendors to make deposits, which are usually always of the same amount so that accounting may be made easier.

1. Miracle, M. and D. Miracle and L. Cohen, "Informal Savings Mobilisation in Africa", *Economic Development and Cultural Change*, July, 1980, vol. 28, No. 4, pp. 701-724.
2. *Ibid.*, p. 718.
3. Lewis, B.C., "The Limitations of Group Action Among Entrepreneurs: The Market Women of Abidjan, Ivory Coast", in Hafkin, N. and E. Bay, eds., *Women in Africa*, Stanford, Stanford University Press, 1976.

kind, the goods that are supplied on credit are usually overpriced. Repayments are usually in cash and only exceptionally in kind, in which case the goods accepted by the lender as repayment are usually underpriced. As we shall see later, trader-lenders are indeed the principal source of interlinked credit, since they often attach conditions to their loans by imposing that the borrower purchase inputs from them or sell them part of his crop at harvest time at a price fixed beforehand (usually underpriced).

Storeowners, equipment suppliers, market vendors and itinerant traders also extend credit to both urban households and small farmers for the purchase of consumer goods, productive inputs, or irregular major purchases (appliances, a motorcycle, a sewing machine, etc.) usually by allowing for deferred payment in regular instalments.

The importance of commercial moneylending is on the rise in many developing countries, as the limit on loans from family and friends is soon reached among the rural and low-income urban households that resort to such practices. Moreover, changes are occurring within the moneylending profession itself. With the advent of urbanisation, new technologies and marketing procedures, it seems that professional moneylending is gradually becoming more an urban rather than rural phenomenon; while, in rural areas, the importance of landlord-lenders is slowly being by more complex arrangements with trader-lenders and storeowners.

b) Mutual Savings and Loan Associations

Informal financial activity may also take the form of groups of individuals organised mutually and subject to rules and regulations of functioning which they themselves have laid down and agreed upon. There are many kinds of informal associations engaged in financial intermediation activities. These may be grouped into two main types: savings arrangements only, and combined savings and credit arrangements.

Associations of the first type, two examples of which are fixed-fund associations and savings clubs, focus primarily on providing savings facilities for their members, who are otherwise barred from formal sector savings services for want of a sufficient sum to warrant the bank operation[23]. Usually, the funds thus accumulated are eventually used for a specific purpose which may or may not be explicit from the outset.

Another reason for participating in mutual savings may be to ensure oneself and one's family of assistance (in kind or in cash) in case of an emergency such as illness, death, accident, theft, fire, unemployment, etc. Mutual aid associations therefore, which also come under the "savings arrangement" category, actually provide a form of informal insurance coverage.

The other main type of mutual scheme is the combined savings and credit arrangement, where the regularity of participation in the savings accumulation process entitles a member to loan facilities from the group which, here again, would not otherwise be available from formal financial institutions. Examples of this type of association include informal credit unions, informal savings and loan associations, and rotating savings and credit associations or ROSCAs.

Finally, alongside those informal arrangements with a "financial vocation" (savings and/or credit services), mention must also be made of self-help organisations in which the services rendered are in kind, through hired work associations, rotating work associations, non-reciprocal work associations, or temporary groupings. Two of the case studies cited such examples: in Zambia, work may be done collectively for the village chief, or for a community development project. The example of hired work associations in this country merits mention here; hired work associations receive payment in kind (maize, usually) or through "beer parties". In fact, for a household, a beer party in exchange for labour is the cheapest way of getting the work done, payment in cash being the most expensive. Moreover, beer parties and communal work are important social occasions for cementing kinship and other social ties with the local community. As for the participants, the alternative use of their own work is not pressing at the time, and as the labour input is not too arduous, it represents an easy way to get beer. There is also an economic reason behind participation in a beer party. These arrangements usually take place between the months of December and March, when some households may be threatened with a maize shortage and for whom beer is a partial food substitute.

In Burundi, temporary groupings are formed to carry out such tasks as planting, house construction, or the clearing of fields. As these types of associations cannot be said to be directly concerned with financial intermediation activity, they are not discussed further in the pages that follow.

The basic structure of mutual savings and/or loan associations in the informal sector is the same: a group of people with a common bond – extended family, friends, residents of the same village or district, workers in the same office or firm, ethnic ties, etc. – join together to pool their individual resources, however large or small they may be, in order to benefit from savings and/or credit facilities in view of expenditures which they cannot assume on their own, or for mutual aid in an emergency. Sometimes, the objective may be to contribute to a community development project. Where the schemes may differ from each other is in conditionality of membership, number of members, amount and periodicity of contributions, form of leadership, use of funds, mode of disbursement of loans, etc. In the sections below, we shall look more closely at the workings of some of them.

i) Fixed-Fund Associations

In a fixed-fund association, each participant contributes savings at regular intervals to a treasurer who holds them for safekeeping and then returns the lump sum at the end of the year or other time-period mutually decided upon. In their simplest form, these groups are strictly savings associations from which no borrowing is allowed. More commonly, however, a portion, if not all, of the amassed savings is lent out to members, sometimes with interest (see Box 2.10). Depending on the rules in force, a prospective borrower must apply for a loan either orally or in writing, and address his request to an officer or to the group of officers of the association, or even to the entire membership itself. Sometimes non-members are also granted credit, always with interest and at a higher rate than for members. Interest income is distributed among the latter.

Fixed-fund associations can provide a source of credit which would not otherwise be available to the participants. At times, they can also fulfil a community development function, as when a portion of the total deposits is earmarked for the purchase of inputs, other equipment or commodities, or for investment in a project which will be of benefit to the entire group, such as the building of a school, road or bridge. Another advantage of these associations is that a saver who lacks the skill or contacts to lend money can count on the officers of the group to handle loans; in addition to the pooling of funds, there is also a sort of pooling of financial skills, with everyone benefiting from the interest income. The main risk with fixed-fund associations, of course, is that members must be assured of the honesty of the group's officers and have confidence in their lending skills and capacity to recover loans.

ii) Self-Help Organisations: Savings Clubs in Zimbabwe

Savings clubs are another example of informal associations which are focused primarily on saving. In contrast to the fixed-fund associations described previously, however, where the amassed funds may be lent if there is such a request, savings clubs are characterised by a marked reluctance to grant loans to individual members, let alone give credit to outsiders.

Box 2.10

INFORMAL SAVINGS AND LOAN ASSOCIATIONS IN BANGLADESH

Informal savings and loan associations are a fairly recent phenomenon in Bangladesh and have not yet reached the "advanced" stage of chit funds in India or ROSCAs in other countries. The trend towards the creation of informal groups has accelerated in recent years, partly as a response to the challenges faced by the rural community both in terms of neglect by formal financial institutions and opportunities created by the adoption of new technologies and marketing procedures, in part due to the efforts of various government programmes and non-governmental organisations (NGOs) to stimulate co-operation and encourage self-help groups. A survey of 472 savings-credit groups by the Asian Development Bank showed that 323 of them were formed spontaneously, 44 were NGO-sponsored and 105 were registered co-operatives. Slightly less than half of them were set up since 1984-1985.

Most associations are formed by small businessmen and traders, followed by those of farmers and fishermen, and the landless. Groups are also formed along kinship lines, religious lines or age groups (youth organisations), thus fulfilling social or religious aims as well as economic ones, while some associations were found to have been set up specifically to extend consumption loans. The average size of groups is about 44 members, although the more successful ones have 5 to 10 participants. Meetings may be held on a daily, weekly, monthly and even a yearly basis. Most of the amassed savings are recycled as loans to members. Women's informal groups often deposit the savings in banks – despite the latter's hesitation to accept small deposits – for lack of alternative "sound investments". In the exceptional case of loans to outsiders, a higher interest rate is charged.

Attempts to use savings-credit associations as conduits for channelling loans to their members from NGOs, government organisations and banks, have led to the dissolution of the group once the source of external funds dried up. Other reasons for the discontinuation of informal associations may include: misappropriation of funds, leadership crisis, and internal power conflict.

Savings clubs are of fairly recent origin, having appeared after formal institutions were already in place in the developing countries. The movement is most advanced in Zimbabwe[24], where it dates back to the 1960s when the first savings club was set up by a Jesuit missionary. No such vast activity exists elsewhere, although lately the movement has spread to southern Zambia and Botswana. Today, it is estimated that there are some 6 000 clubs in Zimbabwe with approximately 140 000 members.

Savings clubs operate autonomously according to the rules set by their own members. They are largely confined to rural areas and operate mostly on a village level. Their underlying objective is the regular mobilisation of small savings for the bulk purchase of agricultural inputs (seeds, fertilizers, pesticides) or household goods and to provide money for seasonal outlays such as school fees. The capital built up through regular contributions is also used for off-farm income-generating activities such as handicraft production, vegetable production, or poultry farming. In some cases, farmers also co-operate for the marketing of their produce[25].

Meetings are held on a weekly basis, and attendance is compulsory. A fine is imposed for tardiness, absence or failure to pay one's contribution (unless there is an acceptable explanation). One of the originalities of savings clubs is that members save individually, that is, they may deposit any amount of their own choosing provided it is not less than a minimum amount set by the club (usually 20 cents). A bookkeeping system using savings stamps means that illiterate persons[26] can also participate and keep track of how much they have saved. Each member is issued a thirty page savings book. Each page has room for twenty savings stamps worth 20 cents each. At each meeting members buy from the treasurer the number of stamps equivalent in value to the amount they wish to deposit and stick them in their savings book. The minimum contribution at each meeting is 20 cents (one stamp) and the minimum withdrawal amount, conditional upon one week's prior notice and approval for it by the group, Z$ 4, i.e. a full page is cancelled[27]. All transactions and dates are recorded in a register, as are the total value of stamps sold at each session and the records of the club as a whole. The triple bookkeeping procedure helps avoid mismanagement of funds.

Most savings clubs have between fifteen and thirty members. Larger groups usually split up because the weaker social cohesion and the longer travelling distance for members make them harder to manage. On the other hand, groups of less than ten members are encouraged to join other, existing clubs in order to avoid a situation where "everyone is a committee member". In effect, the savings clubs are run by an elected voluntary committee of five to seven members: chairperson, secretary, treasurer and their deputies, and a stand-by officer who acts as a security member or "shouter", i.e. maintains order. Because they handle the money and bookkeeping, the secretary and treasurer, in particular, must have had at least a few years of formal education, as well as being trustworthy and honest. They are usually the most wealthy, too, since that makes it more likely that they will be able to refund the collected money if it should be stolen while in their safekeeping[28].

Once a month, those savings clubs which are not too far away from a branch of a formal financial institution deposit the pooled contributions in a group account with a bank, a building society, or the Post Office Savings Bank. In fact, these regular transactions with the formal sector are another characteristic of savings clubs.

In principle, withdrawals are permitted at any time. In practice, though, they are made twice a year: in January to pay for school fees; from September to November for the purchase of agricultural inputs. However, the deposited funds are not withdrawn in their entirety in one year – members prefer to accumulate net funds over time.

Outside these two periods in the year, withdrawals from the accumulated funds are discouraged, especially if it is for consumption purposes. Members must explain why they want the money and are often asked to repay the "loan" – which cannot exceed the borrower's savings deposits – within a given period or are even charged interest in order to accelerate the process of reconstitution of their savings. However, grants and loans may be given to needy members with a pressing short-term liquidity gap (such as illness or funeral expenses) up to a maximum of Z$ 30; reimbursement may not always be required, but, if it is, then it is on generous terms (flexible repayment schedules, no collateral, no interest).

A final characteristic of savings clubs is that part of the accumulated funds are used to organise various off-farm activities on a co-operative or collective basis. These include the production of craft goods or foodstuffs (school uniforms, bread, soap), poultry farming, vegetable growing, or the contracting out of labour, that is, the whole group undertakes to do the weeding and harvesting in other farmers' fields. The additional income thus earned from sales or labour is shared as profit among the members and added to their regular sources of savings revenue.

Generating additional income through the joint efforts of the group is only one of the incentives to join a savings club, and not the most important one at that, according to savings clubs members themselves. The possibility to save small amounts, the savings discipline imposed by participation in the club, the target-saving procedure for the bulk purchase of agricultural inputs are seen as some of the greatest advantages of membership.

iii) Mutual Aid Associations

Informal savings and loan associations grew out of the need amongst certain segments of the urban and rural population for financial intermediation and savings facilities which would allow them to deal in the small amounts within their means. The financial needs thus covered are mostly current consumption or production expenses. However, social and economic activity involves other types of risks – death, illness, unemployment, fire, theft – which pose a threat to income security. Moreover, traditional ceremonies such as funerals or weddings require high financial outlays which a single family is usually unable to assume on its own. Formal social protection institutions do not have wide enough coverage to provide such protection and financial assistance, nor are they flexible enough in most cases to do so.

Mutual aid associations enable their members to accumulate funds which are disbursed – in the form of an indemnity – to a needy member or his family in case of an emergency. The risk elements most often covered are death (funeral expenses) and illness (medical bills), although other contingencies such as fire or theft give rise to joint efforts by fellow members in rebuilding a house destroyed by fire, for example, or helping replace – in part at least – stolen property.

The common bond which brings together the group may be kinship or friendship ties, common place of work or residence, or ethnic ties[29]. These types of associations may be found in both urban and rural areas.

In accordance with a statute which often governs these associations and which is approved and signed by participants, the associations are run by a committee that is not paid for its services. The size of membership may vary over a wide range from the very small groups (10 to 15 people) where members know each other well to the very large groups (on the scale of the neighbourhood, i.e. more than 1 000 people) (see Box 2.11).

Contributions usually consist of an initial registration or entrance fee (which normally increases as time passes) and a fixed periodical payment. Late payment or failure to pay one's fees are sanctioned by a fine. Outright default can lead to expulsion from the group and, as the news spreads quickly, the defaulter may then be barred from joining other mutual aid associations. Sometimes poorer members who cannot pay their dues in cash may contribute in kind, by carrying out some type of service such as digging graves, preparing food and drink, calling members to the meetings or delivering notices to the members. The collected funds are usually deposited in a bank, provided the branch is not too far away, so as to receive interest and avoid the risk of theft, fire or fraud on the part of the treasurer.

The mutual aid and financial assistance which is provided when a contingency occurs may be in cash or in kind and may also involve other non-monetary obligations. In the case of the death of a member or of one of his relatives, for example, a sum of money is paid out

Box 2.11

MUTUAL AID ASSOCIATIONS *"IDIRS"* IN ETHIOPIA

Mutual aid associations, or "idirs" as they are locally known, may be found in both the rural and urban areas of Ethiopia. The actual level of funds mobilised by rural idirs *in comparison to urban ones may be low for a number of reasons. To begin with, the closely-knit local community of rural areas, where the extended family is common, contrasts with the nuclear family structures and impersonal relationships which are characteristic of the urban setting, with very few relatives or friends on whom to rely for help in times of need. Urban dwellers are thus much more "dependent" on* idirs *for protection against the risks of death, illness, theft, fire, in short, any event that may incur a sudden and substantial expense. Secondly, there is a greater opportunity in rural areas than in urban areas for assistance to be provided in kind rather than in cash.*

Nevertheless, the variety of combinations in both urban and rural zones regarding the size of membership, contributions, indemnities, obligations, complex modes of functioning, etc. is illimited, and largely reflects the socio-economic characteristics of the participants, as illustrated by the four different idirs outlined briefly below.

1. **Rural *Idir***

Location:	*Fertile agricultural district 50 kms south of Addis Ababa.*
Membership:	*45 families, dependent on agriculture for their livelihood.*
Frequency:	*Once a month.*
Contributions:	*50 cents. Fines of 25 cents for unjustified absence or tardiness, 50 cents for non-payment of contribution. If balance of total funds amassed falls below 500 Birrs, members are asked for additional contributions.*
Indemnity:	*Death of a member or his wife: 100 Birrs; death of a child or brother, sister, parent who was not self-supporting: 80 Birrs.*
Obligations:	*Attendance at the funeral (fine of 5 to 10 Birrs for absence); one day's cultivation, taken in turns by members, of the deceased's fields.*
Characteristics:	*Insures against a wide range of risks and provides coverage by cash payments as well as the provision of services in kind.*
Additional comments:	*The district in which the* idir *is situated is rich in resources. The participating farmers are financially self-sufficient. The contribution requested is small in relation to their average income.*

2. Urban, Neighbourhood *Idir*

Location: Inhabitants of a neighbourhood of Addis Ababa.

Membership: 300 members of widely differing incomes, social levels, ages.

Committee: Run by an elected committee (every 3 years) consisting of a chairman, treasurer, secretary, auditor.

Frequency: Monthly.

Contributions: 35 Birrs entrance fee; 2.5 Birrs monthly contributions. Funds deposited in an account with Commercial Bank of Ethiopia. Fifty cent fine for absence from meetings or for late payment of contributions. Personal pass books to record payments and fines.

Indemnity: Death of a member or his relative: 100 Birrs if lived at home, 50 Birrs if lived away from home.

Obligations: Attend funeral (fine of 1 Birr for absence).

Additional comments: One of the members, a high-ranking bank official with multiple membership in other idirs as well, confessed that he prefers to sleep and miss the meetings and pay the fine. He joined the idir mainly for socialising within the neighbourhood and to strengthen ties of solidarity with other members.

3. Urban, Office *Idir*

Location and membership: Idir formed by clerks at the head office of the CBE. Most employees are members.

Frequency: Monthly.

Contributions: High entry fee of 350 Birrs. Monthly contributions of 5 Birrs are automatically deducted from salary.

Indemnity: 1500 Birrs for death of a member or his wife; 250 Birrs for death of a child; 150-200 Birrs for other deaths.

Additional comments: Automatic deduction of contributions from salary helps avoid late payment but also reduces social contacts between members. There are weak ties of friendship and little spirit of mutual assistance in a group of this size which holds one general meeting a year at which attendance is not compulsory. Members join because of the considerable sum received in the event of death.

4. Urban, Friends' *Idir*

Location: Friends living in same neighbourhood with similar salaries and standards of living.

Membership:	*Went from 8 to 15 families; limit set to any further growth.*
Committee:	*Run by a committee elected every 2 years. Chairman, treasurer, secretary, and auditor not remunerated for their services.*
Frequency:	*Monthly.*
Contributions:	*Entrance fee of 50 Birrs; monthly contributions of 10 Birrs. Funds deposited with Housing and Savings Bank. Fine of 2 Birrs if absent from meetings without valid reason, 1 Birr fine for tardiness.*
Indemnity:	*150 Birrs for the death of a member, wife, child; 125 Birrs for the death of another relative living at home (100 Birrs if living away from home); 50 Birrs for death of a female servant. In case of accident, illness, unemployment, fire, imprisonment, etc., group decides on the amount of financial assistance within a maximum of 500 Birrs (on basis of extent of loss incurred).*
Obligations:	*Visit ill members; keep bereaved family company during 3-day confinement period (local custom).*
Additional comments:	*In four years of existence, there have been no defaults, one quarrel over the private life of one of the members; the idir has intervened in one death and one imprisonment. Existence of* idir *kept secret because could be considered by neighbourhood as a form of discrimination on the basis of income (there is a fairly high level of contributions and coverage; average monthly savings of members are 200 Birrs).*

to the bereaved family to help pay for funeral expenses and otherwise serve as financial aid. Obligations of a non-monetary nature may include visiting the bereaved family, attending the funeral (sometimes there may be a fine for non-attendance) and, in rural districts, cultivating the deceased's fields for a certain period of time[30]. In the case of other contingencies besides death, the indemnity may be decided upon on a case by case basis and be fixed as a function of the extent of damage and need as evaluated by the group.

To sum up, two final points should be stressed. The first one is that membership of a mutual aid association may be prompted by both social and economic concerns. From the social point of view, meetings are an occasion for members to foster community or group solidarity and exchange information. Indeed, refusal to participate in such schemes could even lead to marginalisation of the individual from the community. Moreover, in some cultures, considerable importance is attached to being able to provide a deceased relative with the proper burial rites and to ensuring that a large number of people will attend the funeral.

The economic considerations have already been outlined above and are, of course, related to coverage of the financial costs in an emergency.

This brings us to the second point which is that by "systematizing" the social obligations for mutual assistance which are prevalent in many developing country societies, mutual aid associations come to operate as a sort of local insurance programme run by a community or group to meet emergency situations[31]. In essence, it is the regularity of one's contributions – to what extent one fulfils the terms of the "contract" – that entitles one to a sum, which does not usually have to be reimbursed, at a time of need.

iv) Rotating Savings and Credit Associations

Rotating savings and credit associations, or ROSCAs, are by far the most extensively documented informal lending mechanisms. It seems they are also the most widespread in the developing countries, and there are many variations on the basic pattern, depending on the area, ethnic group, or country.

The most basic form of ROSCA combines a savings and credit arrangement in the following way. Participants make regular, fixed-amount contributions to a common pool of funds which is then given to each member in turn, usually by lottery. After each member has had access to the fund once, the procedure usually starts again. In essence, the first recipient of the fund gets an interest-free loan, while the last recipient saves over the entire cycle without earning interest (or at a negative rate of interest if inflation is high), receiving in the end the same amount he would have had by saving regularly on his own. The other members alternate between creditor and debtor positions; through their participation, they benefit from the total sum sooner than they would if they were on their own.

The underlying framework for ROSCAs is derived from the time-honoured traditions of close ties and solidarity within the family, village, or community. In urban areas where such ties are, if not weakened, then more difficult to sustain, bonds may be forged around a common occupation or activity (market vendors, shoeshine boys). ROSCA-type arrangements are also used by traders to obtain working capital (see Box 2.12). What is important to remember regarding ROSCAs and other similar types of mutual associations, is that they go beyond the mere financial aims of savings or credit; the regular meetings often constitute important social events for the participants.

Besides emanating from local socio-economic structures, other main ROSCA features include: rules and procedures that are easily understood by the population, a minimum of administrative formalities and hence of transaction costs, and a substantial degree of flexibility and variety of procedures. The number of participants – which may be anywhere from three to more than fifty – and the frequency of meetings at which contributions are made – weekly, fortnightly, monthly – determine the length of the entire cycle of the rotating fund. The amount of contributions also varies; in Africa, ranges of a penny per day to as much as 1 600 dollars per month have been reported[32]. The duration of the loan and the repayment schedule may be one day, several months or even years. Another differentiating factor is the form of leadership and the responsibilities or privileges attached to this function: some groups are small enough to forego the need for leaders, while others elect members to posts of secretary, treasurer, "president", or chairman.

Finally, the area where the greatest margin for innovation and originality lies, is in determining the order of rotation of the fund. Most often, it is done by drawing lots, in which case care is taken in the next cycle to change the order so that it is not always the same members who are last. Sometimes, the newest participants or the more doubtful debtors are actually programmed to receive the fund last. Other times, the organiser, or "president" of the group is the first to receive the collective deposit and subsequently largely dictates the order in which the rest of the members get the fund[33]. Other determining factors may be age or social standing or urgency of need. Sometimes there are provisions whereby a member in need whose lot was not drawn may take the winner's turn, either through negotiation with him or the entire group or by actually "buying" the right to the fund from him. If there is more than one claim to the fund, it may be auctioned off to the highest bidder. The portion of the prize fund which the winning bidder agrees to forego in order to "buy his turn", and which, in essence, amounts to an interest payment on the loan, either remains in the common reserve fund or is distributed among members as interest income.

As we can see, the distinguishing features of ROSCAs are manifold and the variations – on one or more of the aforementioned aspects – even more so. Nonetheless, we can generally distinguish three main types of ROSCAs: i) mutual ROSCAs, which are the most widespread and which are based on solidarity between members who know each other well; ii) commercial ROSCAs, where the funds are collected by an outsider on whose initiative the scheme began, and who acts as banker, levying a commission for his services and ensuring the best possible mix of savings received and loans paid out; and iii) financial ROSCAs in which interest is paid by the person taking up the funds in the form of a commission, or discount, agreed upon by auction. Members may thus influence the order of allocation of the fund in accordance with their needs: those who borrow before their turn pay interest, those who save receive remuneration.

ROSCAs may also be classified according to savings criteria: some function purely on the redistribution principle, while others have a net savings balance at the end of their cycle. This usually implies the existence of a reserve, or "savings" fund within the ROSCA into which a portion of the collective funds or the interest income from the auctioning of turns are deposited and which may be lent to members, with interest, independently of the rotation of the prize fund (as in Indonesia), or serve as a contingency reserve for defaults or other emergencies, or be used to remunerate the group leaders or purchase refreshments for meetings (as in Ethiopia).

Rotating savings and credit associations are a prominant feature of rural areas in Africa. More and more, however, they are beginning to spread to urban areas as well. In Latin America, urban-based ROSCAs are the most documented, although they do exist in rural areas as well. In the Asian countries too, they are often a long-established and predominantly urban phenomenon, although in some countries they are more recent and are developing in rural areas with the help of external agencies, mainly NGOs.

It should further be pointed out that such schemes may concern people from all income groups. In Zambia, the practice is not uncommon among the staff of commercial banks, for example, and it is becoming increasingly widespread amongst low- and middle-income urban dwellers. In Zimbabwe and Mexico, higher-income earners such as businessmen, teachers, ministry officials are also showing an interest in ROSCA-type arrangements, although the aim in this case is most often to help cover prestigious expenses or strengthen social relations rather than for investment purposes.

In all cases the national and regional variants go by different names; ekub, idir, and mahaber in Ethiopia; tontine in Togo; djanggi in Cameroon; chilemba in Zambia and Zimbabwe; susu in Ghana, cheetu-funds in Sri Lanka, and tandas in Mexico, to name just a few.

Box 2.12

SHOESHINERS' AND TRADERS' *EKUBS* IN ETHIOPIA

Among the shoeshiners of Addis Ababa, ekubs *are extremely common. The boys, who are almost always very young (from 14 to 17), usually form groups of 6 to 8 members (sometimes up to 16). The contribution is on a daily basis and varies from 50 cents to 1.5 birrs[1]. There are variable fines for late payers. The meetings and the distribution of funds are weekly and attendance is compulsory. The* ekubs *are run by the oldest member who is not remunerated but has the right to the first draw.*

Most of the members belong to the Gurage tribe which originates in the Shoa region and where their parents still live. They live in the capital with relatives who are often traders residing in the market district.

The assignment of funds is by means of a lottery, the sum won usually being kept by the boy until it is possible to send it to his parents through a relative or friend who is going to visit them. Default is extremely rare on account of the close bonds, both ethnic and occupational, between members, and the fact that they all know each other well.

Trader ekubs, *by contrast, involve a larger membership, higher contributions, and more complex procedures. One of the* ekubs *in the market district had a total of 100 members, mainly shopkeepers with different levels of income but all in the medium to high range and holding current accounts with the Commercial Bank of Ethiopia. The funds in question are utilised for the members' commercial activity, to rebuild a house, or to purchase durable goods (e.g. a car).*

The weekly contribution per member is 102 birrs which is paid to the chairman at his shop, directly or through third parties, and by the date fixed for the meeting. The fine for non-payment is 5 birrs if the person has already received the fund, otherwise 2 birrs. Each member may purchase a maximum of four quotas. Out of each quota, 2 birrs are put aside, one for the contingency reserve fund and one for the remuneration of the chairman and secretary.

Allocation of the fund is by lottery and the winner of the fund has to provide two guarantors. Attendance at the meeting on this occasion is not compulsory; the presence of a minimum number of 50 people is sufficient. For three weeks in a month the fund is allocated by drawing lots, whilst in the remaining week it is "sold" to members, in accordance with the procedure described below.

When the ekub *is formed, persons with an urgent need for funds submit their names to the chairman. Lots are drawn between them in order to determine the order in which they will receive the fund on those occasions when it is "sold" to members. The "sale" of the fund in this case simply means that 5 per cent until halfway through the cycle and subsequently 2.5 per cent is deducted from the total amount of the prize fund before it is disbursed to the needy member.*

The "proceeds" from the sale, or discount, together with the fines and the one birr deducted from each contribution, go into the reserve fund which is used to cover cases of default and also to purchase food and drink for the meetings.

Negotiation of the prize fund among members is also common and takes place at interest rates which vary but usually do not exceed 10 per cent. Sometimes persons participating in the ekub purchase more than one quota with the specific aim of "selling their turn" in the event of a win. In such cases repayment is assured by substituting the name of the creditor for that of the debtor in subsequent draws.

The chairman and secretary deposit the members' contributions in their own personal accounts with the CBE and pay the winner of the lottery with a cheque. Moreover, they have the right to the first two assignments of the funds, thereby enjoying credit for a longer period than the other members. On the other hand they are responsible for the solvency of the members and have to meet out of their own pockets the contributions of defaulting members unless they subsequently manage to recover these from the members concerned. Cases of default sometimes arise.

1. Exchange rate over the period 1981-1987: 2.07 birr per US dollar.

c) Partnership firms

Thus far in our discussion of informal financial operators, we have focused mainly on individuals and associations, which are the two main vehicles of informal financial activity in almost all the developing countries. In some countries, however, the informal sector is rather more complex and evolved, not only from the point of view of structural and operational characteristics but also in terms of the weight it carries in overall financial activity. The Indian case is the most notorious example of this: alongside the individual moneylending and small-group savings and lending activities, there is a whole panoply of "companies" and "corporations" which, despite their formal-sounding denominations, are considered part of the informal financial sector in India.

Hence, in this section, we shall focus on partnership firms, including indigenous bankers and pawnbrokers as well as the various "companies" operating on the Indian informal credit market. We shall also dwell at some length on the case of chit funds, that is, their stage-by-stage evolution from small, rural-based rotating savings associations in kind, to large, urban-based credit companies.

i) The Informal Financial Sector in India

The Indian informal financial sector covers an entire gamut of financial agencies in corporate and non-corporate forms, that are primarily involved in borrowing and lending activities with the public but do not come directly under the control of either the government or the Reserve Bank of India.

The Indian informal financial sector consists of two distinct components: a non-corporate sector, and a company or corporate sector. The non-corporate sector covers indigenous-style bankers, pawnbrokers, partnership firms such as finance corporations, sole proprietary concerns and partnership firms carrying out hire-purchase business and chit fund business, and, of course, the "traditional" moneylenders typical of rural India and other developing countries. The corporate sector is comprised mainly of six types of institutions: loan companies, hire purchase and equipment leasing companies, investment companies, housing finance companies, mutual benefit fund companies, and chit fund companies. (Indeed, most chit funds in India today are corporate entities.)

What distinguishes the Indian informal financial sector from that of other countries is its high degree of institutionalisation, along with the particularity of having a corporate (but still informal) component which could almost be said to have the status of a legalised, "para-banking" sector.

In effect, the first five types of institutions mentioned above which make up the corporate component of the informal financial sector are governed by the Indian Companies Act and must file an annual audited balance sheet in a prescribed form with the Registrar of Companies. However, they are exempted from quite a few clauses of the Act – those regarding interest rate ceilings, for example – while the returns submitted to the Registrar of Companies are in fact highly simplified. Chit fund companies, for their part, come under a separate Act – the Chit Fund Act of 1982 – which seeks to regulate the working of chit funds, to set ceilings on interest rates and total capital sums involved per round, and to provide safeguards for the subscribers.

Yet in both cases, the corporate informal entities are, in practice, subject to very little government interference and hence can be said to still partake of the characteristics of the informal sector.

The operators of the non-corporate segment of the informal sector, by contrast, do not come under the Companies Act but are often registered under the Indian Partnership Act and/or are licensed to operate under the State Moneylenders Act.

The Non-Corporate Component

Among the agents here involved are the indigenous bankers and pawnbrokers, both closely associated with informal lending not only in India but in the Southeast Asian context in general.

Indigenous Bankers: Indigenous banking is an ancient practice that is most developed in India. Indeed, until the mid-19th century, indigenous banks were a central part of the Indian financial system and even provided credit to the government. Their monopoly was broken with the advent of the British because European bankers were then given state patronage. As commercial banks began to grow in the urban centres, the indigenous banker was gradually pushed out to the rural areas where business would soon be contracting again, due to the expansion in rural areas of commercial and co-operative banks under government policy. Today, indigenous banks play an ever more limited, but still significant, role in the Indian financial system.

The different types include Shikarpuri, Multani, Gujarati Shroffs, Rastogi, and Chettiar bankers. These are generally sole proprietorship concerns and rarely partnerships. Indigenous banks are different from formal banks in more than one way. They do not issue cheque books and are more flexible in their terms and procedures. Their offices, located in rent-controlled, cheap accommodations or in the banker's residence, are simply furnished with a mattress spread on the floor and a telephone. In most cases run by a sole proprietor, they are considered financial intermediaries because they both accept deposits and provide loans. According to Holst[34], they finance the bulk of their lending from the deposits received. By contrast, Madhur and Nayar[35] claim that deposits are a small proportion of their advances, i.e. it is mostly the indigenous banker's own capital which is lent out. What both studies do agree on, though, is that indigenous banker activity is shrinking, ceding business either to an expanding formal sector or to the corporate segment of the informal sector.

Pawnbrokers: Pawnbrokers are also typical in India and, more generally, in Southeast Asia. They accept cash from friends and relatives for investment in their lending business which consists of lending money at interest on the security of goods left with them. In Singapore and Malaysia, pawnbrokers are backed by commercial banks[36], and in southern India they compete, often successfully, with nationalised banks[37]. In order to exercise their activity, pawnbrokers in India must take out a licence under the State Moneylenders Act/Pawnbrokers Act, adhere to the interest rate restrictions prescribed by the latter on loans, and submit account books to officials upon demand.

Although the interest rates on loans from pawnbrokers are higher than those of banks and merchant-moneylenders, the former do offer greater ease of access (in part because they consent to forms of collateral which are unacceptable to banks), quicker service, easier valuation procedures and larger loans in proportion to the value of collateral. Loans may be used for productive (hiring of agricultural labour, purchase of fertilizers, reparation of equipment) or consumption purposes (food purchases, consumer durables, ceremonial expenditures).

Finance Corporations: A finance corporation is a financial intermediary set up for making profit from the business of lending money raised by way of deposits or borrowing. It may be a sole proprietary concern, a partnership firm or a private limited or a public limited company. The most common form is a partnership firm registered under the Indian Partnership Act of 1932. About 95 per cent of the total number of such units in India are partnerships and the rest are mainly proprietary concerns.

In a proprietary concern, an individual, alone or in association with the other members of his family, starts the business of lending, after taking out a licence under the State Moneylenders Act. Initially he starts lending his own money, but soon he invites his relatives and friends to deposit their savings with him for which he offers attractive rates of interest. As the business grows, deposits start coming from those outside the circle of relatives. When funds increase, he diversifies his lending business by discounting post-dated cheques, negotiating trade bills and lending to other finance corporations.

In the case of a partnership firm (registered under the Partnership Act), one of the partners is selected to act as manager, for administrative convenience. The partners, who may not exceed ten in one firm, may or may not be related to each other. The initial funds for the business are contributed by the partners as subscription capital, though not necessarily in equal shares. In addition, the partners deposit their savings with the corporation or lend money to it, receiving interest in both cases at a rate slightly higher than the rate given to the public.

The partners individually canvass for deposits to the corporation. All types of deposits (savings, fixed, recurring and cash certificates) are accepted, but the major portion are fixed deposits for periods of one to three years or more. While the corporation accepts deposits from anybody, loans are made only to persons recommended by, or known to, at least one of the partners, who meet frequently to take decisions regarding lending policy. Loans are usually short-term, ranging from 1 to 100 days, except for loans secured against landed property or gold jewellery.

Both the deposit and lending rates of finance corporations are higher than the corresponding rates of commercial banks.

In 1984, all partnership firms accepting deposits came under the Banking Laws Act which prescribed limits on the number of depositors per firm (not more than 25 depositors per partner, excluding relatives of each partner)[38] but did not impose a ratio of owned funds of the corporations and their deposit liabilities. In this respect, it could be said that finance corporations are still within the purview of the informal sector.

The Corporate Component

Before expanding on the case of the Chit Fund Companies, we give below a brief definition of investment companies, loan companies, and mutual benefit fund companies.

An *investment company* is any company which is a financial institution carrying on as its principal business the acquisition of securities.

A *loan company* is any company which is a financial institution carrying on as its principal business the providing of finance whether by making loans or advances or otherwise for any activity other than its own but does not include a hire purchase finance company or a housing finance company.

Mutual benefit funds in India can be defined as "a group of persons united to help one another by contributing specified sums to a common fund which is to be used for lending to these same persons for their benefit" [39]. The collective fund thus constituted is called *nidhi* or permanent fund. These types of associations have an additional, flexible feature in that the *nidhi* (fixed contributions) may be supplemented by deposits from members.

ii) The Case of Chit Funds

Chit funds, also known as "Kuri" or "chitty", are the oldest of the indigenous financial institutions in India. The highly complex and institutionalised chit fund companies of today are actually the culmination of a gradual process of transformation and adaptation of a traditional savings technique which was prevalent in southern India. In examining the history of chit funds, one can distinguish different stages in their evolution which are succinctly outlined below.

The chitty is believed to have emerged out of necessity, before the advent of modern banks and British rule in India. Villagers needed to find a way of storing their surplus produce (or of safekeeping the money from its sale) in between harvests. In the first stage then, a few village households would bring a predetermined amount of rice to the house of the "foreman" – designated to supervise the procedure but not paid for his services – at each harvest time in the year. The total of the rice contributions would be given in a spirit of mutual help, to a needy member chosen by the foreman or by consensus of the entire group. Subsequently, the rice prize began to be allocated by a system of lottery[40].

The next step saw the honorary foreman replaced by an active organiser whose aim was to raise resources for some temporary purpose, such as a daughter's marriage. The organiser would get a number of his friends to subscribe a certain amount of money or rice to the chitty. His friends would bring their contributions to his home where they would be entertained and where lots were drawn to determine the next beneficiary. The process continued until everyone had his turn.

In later developments, when early prize winners failed to make further contributions, the other members began to hold the organiser responsible for all the risks involved in the receipt and disbursal of the prize. In compensation for assuming such responsibilities, foremen began collecting a commission and earned the right to receive the prize in the first round.

With the decline of barter trade and the emergence of money, chit fund transactions increasingly involved money rather than rice or other grains. At the same time, a number of other changes took place. There was a change in the occupational pattern of chit fund participants: in addition to the farmer clientele, traders, merchants and wage-earners began to take an interest in chit funds. Moreover, the underlying purpose of chit funds was transformed; whereas the primary aim of farmers was the accumulation of savings, the primary aim of traders was the opening up of credit facilities.

The simplest form of money-based chit funds was the rotating lot chitty without discount in which the prize fund rotated among members by lottery and was equivalent to the total contributions (or capital of the chitty) less the foreman's commission. The foreman would receive the fund in the first round, and the cycle would end when all the members had received the prize once. In some cases, there was also a provision for members with limited means to take out fractional shares: the subscription value was contributed by more than one member; when their lot was drawn, the prize fund was distributed pro-rata among the members of the "sub-group".

In fact, the simple chit funds described above soon evolved into rotating lot chitties with discounts to compensate members who received the fund late in the cycle. Since prize-winners could earn interest on the amount during the remaining period of the chitty while late prize-winners earned nothing on their savings, a discount was deducted compulsorily, in addition to the foreman's commission, from the prize amount and distributed as dividend among the non-prize winners only.

One remaining weak point in the scheme was the fact that, with the lottery system, prospective borrowers were uncertain of when they would be allotted the fund. Hence a system of auction, or bidding, for the disbursal of the prize amounts was adopted. In fact, exclusive lot chitties (with or without a discount) have practically disappeared, giving place to exclusive auction chitties (or business chitties) which function in the following way. In the first round, the foreman collects the total amount of contributions. At each subsequent instalment, a certain percentage is set aside as the foreman's commission. An open auction is conducted on the rest, and the winner is the subscriber who offers the maximum discount on the fund. Hence the prize amount is equal to the capital of the chitty less the foreman's commission less the discount, which is distributed as dividend to members. Only non-defaulting members can participate in the auction; a member can bid for and obtain the prize amount only once during the tenure of the scheme.

Moreover, a (legal) ceiling is usually imposed on the maximum discount that can be offered: 30 to 40 per cent of the capital on offer. If more than one member offers the maximum discount, lots are drawn between them. Under the auction system then, those members who receive the chitty in earlier rounds are net borrowers, while those who receive it in later rounds are net lenders.

The final stage in these developments is marked by the entry of institutional foremen on the scene. In place of an individual with limited resources and a restricted area of operation there came a board of directors of a joint stock company with abundant resources and no frontiers for business. Indeed, chit funds started spreading to the urban and metropolitan centres, and the capital of the chitty became big enough to attract even medium-sized businessmen or traders. At present, the large majority of chit funds in India are run by companies.

Foremost among the institutional foremen are the commercial banks, for whom the organisation of chit funds presents a threefold advantage: they gain access to the fund that goes to the organiser in the first round, they earn the organiser's commission in subsequent rounds, and it gives them the opportunity to get in touch with potential new customers and attract the chit fund participants as regular depositors. Chit funds often represent a substantial portion of a bank's total business. The profits derived from the chit fund business are a substantial proportion of gross bank earnings (there are cases where chit fund profits saved some banks from operating at a loss).

Other institutional foremen include joint stock companies (public and private, limited) as well as two state-owned corporations established for the purpose of running chit funds.

The number of registered chit fund companies began to rise in 1975, going from 213 in 1974 to 504 in 1979; while chit subscriptions rose from 7 million rupees in 1974 to Rs 373 million in 1979 and Rs 2 081 million in 1982[41]. Furthermore, there are estimates that contributions to chit funds may represent as much as 20 per cent of total bank deposits in southern India, which is a region noted for its banking development.

The Indian government has taken steps to regulate the working of the chit funds and provide safeguards for the subscribers. Comprehensive Chit Fund Acts were introduced in India as early as 1918 and subsequent legislative acts continued through 1975. The most recent and most comprehensive All India Chit Fund Act dates from 1982 and, if implemented throughout the country, should help the chit fund movement grow on sound lines[42].

In conclusion, what characterises the case of Indian chit funds is their stage by stage development from simple rotating mechanisms in kind, through a stage of increasingly sophisticated ROSCA-type arrangements, to eventually culminate in the corporate form of chit fund companies run by institutional foremen. As we have shown, the process was largely spurred on by experience, i.e. incorporating correctives and safeguards, introducing innovations, and effecting modifications to suit the environment in which they operated as well as the changing characteristics and requirements of participants.

B. THE COMPLETENESS OF THE FINANCIAL SYSTEMS

In the preceding section, we presented the different types of banking and non-bank financial institutions that may constitute the formal financial system of a developing country, as well as the various types of informal savings and credit arrangements which may be encountered. Clearly, various combinations – and not necessarily the entire gamut – of both formal and informal instances are present in each particular developing country.

With regard to formal financial institutions, one could expect the presence of a central bank, commercial banks, and state-owned development banks in all cases. This was also confirmed within our sample of case studies. Interestingly, the co-operative or credit union movement was also a feature common to all of the countries studied in our sample. It should be added that our sample included countries where the entire financial sector was nationalised (Ethiopia) or largely nationalised (commercial banks in India) as well as those with a considerable presence of private and/or foreign-owned or joint-venture institutions (Zambia, Zimbabwe, Indonesia).

As for the informal financial sector, it is, by nature, even more closely linked to and influenced by the economic, social and cultural specificity of each country. What distinguishes one country from another in this case is not so much the presence or absence of one or the other type of informal scheme, but rather the national, ethnic, or even village-level variants on the basic structures and concepts underlying informal financial activity.

Against this backdrop, one may try to assess the "completeness" of the financial systems in the sample countries by observing which institutions (in the formal sector) or schemes (in the informal sector) are present and which are not. Such an exercise helps gain an overall picture – albeit a rudimentary one – of the way in which financial intermediation is achieved and how the various needs for finance are (or are not) being met.

Table 2.4 shows the formal, semi-formal, and informal financial operators in each country and confirms the observation that the developing countries are well endowed – as regards formal financial institutions, at least – despite the usual assumptions to the contrary.

Seen from the perspective of the financial system in its entirety – that is, encompassing the formal, semi-formal, and informal components – the countries in our sample possess a vast range of institutions and schemes. Moreover, there seems to be a "symmetry" between the formal and informal sectors in that those countries which are particularly well endowed in formal financial institutions also harbour a substantial variety of informal schemes and operators. This may be taken as the sign of a high degree of financial activity which finds outlets in either of the three "components": formal, semi-formal, and informal sectors.

1. The Formal Sector

Taking the case of the formal financial sector first, the "bird's eye" view of Table 2.4 may give a broad idea of the extent to which short-, medium-, long-term and equity financing needs are met, as well as the attention given to the mobilisation of small savings. For example, it is striking that Mexico has no savings banks nor building societies nor a postal savings network.

The absence of certain types of institutions does not necessarily mean, however, that the corresponding financial needs are not met. It may simply reflect a conception of the banking system or methods of financing which are particular to the country. Moreover, these "missing" functions are often assumed by other bodies. In Mexico, for example, loans for the housing and construction sector are provided not by building societies but by the commercial banks.

The countries which figure in Table 2.4 may be divided into two groups: those with operational financial markets (irrespective of the latter's stage of development) and those without operational financial markets. The presence of financial markets in Zimbabwe, India, Indonesia, the Philippines and Mexico reflects the degree of financial deepening in these countries and is also an indicator of the degree of coherence of their financial systems. Indeed, in these countries one also finds social security institutions, contractual savings institutions (provident or pension funds, insurance companies) and other term-lending institutions, all of which can be expected to participate in financial market activity.

On the other hand, the countries without a financial market – Burundi, Ethiopia, Togo, Zambia – are also those with relatively few long-term finance institutions and in which social security and contractual savings institutions, and other non-bank financial intermediaries are comparatively absent.

2. The "Semi-Formal" Sector

Savings and credit co-operatives and credit unions, classified under the "semi-formal" sector in our taxonomy, were found to be present in one form or another in all our sample countries. Most often – although there are exceptions – they cannot really be considered as part of the formal sector because they are not usually subject to the control of state laws and the related central regulatory activities. Nor are they necessarily part of the informal sector, particularly since they may be run by governmental or non-governmental agencies.

Table 2.4   THE LAY-OUT OF FINANCIAL CIRCUITS IN SELECTED DEVELOPING COUNTRIES

	Burundi	Ethiopia	Togo	Zambia	Zimbabwe	India	Indonesia	Philippines	Mexico
Formal Sector									
Central Bank	x	x	x[1]	x	x	x	x	x	x
Banks and Financial Intermediaries									
Commercial banks[2]	x	x	x	x	x	x	x	x	x
Merchant banks				x	x				x
Savings banks	x	x	x	x			x	x	x
Building societies		x		x	x		x	x	x
Postal savings networks	x			x[3]	x	x	x	x	x
Development banks									
– State-owned	x	x	x	x	x	x	x	x	x
– Private						x	x	x	
Social security institutions	x							x	
Contractual savings institutions									
– Provident/pension funds				x	x	x	x	x	x
– Insurance companies	x	x		x	x	x	x	x	x
Other specialised or non-bank financial institutions									
– Rural banks, specialised rural finance institutions				x	x		x	x	
– Finance companies and other term-lending institutions	x					x	x		
Markets									
– Stocks and bonds					x	x	x	x	x
Semi-Formal Sector									
Co-operatives and credit unions	x	x	x	x	x	x	x	x	x
Informal Sector									
Individual Moneylending									
Non-Commercial (friends, neighbours, relatives)	x	x	x	x	x	x	x	x	x
Commercial									
– Money-based				x	x	x	x	x	x
– Land-based		x		x		x	x	x	x
– Commodity-based				x	x	x	x	x	x

Associations

Savings arrangements (fixed-fund associations, mutual aid associations, funeral societies, etc.) x x x x x

Combined savings and credit arrangements (ROSCAS and variants) .... x x x x x

Self-help groups (ad hoc associations for services in kind) .... x x x x x

Partnership firms (indigenous bankers, finance companies, investment companies, leasing companies, hire-purchase companies, etc.) .... x x x x x

1. Supranational.
2. Includes state-owned, private, foreign and joint venture.
3. Zambia POSB was transformed into savings bank
Sources: Case studies, *IMF International Financial Statistics*, Unctad, and *Government Financial Statistics Yearbook* (1987) (IMF).

In fact, co-operatives and credit unions are often seen as a sort of intermediate stage between the informal and formal sectors, combining aspects of the two: the idea of grouping together to gain access to certain financial services is rooted in local traditions of solidarity; while at the same time, the groups thus formed are gradually drawn into the mainstream of more "officialised", or rather "semi-officialised", circuits.

3. The Informal Sector

The personalisation of lending arrangements and the basic tenet of solidarity are two of the most oft-stressed aspects of informal financial activity. It is thus not surprising to find that non-commercial loans from individuals (and sometimes also from groups) are present in all the sample countries.

As regards commercial moneylending by individuals, the different types of arrangements which prevail closely reflect the economic environment in which they operate. For instance, land-based arrangements appear in those countries where agricultural activity and the system of land ownership are based on a landlord-tenant structure. Money-based arrangements would tend to be more prevalent in countries, or perhaps even in areas within a country, with a high coefficient of monetisation. As for commodity-based arrangements, these would seem to be on the rise, as trading activity in rural and urban areas expands.

Group schemes (savings arrangements, combined savings and credit arrangements, self-help groups) are also widespread in all the countries of our sample, again as a result of deep-rooted traditions of solidarity. By contrast, partnership firms, including indigenous bankers, finance companies and hire-purchase companies, for example, are much rarer; they are most developed in India (and are said to be on the rise in other Asian countries too), although hire-purchase companies are also found in Zimbabwe. These types of informal schemes – one could plausibly use the term "institutions" – are much more complex than the others, as they resemble more closely the structures and operating procedures which prevail in the formal financial sector; yet they still retain the characteristics of being "simpler" and "faster" in their intermediation activity than formal institutions.

Final Remarks

There are two important points which should be underlined. The first concerns the complementary relationship between the formal and informal financial sectors within the overall financial system. Alongside the broad structural similarities on the microeconomic level between the institutions and schemes in each sector (as underlined in Table 2.1, page 2), the similarities in the actual lay-out of the formal and informal sectors can lead to the conclusion that, to a large extent, the informal sector reproduces financial services comparable to those provided in the formal sector[43]. This means that, on the macroeconomic level, formal and informal financial activity exists in parallel; that is to say, those segments of the population that, for one reason or another, do not have access to formal sector institutions, nonetheless have financing needs which are satisfied through informal arrangements (which are often the informal sector counterparts of the denied formal sector service).

The second point refers to the additional qualitative information which Table 2.4 does not show. Alongside the inventory of financial circuits in the countries studied, it is equally important to know, where possible, the share of each type of institution, scheme, operator, as well as the importance of financial markets, in their respective sectors – and better yet between the three sectors themselves, although this is, admittedly, difficult to obtain. The presence of a particular type of organisation is not enough; its share in the overall transactions, in comparison with other operators, can play a determining role in the volume and quality of the resources mobilised as well as in their allocation.

The question of "shares" is a multifaceted one. Within the formal sector, for instance, it may be approached on three levels: *i)* the relative shares between institutions of the same branch, i.e. commercial banks as opposed to savings banks or development banks, market concentration within the insurance sector, etc.[44]; *ii)* the relative importance of banking as opposed to non-bank financial intermediaries, which is notably an indicator of the availability of long-term finance; *iii)* the proportion of resources which transit through (banking and non-bank) financial intermediaries as opposed to markets (valid for those countries with financial markets).

In the case of the semi-formal sector, the share of savings and credit co-operatives and credit unions in overall financial activity is, admittedly, minimal. However, their potential for development varies from case to case. The importance of co-operatives in Mexico, for example, is in no way comparable to that in Zambia.

In the informal sector as well, the various financial arrangements undergo transformations, in structure and in relative "shares", as the economic environment in which they operate changes. In the Philippines, for example, the weakening of the landlord-tenant relationship which followed the implementation of land reform during the 1970s, the rise of absentee landlordism, and the new and profitable opportunities in product and credit markets created by the introduction of new technology, led to a decline in the share of landlords and a rise of that of traders in individual moneylending activities in rural areas.

Estimates of the extent of the informal sector as opposed to the formal one have already been touched upon in Chapter 1. As for a quantitative assessment of the importance of the operators within their respective sectors, it is clear that this is possible mainly – if not only – for the formal sector. This is the object of the next section.

II. THE RESPECTIVE SHARES IN FINANCIAL CIRCUITS

A. CREDIT IN THE DEVELOPING COUNTRIES

In this section, we will present some data on the distribution of financial savings among the various institutions. The figures in Table 2.5 present the share of central banks, commercial banks, savings banks and thrifts, specialised lending institutions, provident and pension funds, insurance companies, mutual funds, trusts, and investment banks in total gross liabilities of the financial system.

Before looking at the distribution of liabilities, it is worthwhile to examine the share of total financial system assets in GNP. This ratio measures the degree of "financialisation" of the economy, in other words, the weight of the monetary and financial sector relative to the real sector (where goods are produced and traded). This ratio of total financial system assets to GNP ranges from a low of 74 per cent in India and 83 per cent in Nigeria to a high of 230 per cent in South Korea and 232 per cent in Malaysia.

Table 2.5 DISTRIBUTION OF FINANCIAL SAVINGS (1985)

All figures represent percentages of total gross liabilities of the financial system.

Country	Central banks	Commercial banks	Savings banks & thrifts	Specialised lending institutions	Provident & pension funds	Insurance companies	Mutual Funds, trusts & investment banks	Total System assets (as % GNP)	Long-Term debt securities & equities (% system assets)	Equities banks (as % system assets)
Africa										
Nigeria	28	57	0	2	1	3	9	83	24	5
Asia										
South Korea	10	54	5	16	0	4	11	230	11	4
Thailand	19	59	7	15	0	1	0	121	20	4
Philippines	35	40	4	16	0	3	3	120	16	3
India	13	55	7	8	7	9	1	74	31	12
Malaysia	10	45	5	18	16	3	4	232	48	24
Latin America										
Brazil	35	31	11	15	2	1	5	210	30	17
Chile	20	63	0	2	11	5	1	115	40	14

Source: Extracted from "Investir dans les nouveaux marchés de capitaux", IFC Capital Markets Department, Forum sur l'émergence de nouveaux marchés financiers, Paris, October 1988.

It is true that when we compare this ratio to the rate of growth of the economy, we find a positive correlation, and this constitutes one of the main arguments of the proponents of financial deepening as a way of fostering growth. But it is also true that correlation does not imply causality.

The degree of financial deepening also depends on the role of financial markets per se. Table 2.5 shows that the share of long-term debt securities and equities ranges from 11 per cent in Korea to 48 per cent in Malaysia. The share of equities in total financial assets also ranges from 3 per cent in the Philippines to 17 per cent in Brazil (see Section B on market capitalisation).

Turning now to the distribution of financial savings, commercial banks represent the largest share in the total of gross liabilities of the financial system. Their share averages 50 per cent. Next come the central banks with shares that can vary from 10 per cent in Malaysia and Korea to 35 per cent in Brazil and the Philippines. The share of central banks indicates the degree of intervention in economic activity by the public authorities.

The specialised lending institution share is composed largely of development banks; their weight varies from 2 per cent in Chile and Nigeria to 18 per cent in Malaysia.

Social insurance schemes and insurance companies represent only a limited share of the liabilities of the financial system. They are significant only in Malaysia and Chile, thanks notably to the role of provident funds in both these countries.

Savings banks and thrifts, when they exist, represent a limited share of gross liabilities, ranging from zero per cent in Chile and Nigeria to 4 per cent in the Philippines to 11 per cent in Brazil. The relative weight of mutual funds, trusts, and investment banks is of the same order, i.e. between 1 and 11 per cent of total gross liabilities.

In Table 2.6, which presents data on the share of domestic credit in GDP (domestic credit here includes claims on central and/or local government, official entities, non-financial public enterprises, the private sector and other financial and banking institutions),

Table 2.6   DOMESTIC CREDIT/GDP

Per cent

	1981	1982	1983	1984	1985	1986	1987
Africa							
Burundi	21.4	21.2	23.2	19.3	19.1	18.7	19.7
Ethiopia	34.6	38.9	41.1	45.4	49.0	51.3	55.1
Togo	29.9	30.0	26.8	22.5	–	–	–
Zambia	65.1	80.8	79.9	81.8	104.7	76.2	43.3
Zimbabwe	32.1	36.6	34.6	30.7	28.4	26.6	–
Asia							
India..........................	42.4	46.2	46.0	50.1	51.9	54.6	–
Indonesia	9.9	13.5	15.0	13.8	15.7	21.1	–
Philippines	41.6	45.9	52.9	39.7	32.6	26.4	21.6
Bangladesh	27.2	26.8	30.3	32.3	32.0	32.4	31.3
Thailand........................	45.3	51.1	59.1	69.3	67.2	67.4	71.9
Latin America							
Mexico	36.1	45.4	38.9	34.9	37.4	44.1	–

– Statistical data unavailable.
Source: International Financial Statistics, IMF, July 1988.

Figure 2.3 **LEVEL AND TREND OF DOMESTIC CREDIT TO GDP RATIO**

Level \ Trend	Rising	Stable	Falling
High	India Thailand Ethiopia	Zambia	
Intermediate	Bangladesh	Philippines Mexico	Zimbabwe
Low	Indonesia	Burundi	Togo

one can observe a large variety of situations. In 1984, year for which figures are available for all the case study countries, domestic credit ranged from a low 14 per cent of GDP in Indonesia to a high 82 per cent of GDP in Zambia.

If one arbitrarily chooses to distinguish those countries with a low, intermediate or high domestic credit to GDP ratio, one finds that India, Thailand, Ethiopia and Zambia have a high ratio; Bangladesh, the Philippines, Mexico and Zimbabwe are in the intermediate range; Burundi, Togo, Indonesia have a low ratio.

Another arbitrary "classification" could be based on the trends in the evolution of this ratio over the period 1981-1987. In countries such as Ethiopia, India, Indonesia and Thailand it increased rather sharply, whereas in Bangladesh, Mexico, Burundi, and Zambia it remained relatively stable, and even decreased in the Philippines, Togo and Zimbabwe.

However, an attempt to correlate the two aspects (level of ratio, trend of ratio) distinguished above leads to inconclusive results. In effect, India, Thailand, and Ethiopia have a high and rising domestic credit to GDP ratio, while Zambia's is high and relatively stable; Bangladesh and Mexico have an intermediate and relatively stable ratio, while that of the Philippines and Zimbabwe is declining; finally, the domestic credit to GDP ratio is low and rising in Indonesia, low and stable in Burundi, and low and falling in Togo. Figure 2.3 helps visualise these observations.

To a certain extent, the inconclusive results stem from the fact that the ratio of domestic credit to GDP reflects both: i) the degree of financial intermediation in a given country, that is to say, the more agents lend and borrow for a given amount of goods and services produced, the higher the ratio; and ii) the importance of public finance deficits, where the government substitutes debt for taxes. It is clear that when claims on government – either through advances from the central bank, loans by deposit money banks, or deposits by postal savings networks, building societies, etc. – are important, global domestic credit levels will appear high.

Table 2.7   SHARE OF CLAIMS ON CENTRAL GOVERNMENT (NET), THE PRIVATE SECTOR, AND OTHER OFFICIAL ENTITIES AND FINANCIAL INSTITUTIONS, AS A PERCENTAGE OF TOTAL DOMESTIC CREDIT

Average for the 1981-88 period

	Africa					Asia					Latin America
	Burundi	Ethiopia	Togo[1]	Zambia[1]	Zimbabwe[1]	India	Indonesia	Philippines	Bangladesh[1]	Thailand	Mexico
Claims on central government (net)	52.7	50.9	5.6	73.6	19.5	45.1	(43.0)	14.0	19.9	22.8	57.4
Claims on official entities ..	12.3	13.6	–	–	–	–	29.8	9.9	22.8	–	–
Claims on private sector	31.8	8.6	92.7	26.4	50.3	51.2	109.2	66.9	50.6	68.9	30.6
Claims on other financial or banking institutions	3.2	26.9	1.7	–	–	3.7	4.0	9.1	6.8	6.5	3.9
Claims on non-financial public enterprises	–	–	–	–	30.2	–	–	–	–	1.8	8.1
Total	100.0	100.0	100.0	100.0	100.0	100.0	100.0	100.0	100.0	100.0	100.0

–   Data does not exist.
( ) Negative figures in parentheses.
1.   Average for the 1981-87 period.
Source: International Financial Statistics, IMF, July 1988.

This means that one must not jump to hasty conclusions: a high share of domestic credit in GDP can indicate just as much a predominance of government (with its deficits) in resource flows as a high degree of financial intermediation (beneficial mainly to the private sector).

Hence it becomes necessary to disaggregate total domestic credit, so as to distinguish the respective shares of claims on central government and official entities, on the private sector and on other financial and banking institutions (see Table 2.7).

In those countries where the claims on central government in domestic credit are high, the domestic credit to GDP ratio is also high, with the exception of Burundi (where claims on central government are high but domestic credit/GDP is low). Similarly, in those countries where claims on central government in domestic credit are relatively low, the ratio of domestic credit to GDP equally tends to be low, with the notable exception of Thailand, where the high ratio of domestic credit to GDP is due more to the importance of financial intermediation than to the weight of central government in financial circuits.

Table 2.7 also shows that the claims on the private sector in domestic credit vary from 9 per cent in Ethiopia to more than 100 per cent in Indonesia (where the government runs a surplus). Indeed, the share of claims on the private sector in total domestic credit can help to assess the degree of financial liberalisation. In Indonesia, the Philippines and Thailand, for instance, and less noticeably in Zimbabwe and India, claims on the private sector exceeded 50 per cent of total domestic credit, whereas in Ethiopia, Zambia, Burundi and Mexico, the ratio was less than one third of total domestic credit.

Finally, domestic credit levels and trends can also be linked to the government's role in mobilising external resources (see Table 2.8). Indeed, there can be an arbitrage between mobilising domestic resources or resorting to external capital flows. For instance, in the case of Togo, government foreign debt represents 109 per cent of GDP, whereas only 6 per cent of domestic credit is channelled to central government. Conversely, in India, claims on central government represent 45 per cent of domestic credit while government foreign debt is less than 7 per cent of GDP.

Table 2.8   GOVERNMENT FOREIGN DEBT/GDP

Stocks

Per cent

	1981	1982	1983	1984	1985	1986	1987
Africa							
Burundi	15.3	17.3	31.5	34.1	33.3	47.4	59.5
Ethiopia	13.8	18.5	21.4	23.8	27.2	30.6	35.3
Togo	81.4	85.9	103.9	109.7	–	–	–
Zimbabwe	12.9	16.3	16.1	21.5	21.0	–	–
Asia							
India	7.7	7.7	7.4	7.2	6.9	6.9	–
Philippines	9.8	11.8	12.7	18.3	–	–	–
Thailand	4.7	5.9	6.3	6.4	9.0	–	–

– Statistical data unavailable.
Source: International Financial Statistics, IMF, July 1988.

Figure 2.4 **GOVERNMENT BORROWING BEHAVIOUR**

		Domestic borrowing	
		Low	High
External borrowing	Low	Philippines Thailand Zimbabwe	India
	High	Togo	Burundi Ethiopia

In other cases, where there is no arbitrage at all, either the government resorts largely to both domestic and external resources (the cases of Ethiopia, Burundi and Mexico, for example), or the government refrains from both domestic and external borrowing (the cases of Zimbabwe, the Philippines, Thailand and Indonesia). Figure 2.4 summarizes and helps visualise these points by cross-comparing government borrowing behaviour regarding domestic and external borrowing.

B. THE IMPORTANCE OF CAPITAL MARKETS

Most developing countries possess a narrow range of financial instruments and markets. This is not wholly unrelated to the fact that, until quite recently, financial sector development was viewed simply in terms of increasing the number of (specialised) financial institutions, while neglecting the dimension of financial market activity[45].

With the exceptions of Brazil, Mexico[46], India, Malaysia, and Singapore, deliberate attempts to develop stock markets have rarely succeeded. However, certain developing countries recently have encouraged the growth of an active capital market by adopting a markedly favourable attitude towards private enterprise. Indeed, some governments advocate a large dissemination of private firm ownership by pressing family-owned enterprises to go public. In specific cases, governments also see the stock market as a possible way of smoothly transferring foreign ownership of capital to domestic ownership[47].

The relative size of market capitalisation largely reflects the stance adopted by governments concerning the degree of liberalisation of the economy. The keener the stance on liberalisation, the more developed the financial market[48]. The importance of the stock market also indicates the degree of decentralisation of the economy. When markets are

Table 2.9   MARKET CAPITALISATION AS A PERCENTAGE OF DOMESTIC CREDIT
IN SELECTED COUNTRIES

	1981	1982	1983	1984	1985	1986	1987
Asia							
India	15.1	13.3	7.6	12.3	15.6	15.6	14.1[1]
Indonesia	1.1	3.1	2.5	0.9	0.8	0.6	0.6[1]
Philippines	10.6	6.5	7.1	6.2	12.1	24.4	26.7[2]
Thailand	6.1	6.9	6.3	6.2	7.4	10.3	14.8[2]
Africa							
Zimbabwe	29.0	16.0	14.3	12.1	28.0	27.1	41.3[1]
Nigeria	11.7	4.7	7.9	8.0	7.6	4.1	–
Latin America							
Mexico	11.7	2.2	5.4	6.2	6.3	10.7	31.5[2]
Brazil	17.8	13.4	22.6	49.9	61.4	–	–

1. Estimated.
2. Estimated, as of October 1987.
Source: Market capitalisation figures from IFC Emerging Markets Data Base.
Domestic credit figures from *International Financial Statistics*, IMF, July 1988.

active, the economy is usually left to decentralised decision units; when markets are weak and dormant, most of the economic power is concentrated in government hands.

Table 2.9 presents the ratio of market capitalisation to domestic credit in selected developing countries. This ratio can be interpreted as the relative weight of market mechanisms versus intermediation mechanisms. It can also reflect the relative weight of the private sector in the economy.

As it can be seen, this ratio varies markedly from one country to another and, for a given country, from one year to the next. The strong variation of the ratio in the latter case reflects primarily the changes in stock prices. In developing economies as in industrialised ones, the 1980s have been characterised by a sharp increase in stock market capitalisation following an important positive change in stock prices. Table 2.9 shows that in most of the countries surveyed (with the notable exception of Indonesia and Nigeria), this ratio has been on the rise throughout the period under consideration.

Turning to the comparison of this ratio from one country to another, it appears that Brazil and Zimbabwe are by far the most market-oriented countries of the sample. The ratio has skyrocketed in Mexico thanks to a very sharp increase in stock prices in 1987, after having plunged in 1982 following the nationalisation of many private companies. It is in Indonesia that the ratio is the lowest, and this contrasts with the situation observed in other Asian countries such as the Philippines and Thailand.

Unfortunately, we do not have more detailed information on the types of financial instruments traded on the capital markets. It would be interesting to know the relative size of the private and public bond markets, as well as that of private shares, and to be able to assess more precisely the role of the government in the capital market itself.

C. THE SHARES IN DEPOSITS AND LENDING

Little data is available on the respective shares of the various financial institutions in deposit and lending activities. Table 2.10 presents the volume of deposits collected by the central bank, commercial banks, merchant banks, savings banks, building societies, postal savings networks, development banks, finance houses, and non-bank financial intermediaries in the Philippines, Zimbabwe, and Burundi.

As it can be seen, not all of the institutions mentioned collect savings in the forms of demand, savings, and time deposits. In the Philippines, only three institutions do so – commercial banks, savings banks, and development banks – but their market shares vary greatly since commercial banks collect more than three-fourths of total short-term savings. As could be expected, commercial banks are more dominant in urban areas than in rural areas (see Chapter 3).

In Zimbabwe, five institutions collect such deposits: commercial banks, merchant banks, building societies, postal savings networks, and finance houses. Market shares here are more evenly distributed, with commercial banks representing more than a third of the market, and building societies and postal savings networks a little less than one fourth each.

In Burundi, five institutions collect savings: the central bank, commercial banks, savings banks, postal savings networks, and non-bank financial intermediaries. Commercial banks dominate the market for demand deposits, but the role of the central bank is far from negligible. Commercial banks also dominate – though less imperially – the market for savings and time deposits, closely followed by savings banks and non-bank financial intermediaries.

Table 2.10 COMPARATIVE VOLUME OF DEPOSITS BY INSTITUTION

Per cent

	Philippines (1982-1983)		Zimbabwe (1984)	Burundi (1985)	
	savings, time, demand deposits		savings and fixed deposits	demand deposits	savings and time deposits
	rural areas	urban areas			
Central bank				17.3	
Commercial banks	72.2	86.8	37.2	73.0	42.4
Merchant banks			9.3		
Savings banks	13.8[1]	7.2[1]		7.4	33.0[3]
Building societies.			23.3		
Postal savings networks			23.0	2.3	
Development banks.	14.0[2]	6.0[2]			
Finance houses			7.2		
Non-bank financial intermediaries					24.6

1. Includes savings banks, private development banks, stock savings and loan associations.
2. Includes rural banks and specialised government banks.
3. Figure of 33 per cent may be further broken down into: 32.4 per cent compulsory savings; 0.6 per cent discretionary savings.
Source: For Philippines and Burundi: case studies. For Zimbabwe: Radke, Detlef et al., "Mobilisation of Personal Savings in Zimbabwe through Financial Development", Berlin, German Development Institute (GDI), 1986, mimeo.

Table 2.11 COMPOSITION OF DEPOSITS AMONG BANKS, BY TYPE OF BANK
AND BY OWNERSHIP

Per cent

	Bangladesh (1984) total bank deposits	Indonesia (1987) time deposits
Nationalised commercial banks	71.1	
State banks		59.9
Specialised banks	5.5	
Development banks		1.1
Foreign and private banks	23.4	39.0

Source: For Bangladesh: case study.
For Indonesia: Bank Indonesia, *Report for the Financial Year 1987-1988*, Jakarta, Indonesia, December 1988.

Some data is also available for Bangladesh and Indonesia (Table 2.11). Public commercial banks collected almost three-fourths of total bank deposits in Bangladesh in 1984, and they accounted for about 60 per cent of time deposits in Indonesia in 1987. It is interesting to note that foreign and/or private banks represent a sizeable share of the market in these two countries.

There is a dearth of data on the respective sizes of the various informal sector "institutions". One of the characteristics of the informal sector is precisely the lack of reliable figures since almost no accounting is done. The only sources we have concern India (Table 2.12). These reveal that Chit Fund companies represent roughly half of the savings mobilised by the informal sector, followed by hire-purchase companies (one third). The other "institutions" operating in the informal sector (Mutual Benefit Funds or *Nidhis,* loan companies, housing finance companies, and investment companies) account only for a small fraction of the market.

Concerning lending by type of institution (Table 2.13), in all four countries surveyed – Burundi, Zimbabwe, the Philippines, Indonesia – the predominant role of commercial banks in lending activity is undeniable. Only in Burundi are they surpassed by central bank lending. At the opposite end of the spectrum, commercial banks in Indonesia accounted for more than 90 per cent of total lending in 1984 (commercial banking in Indonesia is heavily nationalised; in fact the five nationalised commercial banks account for at least three-fourths of total lending).

The relative importance of building societies in Zimbabwe, paralleled by that of development banks in the Philippines, is also of some interest. Finally, it must be noted that the share of non-bank financial intermediaries in overall lending is similar in Burundi, Zimbabwe, and the Philippines: between 12 and 14 per cent of the total.

As for the informal sector, again, the only data we have concerns India. Tables 2.14 and 2.15 show the volume of lending by the corporate and non-corporate segments of the informal sector. Lending activity by the corporate sector is dominated by hire-purchase companies, followed by Chit Fund companies. In the non-corporate segment, indigenous bankers and pawnbrokers represent an average of 70 per cent of total lending activity, as opposed to 30 per cent for finance corporations.

Table 2.12 GROWTH OF DEPOSITS WITH THE CORPORATE SEGMENT OF THE INFORMAL SECTOR IN INDIA

Rs. Crores

Year (March end)	Investment companies	Loan companies	Hire-purchase companies, finance companies	Housing finance companies	Mutual benefit fund (Nidhis)	Chit Fund companies (subscriptions per annum)	Total of columns 2 to 7
1	2	3	4	5	6	7	8
1975	3.5 (7.0)	19.6 (16.0)	40.1 (32.8)	0.7 (0.6)	19.9 (16.3)	33.3 (27.3)	122.1
1976	8.2 (5.8)	28.2 (20.0)	45.2 (32.0)	8.7 (6.2)	20.0 (14.2)	30.8 (21.8)	141.1
1977	5.3 (3.3)	32.2 (20.3)	53.2 (33.6)	10.6 (6.7)	19.8 (12.5)	37.6 (23.7)	158.5
1978	19.5 (10.1)	42.4 (22.0)	60.5 (31.4)	10.7 (5.6)	21.7 (11.3)	35.2 (18.3)	192.4
1979	22.2 (10.4)	47.8 (22.5)	70.0 (32.9)	10.7 (5.0)	24.6 (11.6)	37.3 (17.5)	212.6
1980	19.9 (5.7)	58.2 (16.3)	91.1 (25.4)	14.3 (4.0)	28.1 (7.8)	146.3 (40.9)	357.9
1981	33.9 (8.7)	43.6 (11.1)	111.3 (28.4)	14.6 (3.7)	31.5 (8.0)	156.4 (40.0)	391.3
1982	16.0 (3.5)	33.6 (7.4)	133.3 (29.5)	29.9 (6.6)	31.1 (6.9)	208.1 (46.0)	452.0
1983	13.6 (2.7)	7.7 (1.5)	157.9 (31.7)	56.5 (11.3)	35.6 (7.1)	227.1 (45.6)	498.4
1984	19.7 (2.8)	40.5 (5.8)	153.8 (22.2)	60.1 (8.7)	39.6 (5.7)	380.1 (57.8)	693.8
1985	30.0 (3.3)	57.8 (6.4)	285.5 (31.5)	33.7 (3.7)	60.4 (6.7)	439.2 (48.4)	906.6

N.B. Figures in parentheses are percentages of total.
Source: Growth of Deposits with Non-Banking Companies, *RBI Bulletin*, various issues.

123

Table 2.13 COMPARATIVE VOLUME OF LENDING BY TYPE OF FINANCIAL INSTITUTION

Per cent

	Burundi (1985)	Zimbabwe (1984)	Philippines (1983)	Indonesia[8] (1984)
Central bank	49.0[1]			
Commercial banks	25.2	42.8	59.3	93.4
Merchant banks		6.8		
Savings banks	3.2		10.0[6]	
Building societies....................		21.9		
Postal savings networks	0.8[2]			
Development banks	7.7[3]		18.9[7]	6.6
Finance houses		8.4		
Discount houses....................		7.4		
Non-bank financial intermediaries/specialised financial institutions	14.0[4]	12.7[5]	11.8	

1. Figure can be further subdivided: 48.2 per cent loans to government; 0.8 per cent loans to the rest of the economy.
2. The postal savings network in Burundi grants loans only to government.
3. Figure for loans to the "rest of the economy" (no loans to government).
4. Specialised financial institutions category in Burundi includes: Caisse Centrale de Mobilisation et de Financement; Holding Arabe Libyen Burundais; Société Burundaise de Financement; Fonds de Promotion Economique.
5. Specialised financial institutions category in Zimbabwe includes: state-owned statutory corporations; Agricultural Finance Corporation; Small Enterprise Development Corporation; Zimbabwe Development Bank, Industrial Development Corporation, Private Finance Institutions.
6. Savings banks category in the Philippines includes savings banks, private development banks, stock savings and loan associations.
7. Development banks category in the Philippines includes rural banks and specialised government banks.
8. Figures for Indonesia show the distribution of lending activity between state commercial banks, private national commercial banks, and foreign banks, on the one hand, and the state development bank (BAPINDO) on the other hand.

Source: Case studies.

Table 2.14   VOLUME OF LENDING BY THE CORPORATE SEGMENT OF THE INFORMAL SECTOR IN INDIA

Rs. Crores

Year (March end)	Investment companies	Loan companies	Hire-purchase companies, finance companies	Housing finance companies	Mutual benefit fund (Nidhis)	Chit Fund	Total of columns 2 to 7
1	2	3	4	5	6	7	8
1975	8.5	19.6	160.4	2.8	19.1	30.0	240.4
1976	8.2	28.2	180.8	34.8	19.2	27.7	298.9
1977	5.3	32.2	218.8	42.4	19.0	33.8	351.5
1978	19.5	42.4	242.0	42.8	20.8	31.7	399.2
1979	22.2	47.8	280.0	42.8	23.6	33.6	450.0
1980	19.9	58.2	364.4	57.2	27.0	131.7	658.4
1981	33.9	43.6	445.2	58.4	30.2	140.8	752.1
1982	16.0	33.6	533.3	119.6	29.9	187.3	919.6
1983	13.6	7.7	631.6	226.0	34.1	204.4	1 117.4
1984	19.7	40.5	615.2	240.4	38.0	342.1	1 295.9
1985	30.0	57.8	1 142.0	134.8	58.0	395.3	1 817.9

1. For Investment Companies and Loan Companies, credit deposit ratio is assumed at 100 per cent (i.e. all public deposits are assumed to be used as credit).
2. For Hire Purchase Finance and Housing Finance Companies, the credit is calculated at four times the deposits.
3. For Mutual Benefit Fund Companies, the credit-deposit ratio is 96 per cent.
4. For Chit Fund Companies, the credit-subscription ratio is 90 per cent.
Source: Case study.

Table 2.15   VOLUME OF LENDING BY THE NON-CORPORATE SEGMENT
OF THE INFORMAL SECTOR IN INDIA

Rs. Crores

Year	Finance corporations	Indigenous bankers and pawnbrokers	Total lending by the non-corporate segment
1	2	3	4
1979	554.9	2 883.0	3 437.9
1980	652.2	2 883.0	3 535.2
1981	749.5	2 883.0	3 632.5
1982	861.3	2 883.0	3 744.0
1983	989.8	2 883.0	3 672.8
1984	1 137.3	2 883.0	4 020.3
1985	1 307.2	2 883.0	4 190.2

Source: Case study.

D.   LENDING AND DEPOSIT RATES

Reliable data on interest rates is available only for the formal sector.

Let us focus first on deposit interest rates. Tables 2.16 and 2.17 present the various nominal deposit interest rates in the countries surveyed.

As it is well known, there may be a whole series of deposit rates: money market rate, and deposit rate, Treasury bill rate, government bond yield. Due to different institutional settings, not all of these rates exist in all countries. For instance, when the central bank operates mainly on the money market, there may not be a significant discount rate at the central bank. Likewise, in certain countries, there are only Treasury bills and no government bonds.

The interest rate structure is quite different from one country to another. In Ethiopia, for example, the structure of interest rates clearly reveals the fact that they are fixed by the government. When interest rates are driven more by market forces, their structure appears more complex and reflects the various market clearing mechanisms at work. In the Philippines, for example, in 1987, there was a 200 basis point difference between the discount rate and the Treasury bill rate, whereas this difference amounted to 250 in Zambia and 360 basis points in Thailand. In half the countries of the sample – Burundi, Ethiopia, Togo, Zambia, and the Philippines – the deposit rate is the lowest of all creditor interest rates. In the remaining countries, by contrast – Zimbabwe, Indonesia, Bangladesh, Thailand, and Mexico – the deposit rate is higher than the money market and discount rates, government bond yields, and Treasury bill rates. Comparable data on deposit rates was not available for India.

Table 2.16   STATISTICS AVAILABLE ON NOMINAL INTEREST RATES IN 1987

Per cent per annum

	Burundi	Ethiopia	Togo	Zambia	Zimbabwe	India	Indonesia	Philippines	Bangladesh	Thailand	Mexico
Discount rate/Bank rate	7.00[1-5]	3.00	8.50[5]	14.00[5]	9.00[5]	10.00[5]		9.080[5]	11.25[4-5]	8.00[5]	
Treasury bill rate		3.00		16.50	8.73			11.509		4.39[3]	103.07
Deposit rate	4.00[1]	1.00	5.25	13.23	9.58		16.23[3]	8.202	12.00[4]	9.50[3]	94.28[3]
Lending rate	12.00[1]	6.00	8.00	21.20	13.01	16.50	21.47[3]	13.338	12.00[4]	15.00	–
Government bond yield		5.00			13.87	–				7.46[3]	
Money market rate			8.25		9.10[2]	9.91	14.52			5.94[3]	93.20[3]
Average cost of funds											94.31[3]
Annual inflation rate	7.30	(2.50)	(0.10)	65.90	12.50	8.80	9.30	3.80	9.50	2.50	131.80

–   Statistical data unavailable.
1.   Figure for November 1987.
2.   Figure for fit quarter 1987.
3.   Estimate.
4.   Figure for second quarter 1986.
5.   End of period.
Source: International Financial Statistics, IMF, July 1988.

Table 2.17 INTEREST RATES

Per cent per annum

	1981	1982	1983	1984	1985	1986	1987	1988
Africa								
Burundi								
Discount rate (end of period)	7.00	7.00	7.00	7.00	7.00	5.00	7.00[1]	—
Deposit rate	4.50	5.00	4.50	4.50	4.50	5.96	4.00[1]	—
Lending rate	12.00	12.00	12.00	12.00	12.00	12.00	12.00[1]	—
Ethiopia								
Discount rate	2.80	2.90	3.00	—	6.00	6.00	3.00	3.00[2]
Treasury bill rate	—	—	—	3.00	3.00	3.00	3.00	3.00[2]
Deposit rate	—	—	—	—	6.00	3.50	1.00	1.00[2]
Lending rate	—	—	—	—	8.50	7.25	6.00	6.00[2]
Government bond yield	—	—	—	—	—	6.00	5.00	5.00[2]
Togo								
Discount rate (end of period)	10.50	12.50	10.50	10.50	10.50	8.50	8.50	—
Money market rate	13.35	14.76	12.41	11.79	10.53	8.46	8.25	—
Deposit rate	6.25	7.75	7.50	7.25	7.25	6.08	5.25	—
Lending rate	10.00	11.50	10.50	10.00	10.00	8.83	8.00	—
Zambia								
Discount rate (end of period)	7.50	7.50	10.00	14.50	25.00	30.00	14.00	14.00[3]
Treasury bill rate	5.75	6.00	7.50	7.67	13.21	24.25	16.50	14.50[3]
Deposit rate	6.17	6.00	7.00	7.71	—	—	13.23	11.44[3]
Lending rate	9.50	9.50	13.00	14.54	18.60	27.40	21.20	18.39[3]
Zimbabwe								
Bank rate (end of period)	9.00	9.00	9.00	9.00	9.00	9.00	9.00	9.00[4]
Money market rate	6.83	9.50	9.09	8.90	8.80	9.10	9.10[5]	—
Treasury bill rate	5.70	8.50	8.52	8.49	8.48	8.71	8.73	8.44[4]
Deposit rate	7.46	14.46	12.80	10.30	10.04	10.28	9.58	10.50[4]
Lending rate	19.36	23.00	23.08	23.00	17.17	13.00	13.00	13.00[4]
Government bond yield	11.54	13.00	13.08	13.29	13.26	13.20	13.87	14.00[4]
Asia								
India								
Bank rate (end of period)	10.00	10.00	10.00	10.00	10.00	10.00	10.00	10.00[6]
Money market rate	8.61	7.27	8.30	9.95	10.00	9.97	9.91	10.00[6]
Lending rate	16.50	16.50	16.50	16.50	16.50	16.50	16.50	16.50[6]
Government bond yield	7.15	7.59	7.99	8.65	8.99	—	—	—
Indonesia								
Money market rate	16.26	17.24	13.17	18.63	10.33	13.00[7]	14.52	—

Deposit rate	6.00	8.00	8.00	10.00	18.00	13.40	16.25	–
Lending rate	–	–	–	–	–	21.49	21.47[7]	–
Philippines								
Discount rate (end of period)	6.690	6.300	8.050	12.110	11.500	9.630	9.080	9.110[6]
Treasury bill rate	12.547	13.780	14.231	28.529	26.725	16.081	11.509	14.941[8]
Deposit rate	13.717	13.742	13.581	21.172	18.914	11.253	8.202	12.004[8]
Lending rate	15.335	18.120	19.238	28.195	28.612	17.534	13.338	15.554[8]
Bangladesh								
Discount rate (end of period)	10.50	10.50	10.50	10.50	11.25	11.25[9]	–	–
Deposit rate	12.00	12.00	12.00	12.00	12.00	12.00[9]	–	–
Lending rate	12.00	12.00	12.00	12.00	12.00	12.00[9]	–	–
Thailand								
Discount rate (end of period)	14.50	12.50	13.00	12.00	11.00	8.00	8.00	8.00[8]
Money market rate	17.25	14.95	12.15	13.58	13.48	8.07	5.94[7]	6.87[3]
Treasury bill rate	11.57	11.64	9.35	10.00	11.02	6.76	4.39[7]	–
Deposit rate	12.50	13.00	13.00	13.00	13.00	9.75	9.50[7]	–
Lending rate	19.00	19.00	17.63	18.75	19.00	17.66[7]	15.00	–
Government bond yield	13.06	13.85	11.13	12.41	12.11	9.11	7.46[7]	–
Latin America								
Mexico								
Money market rate	30.77	–	–	49.90	62.40	88.40	93.20[7]	–
Treasury bill rate	29.57	45.75	59.19	49.47	63.36	88.57	103.07	54.51[8]
Deposit rate	28.62	43.62	54.70	48.36	59.48	84.68	94.28[7]	–
Average cost of funds	36.60	40.40	56.65	51.08	56.07	80.88	94.31[7]	–
Lending rate		46.02	63.03	54.73	–	–	–	–

–   Statistical data unavailable.
1. Figure for November 1987.
2. Figure for February 1988.
3. Figure for January 1988.
4. Figure for May 1988.
5. Figure for first quarter 1987.
6. Figure for March 1988.
7. Estimate.
8. Figure for April 1988.
9. Figure for second quarter 1986.
Source: International Financial Statistics, IMF, July 1988.

129

Table 2.18   NOMINAL DEPOSIT RATES, LENDING RATES, AND ANNUAL INFLATION RATES

Per cent

	1981	1982	1983	1984	1985	1986	1987
Africa							
Burundi							
Inflation rate	12.00	5.70	8.40	14.30	3.70	1.80	7.30
Deposit rate	4.50	5.00	4.50	4.50	4.50	5.96	4.00[1]
Lending rate	12.00	12.00	12.00	12.00	12.00	12.00	12.00
Ethiopia							
Inflation rate	6.10	4.40	0.70	8.40	19.10	(9.80)	(2.50)
Deposit rate	–	–	–	–	6.00	3.50	1.00
Lending rate	–	–	–	–	8.50	7.25	6.00
Togo							
Inflation rate	19.70	11.10	9.40	(3.60)	(1.80)	4.10	(0.10)
Deposit rate	6.25	7.75	7.50	7.25	7.25	6.08	5.25
Lending rate	10.00	11.50	10.50	10.00	10.00	8.83	8.00
Zambia							
Inflation rate	14.00	12.50	19.70	20.00	37.40	51.60	65.90
Deposit rate	6.17	6.00	7.00	7.71	–	–	13.23
Lending rate	9.50	9.50	13.00	14.54	18.60	27.40	21.20
Zimbabwe							
Inflation rate	13.20	10.60	23.10	20.20	8.50	14.30	12.50
Deposit rate	7.46	14.46	12.80	10.30	10.04	10.28	9.58
Lending rate	19.36	23.00	23.08	23.00	17.17	13.00	13.00
Asia							
India							
Inflation rate	13.00	7.90	11.80	8.40	5.60	8.70	8.80
Deposit rate	–	–	–	9.50[2]	9.50[2]	–	–
Lending rate	16.50	16.50	16.50	16.50	16.50	16.50	16.50
Indonesia							
Inflation rate	12.20	9.50	11.80	10.40	4.70	5.90	9.30
Deposit rate	6.00	6.00	6.00	16.00	18.00	15.40[3]	16.23[3]
Lending rate	–	–	–	–	–	21.49	21.47[3]
Philippines							
Inflation rate	13.100	10.200	10.000	50.400	23.100	0.700	3.800
Deposit rate	13.717	13.742	13.581	21.172	18.914	11.253	8.202
Lending rate	15.335	18.120	19.238	28.195	28.612	17.534	13.338

Bangladesh

Inflation rate	16.20	12.50	9.40	10.60	10.70	11.00	9.50
Deposit rate	12.00	12.00	12.00	12.00	12.00	12.00[4]	–
Lending rate	12.00	12.00	12.00	12.00	12.00	12.00[4]	–

Thailand

Inflation rate	12.70	5.20	3.70	0.90	2.40	1.80	2.50
Deposit rate	12.50	13.00	13.00	13.00	13.00	9.75	9.50[3]
Lending rate	19.00	19.00	17.63	18.75	19.00	17.66[3]	–

Latin America

Mexico

Inflation rate	27.90	59.00	101.80	65.50	57.80	86.20	131.80
Deposit rate	29.57	43.62	54.70	48.36	59.48	84.68	94.28
Lending rate	36.60	46.02	63.03	54.73	–	–	–

– Statistical data unavailable.
1. Figure for November 1987.
2. See Madhur, S. and C.P.S. Nayar, "Informal Credit Markets in India: Their Size, Structure and Macro Implications", December 1987.
3. Estimate.
4. Figure for second quarter 1986.
Source: International Financial Statistics, IMF, July 1988.

Table 2.19 REAL DEPOSIT AND LENDING RATES[1]

Per cent

	1981	1982	1983	1984	1985	1986	1987
Africa							
Burundi							
Real deposit rate	-6.7	-0.7	-3.6	-8.6	0.8	4.1	-3.1[2]
Real lending rate	0.0	6.0	3.3	-2.0	8.0	10.0	4.4[2]
Ethiopia							
Real deposit rate	—	—	—	—	-11.0	14.7	3.6
Real lending rate	—	—	—	—	-8.9	18.9	8.7
Togo							
Real deposit rate	-11.2	-3.0	-1.7	11.3	9.2	1.9	5.4
Real lending rate	-8.1	0.4	1.0	14.1	12.0	4.5	8.1
Zambia							
Real deposit rate	-6.9	-5.8	-10.6	-10.2	—	—	-31.7
Real lending rate	-3.9	-2.7	-5.6	-4.6	-13.7	-16.0	-26.9
Zimbabwe							
Real deposit rate	-5.1	3.5	-8.40	-8.2	1.4	-3.5	-2.6
Real lending rate	5.4	11.2	-0.02	2.3	8.0	-1.1	0.4
Asia							
India							
Real lending rate	3.1	8.0	4.2	7.5	10.3	7.2	7.1
Indonesia							
Real deposit rate	-5.5	-3.2	-5.2	5.1	12.7	9.0[3]	6.3[3]
Real lending rate	—	—	—	—	—	14.7	11.1[3]
Philippines							
Real deposit rate	0.5	3.2	3.3	-19.4	-3.4	10.5	4.2
Real lending rate	2.0	7.2	8.4	-14.8	4.5	16.7	9.2
Bangladesh							
Real deposit rate	-3.6	-0.4	2.4	1.3	1.2	0.9[4]	—
Real lending rate	-3.6	-0.4	2.4	1.3	1.2	0.9[4]	—
Thailand							
Real deposit rate	-0.2	7.4	9.0	12.0	10.4	7.8	6.8
Real lending rate	5.6	13.1	13.4	17.7	16.2	15.6[3]	—

Latin America

Mexico

Real deposit rate............	1.3	−9.7	−23.3	−10.4	1.1	−0.8	−16.2
Real lending rate............	6.8	−8.2	−19.2	−6.5	–	–	–

– Statistical data unavailable.
1. Real interest rates calculated using the following formula:

$$1 + r = \frac{1 + i}{1 + \pi}$$

where r = real interest rate
       i = nominal interest rate
      π = inflation rate.

2. Figure for November 1987.
3. Estimate.
4. Figure for second quarter 1986.
Source: International Financial Statistics, IMF, July 1988.

Turning to real interest rates rather than nominal interest rates (Tables 2.18 and 2.19), it appears that, generally, real deposit rates were negative in most countries at the beginning of the 1980s, but they became positive from 1983 onwards. However, deposit rates were still negative in real terms in 1987 in countries like Mexico, Burundi, Zambia, and Zimbabwe.

As far as lending rates are concerned, they appear to be markedly different from the deposit interest rates, as can be seen from Tables 2.16 and 2.17. The difference between the deposit rate and the lending rate is generally quite important, reflecting the high cost of intermediation in most developing countries. For example, in 1987, there was an 800 basis point difference between these two rates in Burundi and in Zambia, a 500 basis point difference in the Philippines and Ethiopia. The difference was somewhat less marked in the other countries, at least according to existing data. Let us also recall that the lending rates that are presented in Table 2.16 are calculated on an average-for-period basis. Of course, these rates are distributed around the mean according to the creditworthiness of borrowers and the objectives of financing.

Lending rates appeared positive in real terms in all the countries surveyed in 1987 (Tables 2.18 and 2.19), except for Zambia. The absolute levels of real lending rates appear high. However, a closer look at these statistics reveals that the difference between real deposit rates and real lending rates appears to have remained constant since the beginning of the decade.

No reliable or statistically significant data exists on the lending or deposit rates in the informal sectors of the surveyed countries.

E. THE ROLE OF SOCIAL SECURITY AND INSURANCE

In this section, we will successively present data on social security institutions and on the insurance sector.

With regard to social security, available statistics (Table 2.20) show that the amount of social security and welfare expenditures represents a limited fraction of GDP in most developing countries, a situation which contrasts sharply with that prevailing in industrial-ised countries. In most of the African and Asian countries surveyed, social security and welfare expenditures amount to less than 2 per cent and often to less than 1 per cent of GDP. This share is significantly higher in Latin American countries, where social security and welfare expenditures are between 3 and 12 per cent of GDP.

It is well known that such expenditures are considered to belong to the "superior goods" category and are directly and positively linked to the level and growth of GDP. The data presented illustrates this hypothesis.

A number of factors play a role in determining the level of social security and welfare expenditures, namely the age structure of the population, the number of salaried workers (wage earners), the political orientation of the government, and so on.

In the countries surveyed, the very young age structure of the population helps explain why such expenditures are at their relatively low levels. The proportion of wage earners in the active population is also much lower than in industrialised countries. Finally, the political orientation of the governments appears to be less important than usually presumed.

Table 2.20 SOCIAL SECURITY AND WELFARE EXPENDITURE* AS A PERCENTAGE OF GDP

	1980	1981	1982	1983	1984	1985	1986	1987
Africa								
Ethiopia	1.0	1.2	–	–	–	–	–	–
Togo	–	2.9	2.9	2.6	4.1	–	–	–
Zambia	0.7	0.8	0.8	0.7	0.8	0.5	0.4	0.4[3]
Zimbabwe	2.5	2.0	1.9	2.1	1.7	1.6[1]	1.5	–
Cameroon	0.7	0.8	–	0.8	0.8	–	–	–
Senegal	1.5[1]	1.6	1.5[1]	1.6	1.7	–	–	–
Asia								
India[2]	0.6	0.5	0.6	0.6	0.7	0.8	1.1[3]	1.0[3,4]
Indonesia[2]	0.4	0.3	0.2	0.3	0.3	0.4	0.3	–
Philippines	0.2	0.1	0.2	0.2	0.2	0.3	0.2[3]	–
Bangladesh	0.2	0.4[3]	0.3[3]	n	1.2[3]	–	–	
Thailand	0.5	0.5	0.5	0.6	0.6	0.6	0.6	0.6
Malaysia	1.1	1.5	–	–	–	–	–	–
Korea	1.1	1.0	1.8	0.9	0.9	1.0	1.1	1.1
Singapore	0.3	0.3	0.3	0.2	0.2	0.4	0.5	–
Sri Lanka	5.1	3.7	3.6	3.2	3.0	3.0	2.9	3.1
Latin America								
Argentina	6.7	7.6	5.9	7.3	6.3	7.7[1]	7.0	–
Brazil	6.3	6.7	7.7	7.1	6.4	5.8	6.1	–
Chile	9.0	10.8	14.3	13.6	13.6	12.2	11.3[3]	–
Colombia	–	–	3.0	2.7	3.0	–	–	–
Costa Rica	1.8	2.2	2.1	3.5	2.6	3.2	5.1	–
Mexico	2.8	3.0	3.2	2.7	2.2	2.5	2.4	–
Uruguay	10.6	12.9	16.1	13.0	11.3	10.9	11.3	–

* Social security and welfare expenditure at consolidated central government level.
– Not available.
1. Data does not form a consistent series with that for earlier years.
2. Data includes expenditures on social security and welfare, housing and community amenities, and other community and social services.
3. Data in whole or in part provisional, preliminary, or projected.
4. Estimate.
n: Negligible.
Source: Government Finance Statistics Yearbook, IMF, 1987, 1988.

These schemes are usually not balanced, and can present either very large surpluses or very large deficits. Table 2.21 presents social security fund deficits or surpluses as a percentage of their annual revenues. In countries like Cameroon or Togo in Africa, or Costa Rica in Latin America, or Malaysia in Asia, the social security schemes appear to generate a rather large surplus. In most other countries, these schemes generate heavy deficits. It is clear from this data that social security funds can, if well-managed and well-designed, contribute to the mobilisation of savings. The successful experience of Malaysia proves that social security funds (in this particular case, provident funds) can help boost the savings rate and hence the overall rate of accumulation. Furthermore, when these surpluses are well-managed and efficiently invested, they can help in promoting financial markets.

Table 2.21 CENTRAL GOVERNMENT SOCIAL SECURITY FUNDS:
DEFICIT (in parentheses) OR SURPLUS AS A PERCENTAGE OF ANNUAL REVENUE

	1980	1981	1982	1983	1984	1985	1986	1987
Africa								
Burundi..............	3.4	20.6	–	–	–	–	–	–
Cameroon............	39.5	47.2	42.6	(26.0)	(29.6)	34.3	33.3	–
Senegal..............	18.9	8.6	7.7	(0.8)	(15.1)	–	–	–
Togo	32.2	2.5	18.8	43.6	42.9	51.6	38.7	–
Asia								
Malaysia.............	89.1	92.6	88.2	83.8	82.1	76.6	69.8	60.8
Latin America								
Argentina	(10.4)	0.3	0.8	(16.6)	0.6	(27.1)[1]	(33.3)	–
Brazil	(8.0)	(11.2)	(1.8)	(11.8)	(3.9)	(0.6)	0.1	–
Chile	(28.8)	(74.2)	(143.5)	(170.3)	(202.0)	(221.9)	(231.4)[2]	(255.1)[2]
Colombia	(43.6)	(64.9)	(155.8)	(81.8)	(77.3)	(65.5)[2]	(75.6)[2]	(71.0)[2]
Costa Rica	(20.7)	(17.8)	(21.2)	3.1	6.0	4.5	3.9	–
Mexico ....-...	(31.8)	(20.8)	(21.2)	(8.7)	(5.8)	(8.5)	(10.1)	(1.9)[2]
Uruguay.............	(48.4)	(64.7)	(106.6)	(85.1)	(74.5)	(47.1)	(34.7)	–

– Statistical data unavailable.
1. Data does not form a consistent series with that for earlier years.
2. Data in whole or in part provisional, preliminary, or projected.
Source: Government Finance Statistics Yearbook, IMF, 1987, 1988.

Turning now to the insurance sector (Table 2.22), we find that there are relatively few life and non-life insurance companies in Africa, with the noticeable exception of Zimbabwe. Insurance companies are much more numerous, both in the life and non-life sectors, in Asia, notably in Indonesia, the Philippines, Thailand, and Malaysia. In Latin America, the situation appears to vary: there are numerous insurance companies in Argentina, Brazil, Chile and Colombia, and few in Costa Rica and Uruguay.

However, the number of companies operating in one country is not necessarily an indication of the size of the insurance sector, as one can see by looking at Table 2.23. The share of life insurance premiums in GDP goes from almost nil in Burundi to 3.11 per cent in Zimbabwe and to 4.59 per cent in South Korea. This share is usually less than 1 per cent in most other developing countries. It is worth underlining that the size of non-life insurance markets is usually more important than that of life insurance (see also Table 2.24), but still, it lies in the range of zero to three per cent. Needless to say, insurance markets appear weak in developing countries, and hence the insurance sector contributes only marginally to the mobilisation of savings. Non-life insurance operations do not generate savings (or else only a limited amount); only life insurance operations can generate long-term funds which contribute more or less directly to promoting growth. It is clear that insurance does not play the role it should in the process of savings mobilisation (except in certain Asian countries), and does not contribute to the promotion and dynamism of financial markets.

Table 2.22 STRUCTURE OF THE INSURANCE MARKET IN SELECTED DEVELOPING COUNTRIES

	Year	Number of domestic companies				Number of foreign companies			
		Life Only	Non-Life	Composite	Reinsurance	Life Only	Non-Life	Composite	Reinsurance
Africa									
Burundi	1983	0	1	0	0	0	0	0	0
Ethiopia	1983-84	0	0	1	0	0	0	0	0
Zambia	1984	0	0	1	0	0	0	0	1
Zimbabwe	1983	4	15	1	1	17	8	2	8
Asia									
India	1983	1	5	0	0	0	0	0	0
Indonesia	1984	20	66	0	3	0	0	0	0
Philippines	1984	21	88	n.a.	4	2	14	n.a.	1
Bangladesh	1983	1	1	0	0	0	0	0	0
Thailand	1984	7	58	4	1	0	4	1	0
South Korea	1984-85	6	12	0	1	0	2	0	0
Malaysia	1984	2	39	11	1	2	5	3	0
Singapore	1984	3	20	4	5	3	34	2	11
Latin America									
Mexico	1983	5	41	n.a.	2	0	0	n.a.	0
Argentina	1982-83	2	241	0	1	0	15	0	0
Brazil	1983	0	0	94	1	0	0	3	0
Chile	1983	18	29	0	3	0	1	0	0
Columbia	1983	24	34	n.a.	3	0	0	n.a.	0
Costa Rica	1983	0	0	1	0	0	0	0	0
Uruguay	1983	0	0	1	0	0	0	0	0

n.a. Not applicable.
Source: UNCTAD, Statistical Survey on Insurance and Reinsurance Operations in Developing Countries, 14th January 1987.

Table 2.23   ECONOMIC SIGNIFICANCE OF INSURANCE MARKETS IN SELECTED
DEVELOPING COUNTRIES

	Year	Gross premiums as percentage of GDP	
		Life	Non-Life
Africa			
Burundi	1983	0.00	1.06
Ethiopia	1983-6	0.04	1.33
Zambia	1984	0.90	2.15
Zimbabwe	1983	3.11	1.88
Asia			
Bangladesh	1983	0.09	0.25
India	1983	0.69[1]	0.44
Indonesia	1984	0.17	0.45
South Korea	1984-85	4.59[1]	1.28[1]
Malaysia	1984	0.99	2.15
Philippines	1984	0.40	0.66
Singapore	1984	0.86	1.61
Thailand	1984	0.57	0.54
Latin America			
Argentina	1982-83	0.12[2]	2.10[2]
Brazil	1983	0.14[2]	0.73[2]
Chile	1983	0.92	0.70
Colombia	1983	0.36	0.94
Costa Rica	1983	0.19	1.76
Mexico	1983	0.21[2]	0.65[2]
Uruguay	1983	0.09[2]	1.00[2]

1.   Biased result due to 3-month lag.
2.   Rough estimate due to high inflation rates.
Source: UNCTAD, *Statistical Survey on Insurance and Reinsurance Operations in Developing Countries,* 14th January 1987.

In conclusion, except in a limited number of developing countries, neither social security nor the insurance sector play a decisive role in the collection and accumulation of funds. This is regrettable, when one recalls that a large part of the accumulation in the developed countries during the 19th and 20th centuries was achieved precisely in this manner.

Concluding Remarks

This chapter clearly shows that even if it is possible to draw up a taxonomy of the various institutions, schemes, and agents operating in the developing countries, one is nonetheless far from having satisfactory knowledge of the financial flows taking place. There is an urgent need to draw up a flow of funds account which would, ideally, trace all the actual financial relations between all the agents within the economy.

Table 2.24   DISTRIBUTION OF GROSS PREMIUMS BETWEEN LIFE AND NON-LIFE INSURANCE IN SELECTED DEVELOPING COUNTRIES

	Year	Percentage of gross premiums in	
		Life Insurance	Non-Life Insurance[1]
Africa			
Burundi	1983	0.0	100.0
Ethiopia	1983-84	3.0	97.0
Zambia	1984	29.6	70.4
Zimbabwe	1983	62.4	37.6
Asia			
Bangladesh	1983	26.5	73.5
India	1983	61.2	38.8
Indonesia	1984	27.3	72.7
South Korea	1984-85	78.2	21.8
Malaysia	1984	31.8	68.2
Philippines	1984	42.2	57.8
Singapore	1984	34.8	65.2
Thailand	1984	51.4	48.6
Latin America			
Argentina	1982-83	5.4	94.6
Brazil	1983	15.9	84.1
Chile	1983	56.8	43.2
Colombia	1983	27.9	72.1
Costa Rica	1983	10.0	90.0
Mexico	1983	24.5	75.5
Uruguay	1983	8.5	91.5

1. Includes fire, automobile, transportation and other insurance.
Source: UNCTAD, *Statistical Survey on Insurance and Reinsurance Operations in Developing Countries,* 14th January 1987.

The lack of data on informal financial operations makes it difficult to see how financial flows are related, how a formal loan can give rise to an informal deposit in a ROSCA, or how an indigenous banker can make a formal deposit, and so on. Research should be devoted to better measuring and assessing both the size and orientation of flows, as well as ascertaining their origin and final use. Such knowledge would be useful at the macroeconomic level for decision-makers seeking to define appropriate monetary, financial and investment policies, and at the microeconomic level for financial institutions seeking to better manage their activity.

Beyond the statistical measurement of flows, it is also important to know and understand the practices and modes of functioning of both formal and informal operators. This is the object of the next chapter.

NOTES AND REFERENCES

1. Kitchen, Richard L., *Finance for the Developing Countries*, Chichester, John Wiley and Sons, 1986, p. 119.

2. Kitchen, *op. cit.*, pp. 127-128.

3. This is not always the case, however; indeed, the outflow of rural funds towards urban areas is one of the various issues of rural finance which remains to be addressed.

4. Unesco, *Savings Mobilisation in Developing African Countries*, Paris, UNESCO, 1973.

5. Despite such advantages though, it should be pointed out that private development banks are reputed to be more vigorous, more efficient, and more profitable than their government-owned counterparts, largely because their portfolios are more diversified; because they are, by necessity, more effective mobilisers of savings; and because they are active in capital markets.
    See Gordon, D.L., *Development Finance Companies, State- and Privately-Owned: A Review*, World Bank Staff Working Paper No. 578, 1983. Cited by Kitchen, *op. cit.*, p. 126.

6. World Bank, *Indonesia: Rural Credit Study*, Report No. 4566-Ind., June 1983.

7. Other types of non-bank financial intermediaries may include finance and securities companies, investment corporations, mutual funds, etc. Although such activities may be on the rise in some cases, they are still relatively limited due to the underdeveloped nature of financial markets in most developing countries.

8. Short-term risks are usually financed on a pay-as-you-go basis; long-term risks may be financed by either method.

9. The savings mobilised by these institutions in a given year may be defined as the amount of contributions received less the amount of benefits paid out plus interest income and returns from the investment of surpluses.

10. Should this not be the case, there is a danger that the institutions involved may engage in speculative activities (often in real estate) and/or invest in foreign assets, thus aggravating problems of capital flight.

11. Such schemes may be set up by governments, employers, unions, or private individuals and may be compulsory or voluntary. Indeed, in some countries, the pensions branch of the social security system takes on the form of a compulsory, national level provident fund (as in Malaysia or Singapore, for example) that is run on a funded basis and whereby the benefits received are directly linked to the individual's contributions. Often, though, national (or public) pension schemes tend to veer to pay-as-you-go financing as they expand to include more workers with different income levels. Voluntary, private pension schemes are based of course on funded financing and are administered either by a bank, a life insurance company, or a pension fund manager.

12. Fry, Maxwell, J., *Money, Interest, and Banking in Economic Development*, Baltimore, The Johns Hopkins University Press, 1988, p. 292.

13. *Ibid.*, p. 290.

14. Some of the other types of bottlenecks to capital market development identified by Fry (*op. cit.*, pp. 289-290) in Turkey, but which could be partly or wholly applied to other developing countries, are: weak accounting and auditing capability, interlocking ownership and control of banks and business corporations (often the case in the Philippines), a lack of non-bank financial intermediaries to support capital market activities, an inadequate secondary market, and inadequate supervisory mechanisms.

15. Tun Wai, U and Hugh T. Patrick, "Stock and Bond Issues and Capital Markets in Less Developed Countries", *IMF Staff Papers*, July 1973, vol. 20, No. 2, p. 268.

16. These types of schemes have different names in different countries: savings and credit co-operatives, credit unions, savings and loan associations, "popular banks", "popular funds", etc., are among the numerous appellations which (often) denote the same type of scheme and modes of operation. However, we shall set aside national particularities and use the terms "co-operatives" and "credit unions".

17. In some countries, credit unions were created specifically to mobilise rural savings. The "Banques Populaires" (People's Banks) in Rwanda are such an example.

18. The fact that savings and credit co-operatives and credit unions are administered by elected officers or volunteer members has both advantages and disadvantages. With ownership, control, and benefits in the members' hands, administration costs may indeed by low; however, there is also the risk of financial mismanagement due either to a lack of skills and knowledge or to corruption, with high loan delinquency or embezzlement of funds as potential results.

19. However, many, if not most, of these associations have accounts with banks where the collected savings are deposited, so that these funds are, in effect, introduced into formal financial channels.

20. However, in Rwanda, savings deposits with the "Banques Populaires" represent almost 20 per cent of the country's quasi-money. See Cuevas, Carlos E., "Savings and Loan Co-operatives in Rural Areas of Developing Countries: Recent Performance and Potential", *Savings and Development*, 1988, vol. 12, No. 1, pp. 5-17.

21. Ghate, P.B., "Informal Credit Markets in Asian Developing Countries", *Asian Development Review*, 1988, vol. 6, No. 1, p. 68.

22. *Ibid.*

23. Sometimes, the act of joining together not only gives the individual members of the group the opportunity to save and/or borrow the modest sums that are within their means, but also allows the group as a whole to gain access to formal financial institutions. This is the case, for example, when the amassed savings of the group are deposited in a bank account (group account or an account in the name of the leader or leaders of the group) or when banks themselves employ group lending practices, i.e. disburse block loans to the group which, in turn, decides, according to its own rules, how to allocate the funds among members.

24. For this reason, we shall focus in this section on savings clubs in Zimbabwe.

25. According to a survey by the German Development Institute, the initiative to set up a savings club most often comes from external promoters like extension workers or representatives of companies producing agricultural inputs. These persons also provide training as well as the books and stamps used to record members' savings and withdrawal transactions. They also play a role in the selection of income-generating activities, the wholesale ordering of inputs and the organisation of transport facilities. In the case of sponsorship of a savings club by a firm, sometimes the membership secures participation in the agricultural demonstrations organised by the company. See Radke, Detlef *et al., Mobilization of Personal Savings in Zimbabwe Through Financial Development*, Berlin, 1986, German Development Institute, mimeographed report.

26. The literacy rate is 60 per cent in Zimbabwe (Möller, case study on Zimbabwe for the OECD Development Centre, p. 61).

27. If a member wants to withdraw less than four dollars, he may buy stamps to make up the difference.

28. The German Development Institute report points out that for the treasurer, the husband's character is often taken into account as well; since she is responsible for holding or banking the club's savings, he must be honest too, if the funds are not to be misused. Husbands also agree to their wives' acting as officers, especially when they must attend training courses.

29. According to Mauri, mutual aid associations – known as *idirs* in Ethiopia – first appeared in Addis Ababa as ethnic group associations among migrants seeking to maintain cultural ties with home; but now polyethnic *idirs* are becoming widespread and carry out the opposite function of encouraging national integration among the various ethnic groups. See Mauri, case study on Ethiopia for the OECD Development Centre, p. 51.

30. In fact, the main feature of rural *idirs* in Ethiopia is that they seek to insure members against a wide range of risks and to guarantee coverage not only by cash payments but also through the provision of services in favour of the needy member. Mauri describes a rural *idir*, consisting of 45 families, and the coverage provided. In case of hospitalisation of a member, the others harvest his crop and lend him money without interest, which is repaid at harvest time. If someone's ox is stolen, the others help him cultivate his land until a new ox is bought and give him a lump sum of money towards the purchase. If a member's house is destroyed by fire, the other members help him rebuild it and give him money to buy furniture. See Mauri, *op. cit.*

31. Indeed, the analogy with "formal" social insurance schemes is not as inappropriate as may at first seem, especially from the functional point of view. In the case of Ethiopian *idirs*, for example, the balance of the total sums collected and deposited with the Commercial Bank of Ethiopia fluctuates according to the ratio of contributions to claims (which is also a function of the average age of members) and to particular periods when the number of deaths within the group are abnormally high or low. If necessary, the periodical amount required may be increased, additional contributions may be requested, or the lump sum paid out reduced. This type of adjustment of the sums involved reflects the absence of actuarial calculations in the context of what could otherwise be considered an insurance scheme.

32. Miracle, Marvin P., Diane S. Miracle and Laurie Cohen, "Informal Savings Mobilization in Africa", *Economic Development and Cultural Change*, July 1980, vol. 28, No. 4, p. 709.

33. This is the case in Nigeria, as reported by Isong, Clement N., "Modernization of the Esusu Credit Society", Conference Proceedings, Ibadan, Nigerian Institute of Social and Economic Research, 1958. Cited by Miracle, Miracle and Cohen, *op. cit.*, p. 710.

34. Holst, Juergen U., "The Role of Informal Financial Institutions in the Mobilization of Savings", in Kessler, D. and P.-A. Ullmo, eds., *Savings and Development*, Paris, Economica, 1985, pp. 121-152.

35. Madhur, S. and C.P.S. Nayar, case study on India for the OECD Development Centre.

36. Drake, P.J., *Money, Finance and Development*, Oxford, 1980, p. 141. Wai, U.T., "A Revisit to Interest Rates Outside the Organized Money Markets of Underdeveloped Countries", *Banco Nazionale del Lavoro Quarterly Review*, September 1977, vol. 2, No. 22, p. 298. Cited by Holst, *op. cit.*, p. 124.

37. Harriss, B., "Money and Commodities: Their Interaction in a Rural Indian Setting", p. 235, in Von Pischke, J.D. and Dale W. Adams and Gordon Donald, eds., *Rural Financial Markets in Developing Countries – Their Use and Abuse*, Baltimore, Johns Hopkins University Press for the Economic Development Institute of the World Bank, EDI Series in Economic Development, 1983.

38. Limiting the number of depositors per firm could have adverse effects in the sense that it may contribute to an increase in the number of finance corporations, since it is uneconomical to operate with 250 depositors per firm and since there is no legislation barring multiple partnerships in a number of firms.

39. Madhur and Nayar, *op. cit.*, p. 86.

40. In women's rice chitties, it was not uncommon for the winner of the prize to sell the rice and invest the proceeds in gold ornaments, household utensils or the purchase of a goat or cow.

41. Average exchange rate value 1985-1987: Rs 12.67 = US$ 1.

42. Many developing countries have, in fact, passed some form of legislation on informal lending activities, mainly anti-usury laws. Admittedly, this is going one step further than leaving informal sector operators totally on their own, but the legislation usually serves more as a guideline than as a straitjacket, and one may have some doubts as to how strictly the regulations are, or rather can be, enforced. In India, however, the legislative framework is one of the most comprehensive and all-encompassing, which has led some observers to talk of the "semi-formal" rather than "informal" sector in India.

43. It should be pointed out, however, that there is also a strong role played by cultural factors in determining the financing needs expressed as, for instance in the importance attached to ensuring oneself a proper funeral, which explains the extent of *idirs* in Ethiopia or burial societies in Zimbabwe.

44. Burundi's single insurance company (Société d'Assurances du Burundi – SOCABU), for instance, is a national monopoly that provides mostly automobile insurance and coverage for import-export activities, fire, and other damages; life insurance premiums are notably absent. Such a situation surely has an impact on both the volume of funds mobilised and their allocation.

45. Fry, *op. cit.*, p. 298.

46. According to Fry (*op. cit.*, p. 259), Mexico is one of the few developing countries that has managed to develop a relatively sound securities market, based on a local financial instrument known as the "financiera". This is a long-term, fixed dividend instrument with a competitively high yield; the issuing institution guarantees its repurchase at par (there is a market price floor).

47. Kessler, Denis and Dominique Strauss-Kahn, "Stock Exchanges and Development: the case of the Ivory Coast", in UNDIESA, *Savings for Development*, Report of the Second International Symposium on the Mobilization of Personal Savings in Developing Countries (Kuala Lumpur, Malaysia, 15-21 March 1982), New York, United Nations, 1984, pp. 44-51.

48. On the issue of financial liberalisation and the development of securities markets, it is important to note the on-going "debate". On the one hand, Drake states that "financial liberalisation is most likely to foster the flotation and trading of both corporate and government securities." On the other hand, Gill warns against the risk that financial liberalisation and deregulation that strengthens banks by permitting universal banking, for example, may weaken or even impede the development of bond and equity markets, as banks seek to dominate and stifle competition from the latter. Fry concludes that abolishing "interest rate ceilings is a prerequisite for security market development, but financial liberalisation that results in greater monopoly power for the banks may well impede such development." See: Drake, Peter J., "The Development of Equity and Bond Markets in the Pacific Region", in Tan, Augustine H.H. and Basant Kapur, eds., *Pacific Growth and Financial Interdependence*, Sydney, Allen and Unwin, 1986, pp. 97-124; Gill, David, "Furthering Securities Market Development", Paris, paper prepared for the 11th Annual Conference of the International Association of Securities Commissions and Similar Organizations, 15-18 July 1986; and Fry, *op. cit.*, pp. 281-291.

Chapter 3

OPERATIONS AND PRACTICES OF THE FORMAL AND INFORMAL FINANCIAL SECTORS

In Chapter 2 we focused on and contrasted the structural aspects of the formal and informal financial sectors – what types of institutions or schemes may be found, the functions assigned them, the lay-out of financial circuits – and presented, for the formal sector at least, the respective shares in financial circuits of the various institutions present.

In the present chapter, we shall look more closely at the operational aspects of the two sectors. Table 3.1 presents some of the most salient features of the way in which formal and informal transactions are carried out. In the pages that follow, we shall limit ourselves to a discussion of four main topics: localisation of activity, access to financial services, cost of intermediation, and market interlinkages in the informal sector. With the exception of the latter, these issues will be dealt with in parallel for the formal and informal sectors. Proceeding in this manner will help shed light on the nature of the relationship between the two sectors and on the strengths and weaknesses of each one; from there, the search for possible ways of linking the formal and informal sectors should be facilitated.

I. LOCALISATION OF ACTIVITY

The issue of localisation of activity cannot be approached in the same manner for the formal and informal financial sectors. In the case of the formal sector, it refers to an urban/rural dichotomy or, more specifically, to an urban bias of formal financial institutions in terms of the distribution of their branches over national territory and the (urban) concentration of their deposit and lending activities. In the case of the informal sector, by contrast, localisation refers to the limited radius of activity of informal financial schemes operating in both rural and urban zones. Indeed, informal savings and credit arrangements can be found in both rural and urban areas, but it cannot justly be said of the informal sector that it has a rural or urban "bias". Though in terms of financial activity the informal sector is generally more important in rural areas, with the advent of urbanisation and internal migration to the cities, it is rapidly becoming an urban phenomenon as well. There are even cases – Mexico and South Korea, for example – where the urban informal financial market is much larger than the rural one.

Table 3.1 COMPARISON OF THE FORMAL AND INFORMAL FINANCIAL SECTORS

INFORMAL FINANCIAL SECTOR	FORMAL FINANCIAL SECTOR
1. The informal financial sector provides savings and credit facilities for small farmers in rural areas, and for lower-income households and small-scale enterprises in urban areas.	1. Formal financial institutions totally ignore small farmers, lower-income households, and small-scale enterprises in favour of a large-scale, well-off, and literate clientele which can satisfy their stringent loan conditions.
2. The procedures of informal schemes are usually simple and straightforward; as they emanate from local cultures and customs, they are easily understood by the population.	2. Complex administrative procedures are beyond the understanding of the rural masses and small savers.
3. The informal sector mobilises rural savings and small savings from low-income urban households.	3. Formal financial institutions do not mobilise rural savings or small-scale deposits. Commercial banks could contribute to rural and small savings mobilisation if they had adequate branch networks and if they adopted the relevant procedures.
4. Informal groups operate at times and on days which are convenient for their members.	4. The working days and opening hours of formal financial institutions do not take rural work schedules into account; banks are open at times when farmers are at work in their fields.
5. Informal sector associations accept any amount of regular savings, even the most modest sums which a saver can afford to set aside. The financial techniques on which such informal groups are based lend themselves to the management of a large number of small accounts.	5. Formal sector institutions are selective regarding their clientele, so as to avoid having clients who make only small deposits. Their financial technology is not suited to the management of modest sums from a large number of savers.
6. Access to credit is simple, non-bureaucratic, and little based on written documents. Literacy is not a requisite.	6. Loan application procedures are complex and require reading and writing skills so that a file on the borrower may be established.
7. The simple and direct processing of loan requests allows for their prompt approval and a minimum delay in disbursement. Rejections are rare; but the level of risk is reflected in the interest rate charged.	7. Processing of loan requests is complex, resulting in long delays before final approval or rejection. Even when approval is obtained, loan delivery is slow.
8. Collateral requirements on loans are adapted to local conditions and borrowers' capacity. The conditions may be based either on regular contributions to ROSCAs or on precise knowledge of farm size and/or crops harvested so as to determine the borrower's capacity to repay the loan.	8. Collateral requirements correspond to the situation of the relatively well-off urban-dwellers: deposits or savings accounts in a commercial bank, property which can be mortgaged.
9. Transaction costs are low.	9. Transaction costs are high.
10. Repayment rates are high.	10. Repayment rates are low.
11. Because they emanate from the local environment, informal groups are aware of the problems that members may be confronted with, and therefore they can deal with repayment difficulties in a pragmatic manner. Debt rescheduling is possible.	11. Formal sector institutions do not have close contact with the environment in which they operate. Sometimes they prosecute defaulters, which can have negative social repercussions, while at other times they do not sue for reimbursement, leading borrowers to believe that formal loans are free.

INFORMAL FINANCIAL SECTOR	FORMAL FINANCIAL SECTOR
12. The informal sector has a dense and effective information network at the grass-roots level for close supervision and monitoring of borrower activity – particularly their cash flow – whether they are members of an informal association or not. This contributes to the efficient mobilisation of savings and ensures high loan repayment rates.	12. Unfamiliar with the grass-roots environment, formal institutions are ill-served by a mediocre supervisory and monitoring network, and are unable to gain insight into the activities of their clientele.
13. Within the informal sector, information is widely diffused. The regular meetings of informal savings and credit associations serve as a forum for dissemination of information.	13. Formal sector institutions do not have a good network for dissemination of information. In addition, they are out of touch with the rural masses and make little effort to seek ways of reaching them.
14. The interest paid on deposits in the informal sector compares favourably with that paid in the formal sector, thus providing an incentive for rural and small urban households to save.	14. Some institutions of the formal sector do not even offer savings facilities. Others apply low – or sometimes even negative – real interest rates, thus putting off many a potential saver.
15. The informal sector charges competitive lending rates; though they are sometimes high, this reflects the scarcity of loanable funds. There is little connection between deposit and lending rates.	15. Public institutions charge very low – sometimes negative – real interest rates on loans. Commercial banks apply moderate lending rates which are nonetheless considerably higher than the interest paid on savings. The link between deposit and lending rates is weak.
16. There are no investment opportunities for savings which have been mobilised but which have not been lent.	16. There are investment opportunities for savings which have been mobilised but which have not been lent.
17. The informal sector usually does not keep a written record on the borrowing and/or saving activities of its clientele. When it does, the procedures are relatively simple.	17. The formal sector keeps written records on the activities of clients, although the information recorded is sometimes irrelevant.
18. The volume and availability of loanable funds are subject to seasonal fluctuations.	18. The formal sector regularly has loanable funds available.
19. The informal sector is not subsidised by the government, nor does it receive grants or other forms of support from donor agencies.	19. Formal sector institutions are subsidised by the government and may also receive grants and other support from donor agencies.
20. Savings and credit mechanisms in the informal sector are not geared towards accumulating funds before the peak season when loan requests are highest.	20. A regular supply of funds allows the formal sector to lend at any time of the year. This is not the case with government lending institutions, which are deprived of sufficient funds because of high defaults rates on their loans.
21. Despite the widespread dissemination of information within the informal sector, informal groups are often unaware of new farming methods, and so members do not learn of new techniques which would allow them to increase production levels and raise their standard of living.	21. Formal sector institutions could reach a widely dispersed rural clientele by collaborating with government extension units. In practice, though, they do not resort to such intermediaries and do not provide financial services in rural areas.

Source : Adapted from Obioma, B.K., "Rural Financial Services in Nigeria: Lessons from the Traditional Financial Group Markets", Doctoral Dissertation, Pontifical Gregorian University, Rome, 1983.

Most often, and to a large extent with good reason, the urban bias of the formal sector is the object of criticism, whereas the overt localism of financial activity in the informal sector is perceived as one of the latter's very strengths. However, as we shall see below, both situations must be put into the right perspective, and one must not be led to believe that localised financing is necessarily the "solution" to the regional imbalances in financial activity.

A. THE URBAN BIAS OF THE FORMAL FINANCIAL SECTOR

That there is an urban bias of the formal financial sector can be seen from the need for the public authorities in developing countries to implement special schemes, set up special institutions and otherwise provide incentives (rediscounting facilities or subsidised interest rates) in order to encourage banks to set up shop in rural areas and engage more actively in rural/agricultural lending. These policies have not always met with an unmitigated success. In effect, there would seem to be a sort of de facto specialisation of formal financial institutions in many developing countries, including those of our sample: it is mostly (rural) development banks that operate in rural areas, and then they usually only provide lending facilities; the other formal financial institutions – commercial banks and merchant banks (both national and foreign), building societies, and even non-bank financial intermediaries – prefer to confine their activities to the urban areas. Savings banks and postal savings networks, though of easy access, also may contribute to an outflow of rural savings towards urban zones through their lending policies (savings banks lend mostly for urban real estate purposes) or the absence thereof (postal savings banks do not lend funds). Even co-operatives may be urban-based[1].

The predilection of formal financial institutions for urban areas may be gauged from the distribution of bank branches over national territory and the rural-urban share of deposits and loans. Directly related to, if not at the root of, this geographical bias is also the sectoral bias, that is, the relatively low share of agricultural credit in total bank credit compared to the shares of the industrial, manufacturing, construction or commercial/trade (imports and exports) sectors.

1. The Distribution of Bank Branches

From the point of view of branch distribution, it should be pointed out that in many developing countries, poor infrastructure and communications facilities may render it costly for banks to set up local branches in outlying areas. Thus, the density ratios of banks (expressed as the number of people per institution) in the Philippines, for example, are 18 000 in rural areas and 6 000 in urban areas. In Mexico, where the financial sector is relatively well developed, the density ratio is equally high, at 18 500 inhabitants per bank office; 75 per cent of bank offices are concentrated in the larger cities. Likewise, in Zimbabwe, only 40 per cent of the total number of permanent branches of the Post Office Savings Bank, commercial banks, and building societies were located in areas with 10 000 inhabitants or less.

In some countries, however, the number of rural branches exceeds the number of urban ones: rural branches represent 66 per cent of the total number of bank branches in Bangladesh, for instance; and in the Philippines, despite the disparity in density ratios, this proportion is 60 per cent.

2. The Rural-Urban Share of Deposits and Loans

A large number of rural branches does not necessarily translate into a commensurate share of deposit and lending activity between rural and urban areas, however. To continue with the two previous examples: rural deposits as a percentage share of total deposits with the banking system were, despite the higher proportion of rural branches, only 17 per cent in Bangladesh in 1984, and the corresponding figure for the Philippines in 1983 was 18 per cent.

With respect to credit, the rural share is also dwarfed: Thailand is a classic example, where 80 per cent of total bank credit is accounted for by the Bangkok metropolitan area. Similarly, the highest concentration of credit in Indonesia is in Jakarta and the more urbanised regions of Central and East Java; in Malaysia, it is in Kuala Lumpur and its environs, and in the Philippines, in the greater Manila area[2]. In the latter country, for instance, the bulk of commercial bank deposits in 1983 came from rural areas (72 per cent), yet only 41 per cent of the total was invested there. Likewise, in Mexico, more than 25 per cent of total deposits in 1987 came from rural areas, which received only 7 per cent of total credit in that same year. This is indeed indicative of a net outflow of funds from rural to urban areas.

On the microeconomic level, one may also examine the credit to deposit ratios of rural and urban bank branches, which help to determine whether the latter are net deposit or net credit centres. These estimates are usually available to central banks but are seldom published, for reasons of political sensitivity, as they may reveal the extent to which rural savings are channelled into urban investments. However, we do have the figures for 1983 for the Philippines: the total loan to deposit ratios for all banks were 97.7 for rural branches and 159.6 for urban branches. The gap was even wider in the case of commercial banks taken on their own: 58.3 for rural areas, 140.2 for urban areas.

3. Share of Agricultural Credit in Total Credit

To some extent, the relatively low share of rural areas in overall lending may also be appraised from the sectoral point of view, that is, by examining the share of agriculture in total credit (compared to the proportion allotted to other sectors) and in GDP. The figures here would seem to corroborate the aforementioned findings. For instance, during the 1980s, agricultural loans in the Philippines accounted, on average and in value, for 8 per cent of total loans, whereas agriculture represented 24 per cent of GDP in 1987. In Indonesia as well, the agricultural sector which represented 26 per cent of GDP in 1987, received 8 per cent of total bank credits, while the manufacturing sector accounted for 14 per cent of GDP and received 35 per cent of credits.

The 1985 figures for some of the African countries of our sample also showed a disparity. In Togo, agricultural loans accounted for 2 per cent of total bank credits while agriculture accounted for 29 per cent of GDP. The agricultural sector in Burundi received 4-5 per cent of all medium-and long-term credits (compared with 44 per cent for the construction sector); agriculture represented 59 per cent of GDP in 1987, and industry 14 per cent.

In the Mexican case, the share of agriculture both in total credit and in GDP showed a downward trend. In effect, the proportion of credit channelled towards agriculture by development banks fell from 20 per cent in 1970 to 6 per cent in 1987, and that of commercial banks fell from 13.5 per cent to 7 per cent. Over the same period, the share of agriculture in GDP dropped from 14 per cent to 9 per cent.

4. The Urban Bias of the Formal Financial Sector Reviewed

The empirical evidence – however scanty – presented above on the rural/urban and agricultural/non-agricultural aspects of formal financial activity lends credence to the hypothesis of financial urban bias, which is that "in many (developing) countries ... the banking system, if not regulated to act differently, easily becomes an instrument for siphoning off the savings from the poorer regions to the richer and more progressive ones where (the rates of profit) are high and secure"[3]. In other words, local deposits exceed local credit in the rural areas whereas the inverse is true of urban areas, with the net surplus of rural deposits being transferred to the urban branches.

While the empirical evidence seems to suggest that this is undoubtedly true, it is also important 'to put the phenomenon into perspective. First of all, note must be made of the fact that deposits are only one form of savings and hence excess deposits do not necessarily represent the totality of excess savings. Account must be taken of the flow of total savings in all forms before generalising about the rural transfer to urban areas. Moreover, there are also flows in the reverse direction, that is, urban wage-earners' remittances to relatives back home in the village. Data on such inter-regional transfers is scarce, however; deposits remain the best measurement, and they point to an outflow of rural savings.

Secondly, although the nature of the banking structure does affect the ease with which such inter-regional transfers are made, there are also other reasons behind such behavior on the part of both bankers and the public. Among these are: i) the absence of profitable lending opportunities in rural areas; ii) the high average cost of small transactions, very often compounded by deliberate, low interest rate policies imposed by the monetary authorities; and iii) the limited initiative and decision-making powers conferred upon the managers of local and regional financial institutions. A corollary of the fact that rural branch managers often cannot sanction loans above specified, and usually low, amounts is that a greater number of loans are disbursed from urban branches because customers borrow through the (urban) head offices while maintaining their deposits at the local (rural) branch.

A final argument put forward is that, to a certain extent, the urban bias is unavoidable if the financial system is at all market-oriented, whereby banks allocate resources according to the criterium of maximum returns. Banks transfer resources from surplus to deficit areas; it so happens that the credit-intensity of urban economic activity is greater and that the rates of return on urban credit and investment are higher[4].

In sum, the foregoing serves to show that the urban bias of the formal financial sector may indeed be "supply-determined", i.e. originate in the portfolio behaviour of lending institutions, but that the transfer of financial resources from rural to urban areas may also reflect failures of rural financial markets.

Moreover, one must be careful not to take the parity of share in credit and share in GDP as the ultimate reference. Indeed, a difference between the sectoral and geographical distribution of credit and the shares in GDP should not necessarily be seen in a negative light; the fact that agriculture is allotted a lower share of credit than its share in GDP or than industry may correspond to explicit political and economic policy choices on the part of the public authorities. What one should look for here is the rationale behind this, and see whether or not credit policy is consistent with and serves effectively as a tool in the conception and implementation of overall macroeconomic and sectoral policies.

B. THE LOCALISM OF THE INFORMAL FINANCIAL SECTOR

The localisation of activity in the case of the informal financial sector refers not to a rural-urban dichotomy, as for the formal financial sector, but to the circumscribed area of operations of the various informal savings and credit arrangements which are encountered in both rural and urban areas. Such a "local bias", if it may thus be called, in fact constitutes one of the very strengths of the informal financial sector: since the schemes are set up in response to the specific needs of a particular group of people (borrowers and lenders), they develop and evolve with the circumstances prevalent in the particular rural or urban setting in which they operate. Moreover, limiting operations to a specific geographic area or defined group of people allows for personal knowledge of borrowers and consequently a better assessment of their creditworthiness.

Most, if not all, informal transactions – be they the work of rural-based or urban-based moneylenders, mutual associations or partnership firms – involve a clientele drawn from within a narrow operating radius, as we shall see below.

1. Moneylenders' Clientele

In rural areas, individual moneylending is the work of landlords, farmers, or traders who may or may not be residents of the village in which they carry out their lending activities. Landlords and farmer-lenders most often are local residents. Some farmer-lenders do transact outside their village of residence but this is usually rare since geographic mobility in rural areas tends to be low. Trader-lenders, on the other hand, are more likely to be from outside the borrower's village, especially if they are itinerant traders or produce traders who transport agricultural goods to urban markets.

As an example, let us refer to a 1984-85 survey of 52 villages in the Nakhon Ratchasima province in Thailand, by the Thailand Development Research Institute and the Thai Khadi Research Institute, which estimated the share of credit by types of informal lenders (see Table 3.2). It is interesting to note the substantially lower share of loans from farmers and fixed-income recipients *outside* the borrower's village compared to the corresponding figures from the same types of lenders *within* the borrower's village. By contrast, loans from traders outside the borrower's village outnumbered those from local traders.

Clearly, a resident lender is in a good position to assess a potential borrower's creditworthiness, if only because of the proximity of living and working conditions. Even in the case of outside lenders, however, close knowledge of their clients' financial position is possible for the simple reason that, though they may move from one village to another, the number of villages served is still relatively limited and, moreover, they deal regularly with the same clients.

Personal contacts, a limited geographical area of operations (neighbourhood, marketplace), and regularity of transactions are also at the basis of urban informal moneylending. Neighbourhood storeowners are eventually able to select from amongst their customers those to whom they are willing to extend credit on favorable terms. Mobile bankers operating amongst market vendors in African marketplaces also carve out for themselves a niche in the informal financial market[5].

Thus, in the case of individual moneylenders, both rural and urban, gaining a relatively sound opinion on the financial status of their clients is the result of a continued presence within a delimited area of operations.

Table 3.2   SHARE OF CREDIT BY TYPES OF INFORMAL LENDERS
(Nakhon Ratchasima province, Thailand, 1984-85, 52 villages)

	Share in the Number of Contracts (per cent)	Share of Loan Amount (per cent)
Farmers within the borrowers' village	32.4	28.6
Farmers outside the borrowers' village	4.3	5.3
Traders within the borrowers' village	15.3	12.3
Traders outside the borrowers' village	23.5	20.8
Fixed-income recipients within the borrowers' village	12.0	16.0
Fixed-income recipients outside the borrowers' village	2.3	1.6
Rentier	2.1	2.8
Finance partnerships	1.4	1.5

Source: Thailand Development Research Institute/Thai Khadi Research Institute Survey, cited by Siamwalla, Ammar, 'Thai Rural Credit System: Some Empirical Findings and a Theoretical Framework", mimeo, 1987, p. 16.

2.   The Common Bond in Mutual Associations

If the members of a mutual association (fixed-fund, self-help, mutual aid, ROSCA, etc.) are to know and trust each other well, then this of itself implies some localisation or a circumscribed area of activity.

In rural areas it is again the village (which may also coincide with the ethnic criterion in those cases where it plays a role), and this for very practical reasons: not only does everyone know his neighbour, but attendance at meetings does not require travelling, which can be difficult and costly in terms of money, effort and time.

In the cities, a number of other criteria in addition to the residential one (neighbourhood associations are common) have also emerged. Members of an urban-based mutual association may have a common employer (occupational bonds) or they may practice the same trade or operate on the same marketplace (professional bonds). Sometimes the bonds may be of an ethnic or social nature: in Ethiopia for example, some *ekubs* and *idirs* limit membership to people with a certain income-level (and hence belonging to a certain social class). In all these cases, it is clear that activity is restricted, if not to a certain area (neighbourhood, factory, market, etc.), then to a specific group of people with defined needs and socio-economic characteristics.

3.   Partnership Firms

Partnership firms are, as has already been pointed out, specific to certain countries (mostly in Asia) and are an urban phenomenon. They too confine their activities to a limited area on the city, province, or state level. Whether in corporate or non-corporate form, partnership firms like to know their customers well (and in fact, compared to formal financial institutions, they generally do); customers are usually business acquaintances who must be known, if not recommended, by at least one of the partners of the firm.

Private financiers also want to be able to follow up on pending loans. Since most firms operate as family businesses, it is evident that they cannot spread themselves too thin by extending their operations beyond the limits of the agglomeration they are working in.

Informal financial mechanisms are indeed very localised. But it should also be pointed out that the informal sector's localism does not necessarily imply an absence of variety of the financial services available to users, who often have access, within their circumscribed area of action, to more than one type of scheme or source[6]. Thus there may be more than one moneylender operating within the precincts of a village. Sixty per cent of Thai villages, for example, have from three to five lenders operating in their vicinity. (It should be pointed out, however, that borrowers do not necessarily face a competitive lenders' market, since they may be tied to one particular lender by a previous loan or transaction.)

Similarly, within the same community (the village in rural areas, the neighborhood in urban areas), there may be a number of mutual associations, all operating simultaneously, each with a different size of membership, contribution amounts, frequency of meetings and hence length of cycle. People who have the means for multiple membership thus have the possibility of choosing the scheme or schemes most suited to their affinities and to the variation of their cash flow needs (provided they are accepted by the other members of the group).

As for the different types of partnership firms in urban areas, the variety of financing combinations which they can propose may also be quite extensive.

4. The Pros and Cons of Localised Financing

From the perspective of localisation of activity, the formal and informal sectors would seem to be opposed in the sense that the former drains resources from one region (usually rural) to another (usually urban) while the latter, almost by necessity, operates on the basis of the local use of funds within the given community, region, or otherwise circumscribed area whence they were mobilised. Such a system of localised financing, or "endogenous circulation of capital", presents a number of advantages and disadvantages[7].

There are three main advantages that can be derived from limiting operations to a specific geographic area and/or a defined group of people.

First, as we have seen, personal knowledge of the area and of borrowers allows for a better assessment of creditworthiness and for closer monitoring of outstanding loans. Moreover, it means that the financial services provided and the allocation of resources can be adapted to specific needs, as they appear, within the community. Secondly, the level of involvement and responsibility of the population concerned is usually high, especially in the case of savings and loan associations where, in theory, all participants are committed to maintaining a well-run, viable scheme. Finally, since the mode of financing is that of a "closed circuit", the notion of a link between (prior) savings and credit is reinforced.

On the other hand, one of the disadvantages is that a closed and self-financing circuit at the local or regional level functions within the limits allowed by local capital supply and demand. Indeed, there is a certain "volatility" of deposits and a risk of massive defaults on loans, for example, should a natural disaster hit the whole community at once. A second issue is whether a given community can provide sufficient profitable opportunities for the efficient local use of all the surplus funds collected and available. This leads directly to the third "drawback" of localised financing which is the absence of links with outside sources of funds that could serve to channel resources from surplus to deficit regions (and help solve any occasional liquidity problems, as in the case of a temporary scarcity of funds cited above). Inter-regional transfers are important because the various economic activities, which are not necessarily of the same credit-intensity, are not present in the same proportions in the different regions of one country[8] – hence the regional financing needs (and absorptive capacity) are also different.

Thus it is clear that the issue of the local use of local savings is not itself a simple one, and that it must be placed in a more global economic and financial context. As we have seen, neither the urban bias of the formal sector, nor the localised financing which characterises the informal sector are favourable to an efficient allocation of resources on the macroeconomic level.

In sum, excessive regional imbalances do exist and should be righted so that a greater proportion of the resources mobilised locally are channelled back into their region or community of origin; at the same time though, a certain degree (which still remains to be determined) of inter-regional transferring of resources should not be excluded de facto, as it makes possible the flow of funds from surplus to deficit areas.

II. ACCESS TO FINANCIAL SERVICES

The issue of access to financial services is a central one in the debate on the formal and informal financial sectors. Whether it is on the matter of the characteristics of borrowers (and savers), the size of the sums involved, the use of funds, collateral requirements or lending and deposit procedures, the descriptions which emerge for each case (formal and informal sector) can be contrasted almost on a point by point basis. This stems largely from the fact that the informal financial sector deals with what the formal sector leaves aside by way of deposit and lending activity.

A. CHARACTERISTICS OF CLIENTELE

The characteristics of formal and informal sector clientele are best approached from the viewpoint of the direction of lending by formal and informal operators. Indeed, once the preferred sectors, areas, and categories of clientele are discerned, it becomes fairly easy to identify, along general lines, the different borrower (and saver) groups[9].

Taking up the case of the formal sector first, one notes that the lending policies of formal financial institutions display a triple bias whereby preference is given to: i) the public sector over the private sector; ii) urban areas of activity over rural ones and, by extension, non-agricultural loans over agricultural loans; and iii) large-scale enterprises over small-scale ones, particularly as regards lending to the private sector. Each of these biases may be more or less pronounced in each sample country.

Loans to government and the public sector often outweigh loans to the private sector (crowding out effect). In Zambia for example, the central government is by far the largest beneficiary of domestic credit: in 1986, claims on central government accounted for 80 per cent of total domestic credit and claims on the private sector for 20 per cent. The Mexican government also dominates both the credit and securities markets: in 1987, 78 per cent of total domestic credit was channelled to the public sector (22 per cent to the private sector), while government securities represented 90 per cent of the total value of fixed-rate security transactions[10].

There may be several explanations for this type of bias. Aside from cases where formal financial institutions are statutorily required to invest a certain portion of their resources in government securities or to contribute to the financing of public enterprises or development projects (the case of the National Savings and Credit Bank in Zambia, for example), they may actually choose to allocate their resources in this manner for the relatively lower risk and greater security it ensures, disregarding the fact that higher returns could be obtained from a more venturesome and innovative but no less vigilant lending and/or investment policy. Another reason for such a choice may simply be a lack of profitable investment opportunities in the private sector.

The second bias stems from the preference of formal financial institutions to operate in urban rather than rural zones and to grant non-agricultural rather than agricultural loans. The result is a marked geographical and sectoral imbalance in their lending portfolios. This issue has already been discussed at some length in the previous section. Suffice it to add here that the urban bias can be largely explained by considerations of high operating costs in rural areas. Non-agricultural loans (to industrial, commercial, manufacturing or real estate businesses) are preferred to agricultural ones because they are less risky and provide quicker returns.

Finally, the preference for large-scale borrowers over small-scale ones is manifest in both urban and rural lending. In the case of the Development Bank of Zambia, for instance, it is even explicitly stipulated that the latter's objective is to contribute to the development of economically viable enterprises in various sectors, but not to lend to individuals or small enterprises. Hence, in the urban setting, the financing needs of small- and medium-scale enterprises as well as craftsmen are usually neglected by the formal financial sector.

As for rural/agricultural lending, which in any case is given second place, priority is given to non-agricultural activities based in rural areas and then to medium- and large-scale commercial or export farming. In Zambia, agricultural parastatals and large-scale commercial farmers are the favored borrowers. In the Philippines, agricultural lending is usually limited to export crop plantations or mill-owners. In Mexico, loans for agriculture are directed towards large-scale agro-industrial complexes and medium- and large-scale farmers with access to modern farming technologies. True, efforts are being made in many developing countries to focus on providing financial services to small-scale farmers but, on the whole, their share in total lending activity as yet remains marginal.

As an illustration, a survey conducted in the Philippines in 1974 on the distribution of formal credit by farm size gave the results shown in Table 3.3. Although the figures are rather dated, there seems to be little reason to believe that the situation has greatly changed.

Regarding loans and savings facilities for individuals, little information is available, but it is safe to assume that it is probably the urban-based, higher-income groups along with civil servants who benefit the most from such services.

From the foregoing then, it follows that: i) the formal financial sector primarily serves the upper-income social categories and ii) that its clientele consists mainly of urban-based, medium- and large-scale, public or private enterprises (industry, commerce, manufacturing) and, in the rural areas, of large-scale and usually commercial farming activities.

Table 3.3   DISTRIBUTION OF FORMAL CREDIT BY FARM SIZE
(The Philippines, 1974)

Farm Size (Hectares)	Percent Share of Total Farms	Percent Share in Total Volume of Formal Credit
>1	14	0
1-3	47	19
3-5	24	8
<5	15	72

Source: Presidential Committee on Agricultural Credit, "Financing Agricultural Development: The Action Program (Agricultural Credit Plan 1977-1982)", Manila, 1977.

Turning now to the informal financial sector, which caters to the needs of those denied access to formal financial institutions, the characteristics of its clientele may be contrasted with those of the formal sector point by point. The informal sector does not lend to government or the public sector. It lends to the private sector in both urban and rural areas.

In the urban areas, it covers the working capital credit requirements of craftsmen, independent workers, and small- and medium-scale informal enterprises. In some countries (India, South Korea and Thailand) it is known to have become important in financing the working capital requirements of formal sector manufacturing and trade enterprises. But this is more the exception than the rule. Small borrowers and new borrowers proposing risky ventures (such as the cinema industry in India) or possessing few assets to offer as collateral (for example restaurants) or for whom speed of credit delivery is essential (as in export credit) address themselves to the informal sector. The lower-income urban households also resort to informal financial services, mainly for consumption credit and savings facilities.

In stark contrast to formal financial institutions, informal financial operators are very active in rural areas; in fact, in most countries it is the rural informal sector which is dominant. Moreover, the informal savings and credit schemes are centered on financing the consumption and working capital needs of small farmers.

In summary, the informal financial sector deals precisely with those categories of borrowers and savers that the formal sector neglects, that is, small-scale farmers and rural households, low- and sometimes middle-income urban households, craftsmen and small- and medium-scale urban enterprises.

B.   SIZE OF THE SUMS INVOLVED

Not surprisingly, the size of the sums involved in savings and lending transactions by the formal and informal financial sectors is consistent with the characteristics of their respective clientele.

Large sums are typical of formal financial institutions, so much so that special schemes must be created within the formal sector for small-scale lending and deposit mobilisation.

At any rate, large-scale borrowers often have a need for and can absorb a high loan sum. Moreover, formal financial institutions incur high per unit transaction costs, which is why they often impose minimum deposit, balance and transaction requirements; these conditions can only be met by the higher-income categories, and as such, constitute an entry barrier for the majority of households and for small-scale enterprises.

Conversely, flexibility of operations in the informal sector and the consequent low transaction costs incurred, underpin the capacity and willingness of informal lenders to deal in small sums. It should be further pointed out that many of the borrowers and savers concerned neither have a need for nor would be able to absorb large sums.

Informal savings and lending arrangements usually do not entail any minimum transaction requirements: lenders respond to borrower requests, and ROSCA contributions are set at levels affordable to members. In those cases where there are minimum contribution constraints, provisions may be made for several people to group together and subscribe to one quota (as in Ethiopian *ekubs,* for example).

Unfortunately, there is very little data on the average size of loans in both the formal and informal sectors. One example in the formal sector that can be cited concerns minimum deposit requirements with commercial banks in Zimbabwe, which are around Z$ 40-50[11]. As a very rough assessment of the ability of most depositors to meet these conditions, one may quote another figure: the balance on 55 per cent of all savings accounts with the Post Office Savings Bank (which is geared towards small and/or rural savers) is less than Z$ 20. One may thus infer that the restrictions imposed by the commercial banks do not correspond to small saver capacity or preferences.

The same may be said of small savers in Mexico, who also face institutional barriers: the minimum requirement to open a current or a savings account is the equivalent of US$30-40. According to the 1983-1984 household budget survey, however, around 35 per cent of all households have a monthly income that is less than the minimum wage level which is equivalent to US$100, and in rural areas taken alone, this proportion is more than 50 per cent.

An additional obstacle for small savers in the Mexican case stems from the fact that their savings accounts are eroded by high inflation. In June 1987, 62 per cent of all savings accounts had an average balance of 1 277 pesos which at the time corresponded to US$0.95. In effect, the number of savings accounts barely tops 2 million, and these are held mostly by those members of the middle class who have a long tradition of saving as well as sufficiently high incomes to withstand erosion by inflation.

As for the informal sector, very little information was available on loan sums from moneylenders. One example which may be cited is that of the moneylenders operating in the market-places of Mexico City. Known as "coyotes", these are actually usurers who lend high sums, ranging from US$500-3 000, for a very short-term period, i.e. one day, to traders with short-term cash requirements. The interest rates on these "morning to night loans", as they are known, are around 10 per cent per day.

The range of contribution levels in ROSCAs in several of the sample countries are also of some interest. In some countries, the levels remain rather low: tontine contributions in Togo may range from FCFA 100 per week to FCFA 10 000 per month; while in Zimbabwe, membership fees were between Z$ 0.20 and Z$ 0.50 in 67 per cent of the savings clubs surveyed. In other countries, where ROSCAs are more developed and are becoming increasingly sophisticated, the sums may be substantially greater. *Ekub* contributions in Ethiopia may range from 0.50 birrs per day (small, shoeshiners' *ekubs* in Addis Ababa) to 204 birrs per month (large, traders' *ekubs*). Perhaps one of the most impressive examples in Africa is Cameroon, where tontine contributions in Douala may reach levels of FCFA

500 000 per month in a group of 30 people. Some tontines are also known to involve a total prize lot of FCFA 500 million – a useful lump sum for a large trader in Douala seeking to clear imported goods from customs.

As elsewhere, in Mexico, the contribution levels in *tandas* (the local names for ROSCAs) are a function of the income level of members. Thus contributions may range anywhere from the equivalent of US$13-220 per month (although the *tanda* "prototype" is most probably between US$10-20 per month). For example, *tandas* organised by taxi drivers may call for contributions of US$100-200 a month. In cases of *tandas* organised by higher level income groups, contributions may reach US$450 per month.

C. USE OF FUNDS

1. The Formal Financial Sector

As official policies place the emphasis on productive investment to stimulate economic growth, it is not surprising that most lending by formal financial institutions is channelled into the long-term investment projects of large-scale enterprises, mostly in the industrial, manufacturing, commercial, and often also the construction sectors. By contrast, we have very little information on formal loans to private individuals and on the use of the funds thus received. However, in view of the characteristics of the private clientele of the formal financial sector as described earlier (mostly the upper-income social categories), it may be assumed that loans are requested largely for real estate (housing) or consumption (education, consumer durables, ceremonial expenses, etc.) purposes.

Regarding the motives for saving by formal sector clients, the data was equally scant. We have the results of one survey carried out in India by the National Institute of Bank Management, which are presented in Table 3.4. It becomes clear that, in both urban and rural cases, the most important motives for saving are: provision for emergencies, for old age, for children's education, and for marriage (ceremonial expenditures). In addition, provision for the acquisition of farm assets is a strong motive for rural bank savers.

2. The Informal Financial Sector

While the same motives for saving as those above can be observed amongst informal sector clientele, the debate is much more lively on the use of funds in the informal financial sector, which is often accused of having a negative impact on overall growth and development because it allegedly diverts savings to private consumption and unproductive uses, or to investments having low productivity and development priority.

The use of funds in the informal sector is extremely diverse, and often innovative. Informal savings and credit mechanisms are generally of a short-term and/or seasonal nature; and although much of informal lending is indeed for consumption purposes, empirical evidence shows that funds may be channelled into productive uses as well – sometimes consumption does not even represent the major share.

Consumption lending may be divided into four categories[12]: i) loans for subsistence or emergency reasons (including food during the pre-harvest gap, medical expenses, etc.), ii) loans for housing and education, iii) loans for the purchase of consumer durables, and iv) loans for "conspicuous consumption", i.e. ceremonial expenditures and the like. The

Table 3.4 MOTIVES FOR SAVING BY BANK SAVERS IN INDIA

Motives for savings	(Percentages)	
	Urban bank savers	Rural bank savers
1. Provision for emergencies	82	85
2. Provision for old age	65	62
3. Provision for children's education	63	65
4. Provision for marriage	58	64
5. Provision for festivals	31	31
6. Provision for acquisition of house/property	27	26
7. Provision for consumer durables	26	24
8. Provision for business expansion	23	30
9. Provision for additional income	19	16
10. Provision for pilgrimage	16	14
11. Provision for payment of debts	10	11
12. Provision for acquisition of farm assets	10	46

Source: National Institute of Bank Management, *All-India Savings and Deposit Trends and Patterns: Highlights 1986,* Pune, India, 1987.

"productive" use of funds, on the other hand, may involve the purchase of seeds and fertilizer, or raw materials, or the hiring of labour, in order to keep production (agricultural or artisanal) going.

Most informal lenders and most of the different types of informal savings and credit arrangements are a source of loans for both productive and consumption purposes.

a) Moneylenders

Individual moneylenders may finance basic consumption needs – i.e. the subsistence needs of small farmers in emergencies such as a loss of harvest – or provide loans to cover wedding and funeral expenses. They may also lend for productive purposes to farmers (for the purchase of agricultural inputs) and to artisans and traders (working capital requirements, tools and equipment, etc.).

Private moneylending may sometimes present monthly or yearly cyclical features, depending on how closely it follows the activity cycles of the community. In Zambia, for example, moneylending activity in rural areas normally increases before the harvest season; in urban areas, it is more pronounced in the second half of each month, when money from wages has dwindled.

b) Mutual Associations

Initially, the savings accumulated and the loans acquired through fixed-fund associations and ROSCAs were intended to cover traditional expenses (wedding and funeral ceremonies, in particular). However, these types of arrangements have continuously evolved and adapted themselves to new needs (see Box 3.1) so that today the amassed funds may be used for a wide variety of purposes, ranging from personal needs and consumer acquisitions to major investment undertakings (see Table 3.5).

Box 3.1

MEXICO: USE OF FUNDS IN *TANDAS*

From the late 1970s through to the early 1980s, there has been a noticeable shift in the use of the funds amassed by the "tandas", the local form of ROSCAs in Mexico. This change largely reflects the underlying motives for saving by tanda *participants and has also been influenced to a considerable degree by the inflationary economic environment which currently prevails in the country.*

Based on the answers received in a survey of 50 tandas *conducted in the early 1980s by Velez[1], the use of tanda funds was, in decreasing order of importance, as follows:*

- *savings (i.e. through the pooling of resources, administrative requirements and notably minimum deposit levels of formal financial institutions can be met by the individual member, who deposits the total amount received in a private bank account);*
- *regular, seasonal and/or unexpected living expenses (clothing, education, medical expenses, emergencies, etc.);*
- *ceremonial or other traditional expenditures;*
- *purchase of household goods and/or consumer durables.*

In the course of field work conducted in 1988 for the case study on Mexico, however, the order of priority of the various possible uses was found to be modified:

- *regular, seasonal and/or unexpected living expenses;*
- *purchase of household goods and/or consumer durables;*
- *ceremonial or other traditional expenditures;*
- *savings.*

Thus, a change can be observed on three levels:
- *savers are moving from a medium- to long-term horizon towards a more short-term horizon;*
- *the concept and practice of saving to build up reserves for future use is gradually being replaced by saving for ad hoc outlays;*
- *funds are therefore used mostly for consumption purposes while capital accumulation is neglected.*

One explanatory factor behind this is the fact that the motives for saving in Mexico are largely a function of social class. For wage-earners, who have limited resources and little or no access to formal credit, tandas *are a substitute source of funds that enable them to assume major purchases and unexpected expenses. For the middle class,* tandas *provide a means of sustaining a standard of living at a higher level than that which one's income permits, as evidenced by the use of funds for the purchase of luxury items and the reimbursement of debts. Thus for both lower-income wage-earners and the middle class, although it is for different reasons,* tandas *take on a role of "consumer associations". By contrast, the social function of* tandas *would seem to prevail in the case of professionals and the upper-income social strata where* tandas *are seen as a means of securing oneself a place within a network of social or professional relations (sometimes the bond may even be political). In this case, funds are used mostly for ceremonial expenses, while the tanda takes on the form of a "club" based on the prestige of its members.*

The second variable affecting the use of tanda funds is the inflationary economic environment which has undoubtedly played a role in determining cycle duration as well as contribution levels. In reaction to high levels of inflation (159 per cent in 1987, for example), tanda cycles are short, usually 10 months or less, and sometimes the fund rotates every 15 days. In cases where the cycles are longer, other measures are adopted to deal with the risk of rapid depreciation of funds. For example, commercial (or fixed-objective) tandas, with cycles of 10 to 12 months, are set up for the purchase of imported goods and involve three parties: the seller of the goods in question; the organiser of the tanda; the buyers (members of the tanda). The tanda organiser and seller settle on a price for the goods. A surcharge is put on the price in anticipation of inflation, and the organiser's commission is also included. The level of individual members' contributions is determined as a consequence. As long as inflation remains at a level below that anticipated and accounted for, the excess funds collected are the counterpart of the implicit interest rate charged by the seller to the buyers. This implicit interest rate decreases as inflation rises and as the price for the goods fixed at the beginning of the cycle is approached and eventually exceeded.

1. Velez Ibanez, C.G., "Social Diversity, Commercialisation and Organisational Complexity of Urban Mexican/Chicano Rotating Credit Organisations: Theoretical and Empirical Issues of Adaptation", *Human Organisation*, 1982, No. 41, pp. 107-120.

The personal consumption needs covered by mutual associations may include the purchase of food and clothing, or other household goods; housing costs; the payment of school fees; social, medical or other unforeseen expenses; and the reimbursement of debts. In urban areas, participation in a ROSCA may be the means of financing the purchase of a major consumer good such as a car (one of the uses of funds amassed in *ekubs,* in Ethiopia), a house, furniture, or a household appliance such as a refrigerator.

The recipients of ROSCA funds may also use them for productive purposes. In rural areas, these may include the purchase of land, of agricultural inputs (seeds, fertilizers), oxen, tools or other light equipment, the hiring of labour, or the purchase of vehicles to transport goods. Members of trader rotating funds may use the money to start a business (which often entails buying a shop or a taxi) or buy equipment to expand or diversify their professional activity.

Finally, both ROSCAs and fixed-fund associations – but especially the latter – may earmark a proportion of total deposits or contributions for major investment purposes which benefit the entire community, such as the purchase of heavy agricultural machinery, processing equipment (especially grain-grinding mills), transport vehicles; or the building of a school, road, or bridge. In Ethiopia, for example, regional associations based in towns and bringing together people from a same region, raise funds for the construction of roads,

Table 3.5 USES OF FUNDS BY INFORMAL SAVINGS AND LOANS ASSOCIATIONS: AFRICA

Use	Sierra Leone	Liberia	Ghana	Benin	Nigeria	Niger	Cameroon	Zaire	Congo (Brazzaville)	Ethiopia	Zambia	Malawi
Trade[1]	x	x	x	x	x		x	x		x	x	
Acreage expansion		x		x			x	x				
"Property"				x								x
Buses, trucks, or taxis		x		x			x	x		x		
Bicycles for business					x							
Canoes			x									
Palm groves					x							
Fish nets			x	x								
Grain grinding mill				x								
"Tools"					x							
Seed					x		x			x	x	
Fertilizer				x	x					x	x	
Hire labour					x							
Roads, schools, or hospitals		x		x	x							
Livestock					x		x	x				
Education				x	x		x		x	x		
Brideprice		x		x	x		x	x	x			
Taxes					x		x	x				
Collateral for loan					x		x					
Build houses (use unspecified)			x	x	x		x	x	x	x		x
Improve houses[2]		x		x			x		x			x
Litigation				x	x							
Travel (purpose not specified)	x					x	x	x		x		
Food or clothing				x	x		x		x			x
Bicycles (use unspecified)		x			x		x		x			x
Sewing machines							x					
Radios		x		x			x					
Jewelry		x		x	x		x		x			
Ceremonies (including funerals)		x			x		x		x			
Parties & other entertainment										x		
Medical expenses			x									

1. Includes "buy trade goods", "finance new business", and "build rental houses".
2. Provision of a metal roof specifically mentioned for Benin and Cameroon.
Source: Marvin P. Miracle, Diane S. Miracle and Laurie Cohen, op. cit., p. 716.

schools, bridges, and other infrastructural improvements in the home area. One such association built a 150-mile road from Alem Gena to Wollamo Sodo. ROSCAs can indeed play the role of a development or investment bank.

c) Partnership Firms

Pawnbroker loans are mainly used for productive purposes, that is, to hire agricultural labour, purchase fertilizers, repair equipment, etc. It is not uncommon, however, for them to also cover food expenses, the purchase of consumer durables, or ceremonial expenditures.

Indigenous bankers are geared primarily to urban informal activity, financing the working capital needs of traders and craftsmen in urban areas. Indigenous bankers in India do not lend directly to farmers[13]. It has been estimated that about two-thirds of indigenous banker credit is directed towards the trade, transport, industrial and export activities of small businesses; about one-sixth goes to building construction and another one-sixth is accounted for by personal consumption[14].

The use of funds obtained from the other types of partnership firms is also split between productive (such as fixed investment, i.e. secondhand machinery in manufacturing, or transport assets like trucks) and consumption (including social and religious ceremonies) purposes. The figures available to us concern the case of India.

With the exception of financing provided by Mutual Benefit Funds, trade and business activities draw in the largest share of lending by partnership firms, with an average 43 per cent of total funds. The remaining funds are used to finance a host of activities ranging from exports (an average of 15 per cent of funds), and small-scale industry (8 per cent of funds, on average) to personal consumption (an average 13 per cent of funds). Mutual Benefit Funds are the only institutions which lend a substantial proportion of their funds for personal consumption purposes (65 per cent of total funds lent by MBFs; another 25 per cent goes to building construction and acquisition of landed property).

3. Final Remarks

One of the key characteristics of informal finance is the ability to adapt saving and lending facilities to all different kinds of needs and clientele. Yet one may observe that, often, the choice of informal lender or scheme may be a function of what needs the borrowed (or saved) funds are designed to cover. Mutual associations seem to be by far the most "adaptable" in the sense that they may serve to cover the whole range of potential uses: regular living expenses, emergencies, special purchases, and ceremonial expenditures as far as consumption is concerned; and purchase of inputs and equipment and hiring of labour as regards productive uses. Individual moneylenders also cover financial needs for consumption and productive uses, though in the former case, they tend to be called upon primarily for ceremonial expenses or in times of emergency rather than for "standard" or occasional spending. Partnership firms, for their part, are primarily geared to productive lending.

It should further be pointed out that in the developing countries it is not always easy to distinguish between productive and non-productive uses of funds within the household because business and household activities are often too closely intertwined. For instance, a durable good such as a sewing machine, a car, a truck or a bicycle, may be used for non-productive purposes (personal leisure) or may be used partially or entirely to earn income (such as the marketing of goods).

In a similar vein, Holst[15] argues that food, clothing, and health expenditures could be considered as "labor maintenance" in labour-intensive agricultural production systems or that school fees may be seen as a long-term investment in the improvement of the labour force, as stated by human capital theory.

At any rate, it is clear that the dividing line between productive and non-productive uses of funds in the informal financial sector is not clear-cut.

D. COLLATERAL REQUIREMENTS

The effect of the excessive collateral requirements demanded by formal financial institutions is to turn away a substantial number of potential borrowers. For one thing, farmers are not always able to put up their land for collateral, because it comes under one of the many types of communal land tenure systems, because the sale of land may be forbidden by law (in Mexico), or because tenant farmers and sharecroppers (in the Philippines) do not own the land they work. Small-scale urban enterprises are usually involved in activities with financing needs which banks do not satisfy sufficiently (such as wholesale trade) or in ventures with insufficient assets for collateral requirements (restaurants, film-making, building contractors, etc.). Nor is the collateral within the means of low-income urban households (gold, jewellery, electrical goods and other portable household effects) acceptable to formal financial institutions.

Generally speaking, the "classic" collateral requirements are absent from informal financial transactions. Moneylenders extend credit on the basis of a borrower's previous record of prompt repayment[16]. Sometimes, though, lenders may request a personal guarantee by a third party or demand real guarantees (often, though not exclusively, the case with partnership firms) such as a promissory note, land title, or mortgage deed, or the pledging of jewellery[17].

The above points may be illustrated by the findings of a study by the Technical Board for Agricultural Credit[18] in the Philippines: "Around 80 per cent of the formal loans are secured by a written promissory note and/or guarantor and 20 per cent are secured with either land title or both land title and chattel mortgage contracts. In contrast, 61.3 per cent of the informal loans are transacted with only a verbal promise of farmer-borrowers to pay, and 35 per cent of the informal loans required both a written promissory note and a verbal agreement to sell the farmer's produce to the moneylender. Less than 5 per cent were secured with a land title"[19].

ROSCAs are also based on mutual trust and reciprocity between members who are nonetheless well aware that they are using each other's savings and who thus feel a strong moral obligation to honour their committments. Some ROSCAs also employ institutional safeguards to ensure continued participation of members who win the prize fund early on in the cycle. In a number of African countries (Nigeria, Cameroon, Ethiopia), the receiver of the fund may have to provide either some form of collateral or a guarantor who is acceptable to the rest of the group and who signs that he will assume the receiving member's subsequent contributions should he fail to pay. Sometimes even the guarantor must provide a deed to his land as collateral. The more "advanced" ROSCAs, such as the one in Cameroon, cited earlier, exert pressure on the defaulting borrower by cashing in a check of his for a large sum even though the check is sure to bounce.

Finally, partnership firms are probably the informal instances that are most likely to request some tangible form of guarantee of repayment, which may take the form of portable household effects (the case of pawnshops), promissory notes, bills of exchange, mortgage deeds or a postdated check at the time of loan disbursement for the total amount.

E. LENDING AND DEPOSIT PROCEDURES

If there is one area where the formal and informal sectors can be contrasted point by point, it is with regard to the lending and deposit procedures which prevail in each one.

Beforehand though, it is perhaps useful to say a word about the attempts in several developing countries to implement some sort of legislation on informal financial activities. (The regulation of the activity of formal financial institutions has already been discussed in the previous chapters.)

1. Legislation on Informal Lending

The informal sector is commonly defined as being outside the purview of regulation by the central bank and/or other public authorities. Yet in several of the countries studied, legislation has been passed concerning the lending activities going on in the informal sector, particularly with regard to moneylending and, by extension, usury. The legislation may include directives on the interest rates charged or specify the types of guarantees that can be demanded and the procedures for recovery of a loan in case of default, as well as stipulate the penalties imposed for non-compliance with the law.

In Zimbabwe, for example, although usurious interest rates are claimed to be unusual, they are not unheard of. Under the Usury Act, amended in 1984, a person convicted of such an offence is subject to a fine of either Z\$ 2 000 or three times the capital amount lent, whichever is greater. In December 1986, three messengers at a commercial bank were together fined Z\$ 21 000 for lending at 25 per cent a month.

In Ethiopia, the Law of Loans enacted in 1924 and still valid today is meant to regulate lending transactions in kind and in cash. Among the conditions it stipulates are whether a written document must underpin the transaction or if the presence of witnesses is sufficient, what types of guarantees can be pledged, what procedures can be undertaken for the coercive recovery of the loan and what goods can or cannot be distrained in this regard, and registration of real estate guarantees. It also regulates the level of interest rates – in fact, combatting usury was one of the principal aims behind its enactment – and sets a ceiling of 12 per cent a year. It must be said, however, that all this legislation is not too effective, and despite the regulation of their activity by law, moneylenders get round the legislation with the complicity of borrowers who comply with the call for secrecy for two reasons: one is not to preclude the possibility of obtaining other loans in future, and the other is to avoid revealing to relatives, friends, and colleagues that they are in debt.

As we can see, legislation on savings and lending activity through means other than formal financial institutions may be more or less binding and more or less successful in achieving what is probably the primary aim of protecting borrowers from a potentially exploitative informal credit market.

Perhaps it is the informal sector's inherent flexibility that explains how non-compliance with regulations may be rampant yet remain undetected and hence unsanctioned by the authorities.

2. Contrasting Formal and Informal Procedures

Formal financial institutions do not provide enough incentive to attract clientele, especially small savers and borrowers. The interest rates on deposits are low, and the subsidised loans which are theoretically intended for them are, in practice, not easy to obtain. Lending interest rates in the informal sector are admittedly higher than rates in the formal sector, but then this is partly attributable to the fact that, in many developing countries, formal financial institutions charge administered rates of interest set at artificially low levels by the monetary authorities. Moreover, there is evidence that in those countries with important informal deposit activities – India, for example – the average deposit rates paid by informal financial operators may also exceed the rates paid on deposits by formal financial institutions.

Moreover, the incentives to participate in informal savings and credit arrangements are of both an economic and social nature: not only is it important to build up and maintain a good track record so as to continue to be eligible for future loans, but it is equally important to kindle social ties with one's community, especially in the case of mutual associations. Often, trader associations serve as a forum where businessmen exchange economic intelligence (information on market supply, demand, and prices) or consult with one another on technical and managerial aspects of their activitites.

Formal financial institutions do not take sufficient note of some of the constraints which potential rural or small clients must face and adapt their services to these conditions, while the informal lenders' comparative advantage over the formal sector is that they do, and they do so at each stage of the process – from that of actual access to an institution or operator to disbursement and reception of a loan.

A farmer who wants to deposit funds or apply for a loan, for example, may have to travel a long distance to the nearest bank branch – using often poor and unreliable transport facilities – and still he may not be sure of arriving in time to do his business. It may seem like a minor detail, but a bank's working days and opening hours may play an important role in attracting clients. In Zimbabwe, for instance, savings clubs in fact prefer to deposit their funds with a building society – even though it may be farther away than a post office savings branch – because of the former's more convenient working hours[20]. Indeed, the opportunity cost of the time spent to deposit funds or take out a loan is of prime importance to a farmer.

Informal financial operators, by contrast, are characterised by their local convenience. Borrowers do not have to travel far and long to apply for a loan or receive disbursement, nor savers to make deposits. In fact, it is not uncommon for the operator making the loan or providing the deposit facilities to come to the doorstep of the client. Times and days of operation in the informal financial sector are a function of when a non-resident money-lender (trader or other) passes through the village or when ROSCA meetings are held; but these are usually fixed, by common accord of the parties involved, at frequencies which best suit them.

The bureaucratic nature of formal financial institutions is an additional hindrance in dealing with small clients. Rigid, standardized procedures and the usually excessive red tape and paperwork involved, render them opaque to the user, who often does not understand the purpose of such time-consuming preliminaries.

The strong point of informal transactions is precisely their flexibility. There is usually no paperwork; if there is, it is limited to signing a register upon receiving the fund in a ROSCA, for example, or issuing of individual passbooks for participants to record their contributions, withdrawals, and fines. At any rate, none of this entails filling out innumerable forms. Moreover, the self-imposed rules and regulations which govern informal financial activity are most often derived from local cultures and customs; participants thus understand the procedures, which can in fact be quite complex, and are more willing to comply.

Farmers and other small-scale clients find the setting of banks impersonal and intimidating. Moreover, bank personnel tend to be unfamiliar with the problems and constraints faced by many of those who operate in the informal sector, so that even if lending and deposit procedures were more adapted to informal credit users, the clerks would be of little counsel.

Informal savings and credit activity, on the other hand, is based primarily on personalised relationships between borrowers and lenders, who are well-acquainted with the circumstances which determine the financial needs expressed. Informal users sometimes carry over this aspect of personalised relationships to their dealings with formal financial institutions: farmers in Zimbabwe, for example, always prefer to deal with the same bank clerk who initially received them (see also Box 3.2).

Finally, one of the distinguishing characteristics between the two sectors is that a loan can be – indeed, often is – refused in the formal sector (for lack of sufficient collateral offered by the borrower or because the latter does not satisfy in some other way the eligibility criteria of a special credit scheme, etc.). For a would-be borrower, refusal of a bank loan is still a costly proposition, because considerable time and money was spent in making the application. However, even when a loan request is answered favourably, there may be a relatively lengthy lapse of time between the approval of the loan and its actual disbursement. This delay may be equally "costly" since farmers and other small-scale borrowers usually need credit quickly.

By contrast, almost all loan requests are satisfied in the informal sector, although the level of risk is reflected in the interest rate charged. Furthermore, informal credit is characterised by its rapid and prompt delivery.

3. Confidence in the Financial System

There is another important aspect relevant to formal and informal sector practices: that of user confidence. In effect, the cornerstone of every financial system is the confidence of the public in entrusting their funds to the institutions concerned.

In the developing countries, the population is often distrustful of formal financial institutions, largely from fear of the possibility of bankruptcy, fraud, embezzlement of funds, illegal exports of capital, or bribery on the part of those who run these institutions. Indeed, if such scandals do break out in a country, they cannot but undermine the public's confidence in formal sector institutions and in the integrity and managerial capacity of those responsible.

In this context, it is important to realise that regulation in the formal sector has a prudential function, i.e. that of preventing bankruptcies and fraudulent practices with a view to raising confidence levels in the banking sector. However, excessive regulation of the formal sector can have a counterproductive effect and drive away potential users through the resultant bureaucratisation and lack of transparency of formal institutions: the public is cautious when it does not quite comprehend the on-going procedures. There is, in effect, a delicate balance to be found on the issue of regulation of the formal sector.

In line with the above reasoning then, a priori, confidence in the informal sector, where there is no outside regulation, should be low[21]. However, user confidence seems to be quite

Box 3.2

POPULAR SAVINGS BANKS IN MEXICO

In most developing countries, considerable importance is attached by the population to the personalisation of relationships as regards financial transactions. While it is admittedly difficult for formal financial institutions to apply, let alone sustain, such tactics, there are some cases where formal, or perhaps more appropriately "semi-formal" organisations, have been created in order to try and fulfill such objectives.

The Popular Savings Banks of Mexico are one such example. Created in 1951, these savings and loan organisations deal only with their members (those excluded from formal sector transactions) and function on the co-operative principle, even though they have not been accorded the legal status of co-operatives by the Mexican government (legislation applies only to production and consumption co-operatives). They have set for themselves the objectives of providing savings and credit facilities to members as well as "educating" the latter in more formal-type financial relationships without, however, jeopardising the simplicity, flexibility and rapidity of credit operations. Based on interpersonal relations, the credit committee, and in some cases the director on his own, decide on loans which, once approved, are disbursed within a maximum of one week. This commitment, along with their autonomy in resource allocation and an informal, almost "family-style" structure of operations, underpins the relative stability in the membership of the Popular Savings Banks.

The Popular Savings Banks are run by three executive bodies elected by an assembly. Other than the general manager, the personnel is not paid for its services. In fact, this issue is the object of some debate: should a payroll be established so that "professionals" can be employed, or should the informal character of these organisations be retained? The latter point of view starts becoming questionable when there are 3 000 to 4 000 members in a bank.

The Mexican Confederation of Popular Savings Banks brought together 190 savings banks and accounted for 210 000 members in 1987. Their share in overall financial activity was and is limited, however, and it is being further held in check by rampant inflation and the paucity of financial instruments on offer. For instance, between 1982 and 1987, the amount of savings collected was multiplied by 14, but at the same time prices were multiplied by 24, leading to a substantial loss in the real value of savings and of members' incomes. Under such conditions, with inflation at 159 per cent in 1987, the 20 per cent interest offered on savings accounts is of little attraction, while the funds mobilised in connection with current accounts and time deposits were also negligible.

Clearly, then, it is not the interest paid on deposits which attracts members but the possibility of obtaining credit, on flexible terms, to the tune of three times the amount of one's own deposited savings. In an inflationary context, this is undoubtedly an advantage.

Each PSB has complete autonomy in determining loan conditions. Maximum loan duration is 18 months, though it may in some instances be extended to 24 months.

Generally, members are encouraged to reimburse loans rapidly so that funds may rotate and each member receive a loan at least once a year. In 1987, the average ratio of loans per member was 1.15 and repayment periods did not exceed, on average, 8 months.

Interest on loans in 1987 was subject to a ceiling of 48 per cent although the rate on funds borrowed for productive purposes could reach 60 to 65 per cent. In 1986, more than 50 per cent of total loans granted were for housing purposes, and 30 per cent were channelled to craftsmen and small-scale enterprise for productive investment.

Default on loans is rare and can largely be attributed to the fact that the credit committee knows PSB members – though interpersonal contacts become more difficult as the group grows – and applications are closely studied before loan release, notably from the point of view of the borrower's social and moral standing, his solvency, the purpose of the loan and the guarantees provided (usually the borrower's own deposit or a personal guarantee by a third party).

high in the informal sector, where social and often residential ties link borrower and lender, who are thus in close and constant contact and can more easily assess each other's reliability, and where transactions are founded on traditional procedures and are hence more easily understood.

This is not to say that well-managed and supervised formal institutions do not exist or that fraud is absent from the informal sector. There are cases where the treasurer of a savings association disappears with all the funds, or an indigenous banker goes bankrupt due to bad lending policy, or where the "leaders" of a group take advantage of their position for their own personal benefit rather than looking after the interests of the group.

In India for example, the set-up of chit funds was, like any other association, susceptible to some malpractices, particularly in connection with the prominent position of the foreman who could jeopardise the whole process if he was displeased by something. Most of the problems had to do with the disbursement of the collective fund, which was not done in time, either because of delay or default on instalment payments by members, or because the foreman used the excuse that the receiver was slow in providing a guarantee of his continued participation in the chit fund until the end of the cycle. In the meantime, he could use the funds himself. Generally though, failures due to misappropriation of funds by foremen were few and rare in the case of rural-based, small-sized, individual foreman-type units (due to the close knit relationship between the foreman and members). Malpractices started appearing with the launching of big-sized chit funds in urban areas where anonymity was easier and allowed some institutional foremen (though not the banks or government-owned corporations) to accept non-local members or operate through branches and paid managers, with greater room for indulging in malpractices. Still, even in urban areas, failures have been limited in both number and size.

III. COST OF FINANCIAL INTERMEDIATION AND INTEREST RATES

Measuring the efficiency of formal and informal financial intermediaries cannot be done directly, and must hence be gauged, in part at least, on the basis of cost of intermediation (including transaction costs, administrative expenses, etc.), debt discipline (cost of default risk, recovery/loss rates, etc.), and interest rates (both explicit and hidden interest rates, the spread between deposit and lending rates, intermediation margins, etc.). This gives an indication of their efficiency in allocating resources.

The lack of reliable data for both the formal and informal sectors, as well as the methodological problems involved, make cost comparisons between the two sectors difficult. Most researchers (Bottomley, Drake, Timberg and Aiyer, among others)[22] agree, however, that informal financial operators incur lower transaction costs than formal financial institutions when dealing with small clients (small-scale farmers and enterprises) and are more cost-efficient in minimizing default risk (especially so in the case of mutualist associations).

In the following sections, we shall successively analyse the issues of operating costs and debt discipline in each of the two sectors, as well as the differential formation of interest rates.

A. OPERATING COSTS

1. Operating Costs in the Formal Sector

A common proxy for measuring the cost of intermediation in the formal sector is to estimate total operational costs as a percentage of total earning assets. One thus obtains the minimum average spread between deposit and loan rates required to cover intermediation costs. If the figure is low, then the spread is narrower. In theory, then, wide spreads are a sign of inefficiency (for a given level of uncertainty). Using the balance sheets and income statements for 1987 of the Mexican bank Banamex, for example, we calculated a rate of 3.4 per cent. The corresponding figure for Banca Serfin (also in Mexico) was slightly higher, at 3.7 per cent[23]. This calculation may be made for the banking sector as a whole, in a given country. The limited available data tends to show that the figures are markedly higher in developing countries than in developed countries[24]. More studies are needed on this very important point.

Several factors combine to explain the high intermediation costs characteristic of formal financial institutions in many developing countries: absence of competition, high intermediate input costs, constraining labour contracts, heavy taxation, a more or less constraining regulatory environment.

Generally, the financial and banking sectors of developing countries are less competitive than their counterparts in developed countries; often they are oligopolistic and cartelized. Publicly owned financial institutions are not always profit-driven; in those cases when there are also private financial institutions, there is often excessive specialisation of activity by sector, region, type of borrower or loan, etc., which confers a quasi-monopolistic position on each specialised intermediary (and thus incentives to keep costs down are substantially weakened). Such financial specialisation is often justified on the grounds of efficiency as regards resource allocation, but the potential cost reduction that can be gained through the provision of multiple services should not be neglected. There is in fact a trade-off between mono-service and multi-service financial institutions (economies of scope) and size of operations (economies of scale)[25].

High intermediate input costs, such as the purchase of computerized equipment and its maintenance, advertising expenses, etc. also add substantially to operating costs, as do the policies in force regarding bank personnel. The benefits accorded to an often redundant labour force in the banking sector include very high wages compared to the average wage or to the wages paid in other sectors and, in some countries, security of employment.

Recognition of the importance of finance for development has not necessarily deterred governments from heavily taxing the banking systems, both directly (tax on income, interest witholding taxes, profit taxes, value-added taxes, stamp duties, license fees, etc.) and indirectly (reserve requirements)[26]. The example of the Philippines is a case in point. In this country, a gross receipts tax is levied on the income and capital gains of a bank on a sliding scale, at a rate of 5 per cent for instruments with maturities of less than two years. Lower rates are imposed for instruments of longer maturities, and those of more than seven years are free of tax. In addition, a witholding tax on deposit interest income of 20 per cent is levied. Reserve requirements amount to more than 20 per cent of deposit liabilities; the rates are lower for long-term deposits of more than two years. The implicit tax on reserve requirements stems from the fact that the latter are remunerated at 4 per cent, well below market interest rates. In fact, the World Bank estimated that, in the context of a period of devaluations and inflation from 1983 to 1985, at the margin, these various taxes added 12 percentage points to the cost of financial intermediation in the Philippines.

Though few would dispute the necessity of at least some level of reserve requirements, it is increasingly being conceded that excessive levels may be "harmful" in terms of opportunity cost. At present, there is much discussion on whether interest should be paid on bank reserves. Some countries do so already, though none pay interest on excess reserves, the objective being to keep the opportunity cost of holding such reserves high.

The level of transaction costs in the banking sector is also affected by the regulatory environment. Excessive intervention by the public authorities in a country's financial activity fuels operational costs in more than one way.

Bureaucratic procedures, for one, involving a sometimes excessive amount of paperwork, can be costly in terms of time and effort for both borrower and lender. In addition, formal financial institutions – commercial banks mainly – deal with a large number of changing customers in a wide range of sectors of the economy, so they have a less profound knowledge of their clients' finances and creditworthiness. The costs incurred to acquire the requisite information in order to reduce default risk (especially on loans to small farmers and small-scale industries) obviously raises the unit costs of loan processing. As an example, Villanueva and Saito[27] found that, in the Philippines, the administrative costs of lending to small farmers and small-scale industry were, respectively, triple and double the costs of lending to large-scale industry[28]. The same authors also point out that "one of the reasons for the relatively low administrative costs of Rural Banks (in the Philippines) may be the fact that many of them are owned and managed by those who were originally the local moneylenders." Hence they are able to use "to full advantage their contacts with the local clientele and their knowledge of local conditions and problems."

Of even greater incidence are interest rate subsidies, target lending programmes and, of course, the fixing of deposit and lending interest rates. In effect, when interest rates are subsidised or when lending and deposit rates are administered, this may not induce banks to reduce the spread, especially if the cost of funds for them is set well below the fixed rates at which they lend.

The beneficiary institutions of interest rate subsidies (usually development finance institutions) are provided, in essence, with access to a source of "cheap funds" to carry out their activities. But "cheap funds" may in fact be more expensive than they at first appear, if only because they go hand in hand with centralisation of operations and often complex reporting requirements for special credit lines and/or external funds in order to ensure that funds are effectively channelled towards the stipulated uses.

A consequence of selective credit policies, or target lending, is that the beneficiary institutions tend to concentrate more on lending than on deposit mobilisation, which raises the cost of screening loan applicants. In effect, handling the deposits of their prospective clients would provide the institutions in question with additional information on their clients' cash flow, savings habits, and wealth, while any sudden changes in savings behaviour during the life of the loan could serve as an early warning on potential problems of loan repayment. Furthermore, it is clear that the higher the subsidy on interest rates, the greater the demand for credit, and the stronger the temptation for political interference in the ensuing credit rationing process, which can lead to serious misallocation of resources[29].

Finally, high and rising bank operating costs are closely intertwined with the (often arbitrary) setting of interest rates at levels well below those of the market. In his study of the financial sector in Turkey, Fry[30] remarked that the fixing of deposit and loan rates (and hence the defining of a given spread) brought on non-price competition within the banking sector in the form of proliferation of bank branches, massive advertising expenditures, impressive buildings, etc., with high operating cost ratios as a result. Moreover, he detected that for a given, fixed spread, Turkish bankers displayed little incentive to be efficient, preferring to maintain high costs and keep profits within certain limits for fear that a showing of high profits would incite the authorities to further reduce the gap between interest rates on deposits and loans. It is clear that this question of the spread between deposit and loan rates is actually at the centre of the cost of intermediation issue and hence calls for a closer look at the problems involved.

In many developing countries, both deposit and lending rates are often deliberately set at low levels: deposit rates are frequently negative in real terms; lending rates may be high but they are still lower than what they would be on a free market for deposit and lending rates. The intermediation margins are usually high, but are largely absorbed by operational costs which appear to represent a substantial share of the total[31]. Serious problems arise when operational costs exceed intermediation margins[32]: if interest rates are to be maintained at low levels, subsidies or some other form of injection of funds will be needed to keep the bank solvent; in the absence of these, the bank is exposed to losses and may seek to cover part of the shortfall by charging fees and commissions. Thus the high operating costs imply low productivity levels and affect both savers (who are poorly remunerated) and borrowers.

To conclude this section on operational costs in the formal sector, a word should be said about the potential effects that a shift from regulated interest rates to market-determined deposit and lending rates would bring about. As can be seen from Figure 3.1, a first effect would be that both deposit and loan rates would rise to positive levels in real terms, but such an increase would stay within the limits allowed by competition, which would exert downward pressure on lending interest rate levels and upward pressure on deposit rates. In fact, this would mean that the spread between deposit and loan rates would actually shrink, thus creating an "intermediation margin squeeze". Concretely, this means that financial intermediaries would be forced to curtail their operating costs, i.e. increase their productivity and efficiency levels, in order to maintain sufficient profit levels and face competition effectively. In so doing, the more successful the banks are at reducing transaction costs, the

Figure 3.1. **OPERATIONAL COSTS IN THE FORMAL FINANCIAL SECTOR**

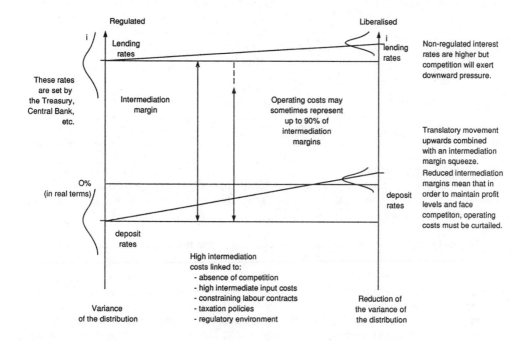

greater the beneficial effects for the community: over time, loanable funds should increase, as should the returns to lenders, while the net cost to borrowers should fall.

Finally, it is important to note that the real interest rate levels shown on the Y axis of the graph are averages: in the case of a regulated financial sector, the variance of the distribution is likely to be much greater than in the case of market-determined interest rates, where averages are much more significant. The third effect of interest rate liberalisation would thus be a reduction of the variance of the distribution of interest rates or, more correctly, the variance would at least be more directly linked to risk and size of loans.

2. Transaction Costs in the Informal Sector

As regards the cost of intermediation via informal financial circuits, the issues involved are of a slightly different nature. Lenders must take into account expenses such as transportation costs, opportunity cost of funds, risks from price uncertainties, marketing margins and sometimes even harvesting costs.

Not unlike formal financial operators, the objective of informal lenders and partnership firms is to maximise the returns on their activities or, put differently, to minimise their costs of lending. While mutual associations may be relatively less profit-driven than the other two types of informal lenders, they too seek to provide efficient and steady savings and credit facilities to their members.

Administrative costs are low in the informal sector because the expenses incurred in setting up and running operations (premises, overhead costs, etc.) are either nonexistent or very small. For instance, moneylenders themselves go to their borrowers' place of work or residence, rather than the opposite. In the case of mutual associations, there are no office space expenses, since meetings are held at the home of the organiser or of one of the members. What counts more in both of the above cases is the travel time needed to the place of transaction. Partnership firms, for their part, have very simple set-ups, with offices located within the lender's residence or in rent-controlled accomodations and often with a telephone as the only piece of equipment. Thus, in most cases, intermediate input costs are minimal as well.

As we have already seen in section II.E. of this chapter, lending procedures are simple and expeditious (sometimes only a matter of minutes), involving a minimal amount of paperwork. Labour costs are virtually nonexistent since each individual lender works for himself, while in partnership firms every partner is expected to contribute to the running of operations. In mutual associations, group officials are either not paid at all or receive a commission fee of 1 to 5 per cent of the distributed fund (this is especially the case in Asia), but the issue of remuneration is decided upon by the group, and not imposed from the outside.

Obviously, figures on the cost of intermediation in the informal sector are hard to come by; but as an example, Timberg and Aiyar's findings on the cost effectiveness of indigenous bankers in India concluded that transaction costs as a percentage of working funds amounted to about 3 per cent, while administrative costs as a percentage of the annual turnover were negligible[33].

As informal financial operations are not subjected to taxation nor to regulations such as those imposed by the monetary authorities on the formal sector, constraints on interest rates, direction and purpose of lending, reporting requirements and reserve requirements are notably absent, as are therefore the costs associated with such constraints[34]. Mutual associations go one step further, collecting and at least allotting, if not disbursing, funds simultaneously (thus the money is never kept idle).

The localisation and personalisation of informal financial activity constitutes the primary comparative advantage for informal lenders because it enables them to acquire information on prospective borrowers and supervise loans cheaply. As a result, the unit transaction costs of small loans tend to be lower in the informal than in the formal sector, and underpin the informal operator's willingness to deal in the small sums within the means of their clientele. In fact, it is widely held that per unit loan transaction costs vary inversely with loan size[35], although this inverse relationship may be less marked in cases of close living and working conditions of lenders (landlords, traders, employers, and storeowners) and borrowers (tenants, employees, and customers), which render supervision costs low and social control easy.

It is also often argued that lower transaction costs in the informal sector stem from the fact that there is greater competition amongst lenders searching to gainfully use their surpluses, competition which is further reinforced by the ease of entry and exit of both lenders and borrowers on the market. It should be pointed out, though, that as a means of countering the risks of default, lenders often resort to tactics of tie-in arrangements, linking the credit transaction with the purchase of inputs or the sale of output (see Section IV). In this case, besides the effect this has on lender competition, the cost of intermediation of informal lenders may be subject to the risks of price uncertainties, while marketing margins and even harvesting costs (in those particular cases where repayment is in kind and is the responsibility of the lender) affect overall costs of intermediation. But these are considerations which have more to do with the issues of debt discipline and debt default, the object of the next section.

B. DEBT DISCIPLINE

1. Arrears, Delinquency and Default in the Formal Sector

Another characteristic of financial intermediation in developing countries is the high cost incurred by arrears, delinquency and default. The share of non-performing assets in the total portfolios of financial institutions in these countries is often quite substantial; arrears can usually be taken to mean that either the institution has financed non-productive investments or that it has failed to press for repayment. The high loss ratios of developing country banks has led to a growing number of government interventions, ranging from restructuring directives to mergers to bail-outs.

Aside from the more spectacular cases, there are also a great number of hidden ones. This is in large part attributable to the fact that the insolvency of these institutions is not always apparent from accounts: for example, non-performing loans are rolled over, or interest may be accrued whether it has actually been received or not, or new loans may be provided to cover unpaid interest. As a result, losses (potential or otherwise) may be understated either deliberately or because of accounting regulations. Statistical information on the share of non-performing loans in banks' total assets is unfortunately not available, apart from some anecdotal examples (see Box 3.3). The general view is that even "healthy" banks can expect to have some non-performing loans, but not on the scale of developing countries, where non-performing loans are now at around 20 per cent or more of total loans.

As far as the question of enforcing loan repayment is concerned, the reduced role of the legal systems in the settling of "disputes" is partly due to the fact that one often finds conflicting legal systems operating in parallel within one same country[36].

In addition, developing country governments are generally reluctant to let formal financial institutions fail, and bankruptcy is indeed rare. Where there is a history of government bail-outs, banks may, as a result, be less hesitant about reducing their provisions for loan losses[37], even doing so to temporarily maintain their solvability and/or hide their current and past losses (what the World Bank calls "cosmetic mismanagement"). Counting on government bail-outs should something go wrong most often proves to be a good gamble, as the World Bank observes.

What are some of the other main reasons behind the high delinquency rates in the formal financial sector? Technical mismanagement, for one, resulting from deficient lending policies or from accounting "patch ups", can play a large role. Deficient lending policies may arise from the mismatching of assets and liabilities in terms of currencies, interest rates, or maturities, or from inadequate credit analysis and screening of borrowers. In developed countries, extensive use is made of collateral (mortgages, floating charges, etc.) and personal guarantees in order to minimise both the probability and the cost of default. Hence the low percentage of annual loan losses of commercial banks in developed countries: typically less than 1 per cent of outstanding balances (which, incidentally, has helped to keep total intermediation costs at less than 4 per cent). Precisely on this issue of collateral, however, financial intermediaries in developing countries are either very lax or they ask for the impossible, especially as regards small/rural borrowers. A further handicap is that

Box 3.3

EXAMPLES OF FINANCIAL DISTRESS

Bangladesh: *Four banks that accounted for 70 per cent of total credit had an estimated 20 per cent of non-performing assets in 1987. Loans to two loss-making public enterprises amounted to fourteen times the banks' total capital.*

Costa Rica: *Public banks, which do 90 per cent of all lending, considered 32 per cent of loans "uncollectible" in early 1987. This implied losses of at least twice capital plus reserves. Losses of private banks were an estimated 21 per cent of capital plus reserves.*

Madagascar: *In early 1988, 25 per cent of all loans were irrecoverable, and 21 per cent more were deemed "difficult to collect". Given the low level of reserves (less than 5 per cent of assets), the banking system as a whole was insolvent.*

Nepal: *In early 1988 the reported arrears of three banks (95 per cent of the financial system) averaged 29 per cent of all assets.*

Sri Lanka: *Two state-owned banks comprising 70 per cent of the banking system have estimated non-performing assets of at least 35 per cent of their total portfolios.*

UMOA countries[1]: *More than 25 per cent of bank credits in the UMOA countries are non-performing. At least 20 primary banks are bankrupt: non-performing credits are almost 6 times the sum of their capital, reserves, and provisions.*

1. The Union Monétaire Ouest Africaine (UMOA), or West African Monetary Union, comprises Benin, Burkina Faso, Côte d'Ivoire, Mali, Niger, Senegal, and Togo.
Source: Extracted from *World Bank Development Report 1989*, pp. 71-72.

although accounting capabilities in developing countries are rather weak, that is often all that banks have to go by in assessing customer creditworthiness. Inappropriate procedures, including delayed loan disbursements, too much or too little credit, unrealistic repayment schedules, etc., may also contribute to high default rates.

Government target lending policies explain in part high loss ratios. First of all, such programmes must obviously set down guidelines regarding aspects like authorised size and types of loans, amount per borrower, disbursement of funds, repayment schedules, collateral requirements, etc. Where this can go awry is that applicants with projects which "fit the general mold" but who may prove to be potentially bad borrowers could benefit from overly favourable conditions, whereas other applicants with a good track record and repayment capacity may be refused loans because their projects are not of the authorised type. Second, selective credit allocation policies may imply excessive risk concentration since a high proportion of loans must be channelled to a designated priority sector, region, or type of borrower. Such regulations also affect lender attitudes towards the importance of loan collection. Under the political pressures to rapidly expand lending to reach set targets, formal financial institutions have more incentives to meet the targets rather than to follow up on and collect loans, which is a costly proposition anyway in terms of time, effort, and resources.

This situation cannot but affect borrower attitudes as well, and weaken their sense of responsibility. When lenders assume that borrowers will not repay and thus take little action to collect loans, borrowers simply confirm these assumptions by not repaying, and this of course has a demonstration effect on other borrowers. Often, borrowers do not distinguish loans from grants, especially when credit is subsidised. Furthermore, if subsidised interest rates are negative in real terms, it may be an incentive to postpone repayment. To quote von Pischke:

> "Unrealistically low interest rates such as those charged by most farm credit agencies in developing countries encourage poor repayment. Little sense of urgency to repay is attached to money provided at a discount. Nominal interest rates exceeded by the rate of inflation actually reward borrowers who delay repayment"[38].

It has been suggested that borrower sense of responsibility might increase if their deposits made up a sizeable share of loanable funds or if the lending volume was conditional on the recovery of past loans. This would induce more commitment on their part, as is apparently the case in the informal sector. It is perhaps no accident that high repayment rates are obtained on those formal schemes which function on principles very close to the group solidarity mechanism prevalent in the informal sector. For example, in a limited liability group loan scheme set up in Malawi (whereby 10 per cent of loans were held as security), 97 per cent of the seasonal credit disbursed between 1969 and 1985 was recovered. Similarly, the Small Farmer Development Programme in Nepal held security deposits of 5 per cent and had a recovery rate of 88 per cent in 1984[39].

Inadequacies in assessing borrower creditworthiness and minimising default costs affects resource mobilisation and allocation in a number of ways. First of all, slow or non-repayment precludes the possibility of recycling funds to other borrowers and towards alternative uses. It may also lead to a perverse phenomenon in credit allocation, to the extent that financial institutions, in compliance with government directives on subsidised credit, may continue to lend to precisely those unprofitable but targeted borrowers, sectors, or regions that account for a large proportion of non-performing loans. Moreover, the new loans extended to large borrowers with solvency problems means that banks are financing the servicing of prior loans rather than new investment. Finally, the "financial distress" of banks exerts upward pressure on interest rates: this means that high interest rates must be charged to new borrowers even though it is clearly unrealistic from the outset to expect any investment, no matter how profitable, to yield returns high enough to allow debt servicing.

2. Debt Discipline in the Informal Sector

We have seen how informal financial operators have a comparative advantage over formal financial intermediaries as regards lower unit transaction costs per loan. They would also seem to have an edge in minimising default rates, despite the absence of a "legal" regulatory framework governing their activities and the fact that collateral requirements are usually minimal, with the exception perhaps of partnership firms, as we have seen. Lower default rates in the informal sector are perhaps a matter of approach: the tactics employed by both lenders and mutual associations in order to minimise expected loan losses involve the closer screening of applicants *ex ante* and the stricter follow-up of loans outstanding *ex post* than is the case in the formal sector. This of course is made possible largely because the transaction costs incurred in so doing are low.

177

a) Moneylenders and Indigenous Bankers

In effect, whether collateral is requested or not, whether loans are secured in some way or not, what lenders are most preoccupied with when assessing a borrower's creditworthiness is his capacity to reimburse the loan rather than the actual purpose of the loan (i.e. the use to which the funds will be put). To this end, the proximity of residence and workplace of lenders and borrowers enables the former to obtain valuable information on the true financial situation of their clients and to continuously monitor their business activities, their payment records vis à vis other moneylenders (lenders exchange information among themselves on bad risks), and even their personal expenditures. Contrary to the often young, inexperienced, urban-raised and urban-educated credit officers of formal financial institutions who have difficulties in communicating with the population in rural areas, for example, local moneylenders cannot easily be misled by farmers about their assets or potential output; and evasive measures on the part of borrowers to circumvent loan contracts and back out of repayment are difficult, in contrast to the anonymity of relations with formal financial institutions where the lender's knowledge of the borrower is primarily through documents.

Another way in which moneylenders seek to minimise expected loan losses is through innovative credit arrangements – namely, market interlinkages (see Section IV) – which enable them to pool and spread their risks by establishing tie-in arrangements between the credit market on the one hand and the land, labour, or product markets on the other (i.e. the credit transaction is linked to the sale of inputs to, or the purchase of output from, farmers; to land tenancy; or other employment arrangements).

Their second safeguard against default is the timely follow-up action maintained until the full sum is repaid. During the life of the loan, the lender can keep tabs on borrowers, first to be sure of the effective use of the borrowed funds, and second to physically be at the borrower's place of work (fields at harvest time, factory on pay day) when repayment dates fall due, so that borrowers cannot put off repayment in favour of other uses. Such close monitoring also means that, should the borrower default, the lender can know the real reason why (death, fire, etc.) and make the subsequent arrangements accordingly. Often, the other community members themselves press potential defaulters to pay for fear that the reputation of "bad debtor" will also rub off on them and jeopardize future access to credit for all.

In a way, it may seem paradoxical that informal lenders, who are more concerned with borrowers' capacity to repay (their future cash flows) than with the actual purpose of the loan (i.e. they are not necessarily averse to granting consumption credit) can actually monitor the use of funds to that end; whereas formal financial institutions, which do attach importance to loan purpose (notably to ensure that funds are used for long-term investment projects), can do little to influence borrower behaviour. Hence the most fundamental difference between formal and informal operators seems to be cost of access to information and monitoring capacity.

Despite all the precautions, bad debts do also exist in the informal sector, more so in some countries than in others. In the Philippines, for example, the incidence of default in aggregate terms is high. Any additional loans must then be secured by a land title or mortgage and the interest rates are double those applicable to the defaulted loan[40]. In south India, 5 per cent of borrowers default on merchant-moneylender loans, and approximately one-fifth of all informal loans from moneylenders and indigenous bankers take longer than agreed upon to repay[41]. Elsewhere in India, bad debts amount to 10 per cent of profits for *Chettiars* (a type of indigenous banker) which, note Timberg and Aiyar[42], compares favourably with the experience of commercial banks for the class of client served. For finance companies, bad debts are 1 per cent of working funds. Legal proceedings to recover bad debts are usually avoided. Besides the expense involved and the difficulty of collecting the awarded sum, lenders are reluctant to "officialise" or uncover their dealings for fear of taxation.

b) Mutual Associations

The two main risks which arise in the case of mutual associations are: the honesty of the group's officers (and notably the Treasurer) and, in the case of ROSCAs, the possibility that early recipients of the fund may subsequently disappear. Although default is generally rare, there are a number of provisions, more or less elaborate, to counter this.

To begin with, ROSCA participants are selective in admitting new members and pay attention to an applicant's savings capacity, credit standing and moral standing before doing so. The information is easy to obtain since the members are all from a small community. Furthermore, participants realise that they are using each other's savings, and the social pressure in case of default is considerable. The news travels fast, and a defaulter runs the risk of being excluded from all other savings and loan associations in the area.

There are also a number of institutional safeguards to minimise default risk. For example, persons of doubtful reputation may be slotted to receive the fund towards the end of the cycle. Sometimes, between drawings, the contributions are collected in instalments, to remind members of their obligations. The distribution of the prize fund may also be deferred or made in instalments[43]. In some ROSCAs in eastern Nigeria[44], contributions per member are increased over the cycle in order to offset the risk and inconvenience of waiting for one's turn until the end of the cycle, as well as the loss in real value through inflation.

Finally, some ROSCAs may adopt a "contingency fund" approach. In Nigeria, some groups hold the first contribution as a reserve to help cover any defaults that may occur in future during the cycle[45]. Cameroonian groups set up a special fixed fund, alongside the rotating fund, to which members contribute each time the group meets. This fixed fund serves to provide a source of credit for members who are temporarily unable to make their contributions to the rotating fund on time[46].

Overall, then, there is an often acute awareness of the need to minimise both transaction costs and the risks of default. Moneylenders, indigenous bankers, as well as mutualist associations have devised a multitude of ways of coping with these issues, based in large measure on the personalised nature of the relationship in informal lending, which is a considerable asset.

Without seeking to deny the importance of transaction costs and default risk, the central issue regarding informal financial activities is, not surprisingly, that of interest rates, their determinants, and lender profit margins. This is one of the most analysed and debated aspects, which we turn to below.

C. DIFFERENTIAL FORMATION OF INTEREST RATES

The question of interest rates in the formal and informal financial sectors is a major topic of debate among academics and policy-makers, even though statistical data on interest rate levels (nominal or real) is notoriously lacking. The information we do dispose of is thus limited to India and the Philippines, and it is somewhat dated; nevertheless, it does help to illustrate some of the main points which will be discussed below. Primarily at issue here are the rates charged by moneylenders (and indigenous bankers, in the case of India), and it is on these that we shall focus.

It is a well-known fact that interest rates in the informal sector are higher than those of the formal sector, and that despite this, repayment rates in the informal sector are higher as well. In India, for example (see Table 3.6), in 1984, the average lending rate of commercial banks was 18 per cent per annum while in the informal sector it was 25 per cent per annum (ranging from 18 to 36 per cent). Higher lending rates were also accompanied by higher deposit rates in the informal sector, with indigenous bankers offering an average rate of 15.5 per cent (ranging from 11 to 22 per cent) compared to the commercial bank rate of 9.5 per cent per annum. As a result, spreads were higher in the informal sector (9.8 per cent) than in the formal sector (8.5 per cent).

In analysing the reasons for the differential in interest rates, one must look to the various components which determine the overall interest rate charged – transaction costs, risk premia, opportunity cost of funds, profits – for both the formal and informal sectors.

In the case of the formal sector, the issue of interest rates has been lengthily discussed, and we have already pointed out that both deposit and loan rates often do not reflect the real cost of loanable funds; in other words, the aforementioned components do not play the role they should in determining the overall interest rate. Moreover, it should not be surprising that subsidised formal sector interest rates are lower than informal rates.

The main issue of debate that remains, of course, is whether interest rates in the informal sector are monopolistic and therefore exploitative or whether they only reflect the real cost of loanable funds. In this regard, two main arguments have emerged.

The first one asserts that informal credit markets are non-competitive and that money-lenders who have monopolistic control are able to extract substantial rents through lending. Proponents of this view underline a number of particularities of informal sector lending to explain the emergence of such lending monopolies. First, moneylenders operate in areas where few individuals have a sufficient amount of loanable funds, while low geographical mobility restrains the entry of new lenders into the credit market, and makes it expensive for prospective borrowers to shop around for alternative credit sources. As a result, the number of potential lenders in a given area is limited, and the degree of market power thus conferred on them may range from pure monopoly (one lender to a village) to some point short of perfect competition[47].

A second feature of the informal credit market is the relative inelasticity of demand for credit with regard to interest rates: for the borrower, often pressured by time constraints, what counts more is the availability of credit rather than its cost. A related aspect is the seasonal fluctuation of financial needs and repayment capacity, particularly in the rural sector, which places temporary strains on interest rates.

One must also remember that the formal and informal sector differ in both the amounts of each transaction and the duration of loans. Informal loans entail small sums for short periods, while in the formal sector it is the opposite. This has implications for the levels of the interest rates charged, since it is well known that "retail (credit) markets" are more expensive than "wholesale" ones and that short-term loans bear higher interest rates than long-term ones. In effect, an informal lender will make a large number of small transactions, charging each borrower each time for the cost of his services. Assuming that this is a fixed charge, it is obvious that, in proportion to the small sum involved in the loan, the rate will appear high. Moreover, as the loan is usually very short-term (sometimes just one day), the daily rate charged also climbs rapidly to very high levels when calculated on a monthly basis.

Table 3.6   AVERAGE LENDING AND DEPOSIT RATES IN
THE INDIAN FORMAL AND INFORMAL SECTORS
(Per cent per annum)

		1979	1984
1. Average lending rate (range)	Formal sector (commercial banks)	16.5	18.0
	Informal sector	23.4 (16-28)	25.3 (18-36)
2. Average deposit rate (range)	Formal sector (commercial banks)	7.3	9.5
	Informal sector	13.7 (10-15)	15.5 (11-22)
3. Spreads (1)-(2)	Formal sector (commercial banks)	9.2	8.5
	Informal sector	9.7	9.8

Source: OECD Development Centre case study on India.

Finally, on the actual interest rates themselves, the effective interest rate paid by the borrower may be even higher than the nominal interest rate would suggest, due to certain practices of informal lending. One of these is the charging of interest on the original amount lent rather than on the unpaid balance. But what makes it especially difficult to ascertain the actual price of credit is the practice of linking the debt transaction with operations in other markets (land, labour or produce). For example, by lending money against the security of standing crops and demanding repayment in output, a lender may take advantage of hidden charges by underpricing the farmer's produce with respect to the market price that is likely to prevail at harvest time. In a similar vein, the agricultural inputs (such as fertilizers, seeds, ploughs, etc.) supplied in a loan in kind may be overpriced, again allowing for hidden charges. This raises the possibility of monopoly profits in the informal credit market. One 1978-79 survey of rural financial markets in the Philippines[48] even tried to assess the extent of "usurious" lending from informal sources, and found that the interest rate charged on around 70 per cent of the loans was in excess of the legal rate (14 per cent at the time) and in excess of actual lending costs (estimated to be at about 22 per cent). Moreover, a considerable 32 per cent of the loans surveyed carried an interest rate of more than 75 per cent. Indeed, in the light of figures such as these, proponents of the position that informal lending is non-competitive claim that the largest component of interest charged by private moneylenders is monopoly profit.

The second, opposing view is that the informal sector is competitive, and hence the market power of informal lenders is considerably reduced. Therefore, the interest rates charged reflect market forces more closely, that is, they reflect the real cost of loanable funds. It is in this context that empirical studies have sought to estimate the share of the various components which determine the cost of loanable funds within the overall interest rate charged. These are: transaction costs, risk premia, opportunity cost of funds, and monopolistic or oligopolistic profits, which are assimilated to any interest charges in excess of the sum of the former three costs[49].

Needless to say, empirical evidence may in fact show differing results. A study by Quinones[50] showed that the high rates of interest in the Filipino informal sector were due mainly to the high risk premia involved. A study by Floro[51] in 1983-84 on rural credit in the Philippines showed on the other hand that the effective monthly rate of interest on linked loans was higher than the rate initially contracted when the different implicit returns, or "hidden charges", to lending were taken into consideration. In marginal areas, the effective interest rate on linked loans (borrower required to sell output and/or buy inputs) was around 5 percentage points higher, and 13 percentage points higher in cases where the borrower was required to render labour services; in developed areas, the same figures were 7 and 22 percentage points higher.

By contrast, another study on the Philippines, by Serrano[52] in 1980-81, argues that when the flexibility and adaptability of informal credit arrangements to the borrower's income flow pattern are taken into account, the interest rates in the informal sector are actually lower than expected, and informal loans are comparatively cheaper than similarly structured formal loans would be. By averaging interest rates throughout the period from the time of loan release to full repayment of the loan, instead of just averaging them on a yearly basis, he finds that the rates on informal loans as a whole fall from 21 to 11 per cent per annum; they decrease from 81 to 48 per cent on traditional-type unlinked loans, and from 10 to 5 per cent on trader-linked informal credits. Moreover, with linked credit arrangements, the interest rate is lowered even further because lenders can reduce the unit cost of lending. Serrano argues that, after all, it may be better for an individual to get non-cash loans from traders (by purchasing items at slightly higher prices) than to borrow cash from moneylenders at even higher interest rates and transaction costs in order to buy the same items.

Despite empirical evidence and irrespective of which viewpoint one subscribes to regarding the monopolistic or competitive nature of informal credit markets, it must be recognised that there is no *single* market rate of interest which can be observed in the informal sector. There is rather a multitude of informal credit arrangements covering a wide range of interest rates. For this reason, it is perhaps useful to look more closely at the four main components mentioned above and at the divergent views on their importance in determining informal interest rates.

1. Transaction and Administration Costs

We have already discussed at some length the issue of transaction costs of both formal and informal lending. Suffice it to say here that transaction costs would most likely enter into an informal lender's calculations if the transaction involved an opportunity cost to his time, for example the "five-six" system in the Philippines where lenders travel around on motorcycles everyday to lend out and collect a large number of small amounts[53]. Otherwise, administrative costs represent a small share in the overall annual interest rate charged: between 1 and 6 per cent in the Philippines in 1981, for example.

2. Risk Premia

Despite the advantages of informal lenders over formal sector operators in information-gathering and follow-up, which helps them to minimise default risk and delayed repayment on loans, the former do in fact deal with riskier loans, due to the nature of their operations. First of all, in contrast to the formal sector, which finances primarily investment projects and capital works, the informal sector mostly caters to short-term credit needs for immediate consumption purposes or the purchase of consumer durables (apart from a few cases of housing and construction loans or community development projects). The interest rate differential between the two sectors thus reflects in part the traditional gap between loans with different maturity dates. Secondly, the borrowers of each sector have different characteristics: at the enterprise level, the formal sector covers the credit needs of medium- and large-scale firms, while the informal sector deals with small-scale enterprise or individual entrepreneurs; at the household level, the formal sector's clients come from the higher-income groups while informal sector borrowers constitute the poorer sections of the population, notably – though not exclusively – the rural masses. Finally, because informal lenders usually operate in a circumscribed area, default risk co-varies, since the farmers are all subject to the same seasonal hazards and fluctuations in crop production.

Informal lender risk-sorting behaviour must be seen in this light. Interestingly, not all informal lenders are necessarily risk averse. In some cases, the arrangement agreed upon in the event of default – for example the transfer of land ownership or usufruct rights – may be of greater interest to the lender than reimbursement of the loan (see Box 3.4).

The importance of the risk premium in the overall interest rate charged thus depends largely on how the lender himself perceives and estimates the potential default rate of his clients. The flexibility of informal credit arrangements allows him to do this almost on a case by case basis, which may help to explain why borrowers seeking loans for "productive" purposes, or those seen as more "creditworthy" (as derived from one's status in the community or by being employed in the modern sector), or those with whom the lender has close ties (friends and relatives) may be given preferential access to or be charged preferential rates on informal loans. Here again, as in the case of variations in transaction costs depending on the type and the degree of closeness of the lender-borrower relationship, there is also a social dimension to the risk component of informal credit transactions, in addition to the economic one.

This is only one of the reasons why assessing the share of risk premia in the overall interest rate charged can give widely varying results. Calculations may be overestimated because they are based on repayment rates and do not include other means by which defaulted loans may be repaid. In addition, much depends on whether calculations are made using the *ex ante* risk estimate (the anticipated risk premium at the time the loan is granted) or the *ex post* estimate (at the time the loan is actually repaid). For example, using data from a 1981 Technical Board for Agricultural Credit survey[54], total transaction costs (administrative costs plus risk premia) of informal lenders would be 19 per cent if the *ex ante* estimate of 15 per cent is used, and 7 per cent if the *ex post* estimate of only 3 per cent is used (administrative costs were calculated at 4 per cent).

3. Opportunity Cost of Funds

It could be argued that lending rates must cover not only transaction costs and risk premia, but also the moneylender's opportunity costs of making capital available, that is, the foregone opportunity of using one's own available financial savings (and sometimes also additional, borrowed funds) for lending rather than for one's own personal use (enlarging the business, placing the money in a savings deposit in a bank, etc.). The importance of the opportunity cost component is thus a function of the lender's principal activity (farmer-lender or trader-lender, as opposed to a "professional moneylender" or indigenous banker)

Box 3.4

THE RISK-SORTING BEHAVIOUR OF RURAL TRADER-LENDERS AND FARMER-LENDERS IN THE PHILIPPINES

Risk-sorting is a procedure common to all lending activities, independent of the source (formal and informal). However, an interesting feature of informal moneylending is that, depending on the type of lender and on the collateral or other arrangements agreed upon in case of default, a lender may or may not be risk-averse. In this respect, the case of the behaviour of trader-lenders and farmer-lenders in rural areas in the Philippines is very typical.

Both types of lenders sort out their borrowers as a function of the circumstances in which they operate. In order to maximise the returns to their trading activities, trader-lenders must find ways of dealing with the high transaction costs and intense competition associated with trading activity. First, they must have a large share of the output market to maintain high utilisation rates of their market facilities (trucks, warehouses, rice-mills, etc.). Second, they are aware of the importance of the time element in the circulation of output to complete the cycle, and thus prefer to have their farmer-borrowers sell their output right after harvest or even repay the loan in kind. As a result, trader-lenders are strongly concerned with their borrowers' repayment capacity. In their eyes, a creditworthy borrower is a farmer with low default-risk who repays in kind, thus ensuring the trader of a supply of produce, reduced market risks and lower transaction costs.

Farmer-lenders, on the other hand, in the face of difficulties associated with land acquisition in the country, are naturally more interested in loans with land collateral. They lend not only to increase their earnings through the returns on interest, but also to accumulate more land or, failing that, to extend their usufruct rights. Imperfect land markets mean that lending is the only way to transfer such rights; if a borrower defaults, the farmer-lender can thus increase the scale of his farm operations, though not necessarily the size of his land ownership. The corollary of this is that farmer-lenders target borrowers with high default propensities: their "ideal" borrowers are poor farmers who put up their land or pledge usufruct rights for collateral and who will be willing to bear the consequences of default.

This difference in the risk-sorting attitude between trader-lenders and farmer-lenders is also reflected in the respective loan terms they apply, such as size of loan, timing of loan release and repayment, and the enforcement of the loan contract and default penalty. Since trader-lenders are concerned about the farmer's capacity to service the outstanding debt, they make the size of the loan a function of the borrower's income, with bigger loans for farmers with a higher income and higher interest rates being charged to farmers with lower incomes and a higher propensity to default, in order to compensate for the risk. By contrast, farmer-lenders make bigger loans at low interest rates to poor farmers who are more likely to default. Such behaviour is contrary to the standard theory of interest rate determination, but there are substantial non-interest returns to be gained from the mortgage of land or the transfer of usufruct rights.

By dealing primarily with the same clients, trader-lenders minimise the need for information-gathering and record-keeping. And in order to minimise loan default, they adjust their lending pattern to farming production cycles. Loans are disbursed at the beginning of the planting period so that the funds will not be diverted to consumption, thus ensuring, to some extent, repayment with the future harvest. At harvest time, lenders often go out to the fields themselves to collect the loan and to prevent the farmer-borrower from evading repayment and/or selling his output to other traders. Delinquent borrowers must either reimburse the previous loan before being granted a new one or pay penalty charges which involve the doubling of the interest rate. Loan terms such as the above may partially explain why repayment rates on trader-lender loans are higher than on formal loans.

For farmer-lenders, the idea of risk is almost irrelevant, so their terms of credit are more flexible. Loans are granted anytime during the production period and there is leniency on the timing of loan repayment. If reimbursement is not possible at harvest time, the defaulted loan is rolled over; from the point of view of the lender, the rescheduling compounded with future defaults merely brings the land-use transfer closer.

In conclusion, then, and in light of the risk-sorting behaviour of trader-lenders and farmer-lenders as described above, it can be said that, from the point of view of credit terms, risk, collateral requirements, and default penalties, informal lenders do not treat their borrowers uniformly. Such behaviour may be particular to only a few countries (especially the case of farmer-lenders, which is contingent upon national legislation on landed property), but it is a dimension of informal lending which one should be aware of when considering policy reforms.

and the economic environment in which the credit transaction takes place. For example, in a technologically stagnant agricultural area where returns to further investment in traditional outputs are low, the opportunity cost of a lender's funds is likewise low. By contrast, it may be even more important than the risk premium as a determinant of the interest rate if investment in one's own farming enterprise is profitable. A study on farmer-moneylenders in Punjab, India, found that the opportunity cost of funds accounted for as much as half the interest rate of 140 per cent charged[55].

Another study on fishing villages in Kerala, India[56], broadened the concept of opportunity cost of funds to include, in addition to returns on investment capital, the subjective value attached to the hoarding of gold, owning one's house, improving one's standard of living (better clothing and diet), or making conspicuous expenditures such as wedding celebrations which are important for an individual's status and prestige within the community. Inclusion of this social dimension, although valid, admittedly makes it more difficult to estimate the opportunity cost of loanable funds in the informal sector.

4. Monopolistic or Oligopolistic Profits

Assessment of the share of monopolistic profits in determining informal sector interest rates is problematic in more than one way. To begin with, it is assessed by deducting from the observed interest rates the assumed size of all the other components. The problem with such a residual approach is that the components themselves are not totally independent of each other. For example, a lender's desire for high profits may be at the root of high interest rate levels, which lead to high default rates on the part of borrowers, resulting in higher risk premiums being charged by the lender[57]. Furthermore, moneylenders themselves do not readily divulge information on their activities or their clients (interest charged, number of defaults, etc.) nor do they keep written records of these, especially in countries with usury laws.

As a result, empirical studies on monopoly profits and informal interest rates have led to different conclusions. A number of surveys concluded that overall, only a small part of the interest rate differential between the formal and informal sectors can be attributed to the presence of monopoly profits. In Ethiopia and Zimbabwe, moneylending at usurious rates is claimed to be unusual. In the Philippines, a competitive moneylending market prevails partly because of the emergence of a new class of lenders during the 1960s and 1970s concurrently with the infusion of low-cost official credit into the rural sector, greater competition from formal financial institutions and the low administration costs of merchant-moneylenders and shopkeeper-moneylenders[58]. In India, too, there was little evidence of monopoly profits. The differential in interest rates could be attributed more to the fact that formal sector institutions are subject to regulations which keep lending and deposit rates down than to the excessive market power of indigenous bankers[59]. The study of Kerala fishing villages, cited earlier, found that borrowers had access to several lenders across geographical zones and that the competition between lenders was centered mostly on the non-price terms of the loan package[60].

Some other studies, however, attribute a much greater share of high interest rates to monopoly profits. A study on moneylenders in Thailand detected monopolistic tendencies[61], as did the case study on Indonesia by Prabowo. There was also evidence in Mexico in the last few years of usurers charging rates of up to 500 per cent (although the high inflation of those years should be taken into account), particularly in situations where credit was needed urgently either to cover an emergency or supplement food supplies (such credit is rarely resorted to for productive purposes).

Although the information dates from 20 years ago, one study attempted to quantify the relative share of each component in the formation of informal interest rates. Based on a worldwide sample, U Tun Wai[62] calculated an average differential of 29 points between formal sector nominal interest rates (averaging at 11 per cent) and informal sector nominal interest rates (the median value of the sample was 40 per cent). Of these 29 points, 5 could be attributed to risk premia and 5 to monopolistic profits, the remaining 19 points accounting respectively for the inelasticity of demand for credit with regard to interest rates, for insufficient collateral or guarantees, for high opportunity costs of funds for the lenders.

A similar endeavour by the Technical Board for Agricultural Credit, in 1981[63], to ventilate the transaction costs and monopoly profits of different types of moneylenders in the Philippines led to some interesting results (see Table 3.7). The annual interest rate charged by all lender types – 56 per cent – could be broken down as follows:

- Transaction costs: 7 per cent;
  - Administrative costs: 4 per cent;
  - Risk premia: 3 per cent;

Table 3.7 TRANSACTION COSTS AND MONOPOLY PROFITS OF DIFFERENT TYPES OF MONEYLENDERS, 1978

In per cent of the amount of loans

Type of Moneylender	Transaction Costs			Annual Interest Charges	Profit Components			
	Administrative Cost	Risk Premium	Total		Opportunity Cost of Capital	Explicitly Charged	Extra Profits "Hidden" Charges	Total
	(1)	(2)	(3)=(1)+(2)	(4)	(5)	(6)	(7)	(8)=(6)+(7)
Farmer	3.04	1.55	4.59	44.83	15.00	17.71	7.53	25.24
Input Dealer	2.35	3.50	5.85	16.17	15.00	(4.99)	0.31	(4.68)
Landlord	3.66	1.98	5.64	47.73	15.00	18.98	8.11	27.09
Palay Trader	3.98	1.67	5.65	67.03	15.00	32.36	14.01	46.37
Rice Miller	5.74	4.55	10.29	14.16	15.00	(11.39)	0.26	(11.13)
Storeowner	6.24	3.64	9.88	69.98	15.00	43.38	1.72	45.10
Full-Time Moneylender	3.56	2.15	5.71	17.00	15.00	(3.76)	0.05	(3.71)
Construction Contractor	5.73	3.63	9.36	37.63	15.00	9.30	3.97	13.27
Handicraftsman	1.73	1.57	3.30	18.90	15.00	0.54	0.06	0.60
Professional	2.94	0.72	3.66	11.78	15.00	(6.88)	0	(6.88)
ALL	4.12	2.97	7.09	55.53	15.00	25.68	7.76	33.44

Source: Technical Board for Agricultural Credit, A Study on the Informal Rural Financial Markets, Manila, 1981, Table 58.

- Opportunity cost of funds: 15 per cent;
- Extra profits: 34 per cent;
  - Explicitly charged: 26 per cent;
  - "Hidden" charges: 8 per cent.

Among the different lender types, *palay* traders extracted the largest monopoly profit (46 per cent), followed by storeowners (45 per cent) and farmer-lenders (25 per cent). However, these estimates only include the hidden charges of underpricing output and do not take into account the overpricing of inputs, underpricing of labour services rendered, and/or the implicit rent on land under mortgage.

On the whole, the difficulty of quantifying informal sector operations and the sometimes contradictory empirical evidence seem to support the proposition that social factors, alongside economic ones, are taken into account by both lenders and borrowers in informal credit transactions. This also provides a partial explanation for the apparent paradox that repayment rates are substantially higher in the informal sector than in the formal sector despite the higher interest rates in the former than in the latter.

It should also be pointed out that there is a contrast between the regulation of interest rates combined with credit rationing in the formal sector on the one hand, and the free but high interest rates and absence of such rationing in the informal sector, on the other. In other words, the imbalances caused by the restricted character of the formal sector are partially alleviated by the informal sector, and, in this sense, it could be said that the high interest rate levels which characterise the informal sector are the consequence of the low interest rates imposed upon formal sector institutions.

Finally, as regards the competitive or non-competitive nature of informal sector lending, it appears that this is a function of such factors as geographical mobility of borrowers and lenders, technological advancement which helps reduce uncontrollable fluctuations in production, active credit policies and keener competition from formal institutions, etc. which vary of course from one country to another.

IV. MARKET INTERLINKAGES IN THE INFORMAL SECTOR

Despite the personalised relationship between informal borrowers and lenders, the problems of information-gathering in the face of uncertainty, moral hazard, and market imperfections have given rise to a wide variety of interlinked contracts in the informal financial sector – with *ex ante* and *ex post* tie-in conditions – to deal with the situation. Available data on this phenomenon concerns primarily the rural informal market.

Market interlinkages in the informal sector refer to tie-in arrangements that may be established between the credit market on the one hand, and the land, labour, or product markets on the other, through the overlapping personae of moneylenders, landlords, employers, or produce dealers.

The main types of linked loans that can thus be identified are: *i)* land-lease and land-mortgage loans, *ii)* labour-related loans, and *iii)* product-related loans, which can themselves be further divided into output-tied loans, input-tied loans, and marketing agent loans.

A. LAND-LEASE AND LAND-MORTGAGE LOANS

Although cases where a landlord or lessor makes a production or consumption loan to a tenant may come under this heading, linked loans in the land market primarily refer to the linkage of credit transactions and the transfer of land occupancy or usufruct rights to the lender. In Indonesia, for example, a small farmer's need for cash may lead him to lease out his land to another farmer. Sometimes the lessor may even work for the lessee as a labourer on his own land. Earnings by the lessee resulting from his use of the land are regarded as interest payments only, while the borrower-lessor must also repay the principal. Ghate[64] characterises such arrangements (*"tabasan"* and *"ijon"*) as usufructuary mortgage.

A different type of transaction *("sewa")* providing long-term credit to farmers removes lender risk since repayment of the loan (in the form of usufruct rights to the land) is made simultaneously with receipt of the cash.

These types of credit arrangements are also frequent in the Philippines, where actual land transfer takes place only in the event of default. However, as this type of credit arrangement does not often involve land titles, the question of legal transferability in fact becomes irrelevant. In most cases, lenders who accept land as loan collateral and enter these types of contracts are interested in land not for its resale value but for its input-augmenting effect in production. As long as lenders are able to enforce their usufruct rights, it makes little difference for the optimum scale of operations that they have only occupancy rights rather than ownership rights[65].

It should be noted, however, that in South Asia, land-linked credit arrangements are often exploited by lenders to keep farmers in a perpetual state of indebtedness, until the longstanding hereditary debt has been paid off.

B. LABOUR-RELATED LOANS

A common form of labour-related loans involves the granting of a consumption loan by an employer on the understanding that it need not be repaid as long as the borrower continues to work for the employer. The underlying motive for such behaviour is, besides maintaining good relations with employees, to ensure a dependable labour supply and attempt to slow down labour mobility. Such arrangements are common between fishing craft owners and crew members in the fishing villages of Kerala, India[66]. Consumption loans without tie-in arrangements but where the employment contract serves as the collateral are also common.

C. PRODUCT-RELATED LOANS

Three main types of product-related loans may be distinguished: output-tied loans, input-tied loans, and marketing agent loans. The latter two were identified in particular in the Philippines and in Mexico (see Box 3.5).

189

Box 3.5

INTERLINKED CREDIT ARRANGEMENTS IN MEXICO

The decline of agricultural financing by the banking sector in Mexico has given rise to the development of informal credit arrangements involving agro-industrial enterprises, agricultural input dealers, local traders, usurers, etc. Usurers and local traders target low-income farmers for whom they represent the only source of credit. By contrast, national and multinational agro-industrial enterprises, as well as chemical and other input suppliers, deal with farmers who grow export or other crops, thus ensuring themselves a source of raw materials for their transformation processes.

Funds are usually obtained by the lending enterprise from commercial or development banks, often at subsidised rates, and are then on-lent to farmer-producers who have concluded an annual contract with the firm in which credit, purchase and marketing of harvest – in fact, the entire production cycle – are simultaneously covered. The oligopsonistic nature of the market allows the agro-industrial enterprise substantial gains, while the farmer benefits from timely and rapid credit delivery, as well as technical assistance and a sure means of marketing of his produce.

Similar credit arrangements are provided by agro-chemical suppliers. In Mexico, about 50 per cent of chemical inputs are supplied by public enterprises, which does not seem to hinder collaboration with informal intermediaries for the provision of finance and the marketing of inputs such as fertilizers, pesticides, etc. Such "commercial loans" do not usually carry an interest rate, but the financial cost is actually already incorporated in the selling price.

1. Output-Tied Loans

Output-tied loans require farmer-borrowers to sell all of their marketable surplus to their lenders at pre-determined but lower-than-market prices, in exchange for the production or consumption credit extended to them before harvest time. Such arrangements are often used by trader-lenders, middlemen farmer-lenders, and processors to guarantee output procurement from farmers even before harvest. An output-credit tie-in arrangement not only forces farmers to sell their goods but also sets the proportion of the harvest to be marketed in the form of loan repayment; such arrangements also ensure lenders priority in the reimbursement of loans at harvest time.

The underlying motive of such lender behaviour, of course, is to secure a higher market share by ensuring oneself of the first claim on farmers' resources as well as to achieve a steady turnover of commodities.

2. Input-Tied Loans

Input-tied loans are credit arrangements requiring the borrower to purchase his inputs (fertilizer, seeds, pesticides, herbicides, etc.) or to rent tractor/thresher services from the lender. In the Philippines, these types of arrangements became prevalent in the 1970s, as a result of the introduction of high-yield varieties (HYVs), especially of rice. The expansion of irrigation and the introduction of other agricultural credit programmes also helped enhance the role of input-tied credit arrangements. Farmers who were unable to borrow from banks but who wanted to apply the new rice technology had to resort to input dealers for credit.

The 1980s, however, saw a decline in the relative importance of input dealers. This was partly due to the occurrence in the early part of the decade of natural catastrophes, such as typhoons and droughts, which raised the riskiness of loans for production investment and shifted the priorities of farmers away from production to consumption loans.

3. Marketing Agent Loans

The emergence of marketing agent loans is related to the drive of traders to expand their share of the output market. Traders seek out middlemen or commission agents whom they can trust, and who know the farmers in the locality, in order to expand the area of their marketing operations. Traders therefore entrust a substantial amount of operating capital in the form of loans to selected rich farmers in order to procure more output from other farmers. With access to large volumes of credit, the rich farmers in turn advance loans to farmers in their locality under the condition that they sell all of their output to the trader-lender associated with the lender.

D. FINAL REMARKS

It is evident that linked credit is one of the most important mechanisms for reducing transaction costs and risk premia in informal lending. In some cases, the control over scarce credit facilities is used by lenders to obtain more favourable terms in other markets. In other cases, lenders first seek to establish contracts in other markets and manoeuvre to gain control over farmers' marketing operations before extending credit to them.

It appears that interlinked credit is more important than non-linked credit and is preferred by both borrowers and lenders. Indeed, Gangopadhyay and Sengupta[67] showed that a farmer would opt to borrow from a trader-lender rather than a professional money-lender, since the former ("linked lender") charges a lower interest rate than the latter ("non-linked lender"). The low interest rate offered by the trader-lender is, however, compensated for by the low price he pays the farmer borrower for the output.

Furthermore, from the point of view of the lender, Floro[68] demonstrated that an "optimising trader" will not engage in trading activity alone, nor will he enter into another activity, such as lending, independently of his trading operations. Engaging in interlinked lending and trading activities is optimal for the trader, who also considers the additional gains of better market position and the reduction of the procurement price of goods.

In the early 1980s in the Philippines, nearly one half of the total volume of linked loans provided by traders required that borrowers sell output to the lender. Sometimes the borrowing farmer had to act as a marketing agent.

As for land-based linked loan arrangements, it was shown that the rich farmer engages in moneylending because it increases his returns not only through interest earnings but also through the opportunity to gain control over the borrower's landholdings relatively cheaply. Slightly more than one third of the total credit supplied by farmer-lenders in both marginal and developed areas actually led to land transfer.

Two main factors augur favourably for the development of interlinked credit arrangements. The first is the reduced costs and risks derived from administering joint activities. The second is the countercyclicality of trader and farmer cash flows, which makes for a natural symbiotic credit relationship.

CONCLUSION

The presentation which was adopted in this chapter on the operations and practices of the formal and informal sectors may be slightly misleading, in the sense that we sharply contrasted the respective characteristics of the formal and informal financial sectors. In other words, the tendency was to underline the differences between the two sectors rather than the similarities. However, it is important to remember that both sectors are present and operate within the same country (and financial system, for that matter); they often deal with the same clientele; and they must face the same global constraints. Thus the "black and white" presentation used here to explain the issues gives way to a reality characterised by "various shades of gray".

It is also important not to adopt a static approach to the issue of financial dualism. In effect, one may ask oneself whether or not there is a movement of convergence or divergence between the formal and informal sectors. Are the differences between the two growing deeper or being slowly effaced over time?

It is our contention that there is indeed a tendency of convergence of the two sectors; it may be slow, irregular, and not uniform on all points – in certain aspects they function along similar lines, in other aspects they still remain opposed – but it is nonetheless a reality. And it calls for reflection on the conditions for improved linkage between them, in view of enhancing and even accelerating this convergence. This is the object of Chapter 4.

NOTES AND REFERENCES

1. In Ethiopia, more than 50 per cent of co-operatives are in Addis Ababa and account for 90 per cent of all the funds administered by the co-operative movement. In Zambia, despite the overt orientation of the credit union movement towards the rural sector, 30 per cent of credit unions are based in urban areas and their savings represent almost 70 per cent of total credit union savings in the country.

2. Chandavarkar, Anand G. "The Financial Pull of Urban Areas in LDCs", *Finance and Development*, June 1985, vol. 22, No. 2, pp. 24-27.

3. Myrdal, Gunnar, "Development and Underdevelopment", in National Bank of Egypt, 50th Anniversary Commemoration Lectures, Cairo, 1965, p. 29. Cited by Chandavarkar, *op. cit.*, p. 25.

4. This is not to say that, in the interests of dynamic growth, allocative efficiency, balanced regional development and welfare, efforts should not be made to redress the situation.

5. Miracle, Marvin P. and Diane S. Miracle and Laurie Cohen, "Informal Savings Mobilization in Africa", *Economic Development and Cultural Change*, July 1980, vol. 28, No. 4, pp. 701-724.

6. For example, Massing and Seibel found that for seven out of sixteen ethnic groups they studied in Liberia, individuals often had access to at least four or more different kinds of institutions for saving or borrowing. See Massing, Andreas and Hans Dieter Seibel, *Traditional Organizations and Economic Development: Studies of Indigenous Cooperatives in Liberia*, New York, Praeger Publishers, 1974, p. 62.

7. For a more detailed analysis of the pros and cons of the local use of locally mobilised funds, see Causse, J., "Necessity of and Constraints on the Use of Savings in the Community in which They Are Collected", in Kessler, Denis and Pierre-Antoine Ullmo, eds., *Savings and Development*, Paris, Economica, 1985, pp. 153-182.

8. *Ibid.*

9. To the extent that savers are potential borrowers, borrower groups (as deduced from the direction of lending) and saver groups will largely coincide.

10. Source for figures: Banco de Mexico, *Indicadores Economicos*, various issues.

11. The official exchange rates of the Zimbabwean, Ethiopian, Togolese and Cameroonian currencies are as follows:

    Zimbabwe: Z$ 1 = US$ 0.60
    Ethiopia: Birr 2.07 = US$ 1
    Togo and Cameroon: FCFA 365 = US$ 1 (FCFA 50 = FF 1)

    The figures for Cameroon are from Haski, Pierre, "La banque saute à Douala", *Libération*, 9 August 1988.

12. Ghate, P.B., "Informal Credit Markets in Asian Developing Countries", *Asian Development Review*, 1988, vol. 6, No. 1, p. 72.

13. Timberg, Thomas and C.V. Aiyar, "Informal Credit Markets in India", *Economic Development and Cultural Change*, October 1984, vol. 33, No. 1, pp. 43-59.

14. Krishnan, R., "The Role of Informal Credit Markets", unpublished manuscript, presented at a seminar of the IBRD in Washington, D.C., 1979.

    Nayar, C.P.S., "Finance Corporations: An Informal Financial Intermediary in India", *Savings and Development*, 1982, vol. 6, No. 1.

15. Holst, *op. cit.*, p. 139.

16. In a similar vein, mobile bankers (most commonly found in West African marketplaces) partly determine the creditworthiness of their trader-clients by the regularity with which they make deposits. In fact, the traders feel this pressure and seem to prefer to deposit the same amount, which facilitates accounting and reduces the possibility of disputes. See Miracle, Miracle, and Cohen, *op. cit.*, pp. 717-719.

17. An interesting practice for securing loans can be found in Ethiopia: if the borrower has an account with the Commercial Bank of Ethiopia, he gives the lender a cheque marked with the expiry date of the loan and covering the entire amount of money involved in the transaction (capital and interest). The lender keeps the cheque until the day of expiry of the loan, when he is paid in cash and returns the cheque to the borrower (rather than cashing it himself directly at the bank).

18. Technical Board for Agricultural Credit (TBAC), *A Study of the Informal Rural Financial Markets in Three Selected Provinces in the Philippines*, Presidential Committee on Agricultural Credit, Manila, 1981.

19. International Bank for Reconstruction and Development (IBRD), *Philippines – Agricultural Credit Sector Review*, Report No. 4117-PH, Washington, D.C., May 1983. Based on the results of a study on informal rural financial markets published by the Technical Board of Agricultural Credit in 1978.

20. Building societies in Zimbabwe come closer to meeting the needs of small savers for two other reasons as well: procedures for opening a group account are rapid and straightforward, and clients may withdraw all their savings at any time and this conforms to the rural saver liquidity preference.

21. The informal sector may escape official control, yet it cannot be said that there is a total absence of rules and organisation governing its activity; the difference of the informal sector is that "self-regulation" is the work of the operators (lenders, savers, borrowers) themselves. The aim of such mechanisms and norms of conduct is to ensure the continuous, if not smooth, running of savings and lending activities in the informal sector. In the case of lenders, it is reflected in the methods they adopt to deal with competition, in their source of information on borrowers, in their ability to impose debt discipline. The primary objective of borrowers and savers (participants of fixed-fund or other mutualist associations) is to find a satisfactory means of meeting their savings and credit needs and ensuring continued access to these mechanisms – hence the social pressure to abide by certain rules of behaviour and the desire to keep up a good track record so as to be eligible for loans in future.

22. Holst, *op. cit.*, p. 131, cited: Bottomley, A., "Interest Rate Determination in Underdeveloped Rural Areas", *American Journal of Agricultural Economics*, May 1975, vol. 57, No. 2; Drake, P.J., *Money, Finance and Development*, Oxford, Oxford University Press, 1980; and Timberg, T.A. and C.V. Aiyar, "Informal Credit Markets in India", *Domestic Finance Studies*, No. 62, Washington, D.C., May 1980.

23. In the case of Banamex, total loans were 14.6 million million pesos. Operational costs were 506 thousand million pesos. Sources: Banamex, *Annual Report 1987*. Banca Serfin, *Annual Report 1987*.

24. Fry, Maxwell J., *Money, Interest, and Banking in Economic Development*, Baltimore, The Johns Hopkins University Press, 1988, p. 271.

25. Meyer, Richard L., "Deposit Mobilization for Rural Lending", paper prepared for the Third Technical Consultation on the Scheme for Agricultural Credit Development (SACRED), FAO, Rome, 17-20 September 1985, p. 11.

26. Fry, *op. cit.*, pp. 273-275; and World Bank, *World Development Report 1989*, Washington, D.C., 1989, pp. 62-64.

27. Villanueva, Delano P. and Katrine A. Saito, "Transaction Costs of Credit to the Small-Scale Sector in the Philippines", Washington, D.C., IMF, DM/78/112, December 1978, p. 18. Cited by Fry, *op. cit.*, p. 267.

28. The expenses are often compensated for by charging various fees at different stages of the procedure, which may be quite long before final disbursement of the loan.

29. Meyer, *op. cit.*, pp. 11-13.

30. Fry, Maxwell J., *Finance and Development Planning in Turkey*, Leiden, Brill, 1972, p. 127.

31. In Mexico's Banamex, for example, operational expenses (506 thousand million pesos) amounted to 44.2 per cent of net income (1 146 thousand million pesos) in 1987.

32. Banca Serfin of Mexico, for instance, had an intermediation margin of 192 billion pesos and operating costs of 300 billion pesos, that is, a shortfall of 108 billion pesos, in 1987.

33. Timberg and Aiyar, *op. cit.*

34. However, leaving the issue of reserves to the discretion of lenders may reduce implicit costs but it can also mean that there is a potential danger of mismatching of maturities of assets and liabilities by informal lenders, which can lead to liquidity problems. In the case of indigenous bankers in India for example, Nayar points out that insufficient risk diversification or a sudden loss of confidence by depositors may even lead to bankruptcy since indigenous banks usually do not have readily available assets nor access to refinancing facilities with the Central bank. See Nayar, *op. cit.*

35. Ghate, *op. cit.*, p. 78.

36. For example, in Indonesia, Dutch law and local adat law differ notably on the issue of land tenure. As a result, it is difficult for banks to foreclose on defaulting borrowers in a context of either unclear or slow or cumbersome legal procedures. (World Bank, *op. cit.*, p. 85.)

37. A World Bank study on financial intermediation found that, in general, development finance institutions made inadequate provision for loan losses. This is partly due to the fact that they are increasingly being used as tools of development policy. In its sample, it was found that the average return on assets would have been negative had realistic provisions been made to cover default costs. See World Bank, "Financial Intermediation Policy Paper", Washington, D.C., World Bank, Industry Department, July 1985. Cited by Fry, *op. cit.*, p. 276.

38. Von Pischke, J.D., "Rural Credit Project Design: Implementations and Loan Collection Performance", *Savings and Development*, 1980, vol. 4, No. 2.

39. World Bank, *op. cit.*, pp. 116-117.

40. IBRD, *op. cit.*

41. Harris, B., "Money and Commodities: Their Interaction in a Rural Indian Setting", p. 235, in Von Pischke, J.D. and Dale W. Adams and Gordon Donald, eds., *Rural Financial Markets in Developing Countries – Their Use and Abuse*, Baltimore, Johns Hopkins University Press for the Economic Development Institute of the World Bank, EDI Series in Economic Development, 1983.

42. Timberg and Aiyar, *op. cit.*

43. Holst, *op. cit.*, p. 134.

44. Banton, Michael, *West African City: A Study of Tribal Life in Freetown*, Oxford, Oxford University Press, 1957, p. 188. Cited by Miracle, Miracle, and Cohen, *op. cit.*, p. 711.

45. Isong, Clement N., "Modernization of the Esusu Credit Society", Conference Proceedings, Ibadan, Nigerian Institute of Social and Economic Research, 1958, p. 113. Cited by Miracle, Miracle, and Cohen, *op. cit.*, p. 710.

46. For an analysis of the saving and liquidity behaviour of tontine participants in Cameroon and the rising importance of the tontine mechanism within the official financial system, see Bekolo-Ebe, Bruno, "Le système des tontines: liquidité, intermédiation et comportement d'épargne", *Revue d'Economie Politique*, juillet-août 1989, No. 4, pp. 616-638.

47. Holst, *op. cit.*, p. 134.

48. Sacay, Orlando and Meliza Agabin and Chita Irene Tanchoco, *Small Farmer Credit Dilemma*, Manila, Technical Board for Agricultural Credit, 1985, p. 89.

49. Bottomley, Anthony, *op. cit.*

50. He calculated risk premium rates of 21, 32 and 43 per cent in 1982 in Bulacan, Isabela, and Camarines Sur provinces of the Philippines. See Quinones, Benjamin, *Explaining Variations in Interest Rates in Informal Rural Financial Markets in the Philippines*, unpublished Master's thesis, University of the Philippines, Los Banos, 1982. Cited by Yotopoulos and Floro, case study on the Philippines for the OECD Development Centre, p. 77.

51. In order to determine the effective rate of interest of lending in the Philippines, Floro used a procedure which calculates the total effective interest rate per month as the sum of: *i)* the nominal interest rate agreed upon at the time of disbursement; *ii)* the price differential between the prevailing market price and the lender's price on the output bought or input sold, net of transportation costs; and/or *iii)* the imputed value of rendered labour service. After adjustment for inflation using the monthly consumer price index, the real monthly interest rates derived confirm that the effective interest rate adjusted for inflation is substantially higher than the initial nominal interest rate agreed upon. See Floro, Sagrario L., *Credit Relations and Market Interlinkage in Philippine Agriculture*, unpublished Ph.D. dissertation, Stanford University, 1987.

52. Serrano, Segfredo, *The Economics of Linking Credit to Other Markets in Camarines Sur, Bicol Region, Philippines*, unpublished Master's thesis, University of the Philippines, Los Banos, 1983. Cited by Yotopoulos and Floro, *op. cit.*, p. 77.

53. Ghate, *op. cit.*, p. 78.

54. Technical Board for Agricultural Credit, 1981, *op. cit.* See Yotopoulos and Floro, *op. cit.*, pp. 80 and 170.

55. Singh, Karma, "Structural Analysis of Interest Rates on Consumption Loans in an Indian Village", *Asian Economic Review*, 1968, vol. 10, no. 4, pp. 471-475. Cited by Ghate, *op. cit.*, p. 79.

56. Platteau, Jean-Philippe and Jose Murickan and Etienne Delbar, *Technology, Credit and Indebtedness in Marine Fishing*, Delhi, Hindustan Publishing Corporation, 1985. Cited by Ghate, *op. cit.*, p. 79.

57. Bhaduri, Amit, "On the Formation of Usurious Interest Rates in Backward Agriculture", in Coats, Warren L. Jr. and Deena R. Khatkhate, eds., *Money and Monetary Policy in Less Developed Countries*, Oxford, Pergamon Press, 1980, pp. 465-477. Cited by Ghate, *op. cit.*, p. 79.

58. IBRD, *op. cit.*

59. Nayar, *op. cit.*

60. Platteau, Murickan, and Delbar, *op. cit.*

61. Lelart, M., "An Unorganised Financial Market: Moneylending in Thailand", *Savings and Development*, 1982, vol. 6, No. 4, pp. 339-365.

62. Tun Wai, U, "The Role of Unorganized Financial Markets in Economic Development and in the Formulation of Monetary Policy", *Savings and Development*, 1980, vol. 4, No. 4.

63. TBAC, 1981, *op. cit.*

64. Ghate, *op. cit.*, p. 81.

65. Mention should be made of the fact that leasing contracts are not confined to land but may actually involve other productive assets such as cattle. For example, a loan in kind in the form of a flock of sheep is repaid through an equal number of offspring, while interest is a share of the proceeds from the sale of wool and meat until the loan is repaid.

66. Ghate, *op. cit.*, p. 83.

67. Gangopadhyay, S. and K. Sengupta, "Interlinkages in Rural Markets", *Oxford Economic Papers*, 1986, vol. 38, No. 1, pp. 112-121. Cited by Yotopoulos and Floro, *op. cit.*, p. 66.

68. Floro, *op. cit.*

Chapter 4

REDUCING THE GAP BETWEEN THE FORMAL AND INFORMAL FINANCIAL SECTORS

The previous chapters have clearly shown that the financial sectors of developing economies are characterised by a high degree of financial dualism. A large share of financial transactions takes place in the informal savings and credit market, a sizeable part of funds are drained and invested by the informal sector. Practices differ markedly between informal mechanisms and formal institutions. The sums involved and interest rates set also differ. As it has been shown, dualism takes on different forms, and is of a specific nature in each country of the sample. This variety of patterns finds its roots in the specific history and the original culture of each developing country.

It is well known that today's industrialised countries were also characterised in the past by a high degree of financial dualism. When reading 18th and 19th century literature, one is struck by the fact that tontines, moneylenders, usurers, indigenous bankers, self-help organisations and charities were playing a very active role at a time marked by the relative absence of commercial banking and insurance. The rise of formal credit and savings institutions, of insurance companies and social security schemes, is actually a rather recent phenomenon dating back from the second half of the 19th century. The coverage of the whole population by formal financial institutions has been achieved only recently, during the last 40 years. The process of expansion of the formal financial sector was achieved partly by replacing informal schemes and partly by drawing informal schemes into the formal financial sphere. Some formal financial institutions in fact stem from what were formerly informal arrangements[1]. There certainly remains a very small informal financial sector in most industrialised countries, but its existence mainly reflects tax avoidance or illegal activities.

History tells us that the reduction of financial dualism is very often associated with economic development and growth, but history does not indicate the direction of the causal relationship. Is the reduction of financial dualism the result of the overall growth of GDP or is the rate of economic expansion partially the outcome of the development of a unified market for financial services? This question may prove to be largely irrelevant, and the two opposing theses can hardly be accepted or rejected outright. Let us simply observe that economic growth and development appear to be closely linked to monetary and financial integration. Let us also stress the fact that the process of integration cannot be achieved quickly: the reduction of financial dualism appears clearly as a long-term phenomenon spanning several decades. It seems that there are no short-cuts in this matter.

The informal financial sector is not an evil, and should not be eradicated in a brutal way: it does indeed play an important and positive financing role in many developing countries. Conversely, the formal financial sector is not a panacea, and should not be simply extended to cover all transactions. There is no such thing as the perfect archetype (which would be the formal sector) and its diametrically opposed antithesis (which would be the informal sector). It seems that it is by transforming both sectors – in other words by "institutionalising" to some extent the informal savings and credit sector and by "deformalising" the formal sector – that a new and more efficient financial sector will appear and evolve.

In this last chapter, we shall first evoke some of the potential effects of financial dualism and the costs and benefits involved. This shall be followed by a brief presentation of the current policy attitudes towards financial dualism in the countries surveyed. Finally, in the last section, we shall formulate a series of recommendations which could contribute to reducing financial dualism and achieving a more homogeneous financial system in developing countries.

I. COSTS AND BENEFITS OF FINANCIAL DUALISM

Should a strategy designed to reduce financial dualism be pursued? This is a crucial question which cannot be sidestepped. One way of approaching the issue is to try to apply a cost-benefit analysis framework. There are two schools of thought in this regard.

One view is that financial dualism has greater benefits than costs since the informal financial sector does, in the final analysis, provide adequate services to outlying areas or to certain fringe segments of the population or to particular types of economic activity that are deprived of access to formal financial circuits. Proponents of this school may agree that there is a gap between the ways in which the formal and informal sectors operate and that this implies certain costs from the point of view of efficiency in the mobilisation and allocation of resources. But they do not actively seek to reduce financial dualism – for them it is more a question of the improvement per se of formal financial institutions and their mode of functioning. In essence, the costs of financial dualism are more than compensated for by the benefits derived from providing services through the informal financial sector.

It is argued that each sector has its own dynamics and that leaving it to competition between them to decide the outcome of how the whole financial system will evolve may in fact be more appropriate than trying to directly intervene in informal financial activities. Another argument put forward in favour of this "laissez-faire and may the best man win" approach is that an active policy to reduce the scope of the informal financial sector may in fact mask other less desirable social or political objectives.

The second, opposing view argues that financial dualism entails considerable efficiency and distributional costs which are borne by at least some segments of the population, if not by the whole population. It is pointed out that financial dualism usually has adverse effects on the mobilisation and allocation of savings and that unequal access to financial services, as well as the distortions resulting from market segmentation, may benefit certain savers, investors, firms or favour certain economic activities to the detriment of others, thereby also exacerbating social and economic inequalities. Proponents of this view believe that the costs largely exceed the benefits implied by the presence of an informal financial sector, and hence an active policy to reduce financial dualism is warranted.

To sum up then, where the benefits are perceived to exceed the costs of financial dualism a policy of laissez-faire may prevail; where costs exceed benefits, ways of reducing the gap may be sought. Whatever one's viewpoint, however, it soon becomes clear that both the benefits and costs of financial dualism are in themselves difficult to assess and estimate, while their exact weighting for deducing their net effect is even more complex, as we shall see below.

A. ASSESSING THE POTENTIAL EFFECTS OF FINANCIAL DUALISM

To gauge the impact of financial dualism on socio-economic activity, there are five elements which may be considered:
- The mobilisation of savings;
- The allocation of resources;
- The efficient use of external funds;
- The effectiveness of macroeconomic and macrofinancial policies;
- The distributional effects of unequal access to financial services (equity concerns).

For each of these five points, we shall evoke the two contrasting views discussed earlier: one which sees financial dualism in general and the informal sector in particular in a more favourable light (benefits exceed costs); and one which stresses their negative aspects (costs exceed benefits).

1. On the Mobilisation of Savings

Those who view financial dualism – or rather the informal sector – with a more favourable eye would argue first that the resource mobilisation aspect of informal financial activity cannot and should not be minimised. Informal sector operators who accept deposits can stimulate savings by offering a higher return to savers than would be obtained on deposits with formal financial institutions, and this for three main reasons:
- Transaction costs are lower and implicit taxation (in the form of administratively fixed interest rates and reserve requirements) is avoided in the informal sector;
- Developing country governments adopt financing policies which lead them to borrow abroad or tap existing savings flows without adequately remunerating savers for their efforts;
- Monetary and financial assets in developing countries are often eroded by high inflation.

Moreover, the difficult access to certain formal institutions, as well as the variability of government policies, do not inspire a high degree of public confidence in formal institutions[2].

It is also stressed that the informal sector provides facilities so that even small savers are induced to accumulate small amounts that would otherwise have been spent for consumption purposes.

Proponents of the opposing view maintain that the level of savings in developing countries is generally far from optimal and that this is in large part due to the importance of financial dualism. To begin with, it is noted that in the informal sector loan transactions are more dominant than deposit transactions – in other words, apart from certain types of mutual associations, the informal financial sector is more significant as a purveyor of (short-term) credit to the small borrower than as a vehicle for small savings mobilisation. In addition, to the extent that it is the lender's own funds with which financial transactions are carried out, it can hardly be said that informal financial activities contribute to saving itself. Even in the case of ROSCAs, the ultimate aim of participation is not so much accumulation per se and/or the accrual of interest as the possibility of obtaining a loan – more often than not for consumption purposes – if needed in the future.

It is pointed out that, because of financial dualism, there is little opportunity, and households show little inclination, to pursue a long-term savings effort and invest in financial assets. Economic agents may prefer to accumulate wealth in kind, the value of which is by definition difficult to estimate. In some cases, capital flight may be an important phenomenon (as in Mexico), with a large part of national savings transiting through the informal sector towards investment opportunities abroad. As a result, both accumulated savings (i.e. household wealth, capital of firms or government assets) and savings flows are very poorly known, while substantial amounts (both in kind and in cash) escape formal channels. This means that official figures on savings rates (whether national, private or household savings rates) are actually an underestimate of the reality. It is argued that they could be much higher than at present if the appropriate reforms were undertaken to make the mobilisation of resources a first priority, in conjunction, of course, with efforts to reduce the existing gap between the formal and informal financial sectors.

2. On the Allocation of Resources

The effects of financial dualism on the allocation of resources may be approached on three levels: geographical, sectoral, and that of project selection.

On the *geographical level*, the question at the centre of the debate is whether or not the resources mobilised are invested (i.e. lent) in the same areas whence they originated. Proponents of the first view point out that formal financial institutions not only invest urban funds in urban areas, but that they drain rural funds to urban areas as well, thus depriving small-scale farmers and other rural-based artisans of working capital financing or other types of loans. The informal financial sector, by contrast, does not perform such transfers.

For those who subscribe to the opposing view, efficient allocation of resources means that loanable funds will be channelled to where there are lucrative investment opportunities; and in most cases, this means urban, as opposed to rural, areas. They point out that the informal financial sector mobilises funds locally and invests them locally, even if more profitable, alternative investment opportunities are available elsewhere (their existence is not usually known of, anyway). Confining what are already small sums of loanable funds to serving investment needs and opportunities in a delimited area is hardly conducive to extensive growth and development on a regional or national scale. The comparative advantage of the formal financial sector is precisely its capacity to transfer resources from surplus regions, sectors, or economic agents to deficit ones; and this function is hampered by the persistence of financial dualism.

Financial dualism at the *sectoral level* entails formal sector lending to priority sectors under advantageous conditions, while the informal sector, in response to unsatisfied demand, directs funds to those remaining sectors and activities, which are accorded low priority – sometimes mistakenly – by selective credit controls or are shunned by banks because of their high risk or insufficient collateral pledged by borrowers. Primarily at issue, however, is the question of the inter-sectoral transfer of resources.

Proponents of the first view argue that for there to be an incentive to save, there must be a direct and visible link between one's savings and the investment it helps to finance (which may be, for example, the purchase of cattle or of one's residence, the starting up of a business, infrastructure needs in the area, etc.)[3]. If the accumulated resources are siphoned off towards investments which benefit other sectors, regions, or segments of the population, then the incentive to save may be substantially weakened. Only when their own accumulation needs are satisfied do people save for investment in other sectors or activities. Hence the line of argument of those who favour maintaining the status quo could be summarised as follows: reducing financial dualism would result in the stepping up of inter-sectoral transfers at the same time that the informal sector's role as a "remedial", alternative source of funds is being eclipsed. These inter-sectoral transfers will therefore limit investment in certain sectors and weaken the savings-investment link. As a result of the disincentive to save, the global rate of accumulation will ultimately decline.

For the proponents of the opposing view, financial dualism presents an obstacle to the inter-sectoral transfers which, in their view, are requisite conditions for growth and development. This line of argument is based on the premise that a given economic sector's savings capacity may not necessarily correspond to its financing needs and that therefore the transfer of resources from traditional sectors in order to finance new sectors that are more likely to serve as "engines" of growth is inevitable, not to say necessary, if growth and development are to be successfully pursued (although such policies should be monitored to avoid excessive imbalances and the perverse effects that could ensue). It is also recalled that, historically, this has been the case in the developed countries, with the agricultural sector financing the development of the industrial sector. Those who subscribe to this thesis maintain that the persistence of financial dualism limits the possibility of effectuating such transfers; for example, if agriculture captures informal savings, this means that industry or other sectors are deprived of potential financial resources. Their viewpoint could thus be presented as follows: reducing financial dualism, i.e. moving towards a more unified financial sector where resources are allocated according to market forces would mean that the inter-sectoral transfers requisite for development would occur spontaneously, and there would be less need for target sector lending policies emanating from the public authorities.

Finally, at the *project selection level*, it is the cost of resources (and its implications for project selection) in the formal and informal financial sectors upon which attention is focused. The general view is that the formal sector is a steady source of cheap funds, while the informal sector is a volatile source, providing funds at varying – and usually high – costs.

In answer to such charges, those who are more amenable to the informal sector stress the fact that the different nature of the projects financed in each sector – in terms of loan size, risks involved, guarantees, etc. – renders the comparison of the cost of resources and project selection meaningless. The fact that the informal sector provides primarily consumption loans (which anyhow are more expensive than loans to enterprises for investment) and finances other small, high-risk projects with little or no collateral required, goes much farther in explaining the high costs observed in the informal sector than does the control exercised over formal financial activities. Hence it is argued that financial dualism does not have any effect on project selection in the informal sector, and that even if financial dualism were to be reduced, the costs of financing small projects in the informal sector would remain high, due to the nature of these projects.

The opposite stand blames financial dualism for distortions in the cost of funds and project selection. It is argued that the artificial structure of interest rates (with low-cost funds available in the formal sector and high-cost funds in the informal sector) and the policy of interest rate subsidies in the formal sector lead to a situation such that the selection of investment projects is not based strictly on financial criteria (of the usual capital budgeting type), but rather on the circumstances under which the loan can be made. In the case of the formal sector, either banks are constrained to finance certain projects, irrespective of their profitability, or they find a means of benefiting from the subsidies while circumventing the legislation on their use. Either way, the initial purpose of the controls is defeated.

In the case of the informal sector, the projects financed are sometimes those that were rejected or ignored by the formal sector, that is, they are much riskier. Allocation of resources by the informal sector is also criticised for being oriented primarily (though not exclusively) towards consumption rather than long-term productive investment purposes and hence not contributing to capital accumulation on the national scale. Even when loans are made to micro-enterprises, it is mostly for working capital purposes rather than for the expansion of business activities.

3. On the Efficient Use of External Resources

Those who hold a more favourable view of the informal financial sector underline its role as a reservoir of funds and operators that makes it possible for those areas, economic activities or individuals denied access to external financial flows to nonetheless continue to function. In effect, the major beneficiaries of external financial flows have most often been the public sector, central governments themselves (budgetary support), or large-scale enterprises.

The counter-argument is that the persistence of a state of financial dualism has led to a wasteful use of external resources, preventing the latter from being channelled to the most productive uses at the grassroots level. Had this been the case, there would now be resources enough to cover the reimbursement of public debt. Furthermore, the combination of heavy foreign debt burdens, a limited tax base, and an extensive informal financial sector make debt reimbursement all the more difficult, not only because of their effect on budgetary and fiscal policies, but also because a share of the sums involved often disappears in the informal sector.

4. On the Effectiveness of Macroeconomic and Macrofinancial Policies

Throughout this study, reference has frequently been made, either implicitly or explicitly, to some of the distortions in the formal financial sector resulting from what have been termed financially repressive policies, probably the most notable of which is a rigid interest rate structure. In most cases, the informal financial sector has played a palliative role in the face of these imbalances. Consequently, those who focus on the positive aspects of the informal sector argue that, since it is to a large extent the inappropriate macroeconomic and macrofinancial policies adopted by developing country governments which created the informal financial sector in the first place, then the latter can hardly be held responsible for the inefficiency of these policies.

The opposing arguments on how financial dualism can deflect the aims of economic, monetary and financial policies (see also Chapter 1), are more numerous and equally persuasive. Money supply is affected by the mode of financing of public debt (the relative role of the Treasury), inflation, and capital flight abroad. A further complication is the flight of funds away from formal channels towards informal ones where control can no longer be exerted over transactions. For instance, an injection of funds into a given monetary base may be reduced by the outflow of currency from formal to informal circuits. With a substantial share of liquidity circulating outside the formal banking sector, aggregates – and hence objectives – are difficult to define. This also means that, in practice, only a fraction of financial transactions are actually affected by the policy measures or directives that are implemented. The monetary authorities cannot ensure depositor security or provide protection against fraud or mismanagement; nor can the central bank serve as a lender of last resort in case of failures[4].

However, the informal financial sector may be indirectly affected by the extent (and effectiveness) of control over formal financial institutions. As regards lending, for example, a restrictive credit policy in the formal sector creates an excess demand for funds which spills over into the informal sector and may or may not bid up the cost of funds there. The informal sector also fills in the credit gap when formal credit schemes in favour of a particular target group or sector are abruptly withdrawn. Savings behaviour too may be affected. For example, if interest rates rise in the formal sector, this should generate an inflow of informal sector savings, at least from those segments of the population who have the possibility of choosing between formal and informal schemes depending on which ones give the highest returns. However, the inverse is equally true: these same savers will channel their funds away from the formal sector towards the informal sector if gains there are higher (for instance, in India, the rates obtained through participation in chit funds are higher than those offered by formal sector banks). This marks the flight of funds from the formal sector to the informal sector where they can no longer be traced for national accounts purposes.

5. On Equity

The issue of equity in the formal-informal financial sector debate revolves around three main focal points: interest rates, access to services and market segmentation.

On the first two questions of interest rates and access to services, it is argued by those who take a favourable stand towards the informal sector that the latter caters to the needs of small-scale savers and borrowers in rural and urban areas who are barred from receiving formal credit; there is thus a "crowding in" effect which helps to explain why lending rates in the informal sector are higher than rates in the formal sector. It is pointed out that interest rates in the informal sector more closely reflect market forces; and not only are lending rates higher, but deposit rates, in those cases where resources are collected by informal operators, are also higher than formal sector rates.

An additional argument is that the credit needs of informal borrowers may be small (in volume and value) but they are no less essential, and some way of meeting them must be found. If this cannot be done through the formal financial sector, then how can it be determined that the alternative to high-cost credit, which would be no credit at all, is better?

Proponents of this view also add that the dividing line between the formal and informal financial sectors is not so clear-cut, and people often have access to both sectors, moving freely from one to the other or combining services from both. In this sense, there may even be a complementary or competitive relationship between the two sectors, depending on each particular case.

Not surprisingly, the main thrust of the opposing argument is that lending rates in the informal sector are excessively high and exploitative. The informal sector's reputation for usury is attributed to the fact that unequal access to funds and market information puts potential lenders in a privileged position to exploit the highly inelastic demand for subsistence credit (and sometimes for conspicuous spending as well), thus drawing borrowers into a spiral of perpetual indebtedness and dissaving. Moreover, it is pointed out that because it is usually the lender's own funds that are involved, much of informal credit goes to uses with high private returns and low social ones (such as speculation in land).

It is also said of the informal financial sector that it may favour over-indebtedness by continuing to lend – at high charges – even when it would be rational not to. In effect, loans are almost never refused in the informal sector, even to those borrowers who, from the outset, do not and will not have the capacity to reimburse, especially if the cost of the loan is high. Critics of the informal financial sector argue that in some cases denying access to credit, irrespective of the rate charged, may not be so irrational or unjust after all, especially if it means avoiding a situation of perpetual indebtedness for the potential borrower.

Under such circumstances, it is argued that disparities are obviously created between those segments of the population with access to formal financial services and those without such access. And it is precisely the lower-income groups to whom the informal financial sector caters who are obliged to pay the higher interest rates which prevail on informal loans. A large fraction of farmers as well as a large number of small- and medium-scale businesses have access only to these expensive informal sources. Hence a substantial share of their profits goes into the pockets of usurers or moneylenders rather than being invested in productive activities or even simply saved.

Finally, there is the question of market segmentation. Proponents of the first view do not necessarily see this in a negative light but rather accept that there is a sort of de facto "specialisation" whereby each sector fulfills the services of its segment: the informal sector deals in small sums, mostly with private individuals and small- and medium-scale enterprises; the formal sector deals in large sums, with the corporate sector and in particular large-scale (usually public) enterprises. The stipulation is that each sector should be left to operate in the domain where its comparative advantage lies.

Proponents of the other view argue that a segmented market creates the possibility of a rent situation for lenders, does not encourage portfolio diversification, and does not allow economies of scale; ultimately, it is the savers and borrowers who bear the costs of these distortions.

B.   DETERMINING THE COSTS AND BENEFITS INVOLVED

Let us recall our initial objective of identifying, assessing, and weighting the potential costs and benefits of financial dualism. There are two main reasons why this aim is more elusive than may at first seem.

First, it cannot always be clearly determined whether financial dualism has a positive or negative impact on the five issues examined above. In presenting the two views for each of the latter, one realises that there are some valid arguments on both sides that cannot be discarded, nor tested for that matter. Such is the case, for example, with respect to the impact of financial dualism on the mobilisation of savings and on equity, for which it is difficult to come down squarely on one side or the other.

By contrast, it is our contention that the impact of financial dualism on the allocation of resources, on the efficient use of external funds, and on the effectiveness of macroeconomic and macrofinancial policies is undebatably negative. Actually, there can be no doubt that a segmented market contributes to a sub-optimal allocation of resources – both domestic and external – on a national scale; nor can it easily be disputed that financial dualism detracts from the impact of macrofinancial policies, when a sometimes substantial share of resources is circulating outside official channels.

The fact that some debatable issues remain is at the root of the second difficulty encountered, i.e. weighting the (positive or negative) effects of financial dualism to deduce the net result. How does one make an arbitrage between the different criteria? How can "efficient use of external resources" be compared with "equity", or "effectiveness of macroeconomic policies" against "mobilisation of savings"? Due to the complexity and the interlocking nature of the issues involved, there is plainly an element of value judgment which comes into play in carrying out such an exercise. The closest one could come to such an objective is thus in-depth analysis, on a country-by-country basis – quantified where possible – in view of settling on an appropriate policy to follow.

Keeping this caveat in mind, let us pursue this line of reasoning and consider the question of policy attitudes. There are three main ones that can be distinguished: "benign neglect", linkage, and integration. If one concludes, upon analysis of a situation in a given country, that the benefits derived from the presence of an informal sector offset the costs, then the policy may be one of "benign neglect" (or laissez-faire), and the government may let events take their course. If one arrives at the opposite conclusion, however, then the aim is a strategy to reduce financial dualism. In this regard, there are two possible roads to follow: linking the formal and informal financial sectors or integrating them and therefore suppressing informal financial activities.

Before examining these three concepts further, let us first try to ascertain the stand of the public authorities in the countries surveyed on the issues of financial dualism, the importance of domestic resource mobilisation, the structure of financial systems, the informal sector, etc.

II. COUNTRY POLICY ATTITUDES

The above discussion would seem to suggest that there are a number of clearly defined policy options regarding financial dualism, three of which have just been evoked, i.e. benign neglect, linkage, and integration. In reality though, very few developing countries have such an explicitly formulated policy. In most cases, one is forced to infer from the policy measures implemented regarding the functioning of the financial system as a whole what the government's stand on financial dualism really is and under which policy option it can be inscribed.

In fact, it would seem that only a limited number of developing country governments have actually set as first priority the reduction of financial dualism. In this section we shall present, in a very sketchy and therefore debatable manner, the respective implicit policy attitudes of a number of Asian countries (Philippines, Indonesia, Thailand, India and Bangladesh), African countries (Ethiopia, Togo, Burundi, Zambia and Zimbabwe) and of the sole Latin American country surveyed, Mexico.

A. PHILIPPINES

Financial policy in the Philippines from the 1950s through to the 1970s made rather extensive use of selective credit controls, low interest rate policies and rediscounting facilities for agricultural lending. The aim was to increase credit flows to stimulate economic growth and investment (especially in the agricultural and export sectors) as well as the growth of financial markets. As informal financial activity was viewed as undesirable, the initial policy adopted was also aimed at hedging it through massive expansion of formal institutions and operations.

However, the negative impact of the strict controls imposed on the financial sector was reflected in declining efficiency levels and the growing dependency of banks on government subsidies and rediscounting with the central bank, rather than on intermediation, for their funds. In addition, low recovery rates of the various special credit schemes often led to their abrupt withdrawal, leaving a vacuum which came to be filled by the informal sector.

Starting in the 1980s, a series of banking reforms were undertaken as part of a larger policy of economic liberalisation. Interest rate restrictions were gradually lifted, rediscounting and loan rates were fully deregulated in 1984, while credit subsidies and credit quotas were being limited. Banking deregulation was promoted to increase the flexibility of formal financial institutions and to test their viability at minimum government support and intervention levels. Also, a more positive stance was taken regarding the potential role of markets (money markets and stock exchange, in particular).

At the same time, a more pragmatic attitude towards the informal sector emerged. The government has gradually come to recognise the utility of informal mechanisms as a possible vector of financial innovation and development, and seems to be aware that liberalisation per se is not sufficient to attract informal financial assets towards formal circuits. The approach adopted entails both a "mimicry option" (i.e. formal sector institutions adopt informal sector-inspired practices) and a "roping-in option", where some sort of link is established between formal and informal intermediaries.

B. INDONESIA

The 1970s were marked by tight control over money supply and the allocation of credit, via regulated interest rates, refinancing policies, credit ceilings, reserve requirements to regulate liquidity, etc.

Since 1983, however, substantive moves towards liberalisation have been made with a view to stimulating domestic savings and promoting more efficient resource allocation. The government encourages the mobilisation of funds from the public through the banking system and capital market.

Measures intended to help promote the role of formal financial institutions included the removal of interest rate and credit ceilings and the easing of regulations on overdrafts, on the classification of credits, on rescheduling. Priority sector lending (in favour of small-scale enterprises, co-operatives, and export activities) through subsidy and rediscount policies was maintained. Monetary management would be carried out through cash reserve requirements, rediscount policies, and open market operations by the central bank. Efforts to promote the activities of other financial institutions (non-bank financial intermediaries, insurance companies, and leasing companies) were also begun.

In order to enhance the attractiveness of the capital market as a source of funds, a deregulation package was introduced in 1987, allowing for easier listing and less stringent profitability requirements to be imposed on enterprises wishing to go public. The market was opened to foreign participation. A parallel bourse, functioning as an over-the-counter market for small and new companies, was also created.

With regard to informal lending, the authorities have enacted legislation prohibiting some forms of informal financial activities (especially those involving the transfer of land use rights) and attempted to regulate others in view of protecting the poorer farmers. This legislation has not proved to be as effective as hoped. The government's policy is to implement institutional credit programmes and promote non-bank financial institutions which would increase institutional credit and thus replace informal credit sources. However, it should be mentioned that the government has adopted the practices of some informal operators, by creating its own governmental pawnshops, for example, which channel government funds to populations traditionally resorting to informal lenders. In addition, savings and loan co-operatives receive supplementary funds from formal institutions such as the Bank Rakyat Indonesia, or from non-governmental organisations.

Overall, financial policy in Indonesia can be considered as being on the road to liberalisation, even if a large number of formal institutions remain government-owned.

C. THAILAND

The case study consulted unfortunately did not provide much information on the official attitude towards the formal and informal sectors. It did express some criticism of the Thai government for ignoring or otherwise entertaining false premises regarding the informal sector, its practices, and its extent (the Thai informal savings and credit sector is in fact far from being the largest in the surveyed countries).

As regards the formal sector, the policy until recently has been quite directorial, enforcing, for example, a ban on the establishment of new banks for the last twenty years. Active sectoral credit allocation policies are also in force, especially in favour of rural/agricultural lending. These have been more successful than similar endeavours in other developing countries largely because of accompanying legislation requiring that leftover funds corresponding to unfulfilled agricultural lending quotas by commercial banks be deposited with the Bank for Agriculture and Agricultural Co-operatives, which itself provides a substantial share of rural credit needs.

At present, and in line with other Southeast Asian countries, Thailand appears to be oriented towards financial liberalisation, accompanied by the will to expand formal avenues – rather than maintaining the status quo – as a means of dealing with financial dualism.

D. INDIA

Initially, the Indian authorities viewed the existence and growth of the informal financial sector as detrimental to economic growth: the informal sector was considered anti-developmental, exploitative, geared to consumption rather than productive investment, and above all incapable of providing an appropriate volume and range of financial services to the population. On the premise that the bulk of accumulation should rest upon formal financial institutions, the control over financial flows has long been considered a requisite, and is reflected in both planning procedures and public ownership of commercial and investment banks.

Accordingly, the scope of formal financial institutions was extended through a substantial proliferation of bank branches, especially in rural areas, consequent to the nationalisation of commercial banks in 1969. Indeed, some success was achieved in substituting commercial bank services for non-corporate informal lending. Efforts were also made to bring the informal sector under the purview of regulations by setting interest rate ceilings on informal lending and defining deposit/borrowed funds to owned funds ratios, although these met with less success.

One can observe, however, a shift in attitude and henceforth in the policy adopted vis-à-vis the formal and informal sectors in India. On the one hand, markets gain greater credence, while on the other, the basic economic rationale of the informal sector, its capacity to satisfy financing needs that are not met by the formal sector, and its role in intermediating between savers and borrowers are increasingly being recognised. In addition, the informal sector tends to impose itself by mimicking formal practices without, however, being submitted to regulations and control from the Reserve Bank of India.

One of the policy implications of this shift in attitude taking hold in India is that the number of bank branches should not be multiplied without first considering the relative cost efficiency of formal and informal mechanisms; rather, proper co-ordination and better integration between the formal and informal sectors should be sought.

E. BANGLADESH

Despite a policy of active expansion of formal financial institutions and greater monetisation of the economy, which should raise the level of financial savings, the extent of saving through formal financial intermediaries is as yet inadequate in Bangladesh. The authorities recognise this as well as the fact that the potential savings of the rural sector are not fully mobilised, primarily because the lack of physical infrastructure and the low incomes in rural areas have a negative impact on the economic viability of rural bank branches.

In dealing with this situation, the government seems to have opted for the "mimicry option", that is, transforming formal institutions or adapting formal (government-sponsored) saving and credit schemes so that they more closely resemble informal mechanisms and practices. At the same time, various government programmes and NGO operations are seeking to stimulate co-operation, encourage individual savers to group together, and inculcate a spirit of self-sufficiency and self-help amongst the rural population. The experience of the Grameen Bank (see Box 4.7) is in keeping with this line of the government's policy.

F. ETHIOPIA

The main implications for the financial sector of the 1974 revolution in Ethiopia were the nationalisation of financial institutions, the planning of financial flows, and the centralisation of decision-making regarding the allocation of credit (in terms of volume and

210

distribution). These measures were to be accompanied by state ownership of financial institutions – so as to ensure a uniformity of policy – and a plurality of banks, with each assigned a specialised role, thereby eliminating competition or structural duplication. As a result of these policies, public savings increased to the detriment of private savings (both in absolute terms and as a percentage of total domestic savings).

The government is aware of the malfunctioning of most of the public financial institutions and of the need to relaunch private (household) savings. Towards this aim, it has opted for the institutional solution, i.e. increasing the territorial coverage of bank branches, assigning the function of mobilising savings from the public to the Commercial Bank of Ethiopia only, and eliminating the alternative channel of financing investment through the securities market, by closing down the embryonic form of stock exchange that had been created in 1965.

The official attitude towards the informal sector, on the other hand, is not the same for individual moneylenders and mutual associations. Moneylender activity is officially condemned, but efforts to suppress it have not been too successful, first because of the clandestine nature of such operations and, second, because of a lack of decisiveness in taking action against them (widespread rumour has it that moneylenders are sometimes protected by influential persons). By contrast, the potential role of mutual associations in financial intermediation is recognised, although little has effectively been done to encourage them to carry out their transactions through banks. The margins for action are admittedly narrow: the lack of knowledge with regard to the quantitative importance and the mechanisms of functioning of such groupings can partly be attributed to the fact that the existence of such associations is usually kept secret. Moreover, no legal status is conferred upon them, nor is there any incentive for them to link up with formal institutions, since real interest rates are negative.

In sum, the Ethiopian authorities see the need for domestic resource mobilisation, but at the same time they still want to exert strict control over financial flows. However, since the informal sector in Ethiopia finds its roots in the excessive control of formal insitutions, the policy led may eventually end up fueling informal activities even more.

G.   TOGO AND BURUNDI

Although it seems that the authorities have not yet formulated an explicit policy towards the informal sector, they do realise that the informal sector may have negative effects on financial deepening if neglected. They do acknowledge, however, the need for lessening the operational constraints on the formal sector. There is also a growing interest in the potential role of co-operatives in providing small-scale savings and lending facilities.

H.   ZAMBIA

As in many other developing countries, official acknowledgement by the Zambian government of the necessity of domestic resource mobilisation is relatively recent, i.e. since the mid-1980s.

Since 1985, one of the priorities of the Bank of Zambia has been to strengthen and deepen the formal financial sector, especially in rural areas. In parallel, the monetary authorities are trying to diversify formal sector activity to include lending to small-scale businesses, and are committed to further strengthening the co-operative movement. Moreover, they have made note of the need to link savings and credit facilities.

Regarding attitudes towards the informal sector, the official ambition is to formalize the rural informal financial sector as much as possible, to reduce its influence, and to bring it directly under the control and supervision of the central bank. A distinction is made between individual moneylenders and mutual associations. The government is officially against exploitative moneylending activity although in practice the stance has been more one of benign neglect. One explanation put forward for this is that the low- and middle-income groups that resort to moneylenders for funds constitute an important political base which the government cannot afford to alienate. The position vis-à-vis mutual associations is also one of relative neglect and ignorance with respect to their importance in informal intermediation activity, although the government is not openly hostile towards them.

Well aware that improving the efficiency of formal financial institutions as a way of reducing financial dualism, boosting the public's confidence in the system, increasing household savings, and ensuring a more efficient allocation of resources, is a long-term prospect, linkage between formal institutions and some informal schemes is an accepted short-term response. Here again, there is some reticence regarding individual moneylenders; in channelling funds to small borrowers through traders and village headmen there is a risk of misuse of funds and a problem of supervision. Linking formal institutions with mutual associations is seen as more "neutral", in that there may be a flow of informal sector funds to formal channels and vice versa without inducing a direct qualitative change in the nature of the informal scheme. Linkage is also sought through strong government support for the co-operative and credit union movement.

In sum, the Zambian approach to financial dualism combines the will to improve the performance of formal financial intermediaries so as to fully substitute the formal sector for the informal sector – which is a long-term objective – with acceptance of formal-informal sector linkages as a second best solution for the short term.

I. ZIMBABWE

The Zimbabwean government controls and directs the financial system via capital participation, legislation, and policy measures including liquidity ratios, the fixation of interest rates, tax exemptions on certain financial instruments, etc. In fact, the rigid interest rate structure, which results in negative real interest rates, benefits the government, which is the largest borrower in the country.

A comprehensive approach to domestic resource mobilisation is notably absent. Indeed, the promotion of personal savings as an important aspect of financial economic development has been virtually neglected. The government's main concern is the development of agriculture and service infrastructure. The vast effort of formal credit expansion actually benefited only a marginal part of the farmer population. From this stems the recent government interest in the savings club movement. The Ministry of Land, Agriculture and Rural Settlement, as well as the Ministry of Community Development and Women's Affairs are involved in endeavours to promote and co-ordinate savings clubs in view of transforming them into credit unions, and integrating them into a nationwide co-operative movement.

On the whole, the authorities view the informal sector favourably, stressing its employment creation ability and the fact that it provides loans to needy groups. However, with the exception of the Savings Club movement, their attitude could be described at best as passive.

J. MEXICO

The Mexican formal financial sector is relatively well-developed, and the authorities seem satisfied by both the structure of banks and the services they offer. However, the banks have serious problems concerning their profitability.

In principle, the nationalised banks are largely autonomous, but in practice, they are tightly controlled by the Secretariat of Finance and the Banco de Mexico (central bank).

An interesting development within the formal financial sector, after the nationalisation of commercial banks in the early 1980s, stems from the attitude of the authorities regarding the degree of freedom of non-bank financial activities: they have allowed very sophisticated private financial entities to develop and actively compete with the nationalised banks.

The attitude of the authorities towards informal finance can be summarised as follows: "Leave it be, so long as it does not undermine the foundations of the formal sector". In other words, the attitude is one of benign neglect, if not total indifference. The lack of documentation on the subject proves the point. Indeed, the only reference to this sizeable sector within the Mexican economy is to be found in studies by American anthropologists.

Nevertheless, in recent years, some efforts have been made – albeit hesitantly – to mitigate the lack of financial sources for small-scale industries and to loosen the hold of usurers ("coyotes") on the latter. Two approaches have emerged in this regard: the first one seeks to integrate informal sector borrowers as rapidly as possible by requiring that they register with the Ministry of Commerce and Industry; the second one, which is the approach of Nafinsa – the largest development bank – does not impose "formalization" on borrowers and expects that economic development will suffice to eventually integrate them. Obviously, it is this second approach which has largely prevailed.

Apart from the marginal measures described above, the authorities show no interest in either the financial activities of "tandas" (ROSCAs) or the informal transactions that take place on produce markets, for example. The argument used to justify this indifference is that the extent of informal finance is negligible and does not pose a threat to formal financial mechanisms.

The attitude of the authorities towards large-scale informal financial activities is in stark contrast to the above. Indeed, they are rapidly taking stock of the dangers of capital flight and other illegal financial transactions in hard currency.

What transpires from the preceding description of government attitudes and country experiences is that there seems to be a growing awareness of at least the presence if not the role of the informal financial sector within the overall financial system. But with the notable exception of the Philippines in Asia, and to a lesser extent Zambia in Africa, most of the countries have not yet formulated, much less implemented, an explicit and systematic policy towards financial dualism. At best, some isolated measures have been taken, as in the two aforementioned countries (and sometimes they may even be contradictory, with new measures actually undoing what the previous ones helped build up), but even so, such efforts can only be ascribed to piecemeal policies for dealing with financial dualism.

In most cases, therefore, benign neglect seems to be the rule: in some cases, this is because the authorities genuinely wish to let things as they are; but in others, it is more because they do not actually pursue an active policy to achieve a more unified and integrated financial sector.

III. STRATEGIES AND RECOMMENDATIONS

In this last section, we shall present and develop a number of policy recommendations aimed at creating a more homogeneous financial sector in developing countries.

In reference to the framework proposed at the beginning of this chapter, these policy recommendations stem from the belief that, on the whole, the costs implied by a persistent state of financial dualism are greater than the benefits derived. In this context, a neutral stand ("benign neglect" or "laissez-faire") on financial dualism is judged untenable and a strategy for reducing financial dualism becomes imperative.

Reducing financial dualism is thus justified on both economic and social grounds. The establishment of a balanced economic, monetary and financial environment is one of the prerequisites, although not the only one, for more regular and balanced growth rates. Above all, it is a prerequisite for re-establishing more self-sustaining growth which is less dependent on foreign factors and less exposed to fluctuations on the international capital markets.

A. INTEGRATION OR LINKAGE?

The obvious question that follows is: which of the two remaining strategies – or policy options – distinguished earlier should one opt for, linkage of the formal and informal financial sectors, or integration of the two?

Let us take the case of integration first. The ultimate goal here is to achieve a single, homogeneous financial system by expanding and transforming the formal financial sector so that it fully absorbs informal financial activities. The aim, then, is to dismantle the informal sector at all costs, disregarding the potential adverse effects that such a "hard integration" approach may have over the longer term.

The strategy of linkage of the formal and informal financial sectors, on the other hand, tolerates a certain degree of financial dualism and seeks not so much to suppress as to reduce the gap between the two sectors by promoting closer links between formal and informal operators on a more systematic scale in order to work through the informal sector as a means of "retailing" formal financial services to areas, sectors or population groups that are difficult to reach. The aim is to preserve and use to advantage the positive aspects of the informal sector while at the same time reforming formal financial institutions.

This approach stems from recognition of the fact that, in addition to its own dynamic for financial intermediation, the informal financial sector plays a supporting role to the formal sector by filling the gap left by the asymmetrical intermediation of the latter. It is pointed out that the rapidity and adaptability characteristic of informal financial transactions would disappear if any outright attempt were made to reduce the informal sector by extending the formal sector and substituting it for the former, as would the principles of solidarity, trust and mutuality – the very basis on which informal savings and credit groups are set up and operated – which are in fact the guarantee of their efficiency. There is thus an indomitable nucleus in the informal financial sector – namely social ties – which would break apart if any attempt were made to formalize that which is informal. As Chandavarkar[5] states, "attempts to formalize the informal sector are liable to fail because its very rationale derives from its informality."

At the same time, partisans of the linkage approach underline the need to loosen some of the constraints on the formal financial sector and thus correct some of the present biases in its intermediation activities. Such measures would include liberalising interest rates (rather than fixing them at a higher level), reducing excessive reserve requirements for commercial banks, removing sectoral allocation policies, etc.; alternative markets for savings (equities, unit trusts, life insurance, pension funds) could also be created or reinforced. However, they stress the fact that it is pointless – worse, counter-productive – to multiply the number of bank branches without considering the relative cost efficiency between the formal and informal financial sectors, and argue instead for greater co-ordination between the two.

At first sight, it would seem that the two strategies described above – integration on the one hand, linkage on the other – are opposed, and hence incompatible, but it is our contention that this is actually a false distinction. In a dynamic context, the two strategies can be seen as sequential, with linkage in the short and medium term preceding integration in the long term; that is to say, until the formal sector can cover the country's financial needs on its own (which is, after all, the ultimate goal in the very long term), the informal sector could be used to do a part of the job, on condition of course that the "exploitative" elements of informal financial activity be weeded out as much as possible. Thus the linkage strategy is seen as a first step towards achieving the goal of a homogeneous financial sector (integration).

Such an approach, which could be termed "soft integration", is based on the premise that letting financial dualism intensify would have negative effects, and so some sort of action to reduce it is warranted, but this action should not be to try and suppress informal finance at all costs, since this amounts to dismantling something operational with no clue as to what will ensue. Rather, the reduction of financial dualism must be done gradually and more through a process of cross-fertilization between the two sectors than through outright substitution – in the initial stages (short- and medium-term) at least. It is against this background that the policy recommendations which follow should be seen.

B. MEASURES TO PROGRESSIVELY REDUCE THE GAP

In more concrete terms, what does "soft integration" entail? The policy recommendations stemming from this perspective involve both macroeconomic and microeconomic measures in view of transforming and improving the efficiency of the formal and informal financial sectors. One may distinguish four series of measures in this regard:

– *A more liberal macrofinancial policy:* It shall be recalled that both the presence and the robustness of the informal financial sector are largely attributed to an excessive regulation in the formal sector. It is not surprising therefore that financial liberalisation measures should appear foremost among the macro-policy reforms advocated.

The line of argument is as follows: liberalising interest rates would encourage the growth of financial assets and liabilities, which would in turn favour institutional development and attract individual borrowers and savers away from the informal sector and inflation hedges towards the formal sector and monetary assets. By gradually widening the range of financial instruments available, narrow, inefficient and fragmented capital markets could develop into wider and more efficient ones. In turn, this would tend to promote economic development.

However, it is also important to note that financial repression is not the sole explanatory factor behind financial dualism and hence financial liberalisation is not the sole "remedy" for reducing it. Other macroeconomic policies which must be reviewed touch upon the issues of money supply, inflation, taxation, exchange rates, etc.

  – *Improving the functioning of the formal financial sector:* There are a number of ways in which in-depth institutional and operational reforms may be achieved. Reshaping the formal financial sector, for example, would entail streamlining existing financial institutions with a view to raising their efficiency levels, and promoting alternative financial instruments, notably by encouraging the development of insurance and social security structures.

At the same time, improving the functioning of the formal sector would also involve what could be called its "deformalization", that is, the expansion of formal sector services to areas heretofore served by the informal sector by adopting some of the latter's own practices and competing it down. This is known as the "mimicry option". By liberalising and deformalizing formal sector activity, the gap between the formal and informal financial sectors as regards lending practices, savings facilities, collateral requirements, etc. can gradually be reduced, thus obviating the need for the informal sector itself and leading to the integration of the informal sector into the formal financial system.

  – *Better organising the informal financial sector:* Financial dualism may also be perceived as but one aspect of the overall structural dualism of the economy (see Chapter 1). In this case, the population's attachment to and preference for traditional values and practices over formal financial services reflects not only the cultural barriers involved but also practical issues such as lack of infrastructure for easy access to banks, illiteracy, unfamiliarity with the handling of money, intimidating bureaucratic procedures, etc.; in short, the people often lack the minimal "technology" which is necessary for access to formal sector services.

Reducing economic dualism would therefore contribute to reducing financial dualism, and it would also be appropriate to act on the informal financial sector itself.

Efforts must focus on gaining better knowledge of informal practices and on providing supportive services to try and improve efficiency. The aim is to eventually "institutionalise" the informal sector, by gradually subjecting it to more and more controls, so that, over time, informal operators will become official entities whose transactions are taxed and regulated, as in the formal sector, and informal transactions will be penalised and eventually suppressed. By targeting informal lenders and the leaders of informal groups (savings and credit associations, co-operatives, etc.) and giving them access to credit lines or other services, for example, formal financial institutions can transmit, through them, to the rest of the population, the mechanics and mentality of formal financial practices and thus rope-in and gradually "formalize" the informal sector.

  – *Promoting closer links between the formal and informal financial sectors:* This would entail identifying the common horizons that exist already and which may take the form of a flow of funds between the two sectors – in both directions – or a common clientele (people with access to both sectors), or a relative similarity from an operational point of view (informal finance companies or social insurance mechanisms, for example). The aim would be to systematise such "exchanges" and promote them on a greater scale. Formal financial institutions would benefit from extending and adapting their intermediation activities by "retailing" financial services through informal operators themselves. At the same time, the informal sector could benefit from closer linkage with formal sector operators, by way of the additional funds and guidance that would be received.

The four series of measures briefly outlined above would all contribute to advancing a "soft integration" process of the formal and informal financial sectors. In this regard, there are two final points which must be underlined. First, it cannot be stressed enough that each of these courses of action are necessary conditions, but not sufficient if taken on their own, for the reduction of financial dualism. For instance, financial liberalisation is not enough to bring down the transaction costs incurred in providing financial services to outlying areas where such basic infrastructural facilities as roads, electricity, telephones, are lacking. By the same token, there is no point in trying to institutionalise the informal sector by bringing it under the purview of precisely those regulations which are at least partially responsible for the inefficiency of the formal sector. Hence it is effectively a combination of all four elements that should be aimed for, as each one seems to form an essential part of an ensemble.

The second point which must be stressed is that reducing financial dualism to achieve a more unified financial sector appears clearly as a long-term prospect spanning several decades. There can be no short-cuts in this matter – even though the problem is a pressing one – not only because both policy reforms and institutional restructuring may run up against an initial degree of inertia, but also because it would be imprudent to try to effectuate a major transformation of the financial system all in one go.

Having thus indicated what we think to be the desirable drift of policy reforms, let us now look in closer detail at some of the concrete measures which could be implemented to this effect.

C. POLICY RECOMMENDATIONS

1. Pursuing Appropriate Monetary and Financial Policies

As has already been pointed out, the constraints influencing financial systems of developing countries are both macroeconomic and microeconomic.

Obviously, any course of action to reduce financial dualism must take into account the overall financial and economic environment in which both the formal and informal financial sectors operate. Thus, an analysis must be made of the characteristics of those monetary, financial, and economic policies likely to promote integration of the formal and informal sectors.

With a view to the long-term integration of the formal and informal financial sectors, it is appropriate to define new aims for monetary policy. A policy of "regulated" interest rates could thus replace a policy of "administered" interest rates. The nuance is admittedly a fine one, and refers to the degree of control exerted by the monetary authorities over the interest rates applied by the banking system. "Regulation" of interest rates could be considered as slightly less authoritarian than "administration" of interest rates; the former would rely more on a system of directives whereas the latter is based more on injunctions. This distinction thus being made, the policy of regulated interest rates would further be accompanied by a policy restricting the money supply and a voluntary exchange rate policy.

The policy of regulating, rather than administering, interest rates has three aims. The prohibition of interest-bearing deposits in the formal sector should gradually be lifted and eventually completely removed. Such a measure would reinforce competition between collecting networks in the formal sector on the one hand, and between those networks and collecting networks in the informal sector on the other. In the longer term, by suppressing regulated deposit rates, it should be possible to increase the combined efficiency of the two sectors with regard to collecting savings.

The main argument in favour of the need to introduce positive real interest rates on demand deposits is based on an analysis of the specific characteristics of developing countries. The reasoning is based on the idea that the level of national income has a positive correlation with real monetary holdings[6]. At first sight this may seem surprising since, according to traditional economic theory, it is usually the opposite phenomenon which occurs.

In order to explain this apparent paradox, it is sufficient to compare the situation of developing countries (where in many cases there is only one item under the heading "assets", to the exclusion of all other financial items), with developed countries, where agents have a whole range of possible investments at their disposal. Nor is it possible to substitute financial assets for monetary assets in developing countries, quite simply because apart from money and other liquid assets, the only other types of assets available are real assets. Thus there can be no portfolio arbitrage.

Positive real returns on monetary deposits could lead to an increase in the volume of bank holdings. This may result from reduced hoarding (reduction of idle holdings), from the recycling in the formal sector of funds which formerly circulated in the informal sector (reduction or even inversion of the gap in the rates between the two sectors), or from a higher rate of retention of capital (cancelling out the interest differential between investments abroad and those in the domestic economy).

Furthermore, positive real returns on monetary deposits is presumed to increase the volume of savings, by protecting the assets of households and firms against inflation and by increasing their financial income. It would appear that the savings rate is more sensitive to the interest rate in developing countries than in developed countries, as can be seen from the results of the econometric studies listed in Table 4.1.

The combined effects of attracting monetary funds to the banks and of increasing the rate of monetary savings would stimulate growth because capital could thus be recycled and mobilised in the context of the whole economy, by means of banking circuits. Such a policy would result in a progressive siphoning off of funds from the informal sector into formal channels.

The liberalisation of creditor rates should be accompanied by a progressive liberalisation of debtor rates in the formal sector without any systematic favouritism towards those with access to the institutions in the formal sector. Thus liberalisation would contribute to a more equal access to credit for those urban entrepreneurs who borrow from lenders and for the rural masses resorting to lenders and credit groups in the informal sector.

In addition, this liberalisation strategy may act as a brake on "rerouting" transactions observed in many developing countries; lenders, pawnbrokers and indigenous bankers will be less likely to borrow at low interest rates from formal intermediaries in order to lend at higher – sometimes prohibitive – rates in the informal sector.

Table 4.1 CORRELATION BETWEEN SAVINGS RATES AND INTEREST RATES IN DEVELOPING COUNTRIES: SOME EMPIRICAL RESULTS

Authors	Country	Variables	Results
Williamson (1968)	6 countries in Asia	National savings and interest rates	Correlations <0 (investment decisions and savings are interdependent in many households)
Gupta (1970)	India	Aggregate savings and real interest rates Savings per capita and real interest rates	Correlation >0 but not significantly 0 Correlation >0
Brown (1971)	South Korea	Level of private savings Level of household savings Level of domestic savings	All correlations are >0, the highest ones are obtained with the average savings rates. Correlations for marginal savings rates are not significant.
		Average rate of private savings Average rate of household savings Average rate of domestic savings (Each rate is calculated from GNP and disposable income)	
		Marginal rate of private savings Marginal rate of household savings Marginal rate of domestic savings and real interest rates on time and savings deposits	
Kim (1973)	South Korea	Elasticity of household savings to interest rates Elasticity of private savings to interest rates	Elasticity = 1.35 Elasticity = 0.48
Frank, Kim & Westphal (1975)	South Korea	Elasticity of household savings to interest rates (period 1955-1970) Elasticity of savings by entrepreneurs to interest rates	Elasticity = 1.82 Elasticity = 0.34
Fry (1978-1980)	7 countries in Asia	Domestic savings rates and real interest rates (period 1960s)	Correlations >0
Giovannini (1983)	7 countries in Asia (the same as Fry)	Aggregate domestic savings and real interest rates (period 1970s)	Correlations <0 in general and not significant
McDonald (1983)	12 countries in Latin America	Elasticity of private consumption per capita to real interest rates	Correlations <0 hence >0 for savings for all countries except Mexico and Guatemala and significant for all countries except Mexico, Costa Rica and Colombia

Source: Fry, Maxwell J., "National Saving, Financial Saving and Interest Rate Policy in 14 Asian Developing Economies", Third International Symposium on the Mobilization of Personal Savings in Developing Countries, Yaoundé, Cameroon, 10-14 December 1984, mimeo.

Finally, liberalising lending rates may be accompanied by reduced quantitative rationing of credit, particularly among the usual clients of the formal sector. This statement must be qualified, however. Without doubt high borrowing rates lead to more rigorous project selection but they can also draw entrepreneurs into selecting increasingly risky investment projects, given the positive correlation between risk and profitability.

It seems pointless to practise a policy of regulated interest rates, if the structure of borrowing and lending rates is not also taken into account. In this context, a reduction of financial dualism would involve reducing the gap between borrowing and lending interest rates, both in the formal and informal sectors.

However, such a monetary strategy is only effective if it is accompanied by deflationary measures. In order to bring about positive real interest rates, nominal rates (at a given rate of inflation), could initially be allowed to increase; however, in a later stage, inflation rates must fall in parallel with nominal rates.

A policy of positive real interest rates also calls for control of the money supply. Reducing dualism, in particular through microeconomic measures in each of the two sectors, eventually leads to more effective control of monetary regulation. In fact, reducing dualism leads to increased monetisation of the economy. Monetary authorities thus have better knowledge and control of monetary flows. In addition, reducing dualism allows for a better understanding of the monetary multiplier[7].

A policy of restrictive money supply would help protect savings against monetary depreciation. The implicit "tax" on deposits would thus disappear at the same rate as disinflation. The government would then have to implement tax reforms in order to secure non-monetary financing of its expenditures. Other inflationary transfers between agents would also decrease, bringing income distribution more in line with that of productivity.

Throughout the period of disinflation, supportive measures could be taken, such as creating financial products with regulated rates, so that they continue to yield overall positive returns.

Finally, the policy of regulated interest rates should be accompanied by an active exchange rate policy.

On the one hand, restrictions on capital movements should progressively be lifted. The risk of capital flight would be lessened to the extent that a policy of positive real interest rates would reduce the gap between interest rates on capital at home and on international markets. Such progressive liberalisation of capital movements would benefit from a concurrent liberalisation of trade flows (in particular, reduced taxation on exports).

On the other hand, it appears desirable to forgo a policy of fixed exchange rates, as this is more or less incompatible with strict control of the money supply. Such action would not of course imply adopting a policy of flexible exchange rates. In reality, most developing countries are open to the world market. In a system of flexible exchange rates, any shock affecting bilateral exchange rates would create imbalances in the foreign trade sector, and hence in the economy as a whole.

Foreign exchange policy is thus situated somewhere between these two extremes. A policy of pegging exchange rates to one currency or to a basket of currencies could be adapted in some cases to the particular situation of developing countries.

Defining new aims for monetary policy does not in itself suffice to promote the ultimate integration of the formal and informal financial sectors. The efficiency of monetary policy is in fact limited when money markets are narrow, shallow and very sensitive to a variation in the volume of transactions. Accordingly, financial markets should be developed in order to bring together those economic agents with financing capacity and those requiring financing.

The matching of financing capacities and borrowing requirements could be made on two levels.

Within formal financial insitutions, the savings and credit functions could – indeed should – be integrated more extensively. In the longer run, multi-purpose financial institutions could be set up; these would provide standardized financial services and, for certain functions, operate along the lines of groups in the informal sector. By standardizing the savings collection and credit distribution networks in the formal sector in this necessarily progressive manner, financial organisations would be able to expand their clientele. This widening of activities would then be reinforced by a decentralisation of services offered to customers.

There can be no doubt that financial markets would also be enlarged as a result of the integration of savings and credit functions within formal financial institutions. However, in-depth development of financial markets would require additional, specific measures; this is particularly so for the organised financial markets such as futures markets for agricultural produce, stock exchanges, mortgage markets, etc. Financial markets have proved to be very efficient in some developing countries (particularly in Southeast Asia), in collecting and distributing savings[8]. The stock exchange which was set up in Côte d'Ivoire has been less successful in collecting savings, but has nonetheless contributed actively to the "Ivoirisation" of the economy[9]. In the same way that dualism should be progressively reduced, the pace for developing financial markets should also be steady without any abrupt changes. A market which has a restricted number of agents and where the volume of transactions is modest is indeed a fragile one.

Lastly, although the public authorities must organise and regulate certain markets, it would appear desirable for the Treasury to progressively disengage itself from the procedures of collection, centralisation, remuneration (interest payments), and allocation of funds.

The measures of monetary and financial policy outlined above should favour the long-term integration of the formal and informal financial sectors. Such measures must also be seen, however, within the framework of a global macroeconomic policy. Thus the necessity of reducing financial dualism entails reformulating certain aims of macroeconomic policy.

Industrial and capital policy should therefore take into account the new aims defined for monetary policy. The gradual removal of administered interest rates could prompt the public authorities to redefine sectoral credit allocation policies as well. Such policies in fact give preferential treatment to certain sectors of activity in accordance with criteria which sometimes defy economic logic. Microeconomic and decentralised selection of investment projects through interest rates should ultimately replace macroeconomic selectivity criteria. This would end the often arbitrary practices of sectoral credit allocation and preferential interest rates; thereupon, the definition and implementation of sectoral development policies would be handled by the budgetary authorities.

In the same vein, it appears difficult to eliminate administered interest rates without also modifying price control policies, which are frequently the cause of distortions in resource allocation. Through a redefinition of global aims in this manner, monetary, financial and economic policies could contribute to reducing financial dualism.

It is often said that such economic, monetary and financial policies are highly likely to increase the domestic rate of savings in those developing countries which decide to implement them. Their efficiency has been the subject of much discussion, and the debate is far from settled. The countries which have applied these measures are mainly Asian (South Korea, Taiwan, Malaysia, etc.). To date, no African countries appear to have set out along this path. Nor is it certain that the experience of Asian countries can be transposed to developing countries situated in other parts of the world.

It appears that the countries which followed this policy have experienced a rise in their savings rate (see Tables 4.2 to 4.4), a fall in inflation and an acceleration in the growth rate, although some observers would see this change as arising not as a result of the policies pursued but rather as a result of other factors.

The liberalisation strategy has been criticised on both analytical and empirical grounds. From the analytical point of view, one may contend that the rate of inflation does not depend upon the money supply and hence that a reduction in price rises may not be achieved through a restrictive monetary policy. Control of the money supply is very difficult in the developing countries due to internal dualism and the constant flight of money abroad. Furthermore, the positive relationship between real cash holdings and growth remains largely obscure. As a result, one may wonder whether money can indeed become a factor of production; in other words, whether an increase in cash balances can lead to an increase of GDP. Finally, the increase of the financial savings which should result from the implementation of a restrictive monetary policy would not be net savings. In effect, this rise in savings levels may actually be the result of an inflow of funds formerly circulating in informal channels[10] or reflect a decline in public savings (due notably to the reduction of the inflationary "tax") which are still the most important component of domestic savings in many developing countries. As for the use of the mobilised funds, private savings are used for the purchase of consumer durables (housing, automobiles, etc.) while public savings are channelled into investments aimed at improving the overall economic and social conditions of the national community.

Regarding the success of those countries in Southeast Asia that have pursued financial liberalisation policies, it is frequently said that these countries in fact benefited, above all, from an influx of cheap capital (and direct investments). Moreover, the increase in the rate of savings recorded would be due to a high concentration of incomes rather than to a policy of positive real interest rates, and the accumulation recorded would hence reflect an increase in the inequality of incomes and wealth.

It is not possible to transpose development models directly from one country to another. Care should be taken to avoid assuming that a policy which has proved successful in one country will necessarily produce the same effects in another country at another time. Nevertheless, the exchange of views and of experiences can only be useful in the search for the appropriate economic, monetary and financial policies to be implemented in individual countries.

2. Improving the Formal Financial Sector

This may entail reforms in the banking sector, "mimicry" of informal sector practices, and the development of social security and contractual savings.

a) Reforms in the Banking Sector

The Third International Symposium of the United Nations on the mobilisation of savings in developing countries, among its final recommendations, adopted, in particular, the following aims: "Financial institutions are called upon to live in symbiosis with their environment if they wish to develop and actively participate in the development process.

Table 4.2   SAVINGS RATES IN ASIAN COUNTRIES

Date	BA	BU	HK	IN	IO	KO	MA	NE	PA	PH	SG	SR	TA	TH
1970	7.1	10.6	25.0	18.2	10.8	17.0	25.8	2.5	13.0	21.2	18.2	18.7	25.6	21.3
1971	3.8	9.2	25.4	18.7	13.8	14.6	22.8	4.0	12.7	20.4	18.5	15.5	28.9	21.0
1972	-3.4	9.9	28.5	18.3	17.0	16.8	20.7	5.0	12.6	19.9	24.3	15.7	32.1	19.3
1973	9.9	10.6	26.4	18.8	19.0	22.5	30.3	5.3	13.4	25.0	29.6	11.6	34.6	22.3
1974	-0.5	9.8	26.1	19.6	24.7	19.5	30.0	3.6	9.6	23.7	29.1	6.3	31.7	22.0
1975	-0.6	8.9	25.3	21.1	22.0	20.6	24.6	4.7	7.2	24.4	28.3	9.9	27.5	20.8
1976	-0.4	9.6	33.6	22.8	22.0	23.7	33.6	7.4	9.5	24.5	32.0	15.8	33.3	20.9
1977	3.7	11.8	30.3	20.9	24.4	27.3	32.6	9.4	9.5	25.2	32.9	17.4	33.6	20.7
1978	2.7	13.9	26.4	23.3	22.4	28.3	31.9	7.6	7.5	23.6	32.6	17.6	35.4	23.3
1979	2.5	18.7	31.1	23.0	28.7	28.7	37.6	8.6	5.9	25.7	34.9	14.7	34.6	23.1
1980	2.5	19.0	31.4	20.0	30.5	24.4	33.3	7.4	6.4	25.0	37.6	10.9	32.8	22.2
1981	1.5	19.5	30.4	20.6	24.3	24.2	27.7	7.0	6.3	25.3	40.0	12.8	31.9	20.5
1982	1.6	15.2	28.5	-	19.3	25.0	26.7	2.0	5.3	22.0	42.3	10.3	30.5	21.6
1983	3.3	17.4	24.5	-	-	-	28.9	-6.4	4.7	20.4	-	-	31.6	20.6

BA   Bangladesh
BU   Burma
HK   Hong Kong
IN   India
IO   Indonesia
KO   South Korea
MA   Malaysia

NE   Nepal
PA   Pakistan
PH   Philippines
SG   Singapore
SR   Sri Lanka
TA   Taiwan
TH   Thailand

– Data not available.
Source: Fry, op. cit., 1984.

223

Table 4.3 MAIN ECONOMIC VARIABLES (AVERAGES FOR 1961-1972)
IN ASIAN COUNTRIES

Country	Sn/Y	Sd/Y	NFI/Y	SF/Y	I/Y	gy	g
BA	7.28	7.04	0.25	3.07	10.35	1.69	1.53
BU	10.44	10.44	0.00	1.83	12.27	2.97	3.00
HK	19.16	19.16	0.00	3.51	22.67	9.31	9.44
IN	15.92	16.62	−0.70	2.14	18.06	3.49	3.39
IO	5.62	6.66	−1.03	4.87	10.49	5.25	4.83
KO	11.48	10.68	0.81	8.94	20.42	7.94	7.93
MA	20.27	22.69	−2.42	−0.97	19.30	4.83	6.60
NE	3.36	1.86	1.50	2.56	5.91	2.38	2.19
PA	11.74	12.00	−0.26	5.69	17.43	5.81	5.99
PH	18.52	19.30	−0.78	1.80	20.32	4.53	5.09
SG	15.56	13.91	1.65	9.19	24.75	4.22	9.24
SR	11.41	12.69	−1.28	4.35	15.76	1.89	4.15
TA	21.49	21.61	−0.12	1.17	22.66	9.67	9.70
TH	19.68	19.68	0.00	2.37	22.05	7.22	7.34

Sn/Y: National savings rate.
SD/Y: Domestic savings rate.
NFI/Y: Net factor income from abroad (as percentage of GNP).
SF/Y: Foreign savings rate.
I/Y: Rate of investment.
gy: Growth rate of real national income.
g: Growth rate of real GNP.

See key of Table 4.2 for country abbreviations.
Source: Fry, *op. cit.*, 1984.

Unless they are adapted to the environment in which they are located, financial institutions will have difficulties in increasing savings deposits or the volume and quality of credits"[11].
This adaptation to the environment may assume many forms:

1. simplified installations in rural areas;
2. simplified procedures;
3. transparency of management procedures;
4. decentralised management;
5. an increased range of financial services;
6. development of new guarantee systems;
7. development of guidance and assistance services.

The financial institutions must adopt communication policies adapted to the environment in which they hope to develop their activities (problems of dialect, ways and customs). The structure of installations in rural areas should be as simple as possible to avoid increasing intermediation costs. In some countries, mobile banks were tried as one way of providing savings and credit services in outlying areas (see Box 4.1).

Simplifying deposit and lending procedures could also be envisaged. Reducing and simplifying the amount of paperwork involved in requesting a loan, developing simple systems for collecting small-scale savings deposits, reducing delays in loan disbursement, introducing greater flexibility in repayment schedules, etc., all these measures would contribute towards making the institutions in the formal sector more accessible to the habitual clients of the informal sector.

Table 4.4 MAIN ECONOMIC VARIABLES (AVERAGES FOR 1973-1983)
IN ASIAN COUNTRIES

Country	Sn/Y	Sd/Y	NFI/Y	SF/Y	I/Y	gy	g
BA	3.49	2.38	1.11	5.73	9.21	4.98	5.12
BU	12.70	14.04	−1.34	4.29	16.99	5.00	5.00
HK	28.55	28.55	0.00	0.88	29.43	7.99	8.02
IN	20.79	21.12	−0.33	1.57	22.36	3.82	4.08
IO	19.67	23.74	−4.07	1.37	21.03	9.68	6.83
KO	22.78	24.42	−1.64	6.36	29.14	6.05	7.45
MA	26.50	30.67	−4.17	1.82	28.31	6.43	6.85
NE	7.02	5.14	1.68	3.74	10.76	2.68	2.89
PA	12.48	7.74	4.73	3.04	15.51	5.86	5.96
PH	23.61	24.07	−0.45	5.16	28.77	4.79	5.35
SG	32.18	33.94	−1.76	9.99	42.17	5.52	7.61
SR	11.76	12.73	−0.98	9.83	21.59	3.15	4.59
TA	32.24	32.50	−0.26	−1.98	30.26	5.09	7.47
TH	20.30	21.63	−1.33	5.03	25.33	5.60	6.30

Sn/Y: National savings rate.
SD/Y: Domestic savings rate.
NFI/Y: Net factor income from abroad (as percentage of GNP).
SF/Y: Foreign savings rate.
I/Y: Rate of investment.
gy: Growth rate of real national income.
g: Growth rate of real GNP.

See key of Table 4.2 for country abbreviations.
Source: Fry, *op. cit.,* 1984.

Transparency of management in institutions is also essential to reinforcing client confidence. Through increased understanding of how an institution is managed, clients can contribute more towards its development and targets. Moreover, by involving clients in management activities, savings and credit organisations are likely to increase their efficiency and the number of potential clients.

As a result of increased independence, particularly with regard to management, financial institutions in the formal sector should be able to adapt more quickly to changing needs. This independence goes hand-in-glove with increased decentralisation within these very institutions themselves, and the encouragement of regional and even local units[12].

Appropriate savings schemes must therefore be developed, particularly for small amounts, in order to extend the range of formal financial services. Another important way of achieving this, in addition to what has heretofore been described, would be to develop products which include both savings and credit aspects. A given amount of savings would automatically confer eligibility for a pre-determined volume of credit. The government could perhaps help advance these objectives by offering premiums to those individuals who are making an active savings effort. This type of formula in fact acts as an incentive to save, and partly solves the problem of guarantees, to the extent that the savings deposits could serve as a guarantee that the loan to which they are linked will be repaid. In addition, formal financial institutions must offer more consumer credit and personal loans. In many cases they leave such loans to lenders in the informal sector. As a general rule, it would appear that multi-purpose financial organisations are more efficient than those with a specialised function.

Box 4.1

MOBILE BANK AGENCIES IN ZIMBABWE

Commercial banks in Zimbabwe have few permanent branches in rural areas. At the instigation of the Reserve Bank of Zimbabwe, and in an effort to improve rural banking services as well as to enable farmers to cash the cheques they receive from the marketing boards in payment for their produce, commercial banks introduced, in 1985, mobile banking services at 60 rural locations.

Although this represents a considerable improvement in the provision of rural banking services, there are still a number of drawbacks which should be mentioned. First of all, mobile bank agencies do not offer the full range of banking services: they cash cheques and accept deposits but do not grant loans. Moreover, the high minimum savings deposit requirements and other restrictions they impose cannot easily be met by the rural population. In this sense, bringing formal financial services closer to the rural populations is not of much help unless access to these services is also made easier.

Not surprisingly, the response of the targeted population has also been poor. Aside from the fact that the introduction of mobile bank units may not have been sufficiently publicised, most of the places served are small and hence the number of potential clients is limited. In addition, at many of the locations served, mobile agencies are not the only ones to offer deposit facilities. In fact, they must compete with the more permanent fixtures of the Post Office Savings Bank, for example, which inspire far more confidence than mobile units. Indeed, the problem with mobile deposit facilities is not only a feeling that "the truck took our savings and went away"; it also reflects an attitude that "deposits require an iron door and a marble countertop".

As a result, when the cost of transport, personnel, and the use of premises is considered, mobile agencies are in most cases an expensive form of banking. Cheques need to be cashed only at certain times of the year, and in most areas deposits are still negligible. Consequently, the commercial banks involved in this exercise are currently incurring considerable losses. In the final analysis, the question of mobile banking agencies must be assessed in light of economic viability as well as development function concerns.

New formulas could be envisaged with regard to guarantees, the absence of which acts as a brake in the granting of loans to potential borrowers in rural areas. Creating a loan-insurance system in the institutional sector could provide guarantees for high-risk, small-account clients. In the same manner, the use of tangible guarantees could be enlarged, based on crops and using sales domiciliation methods. Lastly, futures markets for agricultural produce could be developed to simplify credit arrangements, since both the borrower and the lender would know the amount of future revenues.

SMALL-SCALE DEPOSIT AND LENDING SCHEMES IN THE INDIAN FORMAL SECTOR

The Syndicate Bank in Karnataka State, India, has successfully implemented its Pygmy Deposit Scheme which caters to small-scale savers and borrowers. The "mimicry" aspect of this scheme lies in the small size of the amounts collected by field agents on a daily basis from the doorsteps of customers (street vendors, labourers, village traders). The minimum required deposit is a quarter of a rupee per day. Interest rates paid on these deposits are lower than rates on regular savings deposits on the grounds that collection costs are high and that there is no alternative use for such small sums anyway, other than their remaining idle.

Furthermore, from the point of view of the targeted population, there are two other aspects of the scheme which still make it attractive, despite the low deposit rates. One is that local deposits are used for local investment. The other is that credit and technical assistance facilities are made available to small-scale farmers, retail traders, transport operators, and other professionals.

In addition to the savings and credit services offered, financial institutions could propose complementary guidance and assistance services to their clients. In this way they would serve as an efficient channel for distributing information on prices, markets, production and marketing techniques. In other words, an economic role would be added to their financial one[13] (see Box 4.2).

b) "Mimicry" of Informal Sector Practices

Besides the above seven recommendations, another way for formal financial institutions to extend the scope of their savings and lending activities would be to adopt certain features of informal sector practices. Financial innovation via the "mimicry option" entails first understanding the rationale of informal sector mechanisms and then taking a fresh look at the procedures and requirements of formal institutions in consequence. Sometimes the ultimate objective may be to effectively compete with (and eventually even replace) informal operators in providing small-scale financial services in high transaction cost situations.

There are several ways in which this process may be manifest. For one thing, mutual association mechanisms are often set up by the staff of formal sector banks themselves, with contributions automatically deducted from salaries. Sometimes the initiative may come from the management itself in order to cope with the high number of requests for advances before pay-day. In another case, in Ethiopia, the Commercial Bank of Ethiopia even provides personal loans to its employees to the tune of a three-month advance of salary at 6 per cent interest with repayment in 18 monthly instalments.

Box 4.3

PAWNSHOPS IN SOUTHEAST ASIA

One of the most obvious examples of the "mimicry option", i.e. the adoption of informal practices by the formal sector, is the expansion of government-run pawnshops in Thailand, Malaysia and Indonesia.

Pawnshops are primarily private, family businesses that lend small amounts, mostly for consumption purposes but occasionally for investment purposes, against the collateral of portable household effects which are left with them for the duration of the loan. These tangible guarantees such as gold, jewellery, electrical goods, are not usually acceptable to commercial banks. The size of the loan is a function of the appraised value of the collateral offered. For instance, in Thailand, pawnshops grant loans of up to 80-90 per cent of the appraised value of gold and jewellery, 60-80 per cent of the appraised value of diamonds, 50 per cent of the value of electrical goods.

In Thailand and Malaysia, where pawnbroker businesses must be licensed to operate, interest rates are subject to a ceiling: 2-3 per cent per month in Malaysia, 1.25-2 per cent per month in Thailand.

Private pawnshop activities have apparently proved to be successful enough to warrant the setting up of federal and municipal pawnshops in Thailand, which lend at rates that are competitive with those of private businesses. In Indonesia, the government has a legal monopoly of pawnbroking and, in fact, the growth of government pawnshop business has been impressive, as can be seen from the table below. (The high redemption rates, primarily since 1980, result from the fact that unredeemed pawns are auctioned without delay.) In fact, according to one assessment, government pawnshops in Indonesia proved to be more effective in providing the poor with access to institutional credit than some of the programmes administered by the state commercial banks.

INDONESIA: PAWNSHOP ACTIVITY
Loan figures in Rp billion

	Number of offices	Total loans extended	Redemption	Outstanding loans
1975	441	31	29	8
1976	441	38	35	11
1977	441	46	44	13
1978	446	59	56	16
1979	448	90	83	23
1980	450	110	103	30
1981	463	156	144	42
1982	471	177	175	44
1983	473	221	210	55
1984	474	246	239	62
1985	479	274	271	65
1986	480	330	319	81

Source: Bank Indonesia, *Annual Report* 1987-1988.

Box 4.4

MONEYSHOPS IN THE PHILIPPINES

A phenomenon that has developed in the urban areas of the Philippines is the extension of banking services by a few formal financial intermediaries through "moneyshops". More specifically, the Philippine Commercial and Industrial Bank (PCIB) has launched a "bridge-building" banking mechanism since 1973. The PCIB moneyshop occupies one of the many market stalls in public markets and offers working capital to the market vendors. Similarly to the Grameen Bank in Bangladesh (see Box 4.7), a positive feature of the moneyshop is the easy access to established on-site banking facilities where money can be borrowed easily and conveniently. The convenience is reflected in the fact that the money shop has adjusted its operations to the business patterns in the marketplace. For example, unlike ordinary banks, moneyshops open in the early hours of the morning. Also, daily collections restrain the market vendor from diverting repayment funds to other needs. Collectors go to the borrower instead of awaiting payment at the moneyshop window.

Moneyshops charge an interest rate of about 3 per cent a month. While this is well above the usual bank lending rate, PCIB argues that this is a low rate considering that usurers charged market vendors several hundred percent a month under the "five-six" scheme.

Despite the daily collection system adopted by the moneyshops, the latter carry a significant percentage of loans in arrears or in litigation, considerably higher, at any rate, than the levels usually tolerated by banking institutions. Moreover, the moneyshops have not been as successful as the credit unions in attracting savings. Despite these difficulties, the moneyshop scheme has become a major activity of PCIB and has grown significantly since its inception in 1973.

There may also be cases where the public authorities adopt an informal mechanism outright and set up government-run schemes on that model. For example, we have already seen how commercial banks in India are themselves often promoters of chit funds. Similarly, some governments in Southeast Asia are actively involved in pawnbroker activity (see Box 4.3), while in the Philippines, one bank has initiated its own "bridge-building" banking mechanism (see Box 4.4).

c) Developing Social Security and Contractual Savings

Reducing dualism is not brought about solely by measures concerning banks and credit organisations. Such a policy should include other dimensions, in particular the increasing importance of social security and contractual savings institutions (notably pension funds and insurance), thanks to which the informal sector could gradually be absorbed without compromising any of the social functions which it fulfils.

One of the main characteristics of the informal sector is the intensity and dynamism of the solidarity principle within extended families, village communities, regions and ethnic groups. Groups in the informal sector are in fact a collective organisation against individual and social risks. To this extent, it can be said that there is a large informal insurance sector in developing countries.

If the aim is to reduce dualism, then alternative mechanisms to these traditional means of protection against risk must be found. There are two ways of doing this: either by developing a social security system or developing the contractual savings (and notably insurance) sector.

It should be noted in this context that in countries where there is a large informal sector, social security and insurance systems are not very sophisticated. Only a very small section of the population is affiliated to the social security scheme (civil servants, modern sector wage-earners), and only certain risks are covered. Concerning life insurance, available data suggests that in nearly all developing countries, premiums actually paid account for about 1 per cent of GDP (see Table 2.22 in Chapter 2).

If, through an appropriate monetary and financial policy, the savings and credit functions of the informal sector are eventually institutionalised, then alternative measures must be implemented to ensure that their social functions also continue to be fulfilled.

Attempts to extend national social security schemes run up against major obstacles: difficulties in financing the system through taxation and contributions, difficulties in their administration and management. The anonymity, bureaucracy, and lack of transparency are all factors which combine to make extension unlikely. In this context, new forms of social security could be imagined, based partly on the methods of informal groups (see Box 4.5). In fact, social security authorities could adopt a decentralised structure, with a large degree of independence granted to local bodies.

On account of their flexibility, contractual savings institutions – rather than social security – may be a likely substitute for the spontaneous solidarity found in the informal sector. The positive repercussions of contractual savings institutions on financial development are an additional merit.

As it has already been underlined, contractual savings mechanisms may contribute towards mobilising savings in developing countries, thus increasing the overall amount of savings. Provided they are well organised, these non-bank financial intermediaries, in all countries of the world, generate financing capacity. Furthermore, the savings generated are such that they favour balanced development. It will be useful to recall three characteristics of this type of saving: it is long-term, stable and financial. Thus savings deposits by the insurance sector make it possible to ensure optimal financing of investments and capital. In fact, this type of financing is not inflationary since it does not involve monetary creation; it is stable, and it is less affected by cyclical economic fluctuations.

This is particularly so in the case of organisations dealing with old age insurance. Insurance structures may provide resources for the elderly, although at the present time such persons are frequently cared for by traditional solidarity groups. It therefore seems desirable to develop funded pension schemes or provident funds, which would be managed along the principles of mutuality.

It should be noted here that a substantial part of development financing in the countries of Southeast Asia was generated by funded pension schemes or provident funds[14].

Above all, a developed contractual savings and insurance sector is one of the major prerequisites for developing efficient financial markets. Although insurance organisations (in the widest sense of the word, i.e. including insurance companies, funded pension schemes, provident funds, etc.) are able to mobilise savings, they also make an appreciable

Box 4.5

THE *IDIR* LIFE INSURANCE PROGRAMME IN ETHIOPIA: AN ATTEMPT TO "INSTITUTIONALISE" AN INFORMAL INSURANCE SCHEME

*The **Idir** Life Insurance Programme constitutes an interesting attempt to link directly a formal institution and informal entities with a similar function and mode of operation while maintaining the specificity and (legal) status of each. Indeed, aware of the impossibility of totally replacing informal social insurance mechanisms, the Ethiopian Insurance Company (EIC) tried to find a way of collaborating with the **idirs**. This strategy brought about the creation and launching of the **Idir** Life Insurance Programme (ILI), under which the members of an **idir** agree to pay a certain amount of money to EIC (the premium), and the EIC contracts to disburse an agreed sum of money to the member who finds himself in a situation of need.*

*To be eligible for the programme, an **idir** must meet certain requirements among which are: a minimum of ten members, registration under the Civil Code as an association, authorisation by the Ministry of Public and State Security to form such an association, and a postal address recognised by the Post Office Department.*

*All persons who are dependents of an **idir** member and are permanent residents in the member's house are eligible for insurance protection. Claims are paid immediately after receipt by EIC of documentary proof of an insured person's death. If the delivery of such proof is delayed, the **idir** can pay the claim out of its own funds and obtain reimbursement from the Corporation later. Payment is effected by means of a cheque payable to the order of the policy holder.*

The premium rate per unit of cover is 0.50 birrs, paid monthly by each member. One unit of cover consists of 100 birrs in the event of the death of a member or his wife, 75 birrs in the event of the death of other relatives, and 25 birrs in case of a servant of the household.

*The calculation of the equilibrium premium rate per unit of cover made by the EIC takes into consideration the number of insured persons, their degree of relationship with the member, the death rate in Addis Ababa, and the running expenses of the Corporation. Separate calculations are made for the neighbourhood **idirs** and the office **idirs** in view of the different risks involved (higher average age of neighbourhood **idir** members). The single premium rate applied for all **idirs** is based on the weighted average of the two figures obtained. At the end of each policy year, the experience of each **idir** is evaluated and the premium rate adjusted accordingly.*

*At present, the ILI restricts its activities to Addis Ababa. The policies are distributed through agents and salaried salesmen who are expected to solicit business, conduct the enrollment of **idir** members and their dependents, provide service to insured **idirs** and follow up renewals. In addition, the EIC carries out a substantial advertising and promotional campaign through the mass media and through personal contacts with **idir** committees and members.*

*The programme is still in its initial stage, and it is difficult to forecast how it will develop. At present, only eight **idirs** have joined, so that partly on account of sheer numbers the EIC is suffering losses in administering the programme. This first stage of ILI's operations also confirms that its role is complementary to, rather than a substitute for, the service provided directly by the **idirs**: in practice, a member comes to have two insurance covers, one by the **idir** and the other by the EIC.*

*The programme's strong point is that there is certainly a greater solvency and reliability of the EIC if one considers the cases of insolvency and fraud sometimes encountered in the **idirs**. Furthermore, members have the possibility of diversifying their insurance cover by subscribing to that offered by the EIC. However, the limited territorial spread, the aversion of a large part of the population towards a complex and unfamiliar institution and, most important, a premium/indemnity ratio which is not generally advantageous are among the negative factors which must be mentioned.*

contribution towards reducing dualism through their management of savings. In this context, financial activity through and by the insurance sector is an important vector for what could be called monetary and financial development. Without institutional investors there is no guarantee of regular demand for securities and for stable rates.

3. "Organising" the Informal Sector

There are many possible ways of improving and increasing the degree of institutionalisation of the informal sector. The informal financial sector can become a more efficient structure for collecting savings and distributing loans, particularly in rural areas, than it is at the present time. To this end, extremely flexible types of organisations should be developed, which the present groups and other operating agents in the informal sector can adopt. These new set-ups must allow for the continued existence of the positive characteristics of informal arrangements, while progressively integrating the latter with the formal sector.

Among the characteristics which should be safeguarded in this procedure are the flexibility, rapidity and transparency of procedures. An attempt should also be made to retain the wealth of personal relationships, which are the very basis of the efficiency of informal groups. Lastly, the progressive institutionalisation of the informal sector should be carried out in such a way as to avoid excluding part of its present clientele from savings and credit. Indeed, one of the major pitfalls which must be avoided is that organising the informal sector and linking it with the formal sector could lead to a rise in the overall costs of financial intermediation.

Before considering ways of organising the informal sector, it should be noted that there is a certain degree of controversy concerning the policy to be implemented in this sector. There are those who have strong reservations about the possibility of regulating this sector. Their attitude could be expressed as follows: "It is difficult to control the informal sector

BLOCK LENDING IN THAILAND AND ZAMBIA

Group lending (or block lending) is a technique used by the Bank for Agriculture and Agricultural Cooperatives (BAAC) in Thailand and the Agricultural Development Bank of Zambia for financing small-scale farmers. Group lending by the BAAC usually involves a group of about eight to fifteen farmers, with members jointly liable for one another's debts and with no collateral required for loans. The loans disbursed are partly in kind, to make sure that the money is effectively used to buy supplies.

Group lending procedures by the Agricultural Development Bank of Zambia are more complex. A group consists of 100 farmers, with a leader who is usually a respected elder in the community. Each group is divided into five sub-groups of twenty members, each with a "contact man". Each contact man finds out the credit needs of the individual farmer-borrowers in his sub-group and informs the group leader, who applies for bank credit on behalf of the whole group. Loans are usually short-term and in kind, with a small cash component when necessary. The individual loans are repaid to the group leader who, in turn, transfers the block loan to the bank. By operating on two levels − a first level between the final borrower and the group leader, and a second level between the leader and the bank − there are two main advantages that are derived: one is that there is strong group pressure for repayment of loans; the other is that the bank's transactions costs for group lending are much lower than if each small loan were granted on an individual basis.

precisely because it is born of the absence of regulation"[15]. Others, on the contrary, maintain that it is possible to develop very flexible types of organisation, adapted to each national situation and each type of grouping.

There are several possible measures which would contribute to improving the role of the informal sector in mobilising savings. However, before defining and implementing them, the achievements and numerous functions of the informal financial sector in each country must first be examined in greater detail. On this basis, public authorities could promote training programmes for members and group leaders of savings and credit groups. Such training would allow informal operators to be better informed on financial matters and thus manage more efficiently the collection and, above all, the allocation of savings.

In addition, setting up specialised supportive services for informal groups, such as information on improved marketing techniques, better information on markets, supply of production factors, would facilitate the functioning of informal groups while increasing the productivity of the funds they manage.

In any event, study groups, seminars and case studies should be encouraged to facilitate the exchange of information and experience on how to improve the informal financial sector and its environment.

By drawing on all the experience gained in rural areas, it would be possible to facilitate savings and credit activities by calling on the help of informal groups. Group lending (or block lending) brings together a formal financial institution and a group of borrowers around a single transaction. The decision on how the loan received (by the group as a whole) is to be allocated among members is left to the group itself. The advantage of such arrangements for the group and its members is that they have access to additional funds over and above the limited levels of members' contributions.

For the credit institution, group lending helps resolve the problems of transaction costs and guarantees: dealing with one larger loan instead of several smaller ones reduces transaction costs and provides a more secure guarantee of reimbursement of the loan, as it is now the group as a whole which is responsible (individual guarantees are often insufficient) (see Box 4.6)[16].

Lending groups are one way of drawing informal savings and credit associations closer to formal practices. Let us examine in detail one example of the progressive integration process[17].

The association decides on the appropriate legal structure, and establishes contact with a bank (co-operative, private, or nationalised). The liabilities of the association in relation to the bank are defined in a memorandum. The association receives group loans on behalf of its members; the amount of credit obtained is a function of the amount of savings collected beforehand.

Such savings and credit groups function in the same way as informal groups, namely on principles of solidarity and mutuality. Nevertheless, the links with a banking structure must be clearly defined.

Similar experiences have been described in Lesotho, Nepal (the "Small Farmer Development Project") and in Bangladesh. Indeed, the much cited experiment of the Grameen Bank in Bangladesh is even put forward as a possible model for other developing countries (see Box 4.7).

Finally, it should be mentioned that in many developing countries – and in those of our sample – the co-operative movement is seen as one of the main avenues through which integration of the formal and informal sectors may be brought about[18]. Depending on the country, such institutional links are developed to a greater or lesser degree. They may be limited to a simple function of assistance, including the provision of rediscounting facilities with the Central Bank for credit instruments in the informal sector, or go as far as ensuring national centralisation of funds collected locally.

One of the most promising ways of linking the informal and formal financial sectors revolves around the development of credit unions. The aim of such "banks" is to facilitate access to savings and credit, particularly in rural areas. In order to do this, they have adopted the philosophy of informal groups. Despite the fact that the central office of each bank takes over part of the deposits, these banks retain a certain degree of independence, with the result that they are more easily accepted in rural areas. In this way, credit unions are able to benefit from the large volume of deposits collected by informal groups. This confirms the existence of linkages between the two sectors.

4. Promoting Linkages Between the Two Sectors

It could be said that promoting linkages between the formal and informal financial sectors is made easier by the fact that financial flows already do occur, on a spontaneous basis, from the informal to the formal sector *and* vice versa. Regarding informal flows to the

Box 4.7

SMALL LOANS FOR THE RURAL POOR: THE GRAMEEN BANK OF BANGLADESH

The underlying premise of the Grameen Bank of Bangladesh is that, in order to emerge from poverty and remove themselves from the clutches of usurers and middlemen, landless peasants most need access to credit, without which they cannot be expected to launch their own enterprises, however small these may be. In defiance of the traditional rural banking postulate whereby "no collateral (in this case, land) means no credit", the Grameen Bank experiment set out to prove – successfully – that lending to the poor is not an impossible proposition; on the contrary, it gives landless peasants the opportunity to purchase their own tools, equipment, or other necessary means of production and embark on income-generating ventures which will allow them to escape from the vicious cycle of "low income, low savings, low investment, low income". In other words, the banker's confidence rests upon the will and capacity of borrowers to succeed in their undertakings.

The mode of operation of the Grameen Bank is as follows. A bank unit is set up with a Field Manager and a number of bank workers and covers an area of about 15 to 22 villages. The manager and the workers start by visiting villages to familiarise themselves with the local milieu in which they will be operating and identify the prospective clientele, as well as to explain the purpose, the functions, and the mode of operation of the bank to the local population. Groups of five prospective borrowers are formed; in the first stage, only two of them are eligible for, and receive, a loan. The group is observed for a month to see if the members are conforming to the rules of the bank. Only if the first two borrowers repay the principal plus interest over a period of fifty weeks do the other members of the group become eligible themselves for a loan. Because of these restrictions, there is substantial group pressure to keep individual records clear. In this sense, the collective responsibility of the group serves as the collateral on the loan.

Loans are small – the maximum requested is around 5000 takas per year[1] – but sufficient to finance the micro-projects undertaken by borrowers: rice-husking, mechanic repairing, purchase of rickshaws, of cows and goats, cloth, pottery, etc. The rate on all loans is 16 per cent. The repayment rate on loans is said to be high – 98 per cent – for reasons of group pressure and self-interest evoked earlier, as well as motivation of borrowers.

Although mobilisation of savings is also being pursued alongside the lending activities of the Grameen Bank, most of the latter's loanable funds are obtained from the central bank, on capital markets, and from bilateral and multilateral aid organisations.

Since obtaining the full-fledged status of a bank in 1982, the Grameen Bank has grown considerably: the number of branches rose from 100 in 1984 to 500 in 1988, with an estimated 500 000 clients. These figures are expected to double by 1993[2].

1. Average exchange rate value 1989: Taka 32.27 = US$ 1.
2. Figures quoted from Paringaux, Roland-Pierre, "Petit crédit pour grande pauvreté," *Le Monde*, 18 April 1989.

formal sector, we have seen in a number of cases how the funds amassed by mutual (savings and loan) associations may be deposited in accounts with a formal financial institution, independently of whether or not efforts are made by the latter to attract these deposits. For example, *idirs* in Ethiopia have a savings account with the Commercial Bank of Ethiopia (CBE) or the Housing and Savings Bank; the chairman of a trader *ekub* deposits the contributions received in a current account with the CBE on which he draws a post-dated cheque in favour of the winner[19]. However, since the prize fund is disbursed almost immediately, even if the collected funds are directed into formal circuits, they remain there for a very short time. *Arisans* (savings and loan associations) in Indonesia deposit the collected funds in village units of the Bank Rakyat Indonesia so that the surplus cash is more secure. Savings clubs in Zimbabwe also deposit the amassed funds with a formal financial institution[20].

Ad hoc flows from the formal towards the informal sector, on the other hand, are usually the result of a private, individual initiative whereby a person with access to formal funds may take advantage of his position to lend informally. In Zambia, for instance, members of the upper-income social classes on-lend, through middlemen, to urban and rural small borrowers. Likewise, in Indonesia, lenders may borrow from a bank on favourable terms (under the small-scale investment scheme or the permanent working capital credit scheme, for example) but use only part of the money effectively for investment purposes, the remainder being used for lending.

Furthermore, the similarity of purpose, if not of mode of functioning, of some formal and informal mechanisms should also facilitate a rapprochement. Some informal operator procedures, for example, closely reflect formal sector practices; a notable example is the case of India, where non-bank companies engaged in any sort of activity (a transportation company, for instance) may offer fixed-interest deposit facilities to the public as an alternative means of obtaining resources, i.e. instead of borrowing from a bank[21]. This is not at all far from the idea of financial markets and the issue of securities. Similarly, the concept of social insurance is not alien to informal sector users, as the presence of mutual associations attests; hence, the basis for a more concerted effort to establish social security and insurance schemes is already in place.

The way is thus open for reducing the gap between the formal and informal financial sectors because there are already some common horizons, i.e. a flow of funds from the one to the other and sometimes a relative similarity from an operational point of view. Moreover, it appears that individuals themselves are increasingly making arbitrages between the two sectors. For example, people who have reached the upper limit of their bank loans may seek to supplement them with funds from the informal sector. Other borrowers may resort to informal sources despite their access to formal ones because of the speed of delivery of credit from the former[22]. Efforts should therefore focus on consolidating and systematising these ad hoc initiatives.

Some sources suggest that institutions in the formal financial sector could employ non-institutional operators as local representatives. The latter would act to a certain extent as "financial retailers". Financial retailing reflects the will of formal sector institutions to expand their activity by working *through* informal sector operators because of the latter's lower transaction costs and greater capacity to channel credit to target groups. It entails the provision of credit lines to informal lenders who then on-lend to their own clients, i.e. those borrowers who are denied access to formal financial institutions because of the small sums they request. The intermediary lender may be a professional moneylender or a merchant moneylender (input dealer, output trader, storeowner, etc.) (see Box 4.8).

Box 4.8

"CREDIT RETAILING" IN THE PHILIPPINES

Three of the most important credit programmes which channel government loanable funds to informal lenders are: i) the Quedan Guarantee Fund Board Scheme; ii) the Planters' Product, Inc. (PPI) Special Credit Scheme; and iii) the End Users'/Input Suppliers' Assistance Scheme.

The Quedan Guarantee Fund Board (QGFB) is an agency attached to the Ministry of Agriculture and Food (MAF) which uses the "quedan" or warehouse receipt as a loan guarantee. Traders and millers who borrow from the banking system qualify for the guarantee of 80 percent of the loan value on the basis of grain stocks they hold in a bonded warehouse. The traders and millers, in turn, extend production loans to farmers, subject to the tie-in provision that (a portion of) the grain harvest be sold to a specified quedan operator. Presently, the coverage of QGFB is extended to small grains merchants and farmers who are engaged in small-scale output trading. By providing access to government funds, the QGFB augments the capital base of farmer-moneylenders who, unlike the big and well-established palay traders, have little collateral to offer. Although the QGFB does not receive any government subsidies, it has been able to expand its operations and to leverage its relatively small capital base of 150 million pesos into covering loans totalling about four times that base. This is largely due to a repayment record of 99 percent.

Under the PPI Special Credit Scheme, local input dealers obtain a special credit line at a 12 per cent annual interest rate on the condition that they organise distribution channels for fertilizer and pesticide credit to farmers. It is assumed that with the low cost of fertilizer/pesticide credit, farmers will be encouraged to adopt modern technology and to purchase modern inputs. What remains to be seen, however, is whether hidden charges such as overpricing of inputs occurs, and whether the beneficiary input dealer who had an existing palay procurement mechanism already operating in a certain vicinity will effectively increase his lending operations to a wider number of farmer clientele as a result of having access to more funds.

Finally, the End Users'/Input Suppliers' Assistance Scheme gives informal lenders access to subsidised government loanable funds. It also has a wider reach than the PPI Special Credit Scheme for it lends not only to input suppliers but also to traders, millers, and/or processors of agricultural commodities at concessionary rates. This credit programme involves loan provision to traders and millers (end users) and to input suppliers at a 6 per cent per annum interest rate under the condition that the loan recipients, i.e. the informal lenders, extend production loans to farmers at a 15 per cent per annum interest rate, inclusive of service charges of the agent bank. Repayment of loans is the responsibility of the end users and input suppliers. A penalty charge of 42 per cent per annum is imposed by the agent bank on defaulted loans.

The scheme encourages the use of tie-in stipulations between the informal credit source and farmer-borrowers as a means of effectively enforcing loan repayment. For example, end users who are agricultural processors may advance inputs or optional cash loans to borrowers. Borrowers in turn agree to sell their output to the end user at a purchase price not lower than the government support price. Alternatively, end users may provide initial payment to farmer-borrowers at planting time in the form of inputs with the balance payable upon delivery of the contracted output.

The End Users'/Input Suppliers' Assistance Scheme has a good repayment performance – about a 92 per cent recovery rate – which may be attributed partly to the high penalty rate of 42 per cent for all past due obligations which is much higher compared to the other two programmes mentioned earlier. In addition, input dealers and end users have their own "sorting process" which enables them to be more selective in their choice of borrowers. Trader-lenders prefer to lend to bankable farmer-borrowers with higher incomes and lower default propensities. They also ensure high collection rates by strictly enforcing tie-in arrangements, stipulating certain times for loan release and for loan collection, and imposing penalties on delinquent borrowers.

The three policy schemes which have just been presented tend to highlight one basic process that is already at work in the Philippines' financial system, namely, the interlinkage of the formal and informal credit sectors through the intervention of the banks. Many informal lenders already had credit lines as traders or millers from rural or commercial banks prior to the implementation of these policy schemes. Commercial bankers in fact admit that, in the rural sector, they usually finance only the traders and processors. In some cases, the trader or input dealers are also owners of banks.

Sometimes informal lenders may link up with a formal institution in a different way, by recommending, from amongst their clientele which they know well, a creditworthy borrower to the bank in question[23].

Concluding Remarks

The various country experiences which were used in the above discussion to illustrate some of the macroeconomic and microeconomic measures proposed here for reducing financial dualism, seem to support the idea that it is both possible and realistic to seek to better articulate and integrate the formal and informal financial sectors.

For those who share the view that reducing financial dualism is a necessary course of action, the problem still remains of determining the extent to which it should be reduced. In this regard, the four series of actions discussed above may be pursued to different degrees.

Whatever the objective, however, reducing financial dualism calls for a multifaceted approach based on a far-reaching modification of economic and social behaviour patterns as well as on the appropriate adaptation of structures and procedures. These changes are, by necessity, of a long-term nature for three main reasons. The first reason is that of the confidence which underpins all financial transactions; undermining it by seeking to achieve too much in too short a time will have the well-known catastrophic effects. Secondly, financial transactions are obviously influenced by economic and social structures which are slower to evolve. Finance can contribute to this transformation but it cannot, *per se,* change the rest of the economy. Thirdly, in certain aspects, there still remain some deep-rooted dualistic tendencies in developing economies, notably as regards the close-knit family and social ties at the heart of economic activity, which social security and other contractual savings institutions have difficulty in penetrating.

Reducing financial dualism should hence be centered around a dynamic and long-term policy programme that would be developed by both private agents and the government, and which would be continuously monitored and evaluated to detect and try to remedy any adverse effects of the policy options taken.

CONCLUSION

While it is clear that there is a common goal – improve the functioning of financial systems in developing countries, reduce the need for external funds, ease the debt burden and provide financial services to as wide a population as possible so that people may gradually better their socio-economic condition – it is equally obvious that there are many different avenues to reach it; the ways to be employed are a function of national specificities. In effect, each developing country does not have the same starting point (see Chapters 1 and 2) since financial and monetary phenomena largely reflect historical, political, cultural factors, to name just a few.

One must thus begin by an overview of the structural and operational aspects of the financial systems in place, taking stock of both the formal and informal financial sectors (along the lines of what was done in Chapter 3) in order to define the priorities and take the appropriate options and implement the corresponding measures (such as those discussed in Chapter 4). To this effect, a number of tools of analysis have been proposed for those seeking a better understanding of financial systems in developing countries; and some ways and means for reducing, if not removing, the obstacles to the financing and development of these countries have been suggested.

It is our belief that if developing countries are to recover from the debt crisis and return to a growth path that is more autonomous and stable (and less dependent on external resources), accumulation needs must be financed by domestic resources. Hence the absolute necessity of raising the operational efficiency of financial systems as regards the mobilisation and especially the allocation of internal savings. While it is clear that such a goal is highly desirable, the foregoing analysis seems to suggest that it is also within reach, on condition that priorities are set and the appropriate means employed for a long-term effort to be pursued.

NOTES AND REFERENCES

1. Many co-operative or mutual banks in Europe find their roots in informal mechanisms: in France, the Crédit Mutuel or the Crédit Agricole are examples; in Italy, the Banco San Paolo di Torino stems from the 17th century Monte di Pietà.

2. Wachtel, P., "Observations on Savings by Individuals in Developing Countries," in Kessler, Denis and Pierre-Antoine Ullmo, eds., *Savings and Development*, Paris, Economica, 1985, pp. 17-26.

3. This may be related to the notion of "realism" in the context of developing countries. Financial savings is in effect a very abstract notion: bank deposits or securities, for example, possess nothing of the tangibility of cattle or of hoarded gold or currency.

4. Ghate argues, however, that the incidence of failure in the informal sector is not necessarily higher than in the formal sector, a positive point for self-regulation mechanisms in the informal sector. Chandavarkar pushes the point even further, claiming that "the 'contagion' or 'domino' effect of the illiquidity or insolvency of a single or even a group of intermediaries is not likely to be as deleterious as a similar failure in the formal sector because of their smaller average size and scale of operations". Nevertheless, the issue for an appropriate prudential role for the central bank remains. See Ghate, P.B., "Informal Credit Markets in Asian Developing Countries", *Asian Development Review*, 1988, vol. 6, No. 1, p. 76. See also Chandavarkar, Anand G., *The Informal Financial Sector in Developing Countries: Analysis, Evidence, and Policy Implications*, Kuala Lumpur, Malaysia, South East Asian Central Banks Research and Training Centre, Occasional Papers No. 2, August 1987, p. 35.

5. Chandavarkar, Anand G., "The Non-Institutional Financial Sector in Developing Countries: Macroeconomic Implications for Savings Policies", in UNDIESA, *Savings for Development*, Report of the Third International Symposium on the Mobilization of Personal Savings in Developing Countries (Yaoundé, Cameroon, 10-14 December 1984), New York, United Nations, 1986, pp. 81-86.

6. Shaw, E.S., *Financial Deepening in Economic Development*, London, Oxford University Press, 1973.

   McKinnon, Ronald I., *Money and Capital in Economic Development*, Washington, D.C., Brookings Institution, 1973.

7. Coats, Warren L. Jr and Deena R. Khatkhate, "Money and Monetary Policy in Less Developed Countries: Survey of Issues and Evidence", in Coats, Warren L. Jr and Deena R. Khatkhate, eds., *Money and Monetary Policy in Less Developed Countries*, Oxford, Pergamon Press, 1980.

8. Chandavarkar, *op. cit.*

9. Kessler, Denis and Dominique Strauss-Khan, "Stock Exchanges and Development: The Case of the Ivory Coast", in UNDIESA, *Savings for Development*, Report of the Second International Symposium on the Mobilization of Personal Savings in Developing Countries (Kuala Lumpur, Malaysia, 15-21 March 1982), New York, United Nations, 1984, pp. 44-51.

10. Van Wijnbergen, S., "Interest Rate Management in Developing Countries", Washington, D.C., World Bank, World Bank Staff Working Paper No. 593, 1984.

11. O.N.U., "Conclusions et recommandations", Rapport du troisième Symposium international sur la mobilisation de l'épargne des ménages dans les pays en développement (Yaoundé, Cameroun, 10-14 décembre 1984), édition provisoire, 1985.

12. Ferrari, C. et A. Mauri, "Amélioration des systèmes financiers pour une mobilisation plus efficace de l'épargne dans le cadre de réformes institutionnelles", Troisième Symposium international sur la mobilisation de l'épargne des ménages dans les pays en développement, Yaoundé, Cameroun, 10-14 décembre 1984, mimeo.

13. Von Pischke, J.D. and J. Rouse, "Selected Successful Experiences in Agricultural Credit and Rural Finance in Africa", *Savings and Development*, 1983, vol. 7, No. 1.

14. McGillivray, W.R., "Observations on Contributions to Development by Provident Funds and Social Insurance Schemes", in UNDIESA, 1984, *op. cit.*, pp. 64-69.

15. O.N.U., 1985, *op. cit.*

16. Of course, this is contingent upon the degree of cohesion within the group. There have been cases where the groups were formed quite arbitrarily, i.e. the bank formed groups amongst the people waiting in line at the bank window. Close knowledge of fellow group members and the related principles of solidarity and mutuality are much weaker in such cases, which largely explains the higher rates of default that were registered on such group loans. (Information reported by Charbel Zarour concerning group lending in Senegal; conference on "Informal Financial Markets in Development" organised by the Ohio State University, Rosslyn, Virginia, October 18-20, 1989.)

17. Seibel, H.D. and M.T. Marx, "Linking Formal and Informal Financial Institutions: Indigenous Savings and Credit Associations as Credit Groups", Third International Symposium on the Mobilization of Personal Savings in Developing Countries, Yaoundé, Cameroon, 10-14 December 1984, mimeo.

18. In some cases, the co-operative movement may take on gigantic proportions. In South Korea, the co-operative movement had two million members in 1975: 1 500 multi-purpose co-operatives, 141 single purpose co-operatives. Each basic co-operative had 1 200 members. Whereas at the beginning of the 1960s most of the funds available for lending came from government sources, by the beginning of the 1970s the major part of these funds consisted of deposits from co-operatives. See Adams, D.W. and T.Y. Lee and D.H. Kim, "Savings Deposits and Credit Activities in South Korean Agricultural Cooperatives, 1961-1975", *Asian Survey*, December 1977, vol. 17., No. 12.

19. Cheques are also used by mutual associations as a way of guaranteeing that early winners will continue to participate in the scheme: if a member fails to pay his regular contribution, the cheque is cashed, irrespective of whether the member's bank account can cover it. Cheques may be used as a guarantee of payment in individual moneylending too. For example, in Ethiopia, if the borrower has an account with the Commercial Bank of Ethiopia, he gives the moneylender a cheque with the date corresponding to the expiry date of the loan, for the entire amount of capital plus interest. However, the moneylender prefers to receive cash directly (for reasons of secrecy) and return the cheque to the borrower rather than cash it in for his reimbursement.

20. Moreover, savings clubs are usually established on the initiative of an external promoter – in most cases, extension workers or representatives of companies producing agricultural inputs.

21. Indeed, by offering 10 per cent interest, as opposed to 8 per cent by banks, they often compete successfully with the latter for the mobilisation of resources. The holders of these fixed deposits are creditors of the firm, not shareholders, so that even if the company incurs losses, it still must uphold its obligations of interest payments (not like in the case of a dividend). These issues can be cashed in (via brokers), but usually buyers hold on to them until maturity, using them until then as collateral for loans from banks.

Companies in India resort to this method of financing because it offers them the possibility of access to more funds. In effect, banks are often subjected to certain restrictions regarding their debtor portfolios, e.g. they cannot lend more than a certain proportion of their funds to a single customer. Thus the potential borrower (in this case the company) looks to the market for additional resources, and it does so directly rather than going through the bank.

22. The following letter to the editor of *The Hindu* (Madras, India), which appeared in the issue of 30 September 1973, is a revealing commentary.

"Pawnbrokers and Small Men"

"Sir, many may prefer pawnbrokers to the Nationalized Banks for raising loans, for certain valid reasons. The small men cannot wait for a long time to get their loans. For instance, the other day I approached an agent of a Nationalized Bank to pledge some gold articles worth 3 sovereigns. It happened to be a Saturday. The Bank staff told me to meet them again on the following Wednesday at about noon, as the Bank's appraiser would visit that Bank only on Wednesday. Is it possible for a person to wait up to Wednesday while he needs money badly on Saturday itself? The pawnbrokers, though they are charging exorbitant rates of interest, will lend money as and when it is needed. The Nationalized Banks should make arrangements to enable the small men to get loans at any time on their working day by pledging their goods, if they are to replace usurious pawnbrokers effectively." M. Jagannathan.

See Chandavarkar, Anand G., "Impact of Monetization and Commercialization of the Subsistence Sector on Savings and Credit in Rural Areas", in UNDIESA, *Savings for Development*, Report of the International Symposium on the Mobilization of Personal Savings in Developing Countries (Kingston, Jamaica, 4-9 February 1980), New York, United Nations, 1981, pp. 182-188.

23. In South Korea, informal lenders deposit their funds with a commercial bank which uses these deposits to make a loan to a borrower designated by the informal lender himself. The advantage of such an arrangement for the lender is that he eliminates the risk of default and also receives a premium directly from the borrower; the advantage for the bank is that it increases its market share. See Cole, David C. and Yung Chul Park, *Financial Development in Korea, 1945-1978*, Cambridge, Mass., Harvard University Press, 1983. Cited by Ghate, *op. cit.*, p. 74.

BIBLIOGRAPHY

Adams, Dale W., "Rural Financial Markets: The Case Against Cheap Credit", *Ceres*, January-February 1986, Vol. 19, No. 1.

Adams, Dale W. and Douglas H. Graham, "A Critique of Traditional Agricultural Credit Projects and Policies", *Journal of Development Economics*, 1981, Vol. 8, No. 3.

Adams, D.W. and R.C. Vogel, "Rural Financial Markets in Low-Income Countries: Recent Controversies and Lessons", *World Development*, April 1986, Vol. 14, No. 4.

Adams, Dale W., Douglas H. Graham and J.D. Von Pischke, eds., *Undermining Rural Development with Cheap Credit*, Boulder, Colorado, Westview Press, Westview Special Studies in Social, Political, and Economic Development, 1984.

Akaah, I. and K. Dadzie and B. Dunson, "Formal Financial Institutions as Savings Mobilizing Conduits in Rural LDCs: An Empirical Assessment Based on the Bank Savings Behavior of Ghanaian Farm Households", *Savings and Development*, 1987, Vol. 11, No. 2.

Akintola-Bello, O., "Investment Behaviour of Insurance Companies in Nigeria", *Savings and Development*, 1986, Vol. 10, No. 4.

Arndt, H.W., "The Financial System of Indonesia", *Savings and Development*, 1987, Vol. 11, No. 3.

Arowolo, Edward A., "The Development of Capital Markets in Africa, with Particular Reference to Kenya and Nigeria", *IMF Staff Papers*, July 1971, Vol. 18, No. 2.

Bank Indonesia, *Report for the Financial Year 1987-1988*, Jakarta, Indonesia, December 1988.

Banque Africaine de Développement et Commission Economique pour l'Afrique, *Rapport économique sur l'Afrique 1987*, Abidjan, Côte d'Ivoire, mars 1987.

Barreto de Oliveira, F.E., M.H. Fernandes da T. Henriques et K.I. Betrao, "Le régime de sécurité sociale brésilien: couverture et contraintes", *Revue internationale de Sécurité sociale*, 1987, Vol. 40, No. 4.

Baulier, F., A. Correze, A. Lebissonnais et C. Ostyn, *Les tontines en Afrique: rôles et évolutions*, Paris, Caisse Centrale de Coopération Economique, Notes et Etudes, No. 12, septembre 1988.

Bédard, Guy avec M. Mahon et L. Pickett, "La mobilisation de l'épargne rurale par les institutions de type coopératif et son impact sur le développement local – synthèse de sept études de cas africains", *Archives de sciences sociales de la coopération et du développement*, janvier-mars 1986, No. 75.

Bekolo-Ebe, Bruno, "Le système des tontines: liquidité, intermédiation et comportement d'épargne", *Revue d'économie politique*, juillet-août 1989, No. 4.

Benoit, J. Pierre V., "Artificially Low Interest Rates Versus Realistic or Market Interest Rates", in Kessler, Denis and Pierre-Antoine Ullmo, eds., *Savings and Development*, Paris, Economica, 1985.

Bhatt, V.V., "Improving the Financial Structure in Developing Countries", *Finance and Development*, June 1986, Vol. 23, No. 2.

Bhatt, V.V., "Financial Innovations and Credit Market Evolution", *Economic and Political Weekly*, 1987, Vol. 22, No. 22.

Bhatt, V.V. and Jacob Meerman, "Resource Mobilization in Developing Countries: Financial Institutions and Policies", *World Development*, January 1978, Vol. 6, No. 1.

BIT, *Le coût de la Sécurité sociale*, Genève, BIT, 1979.

Blain, Danièle, "The Push for Viable Institutions", *Ceres*, January-February 1986, Vol. 19.

Blejer, Mario I. et Adrienne Cheasty, "Using Fiscal Measures to Stimulate Savings in Developing Countries", *Finance and Development*, June 1986, Vol. 23, No. 2.

Bonvin, Jean and Rachel Meghir, "Social Security in Developing Countries: A More Active Role in the Economic Development Process", in Institute of Economics Academia Sinica, *Economic Development and Social Welfare*, conference proceedings, Taipei, Taiwan, 6-8 January 1987.

Bouman, F.J.A., "Indigenous Savings and Credit Societies in the Developing World", in Von Pischke, J.D. and Dale W. Adams and Gordon Donald, eds., *Rural Financial Markets in Developing Countries - Their Use and Abuse*, Baltimore, Johns Hopkins University Press, 1984.

Bouman, F.J.A. and R. Houtman, "Pawnbroking as an Instrument of Rural Banking in the Third World", *Economic Development and Cultural Change*, October 1988, Vol. 37, No. 1.

Cartwright, William S., "Saving, Social Security and Private Pensions", *International Social Security Review*, 1984, Vol. 37, No. 2.

Causse, Jean, "Necessity of and Constraints on the Use of Savings in the Community in which They Are Collected", in Kessler, Denis and Pierre-Antoine Ullmo, eds., *Savings and Development*, Paris, Economica, 1985.

Centre de recherche économique sur l'épargne, "Savings and Group Provident Schemes", in UNDIESA, *Savings for Development*, Report of the International Symposium on the Mobilization of Personal Savings in Developing Countries (Kingston, Jamaica, 4-9 February 1980), New York, United Nations, 1981.

Chandavarkar, Anand G., "Impact of Monetization and Commercialization of the Subsistence Sector on Savings and Credit in Rural Areas", in UNDIESA, *Savings for Development*, Report of the International Symposium on the Mobilization of Personal Savings in Developing Countries (Kingston, Jamaica, 4-9 February 1980), New York, United Nations, 1981.

Chandavarkar, Anand G., "Actual and Potential Contribution of Savings Mobilization Institutions to Formation of a Security Market", in UNDIESA, *Savings for Development*, Report of the Second International Symposium on the Mobilization of Personal Savings in Developing Countries (Kuala Lumpur, Malaysia, 15-21 March 1982), New York, United Nations, 1984.

Chandavarkar, Anand G., "The Financial Pull of Urban Areas in LDCs", *Finance and Development*, June 1985, Vol. 22, No. 2.

Chandavarkar, Anand G., "The Non-Institutional Financial Sector in Developing Countries: Macroeconomic Implications for Savings Policies", in UNDIESA, *Savings for Development*, Report of the Third International Symposium on the Mobilization of Personal Savings in Developing Countries (Yaoundé, Cameroon, 10-14 December 1984), New York, United Nations, 1986.

Chandavarkar, Anand G., *The Informal Financial Sector in Developing Countries: Analysis, Evidence, and Policy Implications*, Kuala Lumpur, Malaysia, South East Asian Central Banks (SEACEN) Research and Training Centre, Occasional Papers No. 2, August 1987.

Charmes, Jacques, *Quelles politiques publiques face au secteur informel ?*, Paris, Caisse Centrale de Coopération Economique, Notes et Etudes, No. 23, avril 1989.

Chassagne, Yvette, "Insurance and Development", in UNDIESA, *Savings for Development*, Report of the Third International Symposium on the Mobilization of Personal Savings in Developing Countries (Yaoundé, Cameroon, 10-14 December 1984), New York, United Nations, 1986.

CNUCED, *Les activités du programme spécial en assurances de la CNUCED*, New York, Nations Unies, 1986.

CNUCED, *Les assurances dans le Tiers Monde à la fin des années 70*, Rapport du secrétariat de la CNUCED, New York, Nations Unies, 1981.

Coats, Warren L. Jr. and Deena R. Khatkhate, eds., *Money and Monetary Policy in Less Developed Countries*, Oxford, Pergamon Press, 1980.

Coats, Warren L. Jr. and Deena R. Khatkhate, "Monetary Policy in Less Developed Countries: Main Issues", *Developing Economies*, 1984, Vol. 22, No. 4.

Confédération internationale des Associations de diplômés de l'Institut technique de banque, *L'épargne et sa collecte en Afrique*, Colloque tenu à Yamoussoukro, Côte d'Ivoire (November 1987), Paris, La Revue Banque, Collection Institut technique de banque, 1988.

Copestake, James G., "The Transition to Social Banking in India: Promises and Pitfalls", *Development Policy Review*, June 1988, Vol. 6, No. 2.

Corsepius, Uwe and Bernhard Fischer, "Interest Rate Policies and Domestic Savings Mobilization: A Survey of the Empirical Evidence of Asian Countries", Kiel, Kiel Institute of World Economics, Kiel Working Paper No. 267, August 1986.

CREDOC, *La mobilisation de l'épargne dans les pays en développement*, Paris, 1980.

Croset, Gérard, "La Sécurité sociale en Afrique noire francophone", Paris, Caisse des Dépôts et Consignations, document interne, septembre 1987.

Cuevas, Carlos E., "Savings and Loan Cooperatives in Rural Areas of Developing Countries: Recent Performance and Potential", *Savings and Development*, 1988, Vol. 12, No. 1.

Dasgupta, Arindam, "Some Notes on Formal and Informal Sector Savings Mobilisation in India", paper prepared by the Asian Development Bank for an International Experts' Meeting on Domestic Savings Mobilisation through Formal and Informal Sectors: Comparative Experiences in Asian and African Developing Countries, East-West Centre, Honolulu, Hawaii, 2-4 June 1987.

Datta, Gautam and Parthasarathi Shome, *Social Security and Household Savings: Asian Experience*, Tokyo, Institute of Developing Economies, 1980, mimeo.

Dessal, René, *Risques et financements. Introduction à l'économie de l'assurance*, Paris, L'Assurance Française, 1986.

Di Antonio, Marco, "The Excess Liquidity of Commercial Banking in Ethiopia", *African Review of Money, Finance and Banking* (supplementary issue of *Savings and Development*), 1988, No. 1.

Diaz-Alejandro, Carlos, "Good-Bye Financial Repression, Hello Financial Crash", *Journal of Development Economics*, September-October 1985, Vol. 19, No. 1-2.

Dixon, John, *Social Welfare in Africa*, London, Croom Helm, 1987.

Dooley, Michael and Donald Mathieson, "Financial Liberalization in Developing Countries", *Finance and Development*, September 1987, Vol. 24, No. 3.

Dumont, Jean-Pierre, *L'impact de la crise économique sur les systèmes de protection sociale*, Paris, Economica, 1987.

Eboue, Chicot M., "Epargne informelle et développement économique en Afrique", *Revue économique*, juillet 1988, Vol. 39, No. 4.

Egger, Philippe, "Banking for the Rural Poor: Lessons from Some Innovative Saving and Credit Schemes", *International Labour Review*, July-August 1986, Vol. 125, No. 4.

Erquiaga, Philip, *Improving Domestic Resource Mobilization through Financial Development – Indonesia*, Manila, Philippines, Asian Development Bank, Asian Development Bank Economic Staff Paper No. 40, November 1987.

Euzéby, Alain, "Le rôle de la Sécurité sociale dans la dynamique du développement", *Revue tiers-monde*, octobre-décembre 1977, Tome 18, No. 72.

Fernando, Nimal A., "The Interest Rate Structure and Factors Affecting Interest Rate Determination in the Informal Rural Credit Market in Sri Lanka", *Savings and Development*, 1988, Vol. 12, No. 3.

Fischer, Bernhard, "Rural Financial Savings Mobilisation in Sri Lanka: Bottlenecks and Reform Proposals", *Savings and Development*, 1988, Vol. 12, No. 1.

Floro, Sagrario L., *Credit Relations and Market Interlinkage in Philippine Agriculture*, unpublished PhD dissertation, Stanford University, 1987.

Food and Agriculture Organization of the United Nations, "Savings Mobilization and Institutional Credit in Rural Areas", in UNDIESA, *Savings for Development*, Report of the Second International Symposium on the Mobilization of Personal Savings in Developing Countries (Kuala Lumpur, Malaysia, 15-21 March 1982), New York, United Nations, 1984, pp. 70-73.

"Forum 1988: Emergence de nouveaux marchés financiers", communications au symposium par Maruey Phadoongsidhi (Thailande), Sylvie Trouillez (Brésil), Kodjo Aithward (Nigéria), Youssef Alaoui (Corée du sud), Sophie Kouzmine Karavaieff (Philippines), Yann Cramer (Thailande).

Frimpong-Ansah, J.H., *Mobilization of Domestic Resources for Africa's Economic Recovery and Development*, report prepared for the Symposium of the Annual Meeting of the African Development Bank Group, Abidjan, Côte d'Ivoire.

Fry, Maxwell J., "Savings, Investment, Growth and the Cost of Financial Repression", *World Development*, 1980, Vol. 8.

Fry, Maxwell J., "National Saving, Financial Saving and Interest Rate Policy in Asian Developing Economies", in UNDIESA, *Savings for Development*, Report of the Third International Symposium on the Mobilization of Personal Savings in Developing Countries (Yaoundé, Cameroon, 10-14 December 1984), New York, United Nations, 1986.

Fry, Maxwell J., *Money, Interest, and Banking in Economic Development*, Baltimore, Johns Hopkins University Press, 1988.

Gangopadhyay, S. and K. Sengupta, "Interlinkages in Rural Markets", *Oxford Economic Papers*, 1986, Vol. 38, No. 1.

Gauthier, Michel A., "Les banques de développement en Afrique. Réflexions pour une approche nouvelle du problème", *Marchés tropicaux et méditerranéens*, 17 avril 1987, No. 2162.

Gentil, D. et Y. Fournier, *Coopératives d'épargne et de crédit et voies alternatives au financement du développement rural en Afrique francophone*, Paris, Caisse Centrale de Coopération Economique, Notes et Etudes, No. 18, novembre 1988.

Gerdes, Victor, "Precursors of Modern Social Security in Indigenous African Institutions", *Journal of Modern African Studies*, June 1975, Vol. 13, No. 2.

Ghate, P.B., "Informal Credit Markets in Asian Developing Countries", *Asian Development Review*, 1988, Vol. 6, No. 1.

Ghosh, Arun, "Black Money and Its Impact on Savings and Investment", *Economic and Political Weekly*, August 8, 1987.

Ghosh, Arun, "The Riddle of Savings", *Economic and Political Weekly*, December 10, 1988, Vol. 23, No. 50.

Gilbert, Neil, "Alternative Forms of Social Protection for Developing Countries", *Social Service Review*, September 1976, Vol. 50, No. 3.

Gill, David, "Role of Investment Banking in Developing Countries", *Savings and Development*, 1980, Vol. 4, No. 3.

Gill, David, "Investir dans les nouveaux marchés de capitaux", Washington, D.C., Société financière internationale, Département des marchés de capitaux, communication au Forum sur l'émergence de nouveaux marchés financiers, Paris, octobre 1988.

Gill, David, "Investir dans les nouveaux marchés financiers", *Epargne sans frontière*, décembre 1988, No. 13.

Ginet, Jean-Christophe, "Protection sociale et développement", *Revue française des affaires sociales*, avril-juin 1984, Vol. 38, No. 2.

Giovannini, A., "The Interest Elasticity of Savings in Developing Countries: The Existing Evidence", *World Development*, 1983, Vol. 11, No. 7.

Godfrey, V.N., "A Broader Role for National Provident Funds: the Zambian Experience", *International Labour Review*, February 1974, Vol. 109, No. 2.

Gonzales Arrieta, Gerardo M., "Interest Rates, Savings, and Growth in LDCs: An Assessment of Recent Empirical Reasearch", *World Development*, May 1988, Vol. 16, No. 5.

Goodman, John C., "Private Alternatives to Social Security: The Experience of Other Countries", *Cato Journal*, Fall 1983, Vol. 3, No. 2.

Gruat, J.V., "L'extension de la protection sociale en République gabonaise: consolidation du développement", *Revue internationale du travail*, juillet-août 1984, Vol. 123, No. 4

Gueymard, Y., "Méthodes de mobilisation de l'épargne rurale dans les pays africains", Paris, Ministère des Relations Extérieures et I.E.D.E.S., mimeo.

Haggblade, Steve, "Africanization from Below: The Evolution of Cameroonian Savings Societies into Western-Style Banks", *Rural Africana*, Fall 1978, No. 2.

Harriss, B., "Money and Commodities: Their Interaction in a Rural Indian Setting", in Von Pischke, J.D., Dale W. Adams and Gordon Donald, eds., *Rural Financial Markets in Developing Countries – Their Use and Abuse*, Baltimore, Johns Hopkins University Press for the Economic Development Institute of the World Bank, EDI Series in Economic Development, 1983.

Haski, Pierre, "La banque saute à Douala", *Libération*, 9 août 1988.

Histoires de Développement, Lyon, Cahiers de l'Institut d'Etudes Sociales de Lyon, mars 1988, 1er trimestre, No. 1, numéro de revue consacré au thème "Epargne et développement".

Holst, Juergen U., "The Role of Informal Financial Institutions in the Mobilization of Savings", in Kessler, Denis and Pierre-Antoine Ullmo, eds., *Savings and Development*, Paris, Economica, 1985.

ILO, *Financing Social Security: The Options. An International Analysis*, Geneva, 1984.

IMF, "Interest Rate Policies in Developing Countries", study by the Research Department, mimeo, October 1983.

IMF, *Government Finance Statistics Yearbook*, Washington, D.C., IMF, 1987, 1988, Vols. 11 and 12.

IMF, *International Financial Statistics*, Washington, D.C., IMF, July 1988, Vol. 41, No. 7.

Improving Domestic Resource Mobilization through Financial Development, Manila, Asian Development Bank, September 1985.

International Social Security Association, *Conjugating Public and Private: The Case of Pensions*, Geneva, ISSA, Studies and Research No. 24, 1987.

Kaseke, E., "Social Security in Zimbabwe", *Journal of Social Development in Africa*, 1988, Vol. 3, No. 1.

Kessler, Denis, "Sur les fondements économiques de la Sécurité sociale", *Revue française des affaires sociales*, 1986, No. 1.

Kessler, Denis et Pierre-Antoine Ullmo, "Synthèse du Colloque d'Experts tenu à Paris le 28-30 mai 1984 en vue de préparer le Troisième Symposium des Nations-Unies sur la mobilisation de l'épargne dans les pays en développement", 10-15 décembre 1984, mimeo.

Kessler, Denis and Pierre-Antoine Ullmo, eds., *Savings and Development*, Paris, Economica, 1985.

Kessler, Denis et Pierre-Antoine Ullmo, *Assurance et Développement*, Paris, CEREPI, 1986, mimeo.

Kessler, Denis and Dominique Strauss-Kahn, "Stock Exchanges and Development: The Case of the Ivory Coast", in UNDIESA, *Savings for Development*, Report of the Second International Symposium on the Mobilization of Personal Savings in Developing Countries (Kuala Lumpur, Malaysia, 15-21 March 1982), New York, United Nations, 1984.

Kessler, Denis and Anne Lavigne and Pierre-Antoine Ullmo, *Ways and Means to Reduce the Financial Dualism in Developing Countries: The State-of-the-Art*, report prepared for the OECD Development Centre, Paris, CEREPI, november 1985.

Kharas, H.J. and J. Levinsohn, "LDC Savings Rates and Debt Crises", *World Development*, July 1988, Vol. 16, No. 7.

Khatkhate, Deena R. and Klaus-Walter Riechel, "Multipurpose Banking: Its Nature, Scope, and Relevance for Less Developed Countries", *IMF Staff Papers*, September 1980, Vol. 27, No. 3.

Kim, Wan-Soon, *Financial Development and Household Savings: Issues in Domestic Resource Mobilization in Asian Developing Countries*, Manila, Asian Development Bank, Asian Development Bank Economic Staff Paper No. 10, July 1982.

Kitchen, Richard L., *Finance for the Developing Countries*, Chichester, John Wiley & Sons, 1986.

Kopits, George and Padma Gotur, "The Influence of Social Security on Household Savings: A Cross-Country Investigation", *IMF Staff Papers*, March 1980, Vol. 27, No. 1.

Kropp, Erhard, Michael T. Marx, Ballurkar Pramod, Benjamin R. Quinones and Hans Dieter Seibel, *Linking Self-Help Groups and Banks in Developing Countries*, Eschborn (FRG), Deutsche Gesellschaft für Technische Zusammenarbeit (GTZ) GmbH in collaboration with the Asian and Pacific Regional Agricultural Credit Association (APRACA), 1989.

Lamberte, Mario B. and Joseph Lim, *Rural Financial Markets: A Review of Literature*, Philippines, Philippine Institute for Development Studies, Staff Paper Series No. 8702, January 1987.

Leboucq, Philippe, "Les tontines... un phénomène important et prometteur", *Marchés tropicaux et méditerrannéens*, 6 février 1987, No. 2152.

Le Breton, Philippe, *Les banques agricoles en Afrique de l'ouest. Etude comparative*, Paris, Caisse Centrale de Coopération Economique, Notes et Etudes, No. 24, mai 1989.

Lee, Jungsoo, *Improving Domestic Resource Mobilization through Financial Development: Sri Lanka*, Manila, Asian Development Bank, country study by the Economics office of the ADB on domestic resource mobilization and financial development in Bangladesh, India, Nepal, Pakistan and Sri Lanka, April 1987.

Lelart, Michel, "An Unorganised Financial Market: Moneylending in Thailand", *Savings and Development*, 1982, Vol. 6, No. 4.

Lelart, Michel, "L'association 'Opérations 71-71' de Cotonou... de l'organisation des tontines à la banque tontinière", *Epargne sans frontière*, décembre 1988, No. 13.

Lelart, Michel, "L'épargne informelle en Afrique: les tontines béninoises", *Revue tiers-monde*, avril-juin 1989, Tome 30, No. 118.

Llanto, Gilberto M., "Rural Credit Policy: Do We Need to Target?", *Savings and Development*, 1988, Vol. 12, No. 2.

Mackenzie, G.A., "Social Security Issues in Developing Countries: The Latin American Experience", *IMF Staff Papers*, September 1988, Vol. 35, No. 3.

Masini, Mario, ed., *Profils de finance rurale des pays d'Afrique*, Milan, Finafrica-CARIPLO, 1987.

Mathew, T.I., "Impact of Social Security and Similar Schemes on the Propensity to Save: Implications for Developing Countries," in UNDIESA, *Savings for Development*, Report of the International Symposium on the Mobilization of Personal Savings in Developing Countries (Kingston, Jamaica, 4-9 February 1980), New York, United Nations, 1982.

Mauri, Arnaldo, "The Role of Financial Innovation for Savings Mobilization in Developing Countries", *Savings Banks International*, Spring 1985, Vol. 1.

Mauri, Arnaldo, "Improvement of the Savings Mobilization Process Through Institutional and Procedural Innovations", in UNDIESA, *Savings for Development*, Report of the Third International Symposium on the Mobilization of Personal Savings in Developing Countries (Yaoundé, Cameroon, 10-14 December 1984), New York, United Nations, 1986.

Mauri, Arnaldo and Andrea Calamanti, "A Note on the Role of Securities Markets in Developing Countries in Savings Mobilization", in UNDIESA, *Savings for Development*, Report of the Second International Symposium on the Mobilization of Personal Savings in Developing Countries (Kuala Lumpur, Malaysia, 15-21 March 1982), New York, United Nations, 1984.

McDonald, D., "The Determinants of Savings Behaviour in Latin America", International Monetary Fund, mimeo, April 1983.

McGillivray, W.R., "Observations on Contributions to Development by Provident Funds and Social Insurance Schemes", in UNDIESA, *Savings for Development*, Report of the Second International Symposium on the Mobilization of Personal Savings in Developing Countries (Kuala Lumpur, Malaysia, 15-21 March 1982), New York, United Nations, 1984.

McKinnon, R.I., *Money and Capital in Economic Development*, Washington, D.C., Brookings Institution, 1973.

Meghir, Rachel, "Les institutions de protection sociale et la mobilisation de l'épargne intérieure dans les pays en développement", in Université de Caen, Laboratoire d'Etudes et de Recherches Economiques, *L'Economie sociale dans les pays en développement*, IXe Journées d'Economie Sociale, Actes du Colloque, Caen, 28-29 septembre 1989.

Mesa-Lago, Carmelo, *El desarrollo de la Seguridad social en América latina*, Santiago de Chile, Naciones Unidas, Estudios e Informes de la CEPAL No. 43, 1985.

Mesa-Lago, Carmelo, ed., *The Crisis of Social Security and Health Care. Latin American Experiences and Lessons*, Pittsburgh, University of Pittsburgh, Center for Latin American Studies, Latin American Monograph and Document Series, No. 9, 1985.

Mesa-Lago, Carmelo, "Etude comparative du développement de la Sécurité sociale en amérique latine", *Revue internationale de Sécurité sociale*, 1986, Vol. 39, No. 2.

Mesa-Lago, Carmelo, "Social Security and Development in Latin America", *CEPAL Review*, April 1986, No. 28.

Meyer, Richard L., "Deposit Mobilization for Rural Lending", paper prepared for the Third Technical Consultation on the Scheme for Agricultural Credit Development (SACRED), Rome, FAO, 17-20 September 1985.

Meyer, Richard L. and Geetha Nagarajan, "Financial Services for Small and Micro-Enterprises: A Need for Policy Changes and Innovation", *Savings and Development*, 1988, Vol. 12, No. 4.

Mikesell, Raymond F. and James E. Zinser, "The Nature of the Savings Function in Developing Countries: A Survey of the Theoretical and Empirical Literature", *Journal of Economic Literature*, March 1973, Vol. 11.

Miracle, Marvin P. and Diane S. Miracle and Laurie Cohen, "Informal Savings Mobilisation in Africa", *Economic Development and Cultural Change*, July 1980, Vol. 28, No. 4.

Mittendorf, H.-J., "Mobilization of Personal Savings for Agricultural and Rural Development in Africa", *Mondes en développement*, 1985, Tome 13, No. 50-51.

Molho, Lazaros E., "Interest Rates, Saving, and Investment in Developing Countries, A Re-examination of the McKinnon-Shaw Hypotheses", *IMF Staff Papers*, March 1986, Vol. 33, No. 1.

Mouton, Pierre, *La Sécurité sociale en Afrique au sud du Sahara. Tendances, problèmes et perspectives*, Genève, BIT, 1974.

Mouton, Pierre et Jean-Victor Gruat, "L'extension de la Sécurité sociale à la population non salariée en Afrique", *Revue internationale de Sécurité sociale*, 1988, Vol. 41, No. 1.

Munnell, Alicia H., "Effets des régimes de pensions publics et privés sur l'épargne et la formation du capital", *Revue internationale de Sécurité sociale*, 1986, Vol. 39, No. 3.

Nayar, C.P.S., "Finance Corporations: An Informal Financial Intermediary in India", *Savings and Development*, 1982, Vol. 6, No. 1.

Nayar, C.P.S., "Can A Traditional Financial Technology Co-Exist with Modern Financial Technologies? The Indian Experience", *Savings and Development*, 1986, Vol. 10, No. 1.

Nowak, Maria, *Nouvelles approches en matière d'épargne et de crédit rural pour l'Afrique au sud du Sahara*, Paris, Caisse Centrale de Coopération Economique, Notes et Etudes, No. 5, août 1986.

Obioma, B.K., *Rural Financial Services in Nigeria: Lessons from the Traditional Financial Group Markets*, doctoral dissertation, Pontifical Gregorian University, Rome, 1983.

ONUDI, *Banque et développement dans les années 80*, Comptes rendus choisis du Colloque ONUDI/ Banque mondiale tenu à Zurich, juin 1979, New York, Nations Unies, 1984.

Outreville, Jean-François, *Insurance, Financial Development and Market Structure: Evidence from an International Cross-Section Study (The Case of Developing Countries)*, Geneva, UNCTAD, mimeographed, 1987.

Padmanabhan, K.P., "Why Farmers Default on Loans", *Ceres*, January-February 1986, Vol. 19, No. 1.

Padmanabhan, K.P., "Le crédit bien compris: les prêts ruraux en Inde", *Cérès*, janvier-février 1987, Vol. 20, No. 1.

Paringaux, Roland-Pierre, "Petit crédit pour grande pauvreté: expériences de développement au Bangladesh", *Le Monde*, 17 juin 1989.

Park, Chong Kee, *Social Security in Korea. An Approach to Socio-Economic Development*, Seoul, Korea Development Institute, 1975.

Polak, Jacques J., *Financial Policies and Development*, Paris, OECD, 1989.

Pomareda, Carlos, *Financial Policies and Management of Agricultural Development Banks*, Boulder, Colorado, Westview Press, 1984.

Prabhu, K. Seeta and Avadhoot Nadkarni and C.V. Achuthan, "Rural Credit: Mystery of the Missing Households", *Economic and Political Weekly*, December 10, 1988, Vol. 23, No. 50.

Prabowo, Dibyo, *Some Issues on Informal Credit Markets in Indonesia*, paper commissioned by the Asian Development Bank in preparation of the Regional Study on Informal Credit Markets, mimeo, 1985.

Puffert, Douglas J., "Means and Implications of Social Security Finance in Developing Countries", background paper for *World Development Report 1988*, September 1987.

"Quatre dossiers en économies sociales et développements", *Communautés*, janvier-mars 1986, No. 75.

Quinones, Benjamin R. Jr., "Linkages Between Formal and Informal Sectors in Rural Financial Markets: The Role of Self-Help Groups", *CB Review* (Monthly Publication of the Central Bank of the Philippines), April 1987, Vol. 39, No. 4.

Radke, Detlef *et al., Mobilization of Personal Savings in Zimbabwe through Financial Development*, Berlin, German Development Institute (GDI), mimeo, 1986.

Rahman, Atiq, "Domestic Savings Mobilization through Formal and Informal Sectors in Bangladesh", paper prepared by the Asian Development Bank for an International Experts' Meeting on Domestic Savings Mobilisation through Formal and Informal Sectors: Comparative Experiences in Asian and African Developing Countries, East-West Centre, Honolulu, Hawaii, 2-4 June 1987.

Rahman, Farhana Haque, "The Potential for Domestic Savings", *Ceres*, January-February 1986, Vol. 19, No. 1.

Ramel, Maurice, *La réassurance. Aspects théoriques et pratiques*, Paris, Editions Dulac et Cie, 1980.

Reviglio, Franco, "Social Security: A Means of Savings Mobilization for Economic Development", *IMF Staff Papers*, July 1967, Vol. 14, No. 2.

Reviglio, Franco, "The Social Security Sector and Its Financing in Developing Countries", *IMF Staff Papers*, November 1967, Vol. 14, No. 3.

Ripoll, José, "Les assurances à la Conférence des Nations Unies sur le Commerce et le Développement", *Revue tiers-monde*, juillet-septembre 1973, Tome 14, No. 55.

Rodriguez, Enrique, *Development by Savings Mobilization in Rural Africa*, paper prepared for the Symposium on Swedish Development Cooperation with Sub-Saharan Africa in the 1990s, SaltsjÖbaden, Sweden, 6-8 September 1988.

Rodriguez, Enrique, ed., with J. Pierre V. Benoit, Anand G. Chandavarkar, Uno Tenfält, David Wirmark, *Savings Mobilization in Developing Countries – Guidelines and Facts*, Stockholm, Swedish Savings Banks Association (SSBA), SSBA Development Foundation, November 1988.

Schaefer-Kehnert, Walter and John D. Von Pischke, "Agricultural Credit Policy in Developing Countries", *Savings and Development*, 1986, Vol. 10, No. 1.

Schwefel, Detlef and Reiner Leidl, "Remarks on the Social Meaning of Savings of the Poor", *Development: Seeds of Change*, 1987, Vol.2/3.

Seibel, Hans Dieter and Michael T. Marx, "Linking Formal and Informal Financial Institutions: Indigenous Savings and Credit Associations as Credit Groups", Third International Symposium on the Mobilization of Personal Savings in Developing Countries, Yaoundé, Cameroon, 10-14 December 1984, mimeo.

Seibel, Hans Dieter and Michael T. Marx, *Dual Financial Markets in Africa: Case Studies of Linkages between Informal and Formal Financial Institutions*, Saarbrücken, Verlag breitenbach Publishers, Cologne Development Studies No. 2, 1987.

Shaw, E.S., *Financial Deepening in Economic Development*, New York/London, Oxford University Press, 1973.

Shome, Parthasarathi, "La Sécurité sociale, organisme mobilisateur de l'épargne: l'expérience de la Malaisie", *Revue internationale de Sécurité sociale*, 1978, Vol. 31, No. 1.

Shome, Parthasarathi and Katrine W. Saito, "The Impact of Contractual Savings on Resource Mobilization and Allocation: The Experience of Malaysia", *The Malayan Economic Review*, April 1978, Vol. 23, No. 1.

Shome, Parthasarathi et Katrine A. Saito, "Social Security Funds in Singapore and the Philippines: Ramifications of Investment Policies", *Labour and Society*, January 1980, Vol. 5, No. 1.

Shome, Parthasarathi and Katrine W. Saito, "Investments of Social Security Funds in India and Sri Lanka: Legislation and Experience", *The Indian Journal of Economics*, January 1980, Vol. 60, No. 238.

Shome, Parthasarathi and Lyn Squire, *Alternative Mechanisms for Financing Social Security*, Washington, D.C., World Bank, World Bank Staff Working Papers No. 625, 1983.

Siamwalla, Ammar, "Thai Rural Credit System: Some Empirical Findings and a Theoretical Framework", paper prepared by the Asian Development Bank for an International Experts' Meeting on Domestic Savings Mobilisation through Formal and Informal Sectors: Comparative Experiences in Asian and African Developing Countries, East-West Centre, Honolulu, Hawaii, 2-4 June 1987.

SIGMA, Etudes Economiques, Compagnie Suisse de Réassurances (Zurich):
"Part des primes d'assurance-vie dans le PNB en 1981", août 1982, No. 2.
"L'évolution de l'assurance dans le monde depuis la 2ᵉ guerre mondiale", mars 1984, No. 3.
"L'assurance dans le monde en 1983", avril 1985, No. 4.
"Nouvelles impulsions pour l'assurance-vie internationale", juillet 1985, No. 7.
"La réassurance mondiale: hier, aujourd'hui et demain", octobre 1985, No. 10.
"L'offre de l'assurance dans le moonde en 1985", novembre/décembre 1985, No. 11/12.

St. Rose, Marius, "A Preliminary Assessment of the Impact of Social Security Schemes on the Propensity to Save in the East Caribbean", in UNDIESA, *Savings for Development*, Report of the International Symposium on the Mobilization of Personal Savings in Developing Countries (Kingston, Jamaica, 4-9 February 1980), New York, United Nations, 1982.

Svasti-Xuto, Dusdee, "Relative Merits of Single-Purpose and Multi-Purpose Savings Mobilization Institutions", in UNDIESA, *Savings for Development*, Report of the Second International Symposium on the Mobilization of Personal Savings in Developing Countries (Kuala Lumpur, Malaysia, 15-21 March 1982), New York, United Nations, 1984.

Szmaragd, Jacques, "Adapter l'assurance à l'Afrique", *Journal de l'économie africaine*, Paris, 13 mars 1986, No. 80.

Tamburi, G., "Escalation of State Pension Costs: The Reasons and the Issues", *International Labour Review*, May-June 1983, Vol. 122, No. 3.

Tanzi, V., *Quantitative Characteristics of the Tax Systems of Developing Countries*, Washington, D.C., IMF, IMF Working Paper, November 1983.

Tata, Jayant, *The Promotion of Contractual Savings Institutions*, Washington, D.C., International Finance Corporation, mimeo, July 10, 1984.

Timberg, Thomas and C.V. Aiyar, "Informal Credit Markets in India", *Economic Development and Cultural Change*, October 1984, Vol. 33, No. 1.

Toure, Abdou, *Les petits métiers à Abidjan; l'imagination au secours de la conjoncture*, Paris, Karthala, 1985.

Tun Wai, U, "A Revisit to Interest Rates Outside the Organized Money Markets of Underdeveloped Countries", *Banca Nazionale del Lavoro Quarterly Review*, September 1977, No. 122.

Tun Wai, U, "The Role of Unorganized Financial Markets in Economic Development and in the Formulation of Monetary Policy", *Savings and Development*, 1980, Vol. 4, No. 4.

Tun Wai, U and Hugh T. Patrick, "Stock and Bond Issues and Capital Markets in Less Developed Countries", *IMF Staff Papers*, July 1973, Vol. 20, No. 2.

UNCTAD, *Invisibles: Insurance in Developing Countries. Developments in 1984-1985*, study by the UNCTAD Secretariat, 16 January 1987.

UNCTAD, *Invisibles: Insurance. Statistical Survey on Insurance and Reinsurance Operations in Developing Countries*, study prepared by the UNCTAD Secretariat, 14 January 1987.

UNDIESA, *Administration of Social Welfare: A Survey of National Organizational Arrangements*, New York, United Nations, 1985.

UNDIESA, *Savings for Development*, Report of the International Symposium on the Mobilization of Personal Savings in Developing Countries (Kingston, Jamaica, 4-9 February 1980), New York, United Nations, 1982.

UNDIESA, *Savings for Development*, Report of the Second International Symposium on the Mobilization of Personal Savings in Developing Countries (Kuala Lumpur, Malaysia, 15-21 March 1982), New York, United Nations, 1984.

UNDIESA, *Savings for Development*, Report of the Third International Symposium on the Mobilization of Personal Savings in Developing Countries (Yaoundé, Cameroon, 10-14 December 1984), New York, United Nations, 1986.

United Nations Secretariat, "Development of Stock Exchanges in Developing Countries", in UNDIESA, *Savings for Development*, Report of the Second International Symposium on the Mobilization of Personal Savings in Developing Countries (Kuala Lumpur, Malaysia, 15-21 March 1982), New York, United Nations, 1984.

United Nations Secretariat, "Mobilization of Contractual Savings Through Provident Funds", in UNDIESA, *Savings for Development*, Report of the Second International Symposium on the Mobilization of Personal Savings in Developing Countries (Kuala Lumpur, Malaysia, 15-21 March 1982), New York, United Nations, 1984.

Van Wijnbergen, S., *Interest Rate Management in Developing Countries*, Washington, D.C., World Bank, World Bank Staff Working Paper No. 593, 1984.

Varadachary, Tenalur, "Problems Involved in the Mobilization of Savings of Inhabitants of Rural Areas and of Low-Income Urban Groups in India", in UNDIESA, *Savings for Development*, Report of the International Symposium on the Mobilization of Personal Savings in Developing Countries (Kingston, Jamaica, 4-9 February 1980), New York, United Nations, 1982.

Viksnins, George J. and Michael T. Skully, "Asian Financial Development: A Comparative Perspective of Eight countries", *Asian Survey*, May 1987, Vol. 27, No. 5.

Villanueva, Delano, "Issues in Financial Sector Reform", *Finance and Development*, March 1988, Vol. 25, No. 1.

Vogel, Robert C. and Paul Burkett, *Mobilizing Small-Scale Savings: Approaches, Costs, and Benefits*, Washington, D.C., World Bank, Industry and Finance Series, Vol. 15, 1986.

von Furstenberg, George M., ed., *Social Security vs. Private Saving*, Cambridge, Massachusetts, Ballinger Publishing Company, Vol. 1 in the Series on Capital Investment and Saving (sponsored by the American Council of Life Insurance), 1979.

Von Pischke, J.D., "Rural Credit Project Design: Implementations and Loan Collection Performance", *Savings and Development*, 1980, Vol. 4, No. 2.

Von Pischke, J.D. and J. Rouse, "Selected Successful Experiences in Agricultural Credit and Rural Finance in Africa", *Savings and Development*, 1983, Vol. 7, No. 1.

Von Pischke, J.D., Dale W. Adams and Gordon Donald, eds., *Rural Financial Markets in Developing Countries – Their Use and Abuse*, Baltimore, Johns Hopkins University Press for the Economic Development Institute of the World Bank, EDI Series in Economic Development, 1983.

Wachtel, Paul, "Observations on Savings by Individuals in Developing Countries", in Kessler, Denis and Pierre-Antoine Ullmo, eds., *Savings and Development*, Paris, Economica, 1985.

Wallich, Christine, *Savings Mobilization through Social Security. The Experience of Chile during 1916-77*, Washington, D.C., World Bank, World Bank Staff Working Papers No. 553, 1983.

Wasow, Bernard and Raymond D. Hill, eds., *The Insurance Industry in Economic Development*, New York, New York University Press, 1986.

Wirmark, David, "Saving for Development", address delivered at the Third General Assembly of AFRACA, Arusha, Tanzania, 29 November 1982, reprinted by FINAFRICA.

World Bank, *World Development Report 1989*, Washington, D.C., World Bank, June 1989.

Yoon-Je, Cho, "How the United States Broke into Korea's Insurance Market", *The World Economy*, December 1987, Vol. 10, No. 4.

Yoon-Je, Cho, "Some Policy Lessons from the Opening of the Korean Insurance Market", *World Bank Economic Review*, May 1988, Vol. 2, No. 2.

Yoon-Je, Cho, "The Effect of Financial Liberalization on the Efficiency of Credit Allocation: Some Evidence from Korea", *Journal of Development Economics*, July 1988, Vol. 29, No. 1.

Yotopoulos, Pan A. and Sagrario L. Floro, *Transaction Costs and Quantity Rationing in Informal Credit Markets*, Kyoto, Japan, Kyoto Institute of Economic Research, Discussion Paper No. 264, March 1989.

WHERE TO OBTAIN OECD PUBLICATIONS – OÙ OBTENIR LES PUBLICATIONS DE L'OCDE

Argentina – Argentine
CARLOS HIRSCH S.R.L.
Galería Güemes, Florida 165, 4° Piso
1333 Buenos Aires   Tel. 30.7122, 331.1787 y 331.2391
Telegram: Hirsch-Baires
Telex: 21112 UAPE-AR. Ref. s/2901
Telefax:(1)331-1787

Australia – Australie
D.A. Book (Aust.) Pty. Ltd.
648 Whitehorse Road, P.O.B 163
Mitcham, Victoria 3132   Tel. (03)873.4411
Telex: AA37911 DA BOOK
Telefax: (03)873.5679

Austria – Autriche
OECD Publications and Information Centre
Schedestrasse 7
DW–5300 Bonn 1 (Germany)   Tel. (49.228)21.60.45
Telefax: (49.228)26.11.04
Gerold & Co.
Graben 31
Wien I   Tel. (0222)533.50.14

Belgium – Belgique
Jean De Lannoy
Avenue du Roi 202
B-1060 Bruxelles   Tel. (02)538.51.69/538.08.41
Telex: 63220   Telefax: (02) 538.08.41

Canada
Renouf Publishing Company Ltd.
1294 Algoma Road
Ottawa, ON K1B 3W8   Tel. (613)741.4333
Telex: 053-4783   Telefax: (613)741.5439
Stores:
61 Sparks Street
Ottawa, ON K1P 5R1   Tel. (613)238.8985
211 Yonge Street
Toronto, OM M5B 1M4   Tel. (416)363.3171
Federal Publications
165 University Avenue
Toronto, ON M5H 3B8   Tel. (416)581.1552
Telefax: (416)581.1743
Les Publications Fédérales
1185 rue de l'Université
Montréal, PQ H3B 3A7   Tel.(514)954-1633
Les Éditions La Liberté Inc.
3020 Chemin Sainte-Foy
Sainte-Foy, PQ G1X 3V6   Tel. (418)658.3763
Telefax: (418)658.3763

Denmark – Danemark
Munksgaard Export and Subscription Service
35, Nørre Søgade, P.O. Box 2148
DK-1016 København K   Tel. (45 33)12.85.70
Telex: 19431 MUNKS DK   Telefax: (45 33)12.93.87

Finland – Finlande
Akateeminen Kirjakauppa
Keskuskatu 1, P.O. Box 128
00100 Helsinki   Tel. (358 0)12141
Telex: 125080   Telefax: (358 0)121.4441

France
OECD/OCDE
Mail Orders/Commandes par correspondance:
2, rue André-Pascal
75775 Paris Cédex 16   Tel. (33-1)45.24.82.00
Bookshop/Librairie:
33, rue Octave-Feuillet
75016 Paris   Tel. (33-1)45.24.81.67
    (33-1)45.24.81.81
Telex: 620 160 OCDE
Telefax: (33-1)45.24.85.00 (33-1)45.24.81.76
Librairie de l'Université
12a, rue Nazareth
13100 Aix-en-Provence   Tel. 42.26.18.08
Telefax : 42.26.63.26

Germany – Allemagne
OECD Publications and Information Centre
Schedestrasse 7
DW–5300 Bonn 1 (Germany)   Tel. (0228)21.60.45
Telefax: (0228)26.11.04

Greece – Grèce
Librairie Kauffmann
28 rue du Stade
105 64 Athens   Tel. 322.21.60
Telex: 218187 LIKA Gr

Hong Kong
Swindon Book Co. Ltd.
13 - 15 Lock Road
Kowloon, Hong Kong   Tel. 366.80.31
Telex: 50 441 SWIN HX   Telefax: 739.49.75

Iceland – Islande
Mál Mog Menning
Laugavegi 18, Pósthólf 392
121 Reykjavik   Tel. 15199/24240

India – Inde
Oxford Book and Stationery Co.
Scindia House
New Delhi 110001   Tel. 331.5896/5308
Telex: 31 61990 AM IN
Telefax: (11)332.5993
17 Park Street
Calcutta 700016   Tel. 240832

Indonesia – Indonésie
Pdii-Lipi
P.O. Box 269/JKSMG/88
Jakarta 12790   Tel. 583467
Telex: 62 875

Ireland – Irlande
TDC Publishers – Library Suppliers
12 North Frederick Street
Dublin 1   Tel. 744835/749677
Telex: 33530 TDCP EI   Telefax: 748416

Italy – Italie
Libreria Commissionaria Sansoni
Via Benedetto Fortini, 120/10
Casella Post. 552
50125 Firenze   Tel. (055)64.54.15
Telex: 570466   Telefax: (055)64.12.57
Via Bartolini 29
20155 Milano   Tel. 36.50.83
La diffusione delle pubblicazioni OCSE viene assicurata
dalle principali librerie ed anche da:
Editrice e Libreria Herder
Piazza Montecitorio 120
00186 Roma   Tel. 679.46.28
Telex: NATEL I 621427
Libreria Hoepli
Via Hoepli 5
20121 Milano   Tel. 86.54.46
Telex: 31.33.95   Telefax: (02)805.28.86
Libreria Scientifica
Dott. Lucio de Biasio 'Aeiou'
Via Meravigli 16
20123 Milano   Tel. 805.68.98
Telex: 800175

Japan – Japon
OECD Publications and Information Centre
Landic Akasaka Building
2-3-4 Akasaka, Minato-ku
Tokyo 107   Tel. (81.3)3586.2016
Telefax: (81.3)3584.7929

Korea – Corée
Kyobo Book Centre Co. Ltd.
P.O. Box 1658, Kwang Hwa Moon
Seoul   Tel. (REP)730.78.91
Telefax: 735.0030

Malaysia/Singapore – Malaisie/Singapour
Co-operative Bookshop Ltd.
University of Malaya
P.O. Box 1127, Jalan Pantai Baru
59700 Kuala Lumpur
Malaysia   Tel. 756.5000/756.5425
Telefax: 757.3661
Information Publications Pte. Ltd.
Pei-Fu Industrial Building
24 New Industrial Road No. 02-06
Singapore 1953   Tel. 283.1786/283.1798
Telefax: 284.8875

Netherlands – Pays-Bas
SDU Uitgeverij
Christoffel Plantijnstraat 2
Postbus 20014
2500 EA's-Gravenhage   Tel. (070 3)78.99.11
Voor bestellingen: Tel. (070 3)78.98.80
Telex: 32486 stdru   Telefax: (070 3)47.63.51

New Zealand – Nouvelle-Zélande
GP Publications Ltd.
Customer Services
33 The Esplanade - P.O. Box 38-900
Petone, Wellington
Tel. (04)685-555   Telefax: (04)685-333

Norway – Norvège
Narvesen Info Center - NIC
Bertrand Narvesens vei 2
P.O. Box 6125 Etterstad
0602 Oslo 6   Tel. (02)57.33.00
Telex: 79668 NIC N   Telefax: (02)68.19.01

Pakistan
Mirza Book Agency
65 Shahrah Quaid-E-Azam
Lahore 3   Tel. 66839
Telex: 44886 UBL PK. Attn: MIRZA BK

Portugal
Livraria Portugal
Rua do Carmo 70-74
Apart. 2681
1117 Lisboa Codex   Tel.: 347.49.82/3/4/5
Telefax: (01) 347.02.64

Singapore/Malaysia – Singapour/Malaisie
See Malaysia/Singapore" – Voir «Malaisie/Singapour»

Spain – Espagne
Mundi-Prensa Libros S.A.
Castelló 37, Apartado 1223
Madrid 28001   Tel. (91) 431.33.99
Telex: 49370 MPLI   Telefax: 575.39.98
Libreria Internacional AEDOS
Consejo de Ciento 391
08009-Barcelona   Tel. (93) 301.86.15
Telefax: (93) 317.01.41

Sri Lanka
Centre for Policy Research
c/o Mercantile Credit Ltd.
55, Janadhipathi Mawatha
Colombo 1   Tel. 438471-9, 440346
Telex: 21138 VAVALEX CE   Telefax: 94.1.448900

Sweden – Suède
Fritzes Fackboksföretaget
Box 16356, S 103 27 STH
Regeringsgatan 12
DS Stockholm   Tel. (08)23.89.00
Telex: 12387   Telefax: (08)20.50.21
Subscription Agency/Abonnements:
Wennergren-Williams AB
Nordenflychtsvagen 74
Box 30004
104 25 Stockholm   Tel. (08)13.67.00
Telex: 19937   Telefax: (08)618.62.36

Switzerland – Suisse
OECD Publications and Information Centre
Schedestrasse 7
DW–5300 Bonn 1 (Germany)   Tel. (49.228)21.60.45
Telefax: (49.228)26.11.04
Librairie Payot
6 rue Grenus
1211 Genève 11   Tel. (022)731.89.50
Telex: 28356
Subscription Agency – Service des Abonnements
Naville S.A.
7, rue Lévrier
1201 Genève   Tél.: (022) 732.24.00
Telefax: (022) 738.48.03
Maditec S.A.
Chemin des Palettes 4
1020 Renens/Lausanne   Tel. (021)635.08.65
Telefax: (021)635.07.80
United Nations Bookshop/Librairie des Nations-Unies
Palais des Nations
1211 Genève 10   Tel. (022)734.60.11 (ext. 48.72)
Telex: 289696 (Attn: Sales)   Telefax: (022)733.98.79

Taiwan – Formose
Good Faith Worldwide Int'l. Co. Ltd.
9th Floor, No. 118, Sec. 2
Chung Hsiao E. Road
Taipei   Tel. 391.7396/391.7397
Telefax: (02) 394.9176

Thailand – Thaïlande
Suksit Siam Co. Ltd.
1715 Rama IV Road, Samyan
Bangkok 5   Tel. 251.1630

Turkey – Turquie
Kültur Yayinlari Is-Türk Ltd. Sti.
Atatürk Bulvari No. 191/Kat. 21
Kavaklidere/Ankara   Tel. 25.07.60
Dolmabahce Cad. No. 29
Besiktas/Istanbul   Tel. 160.71.88
Telex: 43482B

United Kingdom – Royaume-Uni
HMSO
Gen. enquiries   Tel. (071) 873 0011
Postal orders only:
P.O. Box 276, London SW8 5DT
Personal Callers HMSO Bookshop
49 High Holborn, London WC1V 6HB
Telex: 297138   Telefax: 071 873 8463
Branches at: Belfast, Birmingham, Bristol, Edinburgh,
Manchester

United States – États-Unis
OECD Publications and Information Centre
2001 L Street N.W., Suite 700
Washington, D.C. 20036-4095   Tel. (202)785.6323
Telefax: (202)785.0350

Venezuela
Libreria del Este
Avda F. Miranda 52, Aptdo. 60337
Edificio Galipán
Caracas 106   Tel. 951.1705/951.2307/951.1297
Telegram: Libreste Caracas

Yugoslavia – Yougoslavie
Jugoslovenska Knjiga
Knez Mihajlova 2, P.O. Box 36
Beograd   Tel.: (011)621.992
Telex: 12466 jk bgd   Telefax: (011)625.970

Orders and inquiries from countries where Distributors
have not yet been appointed should be sent to: OECD
Publications Service, 2 rue André-Pascal, 75775 Paris
Cedex 16, France.

Les commandes provenant de pays où l'OCDE n'a pas
encore désigné de distributeur devraient être adressées à :
OCDE, Service des Publications, 2, rue André-Pascal,
75775 Paris Cédex 16, France.

75490-1/91

OECD PUBLICATIONS, 2 rue André-Pascal, 75775 PARIS CEDEX 16
PRINTED IN FRANCE
(41 91 01 1) ISBN 92-64-13472-7 - No. 44973 1991